...the cold war, democratiza... [become] one of the most crucial iss... international political scene. ...many states are undergoing an ex[tra]ordinary and difficult transition to... democracy. And that transition is de... [influenced] by the international contex... In this first volume of a major new s... [a group of] highly respected scholars fr[om around the] world and se... disciplin... ...role and i... ce of inte[r]national relations in... democratic development... in the Americas and Europe.

Combining the... ...ch set of... ...approaches with... examines the... point of democratic regimes in countries and regions... divers... as Brazil... European, an[d] Central Europe. At the international level the book considers the influence of... international politica... ...the UN... ...wide...

...democratic politics.

OXFORD STUDIES IN DEMOCRATIZATION

Series editor: Laurence Whitehead

. . . .

THE
INTERNATIONAL DIMENSIONS OF DEMOCRATIZATION:
EUROPE AND THE AMERICAS

OXFORD STUDIES IN DEMOCRATIZATION

Series editor: Laurence Whitehead

••••••••••••••••••

Oxford Studies in Democratization is a series for scholars and students of comparative politics and related disciplines. Volumes will concentrate on the comparative study of the democratization processes that accompanied the decline and termination of the cold war. The geographical focus of the series will primarily be Latin America, the Caribbean, Southern and Eastern Europe, and Southern and Eastern Asia.

OTHER BOOKS IN THE SERIES

The International Dimensions of Democratization

Europe and the Americas

....

Edited by
LAURENCE WHITEHEAD

OXFORD UNIVERSITY PRESS
1996

116687

Oxford University Press, Walton Street, Oxford OX2 6DP
Oxford New York
Athens Auckland Bangkok Bombay
Calcutta Cape Town Dar es Salaam Delhi
Florence Hong Kong Istanbul Karachi
Kuala Lumpur Madras Madrid Melbourne
Mexico City Nairobi Paris Singapore
Taipei Tokyo Toronto
and associated companies in
Berlin Ibadan

Oxford is a trade mark of Oxford University Press

Published in the United States
by Oxford University Press Inc., New York

© the several contributors 1996

All rights reserved. No part of this publication may be reproduced,
stored in a retrieval system, or transmitted, in any form or by any means,
without the prior permission in writing of Oxford University Press.
Within the UK, exceptions are allowed in respect of any fair dealing for the
purpose of research or private study, or criticism or review, as permitted
under the Copyright, Designs and Patents Act, 1988, or in the case of
reprographic reproduction in accordance with the terms of the licences
issued by the Copyright Licensing Agency. Enquiries concerning
reproduction outside these terms and in other countries should be
sent to the Rights Department, Oxford University Press,
at the address above

British Library Cataloguing in Publication Data
Data available

ISBN 0–19–828036–X

Library of Congress Cataloging-in-Publication Data
The international dimensions of democratization : Europe and the
Americas / edited by Laurence Whitehead.
— (Oxford studies in democratization)
Includes bibliographical references (p.   ) and index.
ISBN 0–19–828036–X (acid-free paper)
1. Democracy—History—20th century.   2. World politics—1945–
3. Comparative government.   I. Whitehead, Laurence.   II. Series.
JC421.I56   1996   320.9′09′045—dc20   95–45298

1 3 5 7 9 10 8 6 4 2

Typeset by Graphicraft Typesetters Ltd, Hong Kong
Printed in Great Britain
on acid-free paper by
Biddles Ltd, Guildford and King's Lynn

Preface

THIS volume went to press in December 1994, just five years after the dismantling of the Berlin Wall. That anniversary of the West's victory in the Cold War was marked by a series of summit meetings (in Essen, Miami, and Ouro Preto) each of which seemed to signal a new stage in democracy promotion through regional co-operation. In Essen, Germany, the twelve existing member states of the European Union (soon to increase to fifteen) opened the door to the eventual enlargement to include up to ten post-Communist market democracies from Eastern Europe. At the same time, in Miami, Florida, the thirty-four directly elected Presidents and heads of government attending the 'Summit of the Americas' adopted a series of measures intended to 'preserve and strengthen' the community of Western hemisphere democracies, and also set the end of 2005 as the deadline by which this political community would agree on a Free Trade Area of the Americas. In Ouro Preto, Brazil, the four elected Presidents of Mercosur signed a protocol to the founding Treaty of Asunción creating an institutional framework for the emerging common market, which among other provisions established a Joint Parliamentary Commission with not merely consultative, but also deliberative, powers on integration issues.

This volume provides a historically grounded analysis of the significance and limitations of such attempts at 'democracy-by-convergence'. It reconsiders some established ideas about the relationship between domestic and international factors in recent democratization processes. The geographical and temporal scope of the analysis is deliberately circumscribed. The focus is on Europe and the Americas in the late Cold War and early post-Cold War period, for that is where and when such regionally based democratization initiatives have become manifest, and where private and semi-governmental levels of international co-operation in support of democracy (such as the party internationals and political foundations) have the longest track-record and the greatest organizational density. It remains an open question whether these initiatives will live up to current expectations even in these two regions, and more pertinently whether these patterns are transferable to other times and places. Indeed a distinguishing feature of this volume is its stress on regional rather than global processes affecting democratization in individual countries. In particular it emphasizes regional processes of integration or disintegration and convergence or imposition. The two regions singled out for attention here also provide much of the evidence that has been invoked to support the proposition that democracies do not go to war with each other. In so far as this is true it remains an observation restricted in space and time, and yet some have mistakenly erected it into a universal law of international relations. Raymond Cohen's recent assessment of the evidence from what he terms the European and American 'pacific unions' highlights the commonalities and functional equivalences that they now share, and that distinguish them from other regions and other historical periods. His verdict on the issue of war and democracy mirrors the approach of this volume concerning regional co-operation and democratization—'the soundest conclusion to draw from the evidence is that democratic states in the North Atlantic/Western European area, sharing a particular set of historical circumstances and a common cultural heritage, have avoided going to war'.[1] This should not be turned into a timeless universal truth, and nor should the contention that democratic regional communities democratize peripheral states. But the current regional democratic experiments in Europe and the Americas are of sufficient importance to merit in-depth analysis even if they only generate contingent truths.

Even within these constraints this volume has some important omissions. It does not tackle the relationship between the North American Free Trade Area (NAFTA) and the possible democratization of Mexico; it does not say much about specific paths to democracy in Cuba; and it is necessarily inconclusive on the vexed question of the influence of the European Union on the civil war and eventual political transformation within much of what was formerly Yugoslavia. The last two topics are only addressed indirectly in the final chapter, which discusses pariah regimes. These omissions are deliberate, since it is not yet possible to judge how the general approach developed in the first two chapters may relate to the highly uncertain prospects for democracy in these countries.

The arguments advanced in this volume have been under discussion for some time. In 1988–9 the Royal Institute of International Affairs in London invited me to convene a monthly seminar on international support for the new democracies in Latin America. In 1990 I participated in a conference organized by the University of Southern California. Chapter 3 of the present volume is a revised version of my contribution to the resulting A. Lowenthal (ed.), *Exporting Democracy: The United States and Latin America* (Baltimore: Johns Hopkins University Press, 1991).

Chapters 1 and 2 derive from a panel I chaired at the International Political Science Association conference in Buenos Aires in 1991, and a follow-up conference at the Overseas Development Council in Washington DC in 1993. My two chapters on Europe (10 and 13) were originally commissioned by Dr Geoffrey Pridham, Director of the Centre for Mediterranean Studies at the University of Bristol, who published earlier versions in G. Pridham (ed.), *Encouraging Democracy: The International Context of Regime Transition in Southern Europe* (Leicester: Leicester University Press, 1991) and G. Pridham, E. Herring, and G. Sanford (eds.), *Building Democracy? The International Dimensions of Democratisation in Eastern Europe* (Leicester: Leicester University Press, 1994). None of these organizations is, of course, responsible for any deficiencies in the final versions of these chapters published here, but I owe them a great debt of gratitude for their support in these projects. I also wish to thank the Presses just mentioned for their permission to publish revised versions of these chapters.

L.A.W.
Nuffield College, Oxford

Note

1. R. Cohen, 'Pacific Unions: A Reappraisal of the Theory that "Democracies do not go to War with each Other"', *Review of International Studies*, 20/3 (July 1994), 208.

Contents

Notes on Contributors

ALAN ANGELL is University Lecturer in Latin American Politics and a Fellow of St Antony's College, Oxford. His recent publications include 'The Latin American Left since the 1920s', in Leslie Bethell (ed.), *The Cambridge History of Latin America*, vi (Cambridge, 1994).

THOMAS CAROTHERS is a Senior Associate at the Carnegie Endowment for International Peace in Washington DC. He is the author of *In the Name of Democracy: US Policy toward Latin America in the Reagan Years* (University of California Press, 1991).

WOLF GRABENDORFF is Director of the Instituto de Relaciones Europeo-Latinoamericano (IRELA) in Madrid. His publications include articles and books on Latin American International relations and political development. He was previously a Senior Staff Member of the SWP, the international research institute in Ebenhausen.

ANDREW HURRELL is University Lecturer in International Relations and a Fellow of Nuffield College, Oxford. His publications include Andrew Hurrell and Benedict Kingsbury (eds.), *The International Politics of the Environment* (Oxford: Oxford University Press, 1992) and Andrew Hurrell and Louise Fawcett (eds.), *Regionalism and International Order* (Oxford: Oxford University Press, forthcoming).

MICHAEL PINTO-DUSCHINSKY is Senior Research Fellow in Politics at Brunel University, and a governor of the Westminster Foundation for Democracy. His publications include 'Foreign Political Aid: The German Political Foundations and their US Counterparts', *International Affairs*, 67/1 (1991), and 'The Party Foundations and Political Finance in Germany', in S. L. Seidle (ed.), *Comparative Issues in Party and Election Finance* (Toronto: Dundurn Press, 1991).

CHARLES POWELL is a Research Fellow at St Antony's College, Oxford, and also teaches at the Instituto Universitario Ortega y Gasset, Madrid. His latest book is *Juan Carlos of Spain* (London: St Antony's/Macmillan, 1995).

PHILIPPE C. SCHMITTER is Professor of Political Science at the University of Stanford. His recent publications include the edited *Experimenting with Scale in Western Europe* (Cambridge: Cambridge University Press, 1995).

KATHRYN SIKKINK is an Associate Professor of Political Science at the University of Minnesota. Her publications include *Ideas and Institutions: Developmentalism in Brazil and Argentina* (1991), and more recently, studies of human rights, principled issue networks, and the origins and effectiveness of US and European human rights policies towards Latin America.

BASILIOS TSINGOS is a Lecturer in Social Studies at Harvard. As a Rhodes Scholar he completed a D.Phil. in International Relations 'Underwriting Democracy, Not Exporting It: The European Community and Greece' (Oxford University, 1994).

LAURENCE WHITEHEAD is an Official Fellow in Politics at Nuffield College, Oxford, series editor for Oxford Studies in Democratization, and co-editor of the *Journal of Latin American Studies*. His recent publications include 'The Alternatives to "Liberal Democracy": A Latin American Perspective', in David Held (ed.), *Prospects for Democracy* (Oxford: Polity Press, 1993); the introductory and concluding essays in 'Economic Liberalization and Democratization: Explorations of the Linkages', a special issue of *World Development* (August 1993); and 'Prospects for a "Transition" from Authoritarian Rule in Mexico', in Maria L. Cook, Kevin J. Middlebrook, and Juan Molinar Horcasitas (eds.), *The Politics of Economic Restructuring: State–Society Relations and Regime Change in Mexico* (University of California, San Diego: Center for US–Mexican Studies, 1994).

Abbreviations

APF	American Political Foundation
BMZ	Bundesministerium für wirtschaftliche Zusammenarbeit
CAPEL	Inter-American Centre for Election Promotion and Assistance
CDI	Christian Democrat International
CDU	Christian Democratic Union
CONAR	National Refugee Commission (Chile)
CSCE	Conference for Security and Co-operation in Europe
EP	European Parliament
EU	European Union
FELICA	Federación de Partidos Liberales de Centroamérica y del Caribe
FES	Friedrich Ebert Stiftung
IADB	Inter-American Development Bank
ICEM	Inter-governmental Committee on European Migration (Chile)
ICITAP	International Criminal Investigative Training Assistance Programme
IDU	International Democratic Union
KAS	Konrad Adenauer Stiftung
LI	Liberal International
Mercosur	South American Common Market
NAFTA	North American Free Trade Agreement/Area
NED	National Endowment for Democracy
PASOK	Pan-Hellenic Socialist Movement
PSOE	Partido Socialista de Obreros Españoles (Spanish Socialist Party)
SEA	Single European Act
SI	Socialist International
SPD	Sozialdemokratische Partei Deutschland
USAID	United States Agency for International Development
USIA	United States Information Agency

PART I

International Dimensions

Three International Dimensions of Democratization

LAURENCE WHITEHEAD

1. Introduction

Although the establishment and consolidation of democratic regimes requires strong commitment from a broad range of internal political forces, we must not overlook the distinctly restrictive international contexts under which the great majority of really existing democracies ('polyarchies') became established, or were re-established. As a rough indication consider the sixty-one independent states classified by Freedom House as 'free' in January 1990.[1] Thirty of these— beginning with the USA—can trace their democratic institutions to the processes of decolonization from the British Empire. In a further twelve their current political freedoms originated with the Allied victories in the Second World War. Thirteen more states have experienced transitions from conservative authoritarian rule since 1973. (These were all military allies of the United States which had sought to legitimize their undemocratic practices by invoking Cold War justifications.) That leaves only six out of the sixty-one democracies listed not originating either from decolonization, or from the Second World War, or during the recent fading of the Cold War. Of these six democracies only three—Sweden, Switzerland, and the United Kingdom—all geographically insulated and therefore militarily unconquered—seem to originate from domestic processes entirely separate from the international contexts just mentioned. The other three all followed rather distinctive trajectories, but their political institutions were powerfully affected by the Second World War and the Cold War (Costa Rica, Israel, and Venezuela).

Since January 1990 there have been no further decolonizations, and none of the sixty-one 'free states' have to date surrendered their major political freedoms. On the other hand, the collapse of Soviet power triggered a fourth wave of democratizations in Eastern Europe. Subsequently the disintegration of the USSR has created many more new states, some of which (more speculatively) might be classified as relatively free. Similarly, changes have occurred in major parts of Africa, particularly in Angola, Lesotho, Malawi, Mozambique, Namibia, South Africa itself, Zambia, etc. By January 1995 the Freedom House list of 'free' countries had increased by a further fifteen, to total seventy-six. Nine of the additions were formerly Communist-ruled and located in East-Central Europe. This cluster reflected the break-up of the Soviet bloc. Another cluster was beginning to form in post-apartheid southern Africa, although so far only three new 'free' states were listed (Malawi, Namibia, and the Republic of South Africa). In all these latest processes, however they turn out, a balanced analysis will have to give considerable weight to the international context in which they are occurring, as well as to the more strictly domestic forces in play. Indeed in many of these cases it would be artificial to insist on classifying the strategic actors into 'domestic' and 'international' categories (consider the Communist Parties, the Church, UNITA, etc.).

The purpose of this chapter, therefore, is to review the major alternative perspectives available for analysing the international dimension of recent and contemporary democratizations. The emphasis will be on the contrasting logics of the alternative perspectives, rather than on the intricacies of any particular instance, or of the overall historical pattern. However, in weighing up the merits of alternative approaches we should be guided not so much by the logical rigour of one approach or another (let alone by its convenience for formal modelling purposes) as by its capacity to illuminate historical experiences outlined above. These experiences are generally characterized by contingency, subjectivity, ambiguity, and reversibility, all of which tend to be suppressed when one resorts to an unduly formal, rational, or ahistorical mode of interpretation.

The record suggests three main headings under which international factors may be grouped and analysed: contagion, control, and consent. As will soon become apparent there is significant overlap between these three, and also important sub-classifications will be required in order to distinguish between alternative paths and outcomes. Under these three broad headings a variety of actors, processes, and motivations have to be considered. In particular one should distinguish between state-to-state interactions, non-governmental political transactions, and more diffuse social processes. Also, the transition phase of democratization responds to a different logic from that of the consolidation phase.

2. Contagion

Let us begin with a really parsimonious interpretation. It requires no consideration of actors (whether governmental or otherwise), or of their intentions. It needs no investigation into channels of transmission, and no attribution of primacy to either internal or external sources of democratization. It sidesteps all qualitative distinctions between types or stages of democracy. The procedure is first to establish a binary classification of countries according to some simple and schematic objective tests, and then to observe the geographical distribution of the countries classified as democratic, and how it changes over time. As with any parsimonious approach this involves omitting some detail that may help explain observed variations, but the compensating gain is that the procedure is clear, it can be replicated or refined by any practitioner, and it should be possible to establish from the results whether or not the proportion of the variance remaining unexplained is unacceptably high.

This simple procedure uncovers enough clusters and sequences to eliminate the possibility of random association, and indeed it provides remarkably strong support for the strong hypothesis of 'contagion through proximity'. France–Belgium–the Netherlands–Denmark–Norway–Germany–Austria–Italy all within five years (and not counting Finland) constitutes the first sequence. On its own that might be dismissed as an unrepeatable exception, but then we would have to consider Jamaica–Trinidad–Barbados–the Bahamas–Dominica–St Lucia–St Vincent–Antigua–St Kitts all within twenty years (not to mention Grenada and Belize). Another, and different, exception perhaps, but there was also Portugal–Spain, shortly followed by Peru–Ecuador–Argentina–Bolivia–Uruguay–Brazil, all within a decade (followed by Chile, Paraguay, and Haiti shortly after, followed by at least some Central American cases). Then, after 1989, most dramatically, there was Poland–Czechoslovakia–East Germany–Hungary–Romania–Bulgaria, all within little more than a year (not to mention Albania, Slovenia, Latvia, the Russian Republic, or Mongolia the year after that). Finally, we could add a southern African cluster, which arguably began with the decolonization of Namibia in 1990, and culminated in the democratization of South Africa in 1994. Between them those five, restrictively defined, cluster over forty democratizations, i.e. a remarkably high proportion of the countries under observation.[2] There can be relatively few interesting hypotheses in comparative politics that would stand up this well to statistical verification. Moreover the contagion hypothesis can be applied to related but different problems (e.g. sequences of democratic breakdown such as occurred in Latin America in 1947–9 or 1963–6, or in West Africa in the mid-1960s), and most strikingly it even has some predictive power. For example, if Nigeria really were to achieve a successful transition to democracy we can assert with some confidence that the probability of similar developments in neighbouring states would be materially enhanced.

These are pleasing results, particularly in view of the extreme simplicity of the initial hypothesis. But of course they leave unexplained much that should be of interest to those investigating the international dimension of democratization. For example, what determines the boundaries of the clusters just enumerated? Why, for example, were Spain and Portugal not included in the first sequence; why did Guyana deviate from the second; and why is Yugoslavia an exception to the fourth? Despite its intriguing predictive possibilities, on its own the contagion hypothesis cannot tell us how a sequence begins, why it ends, what it excludes, or even the order in which it is likely to advance. For that we need some account, however schematic, of the processes involved. Fairly quickly that enquiry will bring us into areas better studied under the other two headings (control and consent).

But before exhausting the topic of contagion we should relax the most restrictive of our initial assumptions and consider what mechanisms of transmission might produce the sequences observed, without involving the intentionality of any actors, either internal or external.

We are searching, then, for neutral transmission mechanisms that might induce countries bordering on democracies to replicate the political institutions of their neighbours. Such mechanisms would have to affect the attitudes, expectations, and interpretations of the public at large, regardless of whether or not outside agencies intend to produce this effect, and independent of the strategies and calculations of those holding political power within. For example, it would appear that popular attitudes in East Germany were so powerfully influenced by messages transmitted neutrally from the West that democratization became unavoidable, whatever governments or political leaders within or without might have wished or attempted. In turn, information transmitted neutrally about this state of affairs in East Germany produced analogous changes of attitude within the Czech population with comparably irresistible consequences for that regime (whatever its rulers desired) and so on successively. However, when such neutral messages finally reached Belgrade, although they retained their initial force, they received a very different political reading, not I would assume because the transmission had become blurred or was being politically manipulated, but because of a very different Serbian historical consciousness, shaped by their war against Nazi occupation.

If this interpretation is correct it would help to explain the pattern and limits of the contagion process. Such neutral transmission mechanisms might also help to account for the non-participation of Spain in the 1945 wave of democratizations (the Spanish public could see that to follow France and Italy would involve refighting the Civil War), or for the exclusion of Guyana from the West Indian sequence of successful democratizing decolonizations (black opinion in Guyana recognized that for them such a democracy would mean an East Indian majority). Such transmission mechanisms should also be considered when seeking explanations for the alternative paths to democracy selected by adjoining countries. For example (as Charles Powell demonstrates in Chapter 11), Spain's commitment in the 1970s to a 'pacted' democratization was significantly reinforced by the impact on Spanish public opinion of observing the process of Portugal's democratization through 'rupture'. Similarly the highly controlled Chilean process must have been affected to some extent by observation of what had happened a few years earlier when Argentina, Bolivia, and Peru had undertaken much more disorderly transitions.

Perhaps the most striking contemporary example of this process at work involves Cuba, now more isolated than at any time since the revolution, as Grenada, Nicaragua, Panama, and most of its partners in Eastern Europe have all joined the stampede towards representative democracy.[3] Once again this international current is only one factor sapping the confidence and cohesion of the Castro regime; as before it would be artificial to attach a specific weight to this factor viewed in isolation from the other forces acting on the regime. Nevertheless, we can identify a recurrent international contagion effect which appears to operate across a wide range of regime types, and to contribute significantly to many contemporary processes of democratization, just as in earlier periods a similar contagion effect contributed to successive breakdowns of democracy.

In order to carry this analysis further, and clarifying its application to specific countries, one would need to examine the role of the media in magnifying (or dampening) the domestic impact of external developments. A broader and perhaps more fundamental consideration would be the way national historical memories may filter the interpretation of transmissions from abroad. It should never be forgotten that relatively neutral transmissions of information may just as well serve to promote an anti-democratic as a pro-democratic contagion. (Consider the international impact of the information that Franco had rebelled against the Spanish Republic.) The process is as neutral in its value content as in its mechanics. If so, the contagion theory would need to explain why in the post-war world, and in particular during the 1980s, it has been the benign strain of democracy that has proved so virulent, rather than the hitherto equally contagious influence of authoritarianism. It seems to me that this puzzle can be resolved without straying from the confines of the contagion approach, simply by reference to the political and economic success (and therefore attractiveness) of capitalist democracy in the leading centres—the USA, Western Europe, and Japan. It was not always so, of course. In the inter-war period, when these leading countries were attracted to fascism, and when their liberal institutions seemed under threat as a consequence of the Great Depression, the dominant form of political contagion was far from democratic.

3. Control

Thus far we have restricted the analysis to pure contagion effects and neutral processes of transmission. It is somewhat surprising to find how much can be accounted for within this very restrictive framework. But in fact we know, both from the declaratory statements of Western leaders, and from the crude data summarized in the introduction, that at least in the post-war world, democracy is not just like a virus which happens to spread from one organism to another without intentionality. A more appropriate medical metaphor might be to see it as a vaccine. On this view US forces have acted in the Dominican Republic, Grenada, Panama, and (indirectly) in Nicaragua, El Salvador, and Guatemala to innoculate those polities from contamination by Castroism. Washington has always labelled this treatment 'democracy', and in some of these cases independent observers would confirm that in due course it became plausible so to describe the outcome. Similar claims have been made for Greece and Turkey (under the Truman Doctrine), and could indeed be extended to the NATO alliance in general in so far as membership was imposed.

However, as the introduction indicated, since 1945 anti-Communism has not been the only, nor perhaps even the most important, factor motivating some Western governments to impose democratic institutions on a large number of countries where they had the power. The British, in particular, set about exporting the Westminster model of political institutions to most of their former colonies, partly no doubt in order to make the break-up of their Empire more palatable to domestic public opinion. (Here the medical metaphor would be a transplant rather than a vaccine.[4]) As with the American efforts, the results were at best mixed, and in many cases the transplant failed to take, or failed to function in the same way as in its original setting. But this is not the place to dwell on the complications.

The essential point is that approaching two-thirds of the democracies existing in 1990 owed their origins, at least in part, to deliberate acts of imposition or intervention from without (acts, moreover, that were undertaken within living memory). Given this, an interpretation which excludes from consideration the roles played by external actors, their motives, or their instruments of action is bound to produce a highly distorted image of the international dimension of democratization, however good its statistical performance may seem. As always, correlation must be separated from causation. It is not contiguity but the policy of a third power that explains the spread of democracy from one country to the next.

Thus, the five clusters that appeared to validate the contagion approach in Section 2, above, can be re-explained in very different terms once we relax our restrictive initial assumptions, and grant the possibility of explicit external agency.

An extremely simple version of power politics will suffice to account for the four clusters in a very different way from the contagion approach. The first cluster would then express Washington's strategy for consolidating its dominance in Western Europe and Japan following the victories of 1945; the second would reflect an economically and militarily declining Britain's efforts to perpetuate its political and commercial influence; the third would express somewhat comparable American efforts in the more favourable setting of a fading Cold War and continuing US strength in the security realm; and the fourth would simply be attributable to the all-round collapse of Soviet power. Even the southern African cluster could be interpreted in terms of the post-Cold War withdrawal of great-power rivalries.

In this version the speed, direction, limits, and mechanisms of transmission of the democratization process can be accounted for more satisfactorily than under the contagion approach. Thus, for example, the boundaries of democratization after 1945 were rather precisely set by the presence of US forces. This would also explain the observable sequence of regime changes, the speed with which they occurred, and the main processes involved. Similarly, it was only territories within the British Empire that experienced attempts to export the Westminster model (e.g. after Trinidad, Barbados, and St Lucia the contagion skipped over Martinique to Dominica, then skipped Guadeloupe to Antigua). The order and speed of the march towards democracy was set by London's timetable for decolonization, and it was this that largely determined the processes involved. Likewise, developments in Moscow shaped the order and speed of the regime changes in Eastern Europe, which were of course bounded by the Soviet sphere of influence (i.e. spreading to Bulgaria, but not into the Middle East, and reaching less directly into Yugoslavia and Albania). Somewhat similar claims can be made for the third cluster (i.e. the demise of national security states within the US sphere of influence), although in this case the degree of direction from Washington was less apparent, as will be indicated in the next section of this chapter.

As for the southern Africa cluster, during the Cold War both the apartheid regime in Pretoria and the Marxist one-party regimes in Luanda and Maputo received substantial (albeit partly indirect) protection from their respective great-power allies, but faced armed opposition encouraged by their respective great-power opponents. After 1989, however, the great powers co-operated through the UN in promoting policies of reconciliation and democratization. In contrast, in the rest of sub-Saharan Africa, neither these great-power rivalries nor this subsequent switch to pacification operated so powerfully.

These, too, seem satisfying results, but we need to recognize the limitations and paradoxes of this power politics perspective. In particular, how can the relatively permissive and even altruistic act of democracy promotion be derived from the self-regarding and centralizing logic of power politics?

As a first step towards resolving this apparent paradox I would suggest that, although an undifferentiated and single-minded policy of democracy promotion would not be compatible with the maximization of a dominant state's power resources, a more selective and contingent policy might be.

The next step would be to look more closely at the various clusters of democratizations. In two of the five cases under consideration (British decolonization and Soviet disintegration) the aim of the dominant state at the time was not to maximize its immediate power, but to create an international environment that would be relatively less threatening to a former great power in decline in the longer run. In a third case (southern Africa) the collapsing USSR was also attempting to extricate itself from unsuccessful entanglements without indignity. In international politics more broadly conceived, then, there are periods when it may be good policy for a dominant state to be permissive and decentralizing in the territories it influences or controls, even though such a situation is hard to express in the terms of strict power politics theory. This is all the more true if we allow domestic opinion within the dominant state to affect its foreign policy. The single-minded pursuit of power politics abroad normally requires fairly unwavering support for a potentially repressive security apparatus based at home. Domestic interests may feel threatened by such an apparatus, in which case the pursuit of apparently inexplicable altruism overseas may reflect a perceived self-interest in *détente* and the reduction of tension on the internal front. (Cf. British support for decolonization, or French or Portuguese responses to colonial wars. Some of Edvard Shevardnadze's declarations as Soviet Foreign Secretary suggest that similar considerations could be significant even in Moscow.)

However, sustained and effective support for the spread of democracy within a given sphere of influence would require more than just the temporary ascendancy of libertarian factions within an imperial power structure. The libertarians would have to forge and sustain a new foreign policy consensus by demonstrating that the long-run interests of the society as a whole would best be served by relaxing control over previously subordinate territories. There are likely to be two main strands to such a consensus—the security apparatus and its allies will have to be persuaded that the costs of attempting to sustain the old structures of control have become too high, and/or the probability of success has fallen too low; and the political class in general will have to be reassured that the risks and costs of tolerating democratic dissidence and uncertainty are worth bearing.

It was relatively easy to achieve this consensus in post-war Britain, given the presence of the United States as a protector and in the last resort a substitute guarantor of order (the decolonization of Guyana is particularly illustrative here). This goes far towards explaining the thirty or so democratizations through decolonization referred to in the introduction. (The French, the Dutch, and the

Portuguese also decolonized, using European integration as a substitute for imperial grandeur, but without sufficient consensus or control to achieve democratization as well.) By contrast, in the Soviet case, although taken in isolation President Gorbachev's southern African strategy could have been rated a success, the security apparatus in Moscow became so alarmed at the internal repercussions of his decolonizing and democratizing policies in Eastern Europe that it rallied to the August 1991 attempted coup against him. When that failed Yeltsin replaced Gorbachev, and the Soviet Union shrank down to the Russian Federation. Even so, the problem of Russian security remains unresolved, with destabilizing consequences for fragile democracies within Moscow's reach, especially since an eastward expansion of NATO and the European Community will be perceived in Moscow as enhancing the German sphere of influence and marginalizing the Russians.

The other two clusters of democratizations fall within the US sphere of influence, and cannot therefore be analysed by reference to the strategies of great powers in decline. (The wave of democratizations initiated by the Carter Administration may bear some superficial comparisons with British decolonizations but these are secondary resemblances only and will not be pursued here.) During the Second World War (as in the First), Washington made the promotion of democracy a central war aim, and this contributed to America's victory in at least two important respects. It helped to engage a very broad spectrum of domestic opinion in support of the war effort, avoiding the suspicions and divisions that have hampered both earlier and later war mobilizations (e.g. some incursions into Mexico, and of course the Vietnam War). It also contributed to America's success in constructing and sustaining the broad international alliances required for victory. If the European Allies had perceived the USA as just another great power engaged in empire-building, for example, the cohesion of the anti-Axis coalition would have been in jeopardy. As it was both allies and enemies of the US-led alliance were undoubtedly influenced in their war calculations by the expectation that a victorious UN coalition would respect (or restore) national sovereignties and would generally favour the establishment (or re-establishment) of pluralist political institutions in the territories it liberated. If this promise was an important part of the Western Allies' political capital during the war, it held a corresponding political weight among the victors' obligations after 1945.[5]

Fortunately for Washington it proved possible to harmonize these obligations with America's post-war security interests. But although possible, this was far from inevitable, and a great deal of effort and ingenuity was required to achieve this harmonization. For example, the re-democratization of France and Italy was very much in America's interest, provided the resulting governments were stable, were locked into the Western security system, and adopted market-oriented economic policies. But in view of the popular support for the left in these two countries, and the discredit of many on the right due to their wartime complicities, there could be no certainty in advance that America's interest would be well served by these democratizations. The Cold War, the Marshall Plan, and the institutionalization of NATO all involved active leadership and direction from Washington in order to reconcile the Allied commitment to democracy with the more traditional priorities of power politics. Greece and Turkey are of particular significance in this context, because they occupied the grey area between Western Europe (in which the Allied commitment to democracy was most salient, and most easy to reconcile with Western security objectives) and the rest of the world liberated by Western armies (in which the commitment to democracy was either weak, hypothetical, or absent and imperial structures of control were re-established). At least as far as Western Europe was concerned the essential point is that it was both necessary and possible for the Allied forces to relinquish direct control to new democratic regimes without jeopardizing their security, and moreover that it was almost impossible even to consider doing otherwise in view of the pressures on the victors for rapid demobilization and for a return to peacetime normalcy. Western European experience seemed to demonstrate that indirect systems of support could stabilize these newly restored democratic regimes without requiring the maintenance of much overt control.

This sketch of the post-1945 democratizations in Western Europe may seem like straining to explain the obvious, except that we also wish to consider the post-1973 democratizations within the same framework. It must be acknowledged from the outset that the degree of external control was markedly less in this cluster than in any of the other three. After all, in the last resort the Allies had direct military authority at the outset of the Western European democratizations, as had the British when decolonization took place. Moscow had similar capacities—and perhaps a greater disposition to use them—in parts of Eastern Europe (though not in Poland when the democratization process was allowed the longest gestation period). In contrast Washington lacked such direct capacity for control over its authoritarian allies in the 1970s and

1980s. Chapters 4 and 5 analyse some of the consequences for US democracy promotion policies in much of Latin America. (The consequences of Washington's greater capacity for control in the Caribbean basin are considered in Chapter 3.) In general the United States possessed indirect systems of influence and support analogous to those which had helped stabilize and moderate West European democracies after the 1940s. Through the allocation of aid and other economic concessions, through gestures of political support or disapproval, and even through the dense network of military and security ties which bound it to these regimes, Washington could encourage, redirect, or resist democratizing impulses, even if it could not strongly control them.

The next section of this chapter deals with international processes of support and interaction, which is where much of this Carter–Reagan cluster of democratizations should be studied. But even in this group of regime transitions there are some aspects that belong under the heading of control. For example, the Carter Administration proclaimed a general policy of support for democracy and human rights, both within and outside the US sphere of influence. But the US sphere was very wide, and so the question very quickly emerged where to begin (and also, implicitly, where to end). In practice, Washington's initiatives to encourage recent democratizations within its sphere of influence have been consistently selective and contingent. Carter took the lead in the Dominican Republic, but not in Iran; Reagan acted on Grenada rather than Haiti; Bush backed a clean count in Nicaragua, but not in Mexico; and so forth. Some of this selectivity was due to variations in the strength and characteristics of the democratizing actors within individual countries. To that extent it cannot be classified as a product of external control. But considerations of economic and military security, and calculations of political and ideological self-interest, are also very evident as factors explaining the order, rhythm, and intensity of Washington's democratizing initiatives, and to this extent the promotion of democracy has functioned as yet another component in a world-wide system of alliance control.

Certainly, the element of control is less prevalent in these cases than in the other three Cold War clusters discussed previously. It may well be that with the ending of the Cold War, the strengthening of the European Community, and the increasing prevalence of democratic forms of government around the world, this factor will fade away in future years. Perhaps 200 years after Kant's initial contribution to the idealist tradition in international relations[6] his prediction that the spread of 'republican' (today we would say 'democratic') forms of government would gather such momentum as to bring about 'perpetual peace' (the contemporary phrase would presumably be 'the end of history').[7] Or it may be that in the post-Cold War world some regions will come under increased control by democracy-promoting powers (consider not just the 1994 US invasion of Haiti, but also democratic South Africa's involvement in Lesotho), whereas other regions may witness the expansion of non-democratic powers. For example, Hong Kong in 1997, and perhaps eventually even Taiwan, could find themselves incorporated into a still non-democratic China. Whatever we may speculate about the future, this section has shown that in almost all the democratizations that have occurred between the Second World War and the dismantling of the Warsaw Pact, the strategies of regulation and control adopted by the dominant states in the system were of critical importance. External agency, in this sense, represents a major alternative perspective that contrasts with contagion in the account it provides of the international side of democratization.

4. Consent

There remains a third alternative. Once the role and motivations of strategic actors have been admitted into the analysis this can hardly be confined to external agency alone. A comprehensive account would need to incorporate the actions and intentions of relevant domestic groupings, and the interactions between internal and international processes (what Pridham,[8] borrowing from the idiom of Rosenau, called 'linkage politics'). But why do we need a more comprehensive account, with all the additional complexity and confusion it will involve, when contagion plus control seem to have served us so well? The answer I would suggest is that the first two perspectives rest on extremely basic and inadequate conceptions of democratization. To develop a more elaborate and nuanced understanding of the process would require a more subtle and complex account of its international dimension. Otherwise there is no escape from Rousseau's famous paradox about being 'forced to be free'.

A genuine and securely implanted democratic regime requires the positive support and involvement of a wide range of social and political groupings, support that must be sustained over a considerable period and in the face of diverse uncertainties. Such support must be more or less freely given for the term 'democracy' to apply. If so, then it is clearly a misattribution of responsibility to suppose that any real democracy could owe its origin mainly to some act of external compulsion or imposition.

This argument brings us back to the central concerns of the *Transitions* literature, within which, of course, domestic processes were viewed as primary, with international factors generally playing no more than a secondary role.[9] Invasion, or at least military defeat as in the Graeco-Turkish conflict of 1974 or the South Atlantic conflict of 1982, were recognized as exceptions to this generalization, but were considered accidental and infrequent. This perspective reflected both the limited geographical range of the *Transitions* study (southern Europe and South America have been uncharacteristically peaceful areas of the world since 1945), and its methodological inclinations (the focus on coalition-building and on strategic interactions between relatively well-established political forces). Subsequent episodes in Grenada, Nicaragua, Panama, Namibia, Angola, Yugoslavia, etc. highlight the restrictive range of these assumptions. Consequently acceptance of the more elaborate and sophisticated conceptions of democratization, such as those formulated in the *Transitions* literature, still leaves the international dimension in need of reassessment.

Having reviewed the perspectives offered by contagion and control, this section discusses the ways in which international processes contribute to (or impede) the generation of the consent upon which new democracies must be based. It distinguishes between four aspects:

(1) the territorial limits to successive democratizations and their consequences for established alliance systems;
(2) the main international structures tending to generate consent for such regime changes;
(3) the ways in which authentic national democratic actors may be constituted from relatively diffuse transnational groupings;
(4) the role of international demonstration effects.

Territorial Limits

Recent developments in the USSR and Yugoslavia have thrown into stark relief the question of the territorial limits to each democratization, an issue that was barely perceptible to earlier analysts working on Latin America. (With hindsight it could be discerned at least in relation to Belize, Guyana, and the Falklands, but only in a very indistinct form.) The issue is in fact quite general. The establishment of national boundaries is an eminently international act; whereas generating consent for a representative system of government within those boundaries can be regarded as a separate, domestically driven, process. So much time has elapsed in most of Latin America between the completion of the first process and the modern initiation of the second that this polarity may seem natural. In the interim, powerful and sustained processes of national integration have differentiated the various adjoining polities right up to their frontiers. But in most of Europe, not to mention Africa, Asia, or the Middle East, the definition of territorial boundaries and the forging of national identities has been much more recent and/or more bitterly contested, and so has overlapped with (and in many cases redirected) contemporary processes of democratization.

Consider a few examples. When democratic India invaded the Portuguese colony of Goa in 1961, it imposed its democracy and transformed the Goanese political identity. Thirteen years later, when Portugal became democratic, this was extended to Madeira and the Azores (but not to São Tomé, let alone Macau, Angola, or Timor). When Greece restored Karamanlis it was after a war in which the national aspiration for reunion with Cyprus had received a devastating setback (for some, then, this was a truncated democracy). For the GDR, of course, democratization signified the total elimination of a separate East German state. The 'velvet revolution' in Prague gave rise to not one, but two separate, democratic states (although the Hungarian minority in Slovakia might understandably argue that some democracies are more democratic than others). Most of the British decolonizations listed in the introduction involved more or less strained decisions about the territorial limits of the new democracies (for example, Antigua and Barbuda, but not including Anguilla). When the French Fourth Republic foundered it fell in Guadeloupe as much as in Paris. For that matter the democratization of Corsica remains an awkward issue in French politics, just as the democratization of Ulster plagues the British, and Sicily affronts the Italians. In short, the international processes that are fundamental for the establishment and stabilization of national boundaries also carry direct and often powerfully disruptive implications for the composition (and indeed viability) of democratic regimes within those boundaries. The disintegration of Yugoslavia into a range of states, from fully democratic Slovenia to genocidally polarized Bosnia-Hercegovina, may be an extreme case, but it is an extreme case of a widespread phenomenon.

A peaceful international system needs to generate consent (both within and between nations) for a precisely agreed pattern of inter-state boundaries and security alignments. Theoretically it may be that democratic states provide the best machinery for generating such consent, but at least in the transition phase of democratization there is liable to be a high degree of uncertainty about which substantive policy outcomes (including security alignments) will enjoy sustained support. The uncertainty over the future of US bases in democratizing Spain, Portugal, Greece, the Philippines, and South Korea provides one good comparative illustration of this, and the prospective alignment of newly democratizing regimes in Eastern Europe in relation to whatever power structure may eventually be stabilized in Moscow will provide another. Thus, in practice, the early phases of democratization may generate insecurity and tension through the state system, rather than the opposite; and in response the international system may generate resistance to, or conflict over, the precise forms taken by the democratization process in states with insecure national identities. This is an international dimension to the democratization process that may require considerably greater attention than it has received so far.

International Structures of Consent

One strikingly popular remedy for the dangers in question is the creation of regional blocs usually composed of the more successful democratic states, which then offer to support, converge with, or even in extreme cases to incorporate newly democratizing neighbours. In this introductory chapter we will confine the discussion to the European Community, since it constitutes by far the most long-established and ambitious example of this approach to the stabilization of some new democracies. (It is not, in fact, unique: other more recent partial analogues include the Caribbean Basin Initiative, Mercosur, and the 1994 Summit of the Americas, discussed in Chapter 3 below.) Confining our attention, for the moment, to explicit actions of the decision-makers in Brussels, the most powerful of these has undoubtedly been the offer of full membership of the Community to certain European states provided they satisfy a number of conditions, one of which was the establishment of solid democratic institutions. The impact of this 'democratic conditionality' on the consolidation of southern European democracies has already been investigated at length;[10] and is considered further in Chapters 10–12 of this volume.

The question of whether similar conditionality may be extended to certain potential new accessions from Eastern Europe will put this practice to a very severe test, however, as discussed in Chapter 13 below. Even if the EU does decide in favour of eventual further enlargement to the east, this will inevitably be a very slow process, and at least some fragile democracies will be kept waiting indefinitely. Brussels must therefore face the issue of whether it can devise other powerful instruments that will reinforce consent for democracy in those countries where accession is a distant or impossible dream. There are some limited precedents (e.g. EC support for the San José process in Central America),[11] but their impact is very weak compared to the Community's one big prize. Full membership of the European Union generates powerful, broad-based, and long-term support for the establishment of democratic institutions because it is irreversible, and sets in train a cumulative process of economic and political integration that offers incentives and reassurances to a very wide array of social forces. In other words it sets in motion a very complex and profound set of mutual adjustment processes, both within the incipient democracy and in its interactions with the rest of the Community, nearly all of which tend to favour democratic consolidation. Mere aid packages or political advisory missions are far less potent, no matter how well staffed or funded they may be. In the long run such 'democracy by convergence' may well prove the most decisive international dimension of democratization, but the EU has yet to prove that case fully. A second test seems likely to arise in the Western hemisphere, now that the Free Trade for the Americas has been established with a 2005 deadline and relatively clear democratic conditionality.

It remains true that the problem of generating consent for the consolidation of a democratic regime need not have any very obvious or prominent international dimension, so long as the territorial limits, international alignment, and relationship with some dominant democratic bloc of states are uncontentious. But in most cases one or more of these questions does cause difficulty and becomes entangled with the democratization process. When this happens the international dimension becomes unavoidable. For in this case, the various strategic actors whose interactions are central to a *Transitions*-type analysis will no longer act according to a purely domestic logic, unmindful of the external ramifications of their choices. Indeed one could go further, and propose that in such conditions more than a few of the key strategic actors may owe much of their success and effectiveness to their skill in interpreting and reacting to the international repercussions of their actions.

National Democratic Actors

At the outset of most democratic transitions it will be difficult to gauge which of the hastily constituted new groupings and movements within a given country is likely to emerge with real structure, support, and staying power. The origins of these emerging opposition forces typically include a substantial external component (exile clusters, for example, as illustrated in Chapter 7 on the Chilean case), or social movements which enjoyed some degree of international protection through the church, the human rights community, or from a network of fraternal parties overseas. Similar observations may well apply to the new forces emerging from the disintegrating authoritarian regime—technocrats closely associated with the international financial institutions, newspapers aligned with the interests of foreign investors, or possibly even CIA assets (on the one hand) or KGB nominees (on the other).

In short, at the start of many transitions to democracy it can be artificial and misleading to classify all the new strategic actors as ready-made strictly domestic political entities. It is only during the course of the transition itself, and in particular if consolidation proceeds well, that the national authenticity of the various contending forces may become fully established. The evolution of such forces from their often diffuse and semi-dependent origins to fully fledged and unambiguously national political status is in fact a central part of the democratization process. If it remains incomplete or is interrupted then the transition will not proceed to full consolidation. For example, in Nicaragua the Sandinistas had to accept the UNO coalition as an authentically Nicaraguan movement, not under the control of Washington, and the Chamorro government had to reciprocate in its evaluation of the Sandinistas, in order for democratic institutions to become implanted in that society. Likewise for El Salvador, or indeed for more peaceful experiments such as those in Spain and Czechoslovakia. (Indeed, even the democratization of the Uruguayan party system required Blancos and Colorados to shed their Brazilian and Argentine affiliations at the turn of this century.)

If this is correct then a vital international dimension of many democratizations concerns the interactive process by which the external supporters of the various contending political factions step (or are driven) back, relinquishing leverage over their protégés, and lifting vetoes against their competitors. Clearly the fading of the Cold War, and the declining incentives for dominant powers to maintain tight control within their spheres of influence (discussed in Section 3 above), will increase the frequency of these processes. At least as important may be the proliferation of democratic regimes, offering reassurance that this kind of experimentation need not be destabilizing, and providing a denser network of cross-cutting sources of support for pluralism within each polity.

As we have seen, most democratizations involve the assertion of a clearly defined national sovereignty, but not all do. In the case of democratization through incorporation (e.g. Puerto Rico or Guadeloupe) the main strategic actors must shed their national distinctiveness in order to achieve a fully consolidated regime. Some would deny that this route can possibly merit the designation 'democratization', seeing it instead as a betrayal of national identity, but I would leave that for the inhabitants of the territory in question to decide for themselves. What does require stress, however, is that there are high cultural (and probably also political) costs involved in pursuing such a route to democracy. Consequently, if it succeeds at all it will only be after a very protracted process of social adjustment. But then generating consent for a democratic regime is for the long haul, whether achieved through incorporation, convergence, or imposition.

International Demonstration Effects

Finally, there remains one more international aspect of democratization by consent, and it is probably the most fundamental. It concerns international demonstration effects as they affect the underlying distribution of popular preferences and expectations. Clearly this involves returning to the topic of neutral transmission mechanisms already considered in Section 2 above. The emphasis is different here, however, for now the question is not just how information about the establishment of democracy in one country increases the probability of the same occurring in a neighbour—rather it concerns how an almost universal wish to imitate a way of life associated with the liberal capitalist democracies of the core regions (the wish for modernity) may undermine the social and institutional foundations of any regime perceived as incompatible with these aspirations. That is the negative side.

On the positive side it may be (although this is far from certain) that the same international demonstration effects will also serve to generate the consistent and broad-based support needed to bolster fragile new democracies. Contiguity is not the operative variable in this case. Images of the good life in North America or Western Europe may produce equally powerful effects in the Southern Cone as in the Caribbean, in Siberia as in the Baltic states.

What may differ with distance is the ease of mass migration to the major centres of democratic attraction, but if so this will tend to favour the generation of democratic consent in the more distant locations rather than where mass exit offers an alternative to the travails of political accommodation. For example, relatively few Chileans went abroad for political reasons, and most of those always hoped to return. Eventually this gave rise to patterns of mutual accommodation which can be summed up by the attitude that 'despite our differences we are all Chileans, and we will have to learn to live together'. (See Chapter 7, below.) In contrast, the million plus Cubans who migrated to Florida may lack the capacity for accommodation with those who stayed behind, and many of those who left East Germany for West Germany seem ill-equipped to find much political common ground with those who did not. (No doubt, part of the difference here reflects the legacy of Communism, but the evidence from Algeria, say, or Turkey, suggests that that is not the whole explanation and that ease of migration is also vital.)

As indicated by these examples, and by the contrast between regime-destroying and regime-creating aspects of these demonstration effects, there is no simple or uniform process by which the wish to emulate or replicate international liberal capitalist lifestyles is likely to generate consent for democratization in any given society. But the potential scope and power of these demonstration effects seems truly formidable, especially now that the only serious global competitor for international allegiances has crumbled from within. They are likely to increase in intensity with the further penetration of mass media geared to the stimulation of consumer wants, and in view of the prospective advance of regional integration blocs in Western Europe and North America. They therefore transmit a relentless underlying pressure on unresponsive and unsuccessful regimes throughout the periphery. This can become a major international factor in generating consent for democratization, but it can also erode and delegitimize fragile democratic regimes that fail to deliver the improvements in accountability and in living standards that the public are taught to associate with successful liberal democracy.[12] In either case it is an international aspect of democratization that requires systematic attention.

5. Conclusion

This chapter has grouped the international aspects of democratization under three broad headings: contagion, control, and consent.

Although there is inevitably some overlap between them they have been presented as alternative modes of analysis, each with a different structure and each highlighting distinctive features.

The main merit of the contagion perspective is that, operating on the most restrictive of assumptions, and using the simplest possible objective indicators, it proves capable of accounting for some striking regularities. It is, therefore, an acceptable approach for some limited purposes, although it may tend to mislead if extended too far.

The control perspective relaxes the previous restriction on the study of actors and their motivations, but it confines itself to explaining the calculations of the dominant powers. By so doing it links the politics of democratization and the realist or power politics tradition in international relations. Given the importance of democratization processes in contemporary international politics the realist tradition needs to establish some such link. By incorporating the conduct of dominant powers the control perspective adds depth to the observations generated by the contagion approach. It may be of particular value for those seeking to explain how most democratizations begin, and the timing, sequence, and scope of these initiatives. It is less useful in accounting for the subsequent fate of these experiments (except under the special circumstances of democratization-through-incorporation).

To analyse the complexities of the consolidation process requires a third shift of perspective, to the means by which consent may be generated. This involves a more sophisticated conception of the democratization process, including distinguishing between different phases, and alternative paths and outcomes. Naturally, then, it must consider many more variables than the two previous approaches, and the categories of analysis become much more complex than before. Instead of using a few simple indicators it becomes necessary to work with intricate and elusive patterns of strategic interactions which differ subtly from one case to the next. It is not even possible to identify the key actors a priori—rather they constitute themselves in the course of the democratization itself. Small wonder, then, that students of democratization have tended to concentrate on the internal dynamics of institution-building and mutual accommodation, regarding the international component of the generation of consent as generally secondary in importance.

However, this introduction has argued that outside a limited number of South American cases it can be seriously misleading to marginalize the international dimensions in this way. We cannot in general assume consensus over the territorial boundaries within which each democratization unfolds. We should not disregard the possibility that the uncertainties of the transition period will raise doubts about the stability of the regional power balance, and that these international insecurities will feed back into the democratization process. Part of the process of constituting authentically national strategic actors will frequently involve their disengagement from earlier dependence on external protectors. Underlying all these questions of actor-led strategy and interaction will be a distribution of public aspirations and expectations that may owe much of its configuration to the operation of international demonstration effects. One particularly striking illustration of how this may generate consent for democratization is when it is reinforced by the prospect of full membership of the EU. In summary, therefore, the international processes contributing to (or impeding) consent typically deserve sustained attention.

Indeed, whether the appropriate perspective for studying a given issue is contagion, control, or consent it may be artificial to dichotomize the analysis into domestic and international elements. Although there will always be some purely domestic and some exclusively international factors involved, most of the analysis will contain a tangle of both elements. In the contemporary world there is no such thing as democratization in one country, and perhaps there never was.

Notes

1. Freedom House, *Freedom in the World: Political Rights and Civil Liberties* (New York: Freedom House, 1990), 17. This is a rough classification only. The sixty-one free states listed include two with less than 10,000 inhabitants each and also the two halves of Cyprus. Chile, Colombia, Mexico, Nicaragua, Panama, Paraguay, Peru, and Turkey were among the forty-four classified as only 'partly free'.
2. These four sequences by no means exhaust all the possibilities. Consider the Philippines–South Korea–Taiwan sequence in 1985–9, for example, or Papua New Guinea–the Solomons–Vanuatu in 1975–80.
3. M. Boström's focus on the 'contiguous and regional sub-environments' works better for Paraguay than it would for revolutionary Cuba, which, as an island, borders on no other state, and which for thirty years had closer organizational and economic ties with the distant Soviet bloc than with adjacent Latin America. ('Contagion of Democracy in Latin America: The Case of Paraguay', in S. S. Nagel (ed.), *Latin American Development and Public Policy* (New York: St Martin's Press, 1994).) The December 1994 Miami Summit underscored Cuba's isolation by inviting all thirty-four elected leaders of Western hemisphere states,

excluding only Fidel Castro. But the democratization of Cuba is not yet preordained by the international influences outlined above.

4. W. Marvin Will, 'British Institutional Transplants in the New World: The Case of Barbados', paper presented to the Latin American Studies Association, Miami, 1989.

5. Completeness requires some mention of the limitations to this doctrine. Despite Western rhetoric, the armed liberation of North Africa, the Middle East, Indo-China, Hong Kong, and Korea was accomplished without any democratic accompaniment, a fact with consequences that are still unfolding. (For more on the territorial scope and geographical limitations of the various democratizations see the next section.)

6. I. Kant, *Principles of Politics, including Essay on Perpetual Peace*, ed. and trans. W. Hastie (Edinburgh: T. and T. Clark, 1891).

7. 'To Perpetual Peace: A Philosophical Sketch' was written in 1795, before the optimism engendered by the French Revolution had been completely dissipated.

8. Geoffrey Pridham in G. Pridham (ed.), *Encouraging Democracy: The International Context of Regime Transition in Southern Europe* (Leicester: Leicester University Press, 1991).

9. G. O'Donnell, P. Schmitter, and L. Whitehead, *Transitions from Authoritarian Rule: Prospects for Democracy* (Baltimore: Johns Hopkins University Press, 1986).

10. In particular see contributions in Pridham, *Encouraging Democracy*.

11. See L. Whitehead, 'The San José Process and the Identity of the New Europe', in J. Roy (ed.), *The European Community and Central America* (Miami: North-South Center, University of Miami, 1992); IRELA, *Ten Years of the San José Process: A Review of Co-operation between the European Union and Central America* (Madrid: Institute for European–Latin American Relations, 1994).

12. This reference to living standards could open the way to a further discussion, examining the relationship between democratization and economic performance, and assessing the currently fashionable view that it is the international spread of market relations that generates both prosperity and individual freedom in the longer run. The establishment of democratic regimes could be regarded, on an economic determinist version of this argument, as a lagging indicator of the global spread of capitalism. This, then, would provide a fourth international dimension for our consideration—economic liberation. However, the relationships linking democracy, economic performance, and capitalism are by no means so clearly established. For a recent sceptical survey of the literature and an attempt to pin down the relationship that proved inconclusive, see A. Przeworski and F. Limongi, 'Democracy and Development', paper presented at the Nobel Symposium (Democracy's Victory and Crisis), Uppsala University, August 1994. At the same symposium S. S. Bhalla, in 'Freedom and Economic Growth: A Virtuous Cycle?', presented evidence appearing to substantiate the idea of a positive association.

....

2

....

The Influence of the International Context upon the Choice of National Institutions and Policies in Neo-Democracies

PHILIPPE C. SCHMITTER

Few political acts seem more autochthonous than the change from one political regime to another. This shift to a different set of rules and practices governing the exercise of citizenship, the access to power, the conditions of competition for office, and the making of authoritative decisions is not only likely to affect the welfare and security of almost all persons living in a given territory, but it is usually accompanied by an increase in political awareness, a resuscitation of collective symbols, and an assertion of national self-determination. The defunct or deposed regime is frequently vilified as the product either of foreign imposition or of atavistic conditions. The new regime presents itself as an updated and more authentic expression of the true interests and aspirations of the nation. Its proponents, in other words, have an incentive to play down the role of external actors and the impact of international forces.

The transition from autocracy to democracy is a special case in point. By one mode or another, the previous tyrants are overthrown and the event triggers a vast increase in citizen consciousness—it has been termed a resurrection of civil society.[1] Expectations soar and typically focus on national as well as personal goals. The people (or, more accurately, their representatives) assemble; they choose new institutions of self-government and embark on new policies of self-improvement. Whether they do so rationally by evaluating the

As has long been the case with my work on democratization, I have benefited extensively from the encouragement and critical acumen of Terry Karl.

full range of possible rules and selecting those that optimize collective performance and best elicit compliance, or habitually by reinvok-
ing some time-honoured conception of governance that best conforms
to their sense of identity and obligation, is (for the moment) unim-
portant. The implication is still clear: regime change tends to be a
domestic affair; democratization is a domestic affair *par excellence.*

Admittedly, this leaves out those (not insignificant) cases in which
one set of rulers and rules is defeated in war by foreigners who subsequently impose their preferred type of regime upon the vanquished.
Germany (East and West), Japan, Hungary, Bulgaria, Czechoslovakia, Poland, and Romania were compelled to take that route in the
aftermath of the Second World War. The outcomes in Italy, Austria,
and Korea (North and South) were similarly, if less directly, imposed.
But these are typically treated as aberrations.[2] Even where there
is an obvious international element involved in bringing about the
demise of the previous authoritarian regime but which is not followed by physical occupation of national territory by foreigners (e.g.
China, Yugoslavia, Portugal, Greece, and Argentina), it is almost
always presumed that the choice of subsequent institutions and
policies is the product of autochthonous political forces.

The emergent (but burgeoning) literature on democratization
has so far largely reflected this nativist tendency. One of the most
confident assertions in the O'Donnell–Schmitter concluding volume to the *Transitions from Authoritarian Rule* project was that
'domestic factors play a predominant role in the transition'.[3] Not
only does this fly in the face of a substantial (if hardly concordant)
literature that stresses the dependence, interpenetration, and even
integration increasingly embedded in the contemporary world system, but it also seems to clash with some obvious facts surrounding
the more recent transitions that have occurred in Eastern Europe. Would the astonishingly rapid changes in Poland, Hungary,
East Germany, Czechoslovakia, Romania, and Bulgaria in 1989–
90 have even been imaginable, much less gone as far as they did,
without a prior change in the hegemonic pretensions of the Soviet
Union? Would Honecker have been able to hang on to power if it
had not been for a switch in Hungarian foreign policy that allowed
East Germans to transit its territory to seek exile in the West?
And who could have conceived of a regime change in Albania—a
polity virtually without a domestic opposition—in the absence of
the collapse of the other Communist regimes?

Perhaps, it is time to reconsider the impact of the international
context upon regime change. Without seeking to elevate it to the
status of prime mover, could it not be more significant than was

originally thought? Is it not possible that the early transitions in southern Europe and Latin America were peculiarly national, and that those occurring since in Asia, Eastern Europe, and (more tentatively) Africa have been (and will continue to be) more influenced by their external, regional and global, contexts? More specifically, to what extent do variations in these contexts—over time and across countries—impose significantly different constraints upon or open up significantly different opportunities for nascent democracies? How, why, and when do they affect their choice of institutions and policies? What, if any, is the impact of these contextual difference upon the likelihood that these polities will be able to consolidate some form of democracy successfully?

1. Concepts, Theories, and Assumptions

Providing answers to these questions that are valid and generalizable across the large number and dispersed location of contemporary cases of democratization will not be easy. It involves challenging one of the most deeply rooted paradigm divides within political science, that between international relations and comparative politics. It would also require escaping from the confines of area studies and searching for commonalities across quite different cultures, historical trajectories, social structures, economic systems, and levels of development. The existing IR literature is barely any help, consisting mostly of bland reflections on 'linkage politics', 'penetrated systems', 'fusion of domestic and foreign policy', and, of course, 'interdependence'.[4] The regional specialization of most of those who work on democratization deprives them of the knowledge needed to make reliable inter-area comparisons, or encourages them to generalize excessively on the basis of the cases they know best.

Moreover, the international context is a notoriously difficult variable to pin down. On the one hand, it is almost by definition omnipresent, since very few polities in the contemporary world are isolated from its effects. However, its causal impact is often indirect, working in mysterious and unintended ways through ostensibly national agents. On the other hand, while it is usually presented in the singular, i.e. the international context, its actual incidence varies greatly according to the size, resource base, regional context, geo-strategic location, and alliance structure of the country involved. Existing IR theory is relatively good at specifying these

		Basis for action	
		Coercion: backed by states	Voluntary: supported by private actors
Number of actors	Unilateral	Control	Contagion
	Multilateral	Conditionality	Consent

FIG. 2.1. *The 'sub-contexts' of the international context*

conditions at the level of nation-states, but much less well equipped in dealing with phenomena at the sub-national or supra-national levels. In the simplified world of realists, the only actors worth mentioning are nation-states and the only relevant actions consist of their explicit foreign policies: signing treaties; entering into alliances; making diplomatic protests and threats; voting in international bodies; offering or withdrawing economic incentives; and, in the last resort, declaring war and making peace. In the complex world of idealists, a lot of non-state actors: international organizations, human rights groups, foundations, interest associations, media organizations, transnational firms, partisan *internationale*, networks of dissidents, even private citizens have to be taken into account, and their actions can augment, undermine, and even countermand those of the states they belong to. As we shall see, there is reason to suspect that this world beneath and beyond the nation-state has played an especially significant role in the international promotion of democracy.

In Chapter 1 Laurence Whitehead has ventured again into this murky arena of the international context (which he prefers to call 'the international dimension'). In addition to upgrading his assessment of its importance since his earlier work in the *Transitions from Authoritarian Rule* project,[5] he proposes a threefold grouping of the international factors that may impinge upon contemporary democratizations.[6] To his categories of contagion, control, and consent, I would add a fourth: *conditionality*. The defining dimensions are simple, even if their implications are not. On the vertical axis, the key distinction is between unilateral processes of international influence or power in which one actor intentionally or unintentionally affects another, and multilateral ones that involve several, often competing, sources of influence or power and typically work through international organizational rather than purely national channels. The horizontal axis distinguishes between contexts involving at least the threat, if not the exercise, of coercive authority (this is usually the exclusive domain of nation-states, although some international organizations such as the International Monetary Fund, the IBRD, and the European Bank for Reconstruction and Development have also acquired some of this capability) and those whose effect depends on voluntary exchanges. Cross-tabulating these two dimensions produces the four modal sub-contexts.

Whitehead makes an effort at assigning significance to three of these:

(1) contagion, or the diffusion of experience through neutral, i.e. non-coercive and often unintentional, channels from one country to another, he finds present throughout most of the history of democratization;

(2) control, or the promotion of democracy by one country in another through explicit policies backed by positive or negative sanctions, he estimates was present in about two-thirds of the sixty-one cases he considers to be presently democratic;

(3) consent emerges as a more recent category involving a complex set of interactions between international processes and domestic groups that generates new democratic norms and expectations from below. In the extreme, this may lead to an irresistible drive to merge with an already existing democracy (e.g. Germany); in a milder form, it underlies the desire to protect democracy within a given state by joining a regional bloc (e.g. the EU).

Conditionality should be added to the other three as the most recent (and, we shall see, the most rapidly expanding) sub-context for the exercise of international influence. Its hallmark is the deliberate use of coercion—by attaching specific conditions to the distribution of benefits to recipient countries—on the part of multilateral institutions. The *locus classicus* for this kind of behaviour in the past was (and still is) the IMF, although democracy was rarely (if ever) one of its stipulated conditions and those that were imposed were usually kept confidential in order not to offend national sovereignty (or dignity). More recently, it has been the European Community (and, of lesser significance, the Council of Europe) that has insisted upon a certain standard of political behaviour as a condition for membership. Its offshoot the EBRD has been especially up-front about imposing very specific political criteria before loans will be granted. While the practice of conditionality seems largely confined to Europe, there are some signs that other regional organizations, such as the Organization of American States, the

(British) Commonwealth and, even, the Organization for African Unity, have begun to discuss the issue of collective security to prevent unconstitutional regime change.

As we turn now to the theoretical domains in which these factors might be brought to bear, we will try to estimate what (if any) changes have been occurring in international sub-contexts as the locus has shifted from southern Europe to Latin America to Eastern Europe over the past two decades and a half. We will be specifically interested in the extent to which these changes may be promoting or impeding either the transition from autocracy or the consolidation of democracy.

Grosso modo, there seem to be four ways of conceptualizing the dynamics of interaction between the international sub-contexts of power and influence and the varied national cases of democratization. One can adopt a basically functionalist view and interpret the outcome in terms of an adaptation of the latter to independent and inexorable trends in the former. Alternatively, the emphasis could be more historically contingent and focus on the impact of discrete events (or even personalities). Or one can place primary emphasis on the complex, temporally structured interaction between cases and assign primary importance to waves of diffusion and imitation. Or one can take a genetic perspective and emphasize the changing nature and importance of the international context upon different stages of the democratization process. None of these four is mutually exclusive; all may eventually contribute to improving our understanding; each will, however, bring up different variables and generate different hypotheses, and may even lead one to different conclusions.

2. Trends

The most prevalent hypothesis linking the international context and democratization is probably some version of what could be called 'inverted Kantianism'. Immanuel Kant suggested that 'republics' where governments were accountable to their (restricted) citizenry were likely to promote commerce in general and international trade in particular. The development of these exchanges between countries, in turn, would place restrictions on their aggressive behaviour *vis-à-vis* each other. Once all polities had become 'republican', the nature of the international system would shift to 'perpetual peace'.[7]

History was not very kind to Kant's optimistic scenario. Shortly after he wrote his little pamphlet (in 1795), one of his republics

(France) deprived three others (the Netherlands, Switzerland, and Venice) of their independence and distinctive governing form—and transformed itself into an Empire and an autocracy! Nevertheless, the *doux commerce* thesis—that trade tends to produce moderate and accommodative behaviour in both individuals and collectivities—persists.[8] In its more recent versions, however, Kant's causality is inverted. It is argued that the development of mutual exchanges between citizens in different polities during a period of protracted peace tends to produce a demand for republican government. Put in more contemporary terms, increase in international interdependence, especially forms of 'complex interdependence' involving a wide range of types of exchange, leads to the democratization of national political institutions. For example, an assumption of this sort must have underlain Willy Brandt's *Ostpolitik*, as well as European resistance to the US diktat concerning the construction of a gas pipeline from the Soviet Union.

It is, of course, but a small step from this perspective to inverting the dependency theory that was used so extensively to explain the demise of democracy and the rise of bureaucratic-authoritarian regimes in Latin America and elsewhere during the 1960s and 1970s. This would argue that subsequent changes in the content and balance of (inter-)dependencies between centre and periphery had required countries in the latter to adapt their domestic institutions (at least formally) during the later 1970s and 1980s, this time to conform to the new functional requisite of open, free, and competitive politics.

Samuel Huntington has made a quite different, but related point. While rising interdependence remains the necessary condition, the sufficient one concerns the distribution of power within that evolving system of exchanges. Only those countries that are closely affected by existing democracies will be affected: 'In large measure, the rise and decline of democracy on a global scale is a function of the rise and decline of the most powerful democratic states.'[9] As we shall see, this perspective mixes elements of control, i.e. deliberate policy initiatives by the United States, with the effects of contagion, i.e. the example of successful and prosperous democratic polities.

In our previous work on transitions, Guillermo O'Donnell and I firmly rejected all versions of this trendy analysis. It seemed to us that the pattern of external exchanges, the stage of capitalist development, the extent of asymmetric dependencies, and the role of major powers in general and the United States in particular varied so much across the countries of southern Europe and Latin America that we were studying that it was patently erroneous to interpret democratization as a response to some common trend or trends toward interdependence. For the period we were examining, it was the decline not the rise in US power that seemed to open up spaces for political change. As Terry Karl pointed out subsequently with regard to Latin America, it was precisely in those countries where the influence of the United States remained the greatest— the Caribbean and Central America—that the progress towards democracy was the least advanced.[10] Where that major power's option to intervene directly, i.e. militarily, was limited—the Southern Cone of Latin America or the southern edge of Western Europe—or where its leaders were significantly divided on what course of action to follow—the Philippines and Korea—democratization occurred. It has not so clearly followed from the benevolent armed intervention of the US in Panama or Haiti.

What I did emphasize in the introduction I wrote to the southern European case-studies was that a specific form of complex, organizationally saturated interdependence between Spain, Portugal, and Greece (and, to a lesser extent, Turkey) and the rest of Europe (the European Community in particular) did exert a powerful and positive influence upon the subsequent processes of consolidation of their respective democracies.[11] The impact upon the timing and nature of their varied transitions from autocracy was marginal, but once regime change was under way, the networks of public and private exchange that bound these countries to the rest of Europe had a profound effect upon the choice of institutions and policies. Ironically, it was the political weakness (not the strength) of the EC that enabled it to play such a role. Moreover, while the European Union insists on the democratic bona fides of its members, it itself does not meet the minimum criteria for being a democracy. Both these features provide prospective members with greater assurance that they will not simply be outvoted by larger countries that are already members or be dictated to by an overweening supra-national bureaucracy.

Subsequent events in Eastern Europe and the Soviet Union have not compelled me to revise my thoughts about the generic importance of trends. These countries were not characterized by high levels of international interdependence. Their membership of Comecon and unconvertible currencies had the effect of both cutting them off from the mainstream of exchanges within the capitalist world economy and restricting their mutual interdependence. Granted that there was some tendency for commercial and personal exchanges with the West to increase (and a strong desire for even greater increases) and there was the beginning of a mutual recognition process that might have led to closer EC–Comecon relations, it is none the less difficult to assign much causal weight to either. Contrary to Huntington's benevolent assumption about the influence of 'the most powerful democratic states', in Eastern Europe, democratization was triggered (but not caused) by the most powerful autocratic state.

Only by dialectical inversion is it possible to rescue the trend hypothesis: the very prospect that economic interdependence was increasing rapidly between neighbouring countries in Western Europe (especially since the signing of the Single European Act in 1985) could have provided a significant impetus for regime change before the 1992 process would have completed the internal market and left Eastern European outsiders even further behind.

There is another way of resuscitating the 'trend to interdependence' hypothesis that seems particularly appropriate for Eastern Europe and the Soviet Union: it involves switching attention from *doux commerce* to *douce communication*. What if it were not the voluntary exchange of goods and services through trade but the unimpeded transmission of messages through various media that established the basis of interdependence between political systems? Autocracies might still be able to control the physical movement of items and people, but they seem to have lost the capacity to control the flow of information across their borders. Satellite television, free radio, video cameras, computer networks, facsimile and xerox machines, and cellular telephones all seem to have ways of getting around national (or imperial) barriers. Moreover, the content of their messages can be specifically tuned to the process of democratization by disseminating images of individual freedom, self-expression, mass collective action, heroic resistance to tyrants, and so forth. The development of regional and global networks for such transmissions seems to underlie much of what Whitehead has termed contagion and consent in the contemporary international context. It connects societies without the approval or mediation of their governments. With one's neighbours and the world watching, the cost of repression has gone up and, most of all, the potential benefit of resistance has greatly increased. Witness the impact of those images of East Germans trying to climb the walls of the West German embassy in Prague or crossing the Hungarian–Austrian border in droves. Or those joyous people astride the Berlin Wall, or that lonely man in front of the tanks in Tienanmen Square, or Yeltsin haranguing the crowd in front of the Russian Supreme Soviet!

But let us not exaggerate either the reach of this communicative interdependence or its impact upon democratization. Except for the picturesque street theatre of the Portuguese Revolution, the transitions in southern Europe and Latin America were relatively unaffected by it. Perhaps, some regime changes are just less photogenic than others, or mass publics are less interested in what happens in certain parts of the world. In some out-of-the-way places, *vide* Burma and Haiti, the events can be over before the coverage begins. Nor was extensive and unfavourable media attention given to mass protests in the early 1980s that were sufficient to bring down Pinochet. As the Chinese example demonstrates, even with poignant images and ingenious means of transmission, the formula is not infallible. Power is still an irreducible component of the international context and coercion is still a resource available to national autocrats. In other terms, contagion and consent alone are unlikely to be sufficient to bring about democratization—even in conjuncture with favourable domestic forces. Often, regime change will require elements of control and conditionality.

3. Events

No one would deny that major unforeseen occurrences in the international environment have historically had a significant impact upon regime changes in general and democratization in particular.[12] Machiavelli's term for this was *fortuna*, and he confidently assigned 50 per cent of the variance to it. Whatever its proportional contribution in the contemporary setting, we have seen evidence of its role in recent transitions.

The most obvious event is war and, especially, defeat in war. The Portuguese, Greek, and Argentine cases were all affected by unsuccessful efforts by non-democratic rulers at projecting military power beyond their national boundaries—and one could claim that the defeat of the Soviet Union in Afghanistan played a significant role in bringing about the demise of its autocracy.

Second in importance was the change in the international system brought about by decolonization, especially the interconnected events that followed in the aftermath of the Second World War. With the surface of the globe now virtually covered by at least nominally sovereign and self-governing states, there doesn't appear to be much room left for this class of events. Nevertheless, the Soviet Union's (unexpected) willingness to let its Eastern satellites go it their own way in 1988–9 was roughly analogous to the break-up of the British, French, Dutch, and Belgian colonial empires after 1947—even if it was accomplished in a more mutual and peaceful fashion. The event underlying both defeat in war and decolonization in this case was the dramatic realization by the rulers of the Soviet Union that they could no longer sustain their level of international commitments and retain their status as a major power.

It is not yet clear what impact the subsequent collapse of the entire bipolar structure of the international system will have upon the consolidation of democracy in those countries which have undergone a transition, or upon the pressure for regime change in those autocracies that remain in power in Africa, Asia, and, especially, the Middle East. Cuba is obviously an immediate case in point, but there are others which have lost their ability to play the major powers off against each other. Conversely, those which have been liberated by Soviet decolonization—including Russia, the Baltic States, and other ex-Soviet republics—seem to be able to call upon a greater degree of international solidarity and financial support than has been the case since the United States aided in the reconstruction of the fledgling democracies of Western Europe after the Second World War.[13]

4. Waves

Any plotting of the dates when democracies were founded or when they have significantly expanded their practice of citizenship and/or their degree of accountability would reveal a strong tendency towards temporal clustering. There are a few democracies which have followed more idiosyncratic trajectories and timed their changes in seeming disregard for what was happening to their neighbours the United States, Chile, Uruguay, Great Britain, Sweden, the Netherlands, Belgium, Canada, New Zealand, and Australia[14]—but most of them can be placed in one or other wave of democratization.

The first, 1848, was quite spectacular but ephemeral. Most of those affected returned to their previous mode of governance or to an even more autocratic regime in short order. The second major outbreak of democracy corresponded to the First World War and its aftermath.[15] This time not only were new countries carved out of the defunct Austro-Hungarian Empire and the disrupted Russian Empire, but all of them turned to democracy initially.[16] The Weimar Republic replaced the German Reich. Moreover, very important extensions of the franchise and inclusions of new parties into government occurred in those Western European polities that were already partially democratic. The third wave came in the aftermath of the Second World War. Not only were numerous previous democracies liberated to revert to their previous status and new democracies established in West Germany and Italy, but the process of regime change spread far beyond Europe through the process of decolonization in Asia and Africa. Japan and South Korea were given democratic institutions by a withdrawing occupying power. In Latin America numerous dictators, frozen in power by the war itself, were overthrown.[17]

We are currently in the fourth wave of democratization. It began quite unexpectedly and originally in Portugal on the 25 April 1974 and does not yet seem to have crested. Compared to previous ones, it has the following peculiar characteristics.

1. It has been much more global in its reach. It began in southern Europe, spread to Latin America, affected some Asian countries, and literally swept through Eastern Europe. Moreover, from Mongolia to Mali, and Madagascar to Mexico, important changes are still in progress. Only the Middle East seems immune, although even there some change has been occurring in Tunisia and Algeria. Cuba and Serbia stand out in their respective neighbourhoods. (See also Chapter 14, below.)

2. As a consequence of the former, it has affected far more countries and been more thorough in its regional impact. Some parts of the world that were previously almost uniformly autocratic are now almost equally democratic. Cuba and Serbia stand out in their respective neighbourhoods. (See also Chapter 14, below.)

3. It has suffered far fewer regressions to autocracy than in the past. Twenty-seven years after it began, the only clear reversals have come in Burma and China. Thailand seems a rather special case of persistent pendulation in regime type. Haiti is a particularly telling example. Its initial experiment with free and contested elections of uncertain outcome resulted in a reassertion of military power. The democratic trajectory resumed after a short interlude, but again met with a violent overthrow by elements of the armed forces—the outcome of which is not yet certain.

Observing this bunching together of historical and contemporary experiences does not explain their occurrence. The most obvious hypothesis is that the waves of democratization are produced by a process of diffusion. In Whitehead's terms, contagion is the most plausible explanation in the international context, especially when no simultaneous external event is present that could otherwise explain the coincidence.[18] The successful example of one country's transition establishes it as a model to imitate and, once a given region is sufficiently saturated with this mode of political domination, pressure will mount to compel the remaining autocracies to conform to the newly established norm.

This hypothesis is particularly appealing for the explanation of the contemporary, fourth, wave because, on the one hand, the countries affected have not suffered the impact of any common exogenous event such as a world war and because, on the other, the ensuing development of complex communicative interdependence provides greater assurance that the mechanisms of diffusion are working. In fact, the latter observation presents a complication in testing for contagion or diffusion. Previously, the main empirical proof for its presence hinged on geographical propinquity. An innovation was supposed to reach nearby units before it reached those further away. Hence, the observation that democratization in the current wave began in southern Europe and then leap-frogged to Latin America without first affecting North Africa or Eastern Europe that were closer at hand would have constituted a disconfirmation. However, when one considers that modern systems of communication are not so spatially bound and may not even be culturally confined, then the observation is much less damaging. Given the extraordinary simultaneity and omnipresence of these systems, it should be no surprise when its messages are received and responded to in Mongolia before Mali or Mexico.

With this prima facie plausibility in mind, we can turn to the development of further hypotheses. For example, the wave notion leads to the likelihood that the relevance of the international context will increase monotonically with each successive instance of democratization. Those coming later in the wave will be more influenced by those that preceded them. Whether they can be expected to learn from mistakes made earlier is perhaps less predictable, but there may be an advantage to delayed democratization—just as it has been argued that late development had its advantages.

One of the reasons for this momentum effect in the contemporary context has less to do with contagion than with what Whitehead called consent. Each successive case has contributed more and more to the development of formal non-governmental organizations and informal informational networks devoted to the promotion of human rights, the protection of minorities, the monitoring of elections, the provision of economic advice, and the fostering of exchanges among academics and intellectuals—all intended to further democratization. When the first cases of Portugal, Greece, and Spain emerged, this sort of international infrastructure hardly existed. Indeed, some of the key lessons were learned from these experiences and subsequently applied elsewhere. By now, there exist an extraordinary variety of international parties, associations, foundations, movements, networks, and firms ready to intervene either to promote or to protect democracy (see Chapters 8 and 9 below). This suggests a second hypothesis: the international context surrounding democratization has shifted from a primary reliance on public, inter-governmental channels of influence towards an increased involvement of private, non-governmental organizations—and it is the concrete activity of these agents of consent, rather than the abstract process of contagion, that accounts for the global reach of regime change and the fact that so few regressions to autocracy have occurred.

For, however superficially attractive the process of contagion may appear, it rarely bears closer scrutiny. Take, for example, the case of Portugal and Spain. Despite their geographical and cultural proximity and the temporal coincidence of their transitions, it is very implausible to assert that Spain embarked upon its regime change in 1975 because of the prior events of 1974 in Portugal. In fact, the Spaniards had long been waiting for the death of Franco which was the specific triggering event—not the Portuguese Revolution. In many ways, they were much better prepared for democratization than their Portuguese neighbours because they began preparing for it much earlier. At most, it could be claimed that Spain learned some negative lessons about what to avoid during the transition and, therefore, had a relatively easier time of it than might otherwise have been the case. I suspect that detailed evidence of diffusion from southern Europe to Latin America or Asia or Eastern Europe would be just as difficult to provide. Of course, Spain (and, more recently, Chile) seems to have offered a model of successful transition to late-comers and, therefore, encouraged them to venture into uncertain terrain, but this is a long way from being able to claim that Spain actually caused others to change their regime type.

Where the argument for contagion or diffusion is more persuasive is within specific regional contexts. The unexpected (and highly controlled) transition in Paraguay seems to have been influenced by the fact that the country was surrounded by nascent democracies, although Chile under Pinochet held out successfully against such pressures during the 1980s. Pinochet even dared to use the example of the poor performance of Chile's recently democratized neighbours as an argument for voting 'Sí' in the plebiscite that would have perpetuated him in power for another eight years! The fact that he lost that plebiscite suggests (but does not prove) that Chilean citizens were influenced not just by their own democratic tradition but also by the wave that had engulfed their neighbours.

Eastern Europe may provide the best possible case for contagion, even though the initial impetus for regime change was given by an exogenous event, i.e. the shift in Soviet foreign and defence policy *vis-à-vis* the region. No one can question the accelerating flow of messages and images that went from Poland to Hungary to the DDR to Czechoslovakia to Romania to Bulgaria and, eventually, to Albania, or the impact that successive declarations of national independence had upon the member republics of the Soviet Union.

This leads to a third and final sub-hypothesis, namely, that the really effective international context that can influence the course of democratization has increasingly become regional, and not binational or global. Both the lessons of contagion and the mechanisms of consent seem to function better at that level.[19]

Stages, Phases, and Sequences

Democratization proceeds unevenly as changing sets of actors employ different strategies to accomplish different tasks. The process may not always be continuous, gradual, linear, or cumulative, but virtually all attempts to model it refer to the presence of stages, phases, or sequences. The most common distinction has been between a shorter, more intense, uncertain, and eventful period of transition and a longer, less heroic, more dispersed, and deliberate period of consolidation—the contrast between an initial, exciting 'war of movement' and a subsequent, prosaic 'war of position'.

From this staged or phased notion of regime change comes one of the most important general hypotheses linking the international context to domestic political outcomes: regardless of the form (control, contagion, consent, or conditionality) that it takes, external intervention will have a greater and more lasting effect upon the consolidation of democracy than upon the transition to it.[20] Part of the explanation rests on the likely structure of opportunities. During the first phase, the probability of exercising a marginal influence over the outcome may be greater than later when things have calmed down, but the sheer pace of change—coupled in some cases with its unexpectedness—leaves outsiders without the critical information they would need to intervene effectively and without regular channels of influence through which to operate. The rapid pace of internal change tends to out-run the decision-making capacity of most external actors.[21] Moreover, some foreign governments will have been discredited for the realist policies they pursued in relation to the previous autocracy; others whose actions may prove more acceptable within the country can have difficulty in deciding which fractions to support in a context of divided social groups and ephemeral political alliances. To the extent that the transition is related to processes of national liberation and assertiveness, the intromission of foreigners can be especially unwelcome— even if, in this period of high uncertainty, weak domestic political forces may be sorely tempted to look for outside support.

The situation changes once consolidation is under way. The relevant domestic actors have been reduced in numbers and variety, and their positions and resources are better known. The national borders and identities will have been asserted, if not definitively established.[22] Those foreigners who find it in their interest to intervene can do so with greater deliberation and selectivity. The potential marginal impact may have diminished, but so has the risk of backing the wrong forces. Moreover, the *modus operandi* is likely to change from covert actions by foreign governments that are intended to seize upon a target of opportunity in order to influence a particular event through specific inducements or sanctions, e.g. trying to encourage an autocrat to step down peacefully,[23] or to change the outcome of a founding election,[24] towards more open and long-term attempts, often by non-governmental actors, aimed at supporting sets of institutions, e.g. the encouragement of opposition parties, trade unions independent of state authority, or legal organizations ensuring access to justice or the protection of civil rights. These external efforts to penetrate domestic civil society (and even to create a regional or global civil society) may have begun when the regime was still autocratic, but they rarely—if ever—seem to have contributed much to its demise. Whether they can do better to enhance the likelihood of consolidation remains to be seen. The evidence from southern Europe is encouraging in this regard, but one can question its relevance elsewhere, since the regional context provided a unusually rich and multi-layered set of non-governmental exchanges and a powerful incentive for accepting them, i.e. not just full and formal entry into the European Community, but participation in a very vibrant and lucrative European civil society. Democratizers in Latin America have no such prospect and, much as those in Eastern Europe may aspire to integrate with the rest of Europe, the prospect of an immediate positive response is becoming increasingly remote.

The new development in this area is conditionality, especially when practised through multilateral diplomacy and international organizations. Here, the idea is to use the fulfilment of stipulated political obligations as a prerequisite for obtaining economic aid, debt relief, most-favoured-nation treatment, access to subsidized credit, or membership in coveted regional or global organizations. The foreign conditioners should manipulate these incentives—at least in theory—in such a way as to encourage the locals to sustain the momentum of their political transformation and help them over specific critical thresholds: acceptance of existing sovereignties; supervision of free elections; amnesty for political opponents; adoption of specific institutions; refusal to allow non-democratic parties into governing alliances; resistance to military pressures; and tolerance for partisan rotation in power.[25] Not only can any or all of these be made conditional, but domestic politicians may even welcome this interference in internal affairs as an excuse for arguing that their hands are tied and they must go ahead with decisions that may seem unpopular at the time. Moreover, a judicious application of it could be useful in the especially difficult context in which several institutional transformations are simultaneously clamouring for attention. By providing incentives for tackling certain issues first—say, holding elections before removing price controls or privatizing state holdings—the external conditioners could help to ensure a more orderly transition. This assumes, of course, that they have an adequate theoretical understanding of the situation to enable them to determine what should precede what; and that the external institutions at different levels and functional domains are not pushing different priorities and emitting contradictory signals.[26]

Of course, conditionality in economic and monetary matters has long been a feature of the post-war international context, the International Monetary Fund (IMF) being its most active practitioner. What is new is the tying of policy responses to political objectives.[27] Moreover, precisely because of its novelty and its blatant disregard for traditional notions of national sovereignty, there seems to be a propensity for hiding its manifestations behind the façade of multilateral institutions. It seems easier to justify conforming to explicit requests to establish specific political institutions or to perform specific political acts when they come from an international, especially an appropriately regional, organization than when they are demanded by a single government. This effort at multilateral conditionality began with the very first transition in the current wave, but it has gathered momentum as the focus of regime change shifted from southern Europe to South America to Asia to Eastern Europe and, now, to Africa. In part, this may be a reflection that the more recent neo-democracies are more vulnerable in their trading, investment, and indebtedness patterns; in part, it seems to have emerged from an independent process of the accumulation of precedents and organizational capacities at the regional or global levels of the world system.

During a critical phase of the Portuguese transition, an extensive multilateral effort was mounted to ensure that its outcome would conform both to the country's previous alliance commitments and to Western standards of democracy and public policy. This involved mobilizing the formal institutions of NATO (and Portugal's momentary exclusion from its Nuclear Planning Group), the European Community (with a critically timed emergency loan in the autumn of 1975), and the International Monetary Fund (with massive balance-of-payments support), as well as a variety of unilateral (and less public) interventions by the United States and the Federal Republic of Germany. According to one well-informed source, even superpower concertation was brought to bear when President Ford informed Secretary-General Brezhnev at their Vladivostok Meeting that *détente* was off unless the Russians stopped assisting the Portuguese Communist Party in its (apparent) bid for power.[28]

But most expressions of conditionality have been less dramatic and improvised. By far the most important for southern Europe and, now, for Eastern Europe is the firm policy that only democracies are eligible for full membership of the European Union.[29] Needless to say, neither this provision of the Rome Treaty, nor the subsequent Birkelbach Report (1962) of the European Parliament defines precisely what operative criteria are involved. Geoffrey Pridham has suggested that these seem to be (1) genuine, free elections; (2) the 'right' electoral results, i.e. a predominance of pro-democratic parties; (3) a reasonably stable government; (4) leadership by a credible (and pro-European) figure; and (5) the inauguration of a liberal democratic constitution.[30] None of the three southern European applicants were formally admitted to full membership until they had crossed most, if not all, of these hurdles. Which is not to say that their respective democracies were then reliably consolidated. Portugal still had significant, constitutionalized military intromission in policy-making and unstable minority governments; Spain had a weak governing coalition and even suffered an attempted military coup after applying for entry.

Greece is, perhaps, the country that made most intensive use of EC conditionality to assist its unusually rapid transition and consolidation (see, however, Chapter 12 below). Karamanlis anchored his entire strategy upon rapid and full entry into the Community and openly proclaimed that this decision rested on political not economic grounds.[31] This was no doubt facilitated by the strong role the EC (and the Council of Europe) had taken in opposition to the regime of the Colonels, but it should be noted that it was a policy which did not meet with universal approval in Greece. Moreover, Karamanlis coupled his European ploy with a (temporary) withdrawal from NATO. EC officials and member governments responded quickly by unfreezing the association agreement, sending a flock of visitors, and providing emergency aid. They also seem to have pressed for a rapid convocation of national elections.[32] In the cases of Portugal and Spain, the responses of both democratizers and integrators concerning full membership were much more hesitant and lengthy. In the cases of Eastern Europe, where EC entry was placed immediately at the top of the policy agenda by newly elected presidents and prime ministers, the lack of enthusiasm (not to say, veiled opposition) of the twelve member states has been increasingly apparent.[33]

Why this specific form of conditionality has had such an impact is worth exploring further—even though (alas!) no similar regional arrangement exists elsewhere in the world to promote the consolidation of democracy. First, EU membership is expected to be permanent in nature and to provide access to an expanding variety of economic and social opportunities far into the future; second, it is backed up by 'complex interdependence', an evolving system of private transnational exchanges at many levels and involving many different types of collective action (parties, interest associations, social movements, sub-national governments, etc.); finally, it engages lengthy, public, multilateral deliberation and is decided unanimously in the Council of Ministers and by an absolute majority in the European Parliament. This enhances the reputation or certification effect beyond the level attainable via unilateral recognition or bilateral exchanges where other criteria (i.e. security calculations) may override the democratic ones.[34] More than any other international commitment, full EU membership has served to stabilize both political and economic expectations. It does not directly guarantee the consolidation of democracy; it indirectly makes it easier for national actors to agree within a narrower range of rules and practices.

NATO conditionality, for example, has been a good deal less effective. Not only were the authoritarian regimes in Portugal, Greece, and Turkey 'members in good standing' of the alliance, but newly democratized Greece found it expedient to leave the organization—for a brief period. Spanish membership in NATO was much more hotly contested internally than its EC application, and only squeaked through by a narrow margin in a national referendum (and, then, only after the Socialist Party changed its position). Nevertheless, several observers have suggested that the engagement of national militaries in NATO—the external security role, the base agreements, and the funds for modernization and professionalization that are linked to this process—has facilitated the establishment of civilian control over the armed forces in the aftermath of regime change.[35] Again, the absence of such incentives in the functioning of the Rio Treaty in Latin America or after the collapse of the Warsaw Treaty Organization in Eastern Europe points to greater difficulties in these areas.

The members of the Organization of American States (OAS) may, however, be breaking new ground with regard to multilateral conditionality. At their annual meeting in Santiago in June 1991, the foreign ministers of its thirty-four member states—momentarily, all representing democratic governments—agreed to meet in emergency session 'to adopt any measures deemed appropriate' to restore democracy if one of their number were to be overthrown by non-constitutional means. The coup in Haiti, following only three months later, provided an almost perfect case for testing their resolve. The OAS did meet in response to the overthrow of Jean-Bertrand Aristide and voted unanimously to send a high-level mission to Port au Prince, as well as to apply comprehensive diplomatic and economic sanctions. Eventually, after much delay and backstage manœuvring, in September 1994 a Washington-orchestrated international operation culminated in the landing of 20,000 US troops, which were not in the end resisted. On 15 October President Aristide was reinstated in office, to serve out the residual fourteen months of his term, and Haiti embarked on yet another shaky effort to institutionalize competitive electoral politics. The continuing uncertainty in that country makes it difficult to assess what the final outcome will be, but for the first time there exists, at least in embryo, a system of international collective security that claims to protect countries (specifically, democracies) not only from external military aggression but also from internal political overthrow. Were it to become effective—and to be extended to other regions of the world—the entire international context of democratization would be radically transformed.

But why this sudden flurry of attention of collective efforts at ensuring or, better, promoting the consolidation of democracy—especially when previous unilateral or multilateral efforts at making the world safe for democracy met with such a lack of success? It is tempting to refer to the standard variables of interdependence and internationalization, perhaps with a side reference to the grow-ing regionalization of IGOs and NGOs. Moreover, in certain of these regions, democracy at the national level has become the norm not the exception.

While these broad parametric trends and waves no doubt contrib-ute something to the desire to impose conditionality, its feasibil-ity would seem to hinge on major changes in the system of global security. The end of the Cold War and, with it, the loss of external support for anti-capitalist and autocratic experiments in develop-ment has meant that regime changes no longer threaten the global balance of power. Democratic superpowers, such as the United States or Europe collectively, no longer need fear that the uncer-tainty of transition will be exploited by the sinister external forces of world Communism, aimed at undermining their security. On the one hand, this seems to leave insiders freer than before to choose their own institutions and follow their own policies—but only within the narrower constraints imposed by economic interdependence and international norms—on the other, it leaves outsiders freer to intervene when those norms are transgressed or when the inter-ests of interdependence are violated, especially in those *régimes d'exception* where the effort can be orchestrated multilaterally.

Appendix: Propositions and Hypotheses

To facilitate further discussion and research on the impact of the inter-national context upon contemporary democratization, I conclude with an inventory of propositions-cum-hypotheses that are implied by the above analysis. They are neither exhaustive nor inclusive. One could certainly add to them and systematize them further. They are offered as inductive generalizations based on a restricted set of cases and a restricted period of time, not as confirmed empirical findings or invariant deductive con-clusions. For, if there is one overarching lesson to be gleaned from the contemporary international context for democratization, it is that this con-text is subject to rapid change in both the magnitude and direction of its impact!

I. All contemporary regime changes are affected to a significant degree by the international political context in which they occur, even if:

A. This context does not dictate or determine the timing, type or outcome of the transition process.

B. The impact of the international context is normally mediated through national or sub-national actors and processes.

II. Transitions to democracy are more affected by this context since they involve a greater number and variety of actors with a wider range of public and private contacts to that environment. Moreover, once the transition has begun, even more numerous and novel channels of exchange open up as a side-product of the change in regime.

III. The significance of the international context tends to increase over time in the course of a 'wave of democratization' because:

A. Those cases coming later will be influenced (positively and negatively) by their predecessors (especially those in the immediate vicinity);

B. As the wave progresses, new international institutions and arrangements will be formed and apply their efforts to those that follow, *ergo*:

1. Over the course of successive democratizations in a wave, the nature of the international context will shift from primarily governmental and public action toward an increasing role for non-governmental and private institutions.

2. Also, there will be a tendency for the mode of action to change from uni- or bilateral actions towards multilateral efforts.

C. As the number of democratizations increases and is, therefore, geographically more dispersed, the role of actors in the international context will become increasingly explicit—overt rather than covert—and will seek open legitimation, both nationally and internationally.

IV. The most effective context within which external actors can influence democratic processes at the national level is increasingly regional, because:

A. Cultural and geographical propinquity will encourage the formation of denser and tighter networks among neighbouring countries.

B. The contemporary patterns of international interdependence, influenced by the formation of common markets, free-trade areas, and economic blocs, are themselves becoming increasingly regionalized and these multilateral efforts indirectly promote the formation of regionally based NGOs—parties, interest-groups, or movements—that can play a significant role at the national level.

C. Moreover, where such regional trading and policy-making organizations exist and where they restrict membership to democracies, they alone can have a very significant impact, especially upon the processes of consolidation.

V. Existing democratic states tend to believe that it is in their national interests (as well as their national ethos) that other states become democratic, because:

A. Democracies pose less of a security threat to each other.

B. Democracies tend to establish more reliable, extensive, and varied trading relationships with each other.

C. Democracies, however, may fail to act upon their intrinsic preference for other democracies when:

1. The cost of actual intervention is excessive;

2. The risk of failure is too great;

3. The concern for possible changes in national security is significant due to: (*a*) possible defection from an alliance to neutrality; (*b*) a

possible shift to an opposing alliance; (c) possible change to protection-
ist or discriminatory economic or social policies that would negatively
affect national producers.

VI. Transitions towards democracy either occur during or tend to provoke serious crises in a country's international economic relations, which,
in turn, tends to make the consolidation of democracy more difficult. This
is not to argue that:

A. Disillusionment with economic performance, even where severe and
   involving international complications, necessarily dooms the regime
   change to failure, rather:
B. Citizens are less likely (in the present international context) to come
   to believe that an alternative form of political domination (i.e. some
   form of autocracy) would perform better in the international economy
   and would be more likely to focus their negative evaluation upon the
   government or party in power than upon the regime type.

VII. The extent of influence that the international context will have
over the processes of regime change varies with:

A. the size of country
B. its geo-strategic location
C. its vulnerability to specific external flows such as:

   1. indebtedness payments
   2. critical energy or raw-material imports
   3. easily substitutable or subsidized exports.

VIII. The extent of external influence will vary with the stage, moment,
or sequence of the process of regime change.

A. Its potential marginal impact will be greatest during the transition,
   but this is when such an influence will be the most difficult to bring
   to bear effectively.
B. It will be easier and less risky to bring external influence to bear during the consolidation, but this is when the immediate marginal impact
   will be lower (and less visible).

IX. The greater the stalemate between internal political forces, the higher
the likelihood that one or another of them will be tempted to appeal for
external support to break that stalemate, although foreign powers may
prove reluctant to get involved in such a situation.

X. The more that the contending internal forces disagree over basic
foreign policy objectives, the greater the incentive for foreigners to intervene, since the outcome is more likely to produce policy differences that
could affect their interests.

XI. In the contemporary international context, the more open and penetrated the national economy and the more complex its interdependencies,
the more likely it is that regime change—once it occurs—will be towards
democracy, and the more likely that it will result in the eventual consolidation of democracy. This is not to argue:

A. that in an increasingly interdependent world system all regime changes will be in the same direction, or

B. that similar levels or degrees of interdependence will necessarily produce (and reproduce) similar domestic political institutions.

XII. The presence of a powerful democratic superpower (or powers) in the regional environment of a given country will have less of an impact upon the consolidation of democracy than the presence of a viable, expanding multilateral international organization.

XIII. The consolidation of democracy will leave most polities more, rather than less, dependent upon the international context.

XIV. However, the citizenry of these nascent democracies will be more rather than less inclined to accept the interference of foreign actors in their political (as well as economic and social) existence.

XV. Indeed, in certain parts of the world, e.g. Europe, the dispersion and consolidation of democracy opens up the possibility of the formation of a regional civil society that may precede (and eventually precipitate) the formation of a regional polity that will institutionalize democracy at a supra-national level. (Even Europe is still far from this outcome (*pace* the neo-functionalists), but its emergence is worth simulating, and, where possible, stimulating.)

Notes

1. The extent of popular participation and the timing of mass mobilization differ considerably from one mode of transition to another. For a discussion of this variation and its significance, see T. L. Karl and P. C. Schmitter, 'Modes of Transition in Latin America, Southern Europe and Eastern Europe', *International Social Science Journal*, 43/2 (1991), 269–84. For the theme of the delayed resurrection of civil society, see G. O'Donnell and P. C. Schmitter, *Transitions from Authoritarian Rule: Tentative Conclusions about Uncertain Democracies* (Baltimore: Johns Hopkins University Press, 1986), 48–56.

2. For example, protestations to the contrary notwithstanding, no one really expects Panama or Grenada to become models of democratic performance in the aftermath of their conquest by a democracy. The present rulers' origins as *commis* for an external power considerably undermine their legitimacy as representatives of their respective peoples. Similarly, no one seems to have been particularly shocked when various territories liberated by the democratic Allies during the Second World War reverted to colonial and/or autocratic governance: Morocco, Algeria, Tunisia, Libya, Ethiopia, Indo-China, and Indonesia. South Korea and the Philippines demonstrate that even where a considerable effort at the transfer of institutions is made by the retreating power, the outcome is not always stable democracy. Nevertheless, there is the very interesting case of the Dominican Republic, where

armed intervention by the United States has been followed by continuous competitive and open politics. Cf. R. Espinal, *Autoritarismo y democracia en la política dominicana* (San José: Centro Interamericano de Asesoría y Promoción Electoral, 1987).

3. G. O'Donnell and P. C. Schmitter, *Transitions*, iv. *Conclusions*, 19.
4. For a critique of this literature and of the treatment of international variables by students of regime transition, see G. Pridham, 'Democratic Transition and the International Environment: A Research Agenda', Centre for Mediterranean Studies, University of Bristol, CMS-Occasional Paper no. 1 (February 1991), revised as Chapter 1 above.
5. L. Whitehead, 'International Aspects of Democratization', in O'Donnell, Schmitter, and Whitehead (eds.), *Transitions*, iii. *Prospects for Democracy*, 3–46.
6. 'The International Dimension of Democratization: A Survey of the Alternatives', paper presented at the XVth Congress of IPSA, Buenos Aires, 21–5 July 1991.
7. For a discussion of Kantianism in the context of contemporary regime change, see P. C. Schmitter, 'Change in Regime Type and Progress in International Relations', in E. Adler and B. Crawford (eds.), *Progress in International Relations* (New York: Columbia University Press, 1991), 89–127.
8. It also antedated Kant's application of it to the international realm: cf. A. O. Hirschman, *The Passions and the Interests* (Princeton, NJ: Princeton University Press, 1977).
9. 'Will More Countries Become Democratic?', *Political Science Quarterly*, 99/2 (summer 1984), 206–7.
10. 'Dilemmas of Democratization in Latin America', *Comparative Politics*, 23/1 (1990), 1–21.
11. This has subsequently been explored in G. Pridham, 'The Politics of the European Community, Transnational Networks and Democratic Transition in Southern Europe', in G. Pridham (ed.), *Encouraging Democracy: The International Context of Regime Transition in Southern Europe* (Leicester: Leicester University Press, 1991), 212–45.
12. Cf. Göran Therborn, 'The Rule of Capital and the Rise of Democracy', *New Left Review*, 103 (May–June 1977), 3–41.
13. The reason for this seems rather obvious and closely linked to the nature of the international system. These ex-enemies in Eastern Europe and the Soviet Union occupy a much more salient position in calculations of global security than do the friendlier, but less strategically located, countries of Latin America, Africa, and Asia. The prospect that they can be somehow pacified or normalized via foreign aid, advice, and concessions appears to offer much greater and longer-term returns on the policy investments of established democracies. Ironically, if successful, this depolarization is likely to decrease the attention and resources devoted to other needy cases of nascent democratization, since it will have removed the element of great-power rivalry.

14. Even Switzerland, that oldest and most original of democracies, experienced significant changes in its ruling structures during periods that roughly corresponded to waves of democratization in neighbouring countries: 1849, 1872, 1917–20, and 1947.
15. It is possible to detect a mini-wave in the early 1870s which had a lasting effect on such countries as France, Switzerland, Italy, and Denmark, and a more ambiguous one in Germany and Austria–Hungary. The real subject-matter of this wave, however, was state-building and state reorganization, with democracy as an almost incidental by-product. Cf. C. Maier, 'Lines of Force or Thought: Redefining Authority, Interest and Identity in the Era of High Nationalism', in P. Schmitter (ed.), *Experimenting with Scale in Western Europe* (New York: Cambridge University Press, forthcoming).
16. By 1938, however, only one of them persisted in this status: Czechoslovakia. Finland carved itself out of the former Russian Empire; Norway out of the dual monarchy with Sweden — and both of these remained democratic.
17. Most of these post-war democratizations in Latin America were abortive. By the mid-1950s authoritarian rule had re-established itself almost everywhere, with the exception of Costa Rica. In the late 1950s and early 1960s, there was another, strictly regional, wave which corresponded roughly with the Alliance for Progress and led some observers to believe that the United States could effectively control regime outcomes in that part of the world. At one point in 1961, only Paraguay, Nicaragua, and Cuba had non-elected governments. Just two years later, beginning with Honduras and Brazil, the direction of change reversed itself, and democracy once again became the exception rather than the norm in the region.
18. The fact that two of the four waves coincided with an international war that directly affected all of the democratizing countries reduces considerably the plausibility of a thesis that diffusion or contagion alone were involved.
19. Extra-regional powers seem to have learned this lesson. Most of the US interventions in the delicate early years of the Portuguese transition were channelled through friendly European powers, just as much of the American aid for Eastern Europe is stated to pass through the European Bank for Reconstruction and Development.
20. One could go further and suggest that the relation is parabolic: low during the initial transition, building up to its maximum effect during the consolidation, and, subsequently, declining once national political institutions are functioning normally and, hence, capable of asserting both their internal and external sovereignty.
21. This point should not be exaggerated. When their security relationships appear to be jeopardized, external powers can find overt and, especially, covert means for intervening decisively at very short notice. And they can not only find, but even create, almost *de toutes pièces* the domestic interlocutors they need. Italy in the crucial years leading

up to the elections of 1948 and Portugal during the very uncertain spring and summer of 1975 were cases in point, where it can be claimed that the outcome in terms of regime type might have been different were it not for the rapid and deliberate intervention of foreign actors. Cf. R. Leonardi, 'The International Context of Democratic Transition in Postwar Italy: A Case of Penetration'; W. C. Opello, jun., 'Portugal: A Case Study of International Determinants of Regime Transition', both in Pridham (ed.), *Encouraging Democracy*, 62–83, 84–102.

22. This primordial element of transitional uncertainty—the absence of an accepted delimitation of the territorial and cultural parameters of the national political unit—may persist for some time. Indeed, until it is resolved, little or no progress can be made on the more concrete aspects of consolidation, and foreign intervention remains a highly risky proposition. The most obvious (and obtrusive) external action at the governmental level would be to recognize the contested sovereignty of the pre-existing unit, or that of its previous sub-components. While this issue has not arisen in southern Europe (with the possible exception of the Basque Country in Spain) or in Latin America, it is crucial to the role of external powers in several Eastern European cases. The cautious attitude of the EU countries with regard to the Baltic Republics, and their initial refusal to recognize the break-away republics of Yugoslavia or the other Soviet republics, are evidence of how sensitive this issue can be at the level of existing states. In the irrealist world of contemporary international relations, this has not, however, prevented private initiatives and non-state actions from promoting the formation of these sub-units—often with considerable success.

23. The examples of US intervention in Nicaragua to encourage Somoza to step aside peacefully and in the Philippines to depose Marcos offer contrasting evidence as to the efficacy of such efforts.

24. The Italian elections of 1948 were, perhaps, an extreme example of this sort of intervention, and covert US support for a Christian Democratic victory succeeded in making that party the dominant political force until the present day.

25. I have seen a reference somewhere to the fact that Turkey even allowed representatives from the Council of Europe to make unannounced inspections of local police stations in an effort to convince foreigners that it was respecting the civil rights of its citizens!

26. For a further discussion of the importance of timing for the process of consolidation, see P. C. Schmitter, 'La Consolidación de las democracias: procesos, ritmos, sequencias y tipos', in J. R. Montero (ed.), *Democracia* (Madrid: Siglo XXI, forthcoming). On the impossibility of resolving the problem of simultaneous transitions in economic, social, and political structures, see C. Offe, 'Capitalism by Democratic Design? Democratic Theory Facing the Triple Transition in East Central Europe', *Social Research*, 58/4 (winter 1991), 865–92.

27. In 1991 the IMF found itself embroiled in a controversy over political conditionality when one of its functionaries is alleged to have remarked that Brazil would only receive a stabilization loan if it changed its constitution to eliminate a provision guaranteeing individual states a share of federal tax revenues: V. Griffith, 'Brazil Suspends IMF Talks in Negotiator Row', *Financial Times* (24 July 1991).

28. Cf. T. Szulc, 'Lisbon and Washington: Behind the Portuguese Revolution', *Foreign Policy*, 21 (1976), 3–62; also T. Bruneau, 'As dimensões internacionais da revolução portuguesa: apoios e constrangimentos no estabelecimento de democracia', *Analise Social*, 18/72–4 (1982–3), 885–96. According to another account, Helmut Schmidt, Giscard D'Estaing, and Harold Wilson all discussed Soviet commitments in Portugal with Brezhnev 'with a view to trying to get them scaled down': see T. Benn, *Against the Tide: Diaries, 1973–76* (London: Hutchinson, 1989), 423.

29. To which one should add that even those countries which have previously negotiated some associate status are likely to find it jeopardized if they revert to authoritarian rule. The Greek Colonels who seized power in 1967 faced a freezing of Greece's developing relationship with the EC, as discussed in Chapter 12. These were only lifted in September 1974, shortly after their overthrow, and even before the first democratic elections were held. One should note, however, that several (if not most) of the countries in the African, Caribbean, and Pacific programme of the EU would not qualify as democracies.

30. Pridham, *Encouraging Democracy*, 235.

31. Ibid. 226. Also S. Verney and T. Couloumbis, 'State–International Systems Interaction and the Greek Transition to Democracy in the mid-1970s', in Pridham, *Encouraging Democracy*, 103–24.

32. Verney and Couloumbis, 'Systems Interaction', 117.

33. The creation of the European Bank for Reconstruction and Development (EBRD), with its quite explicit commitment to conditionality, raises the prospect that the EU may be able to influence the choice, timing, and sequence of institutions in Eastern Europe without extending the immediate prospect of full membership. The initial funding is substantial (if far inferior to the sums required), but it is not yet clear how conditionality will be exercised—especially in a body of such heterogeneous composition. Another possibility is that the Union may relax its insistence on the *acquis communautaire* on all new members accepting the complete accumulation of collective obligations, and create a multi-track system which would contain incentives for partial compliance with Union norms: cf. P. C. Schmitter, 'Interests, Powers and Functions: Emergent Properties and Unintended Consequences in the European Polity', unpublished paper, Center for Advanced Study in the Behavioral Sciences, Stanford, Calif., April 1992.

34. The persistent Greek opposition to Turkish membership on grounds other than regime type suggests that such security calculations can

interfere with the choice process, although there is no convincing evidence that the other EU members wish to allow Turkey in their ranks.
35. See F. Agüero, 'The Assertion of Civilian Supremacy in Post-Authoritarian Contexts: Spain in Comparative Perspective', Ph.D. diss. (Duke University, 1991).

....

PART II
....

The Americas

In Chapters 3 to 9 we review a range of international processes which have contributed to the transformation of the Western hemisphere from a continent in which a majority of the regimes were openly anti-democratic (mostly military dictatorships) twenty years ago, to one in which by the time of the Miami Summit of December 1994 it was only a pardonable exaggeration to claim that thirty-four out of the thirty-five states were operating some sort of more or less democratic (multi-party competitive electoral) form of government. As indicated in the Preface, not all the international dimensions can be given balanced consideration here: some key imponderables, such as the relationship between NAFTA membership and the possible democratization of Mexico, require more historical perspective than is currently available. Indeed, the completion and durability of the whole democratic community of the Americas proclaimed at the Miami Summit will remain speculative until tested by time. As economic integration proceeds this may knit together a dense network of transnational alliances and commitments which reinforce the convergence around democratic norms; but it could also turn out that growing economic interdependence raises the costs to the democratic majority of sustaining disincentives against member states which relapse into semi-, and even explicit, anti-democratic practices. (As we shall see when we turn to the European section of this volume, contrasting histories of EC relations with Greece and Turkey indicate that in some circumstances virtuous circles of convergence may have their vicious circle counterparts.) Whereas the Maastricht Treaty contains an explicit commitment to democracy and involves some definite pooling of national sovereignty, neither of these elements is written into the Free Trade Area of the Americas proposal, which remains essentially an economic association of states. How far this contrast will affect the respective prospects for democratization in the two regions remains to be seen.

In an attempt to avoid the pitfalls of democratic euphoria and teleology, this part adopts a selective and historical approach to the international dimensions of recent democratizations in the Western hemisphere. The present chapter develops the idea of 'control', proposed in Chapter 1. It therefore focuses mainly on those smaller countries in the Caribbean Basin which have been the privileged targets of what may be called 'democracy by imposition', orchestrated essentially (and for the most part unilaterally) by successive governments of the United States. Chapter 4 provides a contrasting study of President Carter's human rights policy towards three Latin American military regimes over which Washington could exert scant control; in part because in the midst of the Cold War these were national security regimes which saw themselves as engaged in all-out internal wars against subversion, and in part because, in contrast to the Caribbean cases, they were countries with strongly established traditions of national sovereignty. Given these contrasting focuses, it is interesting to note some similarities in the findings of the two chapters. In superficially similar situations the effectiveness of US policies turned out to vary rather widely. These diversities of outcome reflected the distinctive national traditions of each country, as well as differences of timing, balance, and commitment on the part of Washington policy-makers. In general, however, these two chapters give little reason to dissent from the verdict of G. Pope Atkins: 'US attempts to extend the practice of representative democracy and protection of human rights have been ambiguous and vacillating. When resources have been committed to the goal of democratic development, it has usually been viewed as an instrumental objective aimed at achieving one or the other of the long-range goals',[1] namely, the maintenance of political stability and the prevention of foreign control. In all cases the impact of democracy-promoting policies needs to be assessed over the very long run, given that it is the political self-definition of entire national communities which has to be modified, rather than simply the conduct of individual rulers.

Chapter 5 reviews the range of US aid policies geared to political development in Latin America during the Reagan years. It draws attention to the lack of historical perspective informing such policies, and to the superficial nature of Washington's understanding of the complex and varied national realities to which these policies were addressed. Here, too, the underlying message is that effective and lasting international support for democratization must involve a shift from the perspective of control to that of consent.

Chapters 6 and 7 offer contrasting country studies which highlight the subtlety and distinctiveness of national traditions in different South American republics. Brazil, as a vast continent-nation, ruled with some success for twenty years by a military establishment inspired by a sense of geopolitical mission, was perhaps the least amenable to any form of control of all the countries under review here. Nevertheless its path to democratization was affected by a variety of interactions and indirect external influences, which can be seen more clearly because they were not overshadowed by more intrusive forms of pressure. Chile, by contrast, has long sought to counter its geographical isolation by projecting a powerful image of national engagement in international, and particularly in European and North American, political and economic debates. Allende's 'Chilean road to socialism' sought to make the country an international showcase for that political philosophy, and the Pinochet dictatorship was equally active in promoting itself as the exemplar of the opposite view. In the course of that division, large cohorts of talented Chileans went into exile in various parts of Europe and the Americas. Chapter 7 directs our attention to the importance of this easily overlooked international dimension of the Chilean redemocratization process. In their different ways these two chapters both highlight the fact that battles over the course and content of democratization were also in no small measure struggles to promote one or other redefinition of the country's national and international identity, a vital aspect of political integration in such patriotic societies.

Chapters 8 and 9 complete Part II on the Americas by drawing attention to yet another, and analytically separate, international dimension of democratization. Transnational linkages between apparently like-minded parties and social organizations cannot easily be subsumed under any of the three headings proposed in Chapter 1. They are too targeted and purposive to be analysed in the language of contagion; and mostly too polycentric and invertebrate to meet the requirements of control. To some extent they can be considered under the rubrics of consent, and convergence, but with the qualifications that each party international has been engaged in sometimes quite fierce rivalry with its competitors (e.g. in Nicaragua and El Salvador), and that there has often been a marked lack of congruence between the stength and orientations of the internationals and the composition and objectives of their affiliates in any given country. Nor are these non-state actors able directly to apply conditionality, as discussed in Chapter 2, although their influence in the European Parliament, and their ability to offer or withhold funds from the party foundations, do give them some partial and indirect leverage. Notwithstanding these complications, in much of Europe and the Americas there has been a sufficiently shared tradition of political discourse and identification to make these into sometimes quite powerful non-state support channels. However, as the two chapters in this volume make clear, these Europe-based transmission mechanisms are not immune from many of the weaknesses and limitations we have found in the Washington-based agencies, and their impact is very variable over time and place. Their cultural limitations as international democratizing agencies can be seen most clearly at the fringes of Europe (e.g. in Turkey, the Balkans, and Islamic North Africa). Even in Latin America they have a very uneven presence, and with the near collapse of the old internationally aligned party system in Venezuela in the early 1990s their influence in the Caribbean has contracted dramatically.

Note

1. G. Pope Atkins, *Latin America in the International Political System*, 2nd edn. (Boulder, Colo.: Westview, 1989), 111–12.

3

The Imposition of Democracy: The Caribbean

LAURENCE WHITEHEAD

1. The US and Democracy Promotion in Latin America

HISTORY indicates that democracy is quite frequently established by undemocratic means. This is especially true of the history of US foreign relations, which have frequently involved the promotion of democracy by force of arms. France, Italy, Japan, and West Germany all acquired or reacquired democratic institutions under the tutelage of American armed forces. So, the 'imposition' of democracy is no contradiction in terms, at least not in the US political tradition. In fact one feature distinguishing the United States from all previously dominant or hegemonic powers is its persistent and self-proclaimed commitment to the promotion of democracy as an integral element of its foreign policy, and its long-standing confidence that 'all good things' (US influence and security, economic freedom and prosperity, political liberty, and representative government) tend naturally to go together. With such confidence and assertiveness rooted in the American tradition, and with some remarkable successes available as confirmation of their initial intuition, policy-makers in Washington are disinclined to believe that 'democracy by imposition' is a concept containing any particularly intractable contradictions. On this issue, however, the perceptions of most Latin American policy-makers are strikingly different.

For, although a democratic regime may originate from an act of external imposition, it will subsequently be necessary to secure the withdrawal of intrusive foreign influences if the democracy is eventually to take root and to secure the trust and acceptance of the national society in question. Unfortunately this intuitively plausible

model of the democratization process assumes the prior existence of a well-defined nation-state in which no major problems of
national identity remain pending. It also implicitly views the act
of imposition as an isolated event, rather than as one episode in
a protracted sequence of interactions between a dominant nation
and a subordinate one. Neither of these assumptions can be safely
made in relation to the United States and Latin America, which
is why the imposition of democracy in the region has often proved
a problematic and frustrating experience. In fact, as discussed in
this chapter, the broad notion of 'imposition' may embrace a considerable variety of distinctive forms, each with its own logic and
consequences. Three variants are considered here: incorporation,
invasion, and intimidation.

For most of the present century, and in particular since the
1940s, the United States has occupied a dominant position in the
affairs of the Western hemisphere. Its ascendancy has been not
only economic, demographic, and military but also political, ideological, and to some extent even cultural. In contrast to the position of the majority of dominant ('hegemonic') powers in the course
of world history, US ascendancy over its neighbours has been underpinned by a series of shared values, traditions, and assumptions.
These were all liberal republics, at least in origin and rhetoric; they
were all sheltered by the wide Atlantic from the internecine struggles of Europe, a region from which the dominant élites nevertheless
drew much of their inspiration. For the most part these were under-
populated rather than overpopulated territories, with corresponding opportunities for geographical and social mobility. Although
Latin America contained large areas of poverty, overcrowding, and
misery, there was also considerable economic dynamism and modernity. Both private enterprise and public welfare provision, such
as that for education, were considerably more advanced than in
most of the Third World, and they were well-established much
earlier.

In short, by world standards this was quite favourable terrain
for the implantation of conventional liberal democracy. And indeed
democracy did flower here—in Uruguay before the First World
War; in Argentina in the 1920s; in Chile from the 1930s; in Costa
Rica after 1948; in Colombia and Venezuela since 1958; and more
generally in the 1970s and 1980s. Moreover, throughout this whole
period the United States, as the dominant power, proclaimed the
promotion of democracy to be one of its enduring regional priorities.
Both Latin American and North American predispositions favoured
the generalized establishment of liberal democracy, and that is what

we are now witnessing with only a few laggards. Indeed, the December 1994 Summit of the Americas in Miami brought together no fewer than thirty-four directly elected presidents and heads of government 'to preserve and strengthen the community of democracies of the Americas'. President Castro of Cuba was the only ruler to be excluded as undemocratic (although the electoral credentials of Presidents Balaguer and Fujimori might also have been questioned).

However, the establishment in Latin America of democratic regimes has been a protracted and uneven process, with many shortcomings. Particularly in the smaller republics of Central America and the Caribbean neither the method nor the content of US policy has corresponded at all closely to that implied by the liberal terminology just reaffirmed at the Summit of the Americas, nor have the traditional élites and military establishments of most of these countries shown much inclination to promote non-exclusionary politics.

The most notorious instances of US interventions that were directly detrimental to democracy (Guatemala in 1954, Guyana in 1963, and Chile after 1970) can be largely attributed to the Cold War, but such episodes form part of a much longer history, which both preceded the Soviet challenge and extends beyond it. Thus, for example, both in 1915 and again on 19 September 1994 (just before the Miami summit) the USA landed Marines in Haiti to dislodge unacceptable governments there. Fortunately in the most recent instance this result was achieved with very little bloodshed and subject to an international mandate. Indeed, the immediate effect was to reinstate a democratically elected President. So there is a prima facie case that in the aftermath of the Cold War, democracy promotion in the Caribbean and Central America could begin to assume a more law-abiding and multilateral form, as proclaimed at the Summit of the Americas. On the other hand, Washington's apparent success in Haiti was a close call, the full results of which remain to be seen. Its multilateral character disguised a strong imbalance between US priorities (particularly to stem the flow of Haitian illegal immigrants) and the preoccupations of most other American states, and required a strained interpretation of the UN Charter.[1] Washington was also constrained to turn a blind eye to fraudulent electoral practices in the neighbouring Dominican Republic in order to maintain pro-democratic unity over Haiti. Thus, it is still too early to proclaim a liberal democratic end of history (or an end of US impositionism in the Caribbean) at the end of the twentieth century.

Rather than speculate on the future this chapter reviews evidence from the fairly recent past. It examines why, if the United States has generally favoured democracy promotion for so long, and if US influence in the region has been so great, and if the underlying local realities have been relatively favourable—why then have the results been so slow, uneven, and modest? For clarity this chapter concentrates on one aspect of the US record of democracy promotion: its reliance on various methods of imposition, particularly in those countries where the relative power of the United States is most overwhelming.

The point can be put provocatively, but not unfairly, as follows. There is only one place in Latin America where a strong consolidated liberal democracy has been established largely as a result of a sustained US commitment to that end. (The reader unable to identify the place in question may wish to skip a few pages to solve the puzzle.)

The interpretation proposed in this chapter derives from the assumption that not all good things necessarily go together. Where the promotion of democracy reinforces political stability, creates profitable business opportunities, and excludes rival powers from any real influence within a given territory (as in the exceptional case to be discussed), strong and sustained support for democratization may be expected from Washington. But what if democracy promotion might destabilize a key ally (as in Mexico in 1988)? What if the local electorate supports parties or policies hostile to US business interests (Guatemala in 1950 or Chile in 1970; and almost Brazil in 1989)? What if the 'institutionalization of uncertainty' implied by an open democratic contest includes uncertainty over the future international alignment of a strategic neighbour (Jamaica in 1980; or, prospectively, Nicaragua in 1996)? In all such cases both history and theory would suggest that Washington's commitment to the goal of democracy promotion could be expected to waver; and that at least some part of the US policy-making apparatus would be tempted to disregard democratic niceties in pursuit of the more urgent goals of stability, a good business climate, and the preservation of US ascendancy in the region.

In South America during the 1980s the conflict between democracy promotion and other US foreign policy goals was attenuated as the Cold War faded, and as the debt crisis impelled southern hemisphere governments of all persuasions to compete in attracting scarce foreign capital. Even so, many in Washington were reluctant to destabilize friendly authoritarian regimes. In fact, the sharp distinction made in the early 1980s between 'authoritarian' and 'totalitarian' variants of undemocratic politics had the effect of deflecting pressure against the former. However, the Argentine military regime destabilized itself by precipitating the Falklands–Malvinas war, and the Uruguayans achieved a similar result by holding and unexpectedly losing a plebiscite. As the decade progressed, the argument about destabilization shifted, for it became increasingly clear that rigid defence of an authoritarian status quo was likely to be more destabilizing than a controlled and gradual liberalization. Even where the eventual outcome of liberalization was likely to be full democratization, with all the risks and uncertainties that that might entail, almost any incoming civilian government would be driven to mend its fences with Washington by the severity of the socio-economic problems it would inherit, and by the need to circumvent the potential veto power of vested interests left over from authoritarian rule. Thus the United States had less to fear from South American democratization in the 1980s than would have been the case a decade or two earlier. It also had relatively limited influence south of the Caribbean and therefore prudence dictated that if democratization was coming anyway, Washington would be well advised to anticipate and herald the change.

Conditions were different in the Caribbean Basin and on the Central American isthmus, however. There America's Cold War reflexes still predominated during the 1980s. Even after fears of Soviet intentions were assuaged by Gorbachev's new policies, Washington policy-makers remained affronted by Castro's Cuba, and by the challenges from Havana that they still perceived in El Salvador, Nicaragua, and Panama. Several of America's allies still seemed vulnerable to destabilization if too much was demanded of them in the areas of human rights and respect for political pluralism. Although by the 1980s US investments were generally far less important than they had been in earlier periods, this part of Latin America had become quite intimately linked to the US economy via migratory flows, the concessionary trade links encouraged under the Caribbean Basin Initiative, and large-scale illegal transactions concerning narcotics, armaments, and money-laundering. In contrast to South America, therefore, the promotion of democracy in the Caribbean Basin still had the potential to clash quite fundamentally with Washington's other more traditional foreign policy priorities. Moreover, the inequalities of power between the USA and many of the region's mini- and micro-states was far greater than in most of South America, and the interventionist tradition was far more strongly entrenched. It is here that the US capacity to 'promote democracy' in foreign lands should be at its greatest; and it is here that the USA has the longest track-record of 'teaching good government', including by direct occupation and military imposition.

This chapter therefore examines three selected examples of the imposition of democracy in those parts of the Caribbean Basin where US ascendancy has been longest and greatest. The object is to determine under what conditions (and with what limitations) Washington has succeeded in achieving this proclaimed policy goal; and therefore what kind of democracy is likely to be favoured by a massive and unilateral deployment of US power in the region. This is an exercise in recent comparative history, but, as noted briefly in the conclusion, it also has implications for the 1990s, particularly in relation to the still-pending issue of Cuba. Three methods of imposition have been selected for comparison: incorporation, invasion, and intimidation. This highlights the contrast between US and European Union approaches to democracy promotion in adjoining territories. Whereas the decision-making processes of the United States tend to favour democracy promotion by imposition, the European treaty structure precludes such an approach.

2. *Democracy Promotion through Incorporation: Puerto Rico*

The one Latin American country with a fully consolidated democratic regime where the United States has played a consistent, sustained, and determining role in the democratization process is of course the Commonwealth[2] of Puerto Rico. Yet this spectacular example is overlooked in the literature, perhaps simply because it is so easy to forget that Puerto Rico is indeed a Latin American country, or more seriously perhaps because the political price paid for this US support—namely, the absence of sovereignty—is unwelcomely high. But in fact the Puerto Rican experience cannot be dismissed at all lightly, for although it is such a rare case of 'success', it actually dramatizes in an extreme form processes of imposition that can also, as we shall see, be observed elsewhere.

In the exceptional case of Puerto Rico there is no ambiguity about the use of the term 'imposition' to describe the first phase of American policy. Whereas in Cuba and in Panama US intervention was at least nominally in support of local forces fighting for national liberation, the US seizure of Puerto Rico from Spain in 1898 was a straightforward act of colonialism. Cuba and Panama were both allowed a degree of semi-independence in the early 1900s, whereas fifty years were to elapse before Puerto Rico's colonial status began to shift. Even now the eventual outcome (labelled here democratization-through-incorporation) is by no means complete. However, if we take incorporation as the essential pattern, then the US contribution to Puerto Rican democracy can be compared with the experience of Hawaii, or with the French role in Guadeloupe and Martinique, not to mention various British colonies such as Bermuda. In all these instances it seems that the domestic entrenchment of representative institutions has been forcefully promoted by a metropolitan power whose permanent involvement and commitment precludes the possibility of self-determination. In other words, they all appear to involve some kind of trade-off between sovereignty and external support for democracy.

The Puerto Rican experience provides a model case. Here we shall briefly consider the nature and scale of the US contribution to Puerto Rican democracy; the reasons why it was more durable and effective than elsewhere in Latin America; and the consequences for the regime both positive (strong consolidation) and negative (insecurity over political identity, lack of national authenticity). In the light of this discussion some conclusions can be drawn about the type of democratization likely to arise from such strong external involvement, and about the applicability or otherwise of this broad approach in other parts of Latin America.

Political parties, representative institutions, and competitive elections existed in colonial Puerto Rico long before the landing of US troops in July 1898, although the Spanish imperial authorities retained the right to veto local laws. On the other hand, starting in 1812, Puerto Rican deputies were seated in successive Spanish Cortes and could vote on all legislation (a contrast to the present situation, in which the island's commissioner in Washington may vote in committee but has no vote on the floor of Congress). However, this system of representation was far too restricted to qualify as a modern democracy. Whether one would have developed in the absence of US intervention is a tantalizing but unanswerable question. (It could also be asked of Cuba, Panama, the Dominican Republic, and other countries.) At any rate, in 1898 the Spanish system of representation appears to have commanded little loyalty, and most Puerto Ricans are said to have welcomed the American troops, accompanied as they were by the promise 'to give to the people of your beautiful island the largest measure of liberty consistent with this military occupation . . . to promote your prosperity and bestow upon you the immunities and blessings of the liberal institutions of our government,' according to the US military proclamation of 28 July 1898.

From 1900 onwards US law guaranteed islanders the right to elect mayors and the lower house of a legislative assembly (on a restricted franchise), but executive power was vested in nominees from Washington. Since 1917 Puerto Ricans have enjoyed American citizenship (including liability to the military draft), and there has been an elected bicameral assembly with some authority over the cabinet. From 1948 onwards the governor has been directly elected. However, these American citizens cannot vote in presidential elections, and the island's elected authorities lack various attributes of sovereignty, such as the powers to set tariffs, to enter into international economic agreements, and to control the immigration of foreign (non-US) citizens. Although the island has its own electoral commission and its own supreme court, the ultimate arbiter of disputed local elections, like that of 1980 (and indeed of all constitutional issues), remains the US Supreme Court. Other matters of vital concern to the islanders, such as the Internal Revenue Code and the funding of the US welfare system, are also decided in Washington without their participation. It is true that they can vote from time to time in plebiscites to determine possible changes in their constitutional status—for example, in 1967 39 per cent voted to apply to Washington for statehood, and 46 per cent did so in the 1993 plebiscite. But the power of decision on such changes remains vested in the US Congress, and such tests of Puerto Rican public opinion are no more than advisory, albeit of great moral force. This, then, is the current status of Puerto Rican democratic institutionality.

So in what sense does Puerto Rico have a 'fully consolidated democracy', and what was the US contribution to the consolidation process? There is as yet no clear consensus on what constitutes the 'full consolidation' of a democratic process, but by most criteria Puerto Rico ranks ahead of almost every other Latin American and Caribbean country. The closest rival with full sovereignty is Costa Rica. Elsewhere[3] I have argued that one partial but very revealing test of whether a fragile democracy has become fully consolidated is to ask whether the citizens of a long-established and secure democracy would feel unthreatened by an act of political unification or incorporation. By this standard the European Parliament in Strasbourg implicitly judged Portugal, Spain, and Greece to have fully consolidated democracies by the 1980s (but not Turkey). Likewise the US Congress made this judgement about Hawaii in 1959. Since neither the plebiscite of 1967 nor that of 1993 produced a majority for statehood we do not know whether Puerto Rico would have passed this test in the US Congress although in both years the case would have been pretty strong. On this basis, then, Puerto Rican democracy has long been remarkably 'consolidated'. This is not a claim that can yet be safely made about, say, the Dominican Republic or Venezuela.

By more conventional criteria Puerto Rico established a modern electoral democracy in successive stages. Female suffrage was obtained in 1932; universal adult suffrage in 1936; the exchange of votes for favours became less common after 1940; promotion by merit began to replace the spoils system of public employment in 1947. The US Congress was, of course, directly responsible for progress while the island remained a colony. Then with the 1952 constitution the local legislature established a strong legal framework for electoral competition. (It is worth noting that, whereas in the British Caribbean democratic structures were created from above by the less-than-democratic method of imperial orders in council, in Puerto Rico this was the work of a popularly constituted constitutional convention.) The organization of a well-structured majority party, the Partido Popular Democrático (PPD), no doubt facilitated this process of institution-building. US support was ensured when the PPD politically isolated and neutralized the once-powerful independence movement; thenceforth the best way for Washington to stabilize the power of its Puerto Rican allies was to back their democratization project.

In due course a second more conservative party, the Partido Nuevo Progresista (PNP), gained sufficient electoral strength to constitute a genuine alternative to the PPD, this time by advocating full statehood. The governorship has alternated between these two parties in successive elections (in 1968, 1972, 1976, and 1984). Control of the legislature has also passed back and forth in a normal manner. Minor parties have also established niches for themselves (in part because Puerto Rican law provides for minority-party representation on local councils), and the political commitment of the electorate is confirmed by the extremely high levels of turnout that characterize most elections, even after the voting age was lowered to 18 in 1971 (an estimated 88.3 per cent in the 1980 governorship election, for example, compared with the 59.2 per cent of the US voting-age population who reported voting in the presidential election held on the same day).[4] Since 1977 Puerto Ricans have also participated in the primaries organized by the two main US parties to select their presidential nominees. As already noted, the law also provides for the possibility of holding plebiscites, as was done in 1952 and 1967 on the status issue.

In view of this record it is hard to dissent from the conventional judgement that Puerto Rico has established a free and democratic system of political representation. Freedom House, for example, considers that in 1985 Puerto Rico was one of only 10 non-sovereign territories (out of 55) to enjoy full civil liberties (only 20 out of 167 sovereign states met this condition). In the non-sovereign territories of the Caribbean only the Netherlands Antilles and the British Virgin Islands reached the same standard, and in the sovereign states of Latin America and the Caribbean only Belize, Costa Rica, and St Kitts were rated as highly.[5] For the sake of realism it must also be mentioned, however, that when in 1981 the Puerto Rican supreme court ruled in favour of the PPD and against the PNP in an election dispute, the PNP governor accused it of blatant partiality, arguing that six of the seven judges had been appointed by the PPD. He therefore appealed the case to the US Supreme Court (claiming that the matter was a civil rights rather than an electoral issue and was therefore subject to federal law). Eventually the Washington court upheld the original Puerto Rican court judgment.

As this appeal to the US Supreme Court indicates, the whole process of democratization in Puerto Rico has been continuously stabilized and guaranteed by the institutions of the United States. Certainly the islanders and their political leaders have played leading and for the most part constructive roles in this process, but always within a framework provided from outside. Even the electoral timetable is set by the rhythms of Washington. Indeed one reason why Puerto Rican democracy receives so little international recognition is that gubernatorial election results coincide with and are therefore swamped by simultaneous US presidential results. So this case represents a clear exception to the generalization that in post-war Latin America democratizations are internally driven, with external factors playing only a secondary part.

Why was US support for democracy so much more durable and effective than elsewhere in Latin America? Obviously the 1898 invasion denied external powers access to the island and thus removed a competing foreign policy concern. The key step was the Jones Act of 1917, by which the US Congress conferred citizenship (albeit 'passive'—that is, without congressional representation). This was regarded as an irrevocable step. It made young Puerto Rican men liable for US military service and therefore eligible for the benefits conferred on ex-servicemen. Unsurprisingly, then, the island also became an indispensable element in the US naval system. The Jones Act also implied a general right to travel and work on the mainland without fear of deportation. Of course, these political arrangements were linked to an economic settlement. These passive citizens would be exempted from federal taxation as well as from congressional representation. Even prior to the 1952 constitution, therefore, the island possessed a degree of fiscal autonomy (it could raise its own taxes, and grant its own tax exemptions), while at the same time enjoying duty-free access to the huge mainland market for its goods, and relying on the US Federal Reserve to provide its currency and to conduct its monetary policy.

In short, Washington has undertaken a succession of economic, strategic, and political commitments to Puerto Rico that are much more far-reaching and irrevocable than any other obligations it has shouldered in Latin America. US business interests enjoy the full panoply of legal guarantees available on the mainland; so Washington is not cross-pressured between democracy promotion and business promotion. Puerto Rico's small population and peculiar history made it possible for the United States to accept such obligations in this case, precisely because no general precedent would be set. It seems unlikely that American policy-makers could seriously have offered similar arrangements to larger or more indigestible Latin republics (such as Cuba). But in the unique case of Puerto Rico, Washington was willing to undertake such massive and durable (if lopsided) commitments that the United States effectively underwrote an American-style democratization of the island.

What, then, were the costs and benefits of this method of democracy promotion for Puerto Rico? The political benefits have already been outlined—a stronger system of civil rights, a securer rule of law, and a more firmly entrenched system of electoral pluralism than almost anywhere else in Latin America. The economic benefits must also be mentioned, for the stability of the political system has been powerfully reinforced by the accompanying experience of considerable relative prosperity. Income levels have risen well above the Latin American norm (and now approach half those of the poorest state in the union, Mississippi): Puerto Rico is sheltered from the inflation, debt crisis, and International Monetary Fund (IMF)-imposed austerity programmes of its neighbours (for example, government borrowing benefits from a federal guarantee). Living standards have risen to such a point that by 1982 minimum wages on the island could be raised to the federal level. However, there is a negative side to the economic record. High unemployment is a predictable counterpart to high minimum wages. The federal food stamp programme provides a costly safety-net for the poor. But the most important cushion has come from the unrestricted right to emigrate to the mainland, where about two-fifths of all islanders now reside. Were it not for some very expensive subsidies to Puerto Rican industry (notably tax breaks for US firms investing on the island), unemployment and/or emigration would be even higher. Federal transfers, welfare payments, and tax concessions account for about a quarter of the island's regional income, and of course the laws governing inflow are written by a legislature in which the islanders have no vote.

The political price of such a democracy is therefore a considerable loss both of sovereignty and of formal representation. Puerto Ricans sent to fight in Vietnam had no voice in America's debate over the war; their rights to abortion may be curtailed or extended by the decision of others; decisive elements of economic policy are fixed by mainlanders without their concurrence; their elected representatives have no voice in international economic forums. From the standpoint of democratic theory these are serious imperfections, signifying that some US citizens have formal rights that are gravely and permanently impaired compared with those of the majority. In place of the ethic of citizen autonomy, with rights and duties conventionally balanced, Puerto Rican democracy rests on a constrained and dependent form of citizenship with special exemptions excused by the provision of unilateral subsidies. In fact this is a democracy based on the acceptance of second-class citizenship. According to theory, such a formula should breed both resentment and irresponsibility. In practice, the main result seems to have been to generate a persistent obsession with the status issue, and an associated insecurity over the island's real social identity. Although this chapter has classified the islanders as a Latin American people, in many respects they still find themselves in an international limbo.

What lessons can we draw from this example of strong US involvement in democracy promotion? Above all, the Puerto Rican path to democracy is most unlikely to be repeated. The US Congress will almost certainly not grant citizenship (and the unrestricted right of entry) to any other Latin American people or nation in the foreseeable future. The only wholly democratic outcome consistent with the extension of US citizenship would be full Puerto Rican entry into the union as an additional state. However, the pro-statehood PNP suffered a considerable setback in November 1993, when a plebiscite on the status issue recorded a narrow preference for the status quo (48.4 per cent) as opposed to incorporation into the USA (46.2 per cent). (The third alternative—independence—received only 4.4 per cent support, and the turnout was an impressive 80 per cent.) Even if Puerto Rico does in the end achieve US statehood it will only occur after an extremely protracted inter-regnum. Almost a century has already elapsed since the military proclamation of July 1898, and still opinions remain divided, both within the United States and on the island, about the shape of the eventual constitutional settlement. If Washington is to promote democracy strongly in other parts of Latin America, it will almost certainly seek a shorter route, and one that can be traversed at lower cost to the US taxpayer. For their part Latin American beneficiaries of such strong US support will presumably seek to achieve a greater degree of sovereignty at a lower cost in terms of social identity.

3. Democracy Promotion through Invasion: Panama

It would be rash to anticipate the unfolding consequences of the December 1989 US invasion of Panama, but some inferences can be drawn from that country's now quite lengthy past. Because of the Canal, and because of all the history associated with it, we can be fairly sure that Washington will continue to seek a strong influ-ence over the course of Panamanian politics. If the US commitment to democracy promotion is anything like as strong as declaratory statements suggest, Panama is second only to Puerto Rico (perhaps equal with Nicaragua) as a country where one would expect that priority to materialize.

In November 1903 Panama broke away from Colombia under the protection of US gunboats. The new republic received prompt recog-nition and financial assistance from Washington, and in return granted the United States extensive concessions over the proposed Canal route. In theory US military action responded to Panamanian aspirations and sheltered a sovereign and liberal new regime.

However, on 16 May 1908 Secretary of War Taft wrote to Presid-ent Theodore Roosevelt about a proposed treaty with Panama:

We should be given direct control over the elections, so as to permit us, should we desire, to intervene and determine who is fairly elected. This I agree detracts from the independence of the 'Republic' but as the Republic has not shown itself competent in this regard, we are justified . . . to protect our own interests.[6]

This American supervision persisted until the Great Depression. But in January 1931 a Panamanian president was surprised to find his appeal for US military assistance against his political rivals unanswered. 'The old political hierarchy, which had survived for nearly three decades by periodic threats of American intervention, suddenly found itself discredited. In the ensuing campaign for the Panamanian presidency, no candidate solicited American endorsement.'[7]

Under the Good Neighbour Policy of the 1930s Washington to some extent backed away from this degree of external supervision, signing a new Canal treaty in 1936 that somewhat increased the Panamanian government's room for manœuvre. On the political front, in place of gunboat diplomacy the United States sought to substitute good neighbourly abstention from direct involvement in Panama's electoral processes. But this policy proved quite as problematic as the one it displaced, because in Panama, as in other former US protectorates, the political forces that moved to fill the space created by Roosevelt's self-denying ordinances were less than wholly democratic. By the time of the tense elections of April 1948, Secretary of State Marshall was straining to avoid US intervention.[8]

The 1948 election revealed in the starkest terms the contrast between what Washington could achieve in conditions of direct rule in Puerto Rico and what American policy-makers would have to contend with in an ex-protectorate where the national police had been allowed to acquire an identity of its own. At first Colonel Remón of the national police chose to support a fraudulent electoral outcome, and both the electoral tribunal and the supreme court of Panama fell into line with this decision. The United States, following the policy of non-intervention, also accepted this outcome. Within eighteen months, however, Colonel Remón decided that his interests would be better served by a reversal of position. Disregarding Panama's supreme court, in November 1949 he forced the incumbent president to resign and summoned the elections board to recount the 1948 results. 'In hours the Board found pro-Arias votes it had been unable to find in weeks after the 1948 balloting.'[9] US Ambassador David was left to fulminate:

While action [by] Remón and Arias may evidence flattering confidence [in the] reality [of] our non-intervention policy, it shows also a cynical disregard of principles democratic and otherwise, and complete disdain for our oft repeated expressions of policy. It is believed Remón and his gangster associates are incapable of understanding international implications. Apparently it is their idea that they can be brazen about their illegal procedure and yet insist we recognize decisions forced upon their judicial and legislative branches. . . . Since we let it be known we would be guided by action of National Assembly and Supreme Court, it would be logical to do so, stating US government therefore recognizes (deposed) Charis as constitutional president and is prepared to proceed with conduct of normal business once illegal interference by force ceases to impede. This course should not, however, be taken unless we are prepared to take a determined stand and see it through.[10]

The ambassador's recommendation was not adopted, however, in part because the internal legality that it invoked was so unreal. Within three days the State Department had concluded that Arias was in control, at which point a very different view of the 1948 election emerged: 'There can be no doubt that he won the election last year and was cheated out of the Presidency by the fraudulent actions of the electoral jury.'[11] In the absence of full US control over internal political processes, there was no way that even the sincerest and most single-minded Washington supporter of Panamanian democracy could sidestep the reality of competing partisanships and fragmented legitimacy.

In reality, of course, any concern Washington might have felt for democracy in Panama was always overshadowed by the higher priority of preserving the security of the Canal Zone. US policy documents record a close and continuing interest in the internal politics of the republic, but this was always viewed from the standpoint that a friendly and secure pro-American administration would be the best guarantor of Washington's overriding security interests. On the many occasions where that priority conflicted with an even-handed concern for the sovereign democratic order, the issue of democracy took second place. All Panamanian political factions understood that reality and conducted their activities accordingly. Thus, regardless of all the rhetoric in favour of democracy and non-intervention, the objective structure of these power relations was systematically weighted against the consolidation of a democratic order. This goes far to explain why from initially fairly similar points of departure, at the turn of the century the Panamanians made virtually no progress in the establishment of democratic institutions, whereas especially since 1950 the Puerto Ricans achieved major cumulative advances.

The Panamanian electoral process of 1948–9 deserves reconstruction because it anticipates so much of the experience of the 1980s. It therefore demonstrates the existence of a systematic pattern of political interaction between the United States and Panama that cannot simply be attributed to the criminality of General Noriega; and since this pattern of political behaviour is entrenched, the task of averting future repetitions of the cycle will require far more than just the seizure and imprisonment of one military leader.

In May 1984, as in May 1948, a hard-fought presidential election ended fraudulently. The head of the electoral tribunal resigned rather than certify the results, which were imposed by the National Guard under the direction of General Noriega; international observers described them as rigged, but the US State Department accepted them at face value. The incoming president was more acceptable to Washington than his electorally more successful rival—indeed US policy-makers appear to have played an important role in selecting and nominating him. In any case the State Department feared a coup if the pro-government candidate lost the first election held in sixteen years. Even with the benefit of hindsight the chief US policy-maker, Elliott Abrams, still defended the endorsement of a fraudulent outcome, which in his view 'seemed to help propel Panama into the flow towards democracy that is powerfully moving the hemisphere'.[12] In 1985, as in 1984, the illegitimate civilian president attempted to assert his authority against the National Guard that brought him to power. The results were the same, as was the initial US response. Abrams later conceded that the forced resignation of the president was a setback to democracy, but consoled himself with the observation that 'constitutional procedures were followed, at least formally, and Panama remained an open society'.[13] In the ensuing four years Panama was headed by a succession of nominal presidents while real power was retained elsewhere. As in 1948–51, conflicts of jurisdiction escalated and political institutionality degenerated, until following an even more fraudulent election in May 1989, the United States recognized a government in hiding and finally in December 1989 resorted to armed intervention. The stated grounds for this invasion by 26,000 US troops were, first, to safeguard the lives and property of American citizens; second, to terminate General Noriega's drug-trafficking; third, to 'restore democracy' in Panama; and fourth, to maintain the normal operations of the Canal. It is the contention of this section that the first, second, and fourth goals on this list express the tenor of US–Panamanian relations far more typically than the third; the method they imply is imposition, a method that would be far less appropriate if the principal goal of policy was democracy promotion.

The record of US policy towards Panama in the 1980s culminating with the 1989 invasion leaves plenty of room to argue, with the benefit of hindsight, that some alternative choice of policies would have been more effective, more prudent, more principled, or even more supportive of Panamanian democracy. While that may be so, the critical point is that, despite all the advantages available to Washington policy-makers, and despite their strong interest in shaping a favourable political outcome in Panama, their choices were all sub-optimal, and their capacity to reshape Panamanian political processes proved once again to be remarkably limited. In the absence of stable and autonomous legal institutions (which might sometimes clash with immediate US security interests), and in the presence of a perverse pattern of reactions established over several generations through which Panamanian leaders learned how to play off what Washington said about their country against what it really meant, the United Sates was reduced to the starkest and most unattractive of alternatives: either to endure continuing ridicule and defiance from a patently oppressive and corrupt former protégé, or to intervene unilaterally and with massive force in the hope of establishing a fresh beginning.

Although the first eighty-seven years of US–Panamanian relations have not proved very productive from the standpoint of democracy promotion, there are those who regard the December 1989 invasion as the start of a bright new era. Such claims should never be dismissed out of hand. Just as the directly colonial phase of US–Puerto Rican history gave way to a somewhat more equitable relationship in the 1950s, similar possibilities should be considered in Panama. This chapter does not exclude that hypothesis but merely argues that it will take some time before we can judge. Meanwhile the legacy of the past will continue to impede the prospects for authentic and durable democracy promotion in Panama. The security of the Canal, although less vital to the United States than in earlier years, will continue to preoccupy Washington policy-makers as much as the health of Panamanian democracy. If the two priorities were ever again to conflict, the United States would again seek above all else to protect the Canal. After all, America's power, its prestige, and even the lives of its soldiers have just been reinvested in that enterprise.

In the wake of any invasion, the first priority of the occupying force will naturally be to protect the security of its nationals and to make the outcome of the invasion irreversible. Where the aims of the invasion are temporary, and coincide with the wishes of the local population (as in the Grenada 'rescue mission' of 1983), the occupying force may subsequently manage to withdraw, leaving a well-functioning democracy behind. But in Panama the situation is not so clear-cut, in part because American nationals are not about to be withdrawn from the Canal Zone; in part because despite the abolition of the National Guard a security force will still be needed; and in part because the Panamanian economy will continue to revolve around supplying 'services' within this dollar zone and as an adjunct to the entrepôt functions of the canal. Therefore the post-invasion regime will continue to grapple with very similar problems to those that impeded democratization before 1989.

If drug-trafficking, money-laundering, and arms-dealing are no longer to provide the basis of the Panamanian economy, how can an independent democratic government achieve reconstruction and the restoration of confidence after the dislocation caused by the US sanctions and invasion? Since the new post-invasion Endara government (which based its legitimacy on 1989 election results that were annulled before the count was complete) lacked sufficient authority or resources of its own, it was forced to depend once more on the protection of Washington. But a restoration of the 1903–31 protectorate system was not an option in the post-Cold War world. Since, of course, Washington has no wish to incorporate Panama (as it had incorporated Puerto Rico) the problem of anti-US nationalism within a sovereign Panama was almost bound to resurface as a source of inter-state tension. The enterprise of promoting the appearance of national sovereignty while intrusively supervising the substance of local politics is an inherently conflictual undertaking. In the event, in November 1992, when President Endara held a plebiscite on constitutional reforms that might have stabilized the post-invasion balance of political forces, the electorate rejected the package by a majority of almost two to one. By the end of his term of office Endara was reduced to issuing undignified protests against what he described as a disrespectful US stance towards his office; and in the 1994 elections it was the traditionally nationalist Partido Revolucionario Democrático (pro-Noriega in 1988) that won the presidential election, albeit under a conciliatory leadership. There is continuing potential for US–Panamanian friction, not only over such timeless issues as drug-trafficking, money-laundering, and law enforcement, but also in relation to the still fraught issue of the Canal, which, according to the Carter–Torrijos Treaty of 1978, should revert to Panamanian control at the end of 1999.

Thus, an objective assessment of the effects so far of America's massive presence in Panama offers little encouragement to those who suppose that all good things come readily together. Democracy promotion does not necessarily accompany the projection of US power, least of all when that result is sought on the cheap, without any dilution of Washington's other purposes, and without much understanding of the perverse psychology engendered by a combination of formal sovereignty with real dependency.

4. Democracy Promotion by Intimidation: Nicaragua

Our third example of democracy promotion in the Caribbean Basin is Nicaragua. Here, too, the United States has an extremely long track-record; again Washington's power in relation to any government in Managua is potentially overwhelming. Although in the nineteenth century there was some thought in the United States of incorporating Nicaragua, that notion has had no currency in the twentieth; and since the 1920s the idea of invading Nicaragua has been distinctly out of favour with US military planners. There was a US military presence from 1912 to the Great Depression, and the United States did propose in 1979 that the Organization of American States (OAS) might send a 'peacekeeping force' to prevent the Sandinista revolutionaries from seizing full power (along the lines of the successful US intervention with OAS approval in the Dominican Republic in 1965). Throughout all these episodes the defence or promotion of democracy has been repeatedly articulated as a justification of American policy towards Nicaragua. In a similar way it is currently claimed that the February 1990 elections vindicate hotly contested assertions made throughout the Reagan Administration concerning the democratic purposes of the 'covert' or 'Contra' war against the Sandinistas, launched in November 1981, and sustained for more than eight years thereafter. So, does the recent history of US–Nicaraguan relations demonstrate the efficacy of Washington's strategy of democracy promotion through intimidation, or does it more nearly resemble the pattern just sketched of US–Panamanian interactions?

Once again we are dealing with a long history. Over several generations the United States has exerted its extensive influence in Nicaragua in ways that have not served to generate political consensus or to encourage respect for democratic norms. In the second and third decades of this century, the Marines were used to prop up strongly contested governments in Managua. For example, they supervised and administered the 1928 elections against a substantial military and political challenge from the revolutionary general César Augusto C. Sandino. In American eyes he was a 'bandit,' but to many Nicaraguans and to a wide swathe of Latin American opinion he was a more authentic political leader than the Nicaraguan party leaders who had consented to elections on Washington's terms. Latin American disbelief in Washington's ostensible commitment to democracy in Nicaragua was reinforced by US conduct during the almost half-century of the Somoza dynasty. As in Panama, Washington attempted a stance of non-intervention in

Nicaragua's internal affairs, and as in Panama this provided undemocratic armed forces with a licence to commit abuses and to pursue
personal enrichment with political impunity. Successive American
administrations hesitated to criticize such a well-entrenched ally
(with good friends in Congress), especially since he could be counted
on to endorse Washington's most controversial foreign policy initiatives. To lock in US support the Somozas took care to neutralize the
democratic centre in Nicaragua, always presenting Washington with
the choice between an undemocratic but reliable right, or a radical
and potentially 'disloyal' left.

The Sandinista revolution of 1979 was a logical outcome of this
long history. The many nationalist and radical currents of opinion
that had been suppressed by the Somozas resurfaced under the
umbrella of the Sandinista Front. Although the bulk of the Front's
leadership was Marxist-inclined, and although many of the key figures had been trained or influenced by Cuba, the rigid and repressive nature of the Somoza regime enabled the Sandinistas to build
a broad alliance, with centrists attracted by the promise of democratic elections, a mixed economy, and non-alignment. According
to the official US view, Washington's policies of 'intimidation' during
the 1980s were in fact intended to force the Sandinistas to honour
these original promises, and that is the result they are said finally
to have achieved in the February 1990 elections that displaced the
Sandinistas from government.

On closer inspection of the record of US intimidation of Nicaragua
during the 1980s the picture is less clear-cut. To avoid misunder-
standings it must be stated at the outset that the Sandinista Front
chose to overplay its hand, attempting to consolidate a far more
radial political and economic order than that initially promised.
Thus it was not only Washington but also Managua that chose the
path of continued polarization in the 1980s. Although the Sandinista
strategy may seem explicable in view of the long preceding history of US–Nicaraguan relations, it was not entirely forced upon
them (certainly not by the Carter Administration). They therefore
bear considerable responsibility for the ensuing consequences, which
included missing the opportunity to promote national reconciliation and democratization.

That said, let us turn to the topic of this chapter, which concerns
the US role. Let us consider first the motives, then the methods,
then the results of the US response. This policy of intimidation
was motivated by a variety of considerations, among which concern
over the quality of democratic governance in Nicaragua was not, to
put it mildly, always foremost. Initially, policy was shaped by the

pressures of the Carter–Reagan election campaign, in which a dominant theme was the need to reassert American self-confidence and international leadership. In this setting Nicaraguan realities were compressed to fit into the terms of a debate set by the Iranian hostage crisis. After Reagan's victory campaign, perceptions continued to override reality and the 'Nicaraguan threat' was inflated to improbable proportions. The genuine issue that underlay mounting US hostility towards Managua was the fear of a second revolution in neighbouring El Salvador. It was to cut off supplies to the Salvadorean guerrillas rather than to promote democracy in Nicaragua that the 'Contras' were initially funded by the National Security Council in November 1981. (After all, Washington was at that time sheltering a regime in El Salvador whose democratic credentials were at least as dubious as those of the Sandinistas.) As the Contra war expanded, US objectives became more complex and difficult to decipher. One possibility was certainly the armed overthrow of the Sandinistas, and it remains extremely questionable whether that would have heralded a new dawn of democracy in Nicaragua. (The precedent of Guatemala in 1954 hardly seems encouraging.) Another was simply to isolate and discredit the Sandinista model, so that no other Central American republic would be tempted to follow that example. (Again, the democratic content of this outcome would seem questionable.)

By 1984, with the Salvadorean regime becoming more stable and respectable, and with the Grenada 'rescue mission' accomplished, the theme of democratizing Nicaragua became much more prominent and explicit. To the Reagan Administration the promotion of democracy in Nicaragua had one great advantage over all other possible justifications for the Contra war. With any other war aim, the danger existed that the Sandinistas would accept US demands, and the administration would therefore come under pressure to call off hostilities before the regime in Managua had been toppled. 'Democracy', by contrast, could be promoted as an unimpeachable goal that would attract the support of many waverers. Under Reagan the State Department would adhere to a definition of the term designed to ensure that no form of Sandinismo, however toned down, would ever qualify, just as no form of façade democracy in El Salvador would ever be allowed to disqualify.

This may seem a harsh and uncharitable explanation of Washington's motives in the mid-1980s. But we cannot overlook the fact that in November 1984 the Sandinistas did finally honour their 1979 pledge and hold national elections, and that various respectable foreign observers considered these acceptable. If the United

States had genuinely sought the strengthening of democracy in Nicaragua, would it have pressured the leading opposition candidate to stand down, and would it have disdained to see any merit in this electoral process? The trouble with these elections from Washington's point of view was not that they were fraudulent (we have seen that fraudulent elections held in Panama at that very time were praised as a step towards democracy). It was that even under clean elections the United States believed the Sandinistas would probably win.

During the 1980s the Sandinistas were progressively weakened by the long US campaign of harassment against them, but they were never toppled by the Contras, and no US invasion ever came. Their response to the demand for democracy was to offer to extend political freedoms if the campaign of harassment abated, but to curtail them if US hostility put Nicaragua's national security at risk. This can be viewed as just a question of tactics, but it also reflected an underlying disagreement about the kind of democracy that might be established. The Sandinistas might be willing to move towards democracy-with-sovereignty, but as the very name Sandinista implied they could not contemplate democracy on Puerto Rican terms, or of the post-Panama-invasion variety. The Reagan Administration, by contrast, seems to have defined democracy to require congruence with American interests. A sovereignty that clashed with US priorities was unlikely to be regarded as acceptable. Since the end of the Reagan Administration the United States has somewhat softened its position on such questions, but it remains to be seen how Washington would react to some future Sandinista electoral victory. Thus, it cannot be said that pure democracy promotion motivated US policy towards Nicaragua in the 1980s.

Even if the motives for US policy had been straightforwardly democratic, the methods chosen were not. As we have seen, there was never any intention to incorporate Nicaragua into the democratic system of the United States, and although invasion may at times have been contemplated, this method was also ruled out by the time of the Irangate scandal. Therefore Washington resorted to less direct methods of pressure, including covert operations, economic sanctions, and political warfare—'intimidation' for short. But intimidation is inherently a blunt instrument. It does not destroy but merely cows. So the result of a successful act of intimidation is more likely to be purely formal compliance than willing co-operation. In addition, because intimidation stops short of complete destruction of the enemy, it leaves open the option of continuing defiance regardless of cost, so intimidation risks destroying the social prerequisites for democratic compromise and accommodation. Moreover, the Reagan Administration's acts of intimidation were also often prima facie undemocratic in domestic US terms (deceiving Congress, misleading public opinion, diverting funds, etc.). Reliance on such methods broadcasts an example that hardly squares with the ostensible goal of democracy promotion. In fact, whereas democracy promotion through incorporation is likely to strengthen the democratic institutions of the metropolitan power (by generalizing and reinforcing them), democracy promotion through intimidation is more likely to damage the qualities of trust, co-operation, and lawfulness in the home democracy, to lower its international reputation, and to breed cynicism and opportunism in the target country.

These are objections in principle to the practice of democracy promotion through intimidation. Nevertheless in practice, it may be asserted, the Reagan Administration achieved the desired results, and these were unlikely to have been accomplished by any alternative approach. As in the case of Panama, it may be too soon to judge. A great deal will depend upon what is considered to count as a 'successful democratization' in Nicaragua—and on who controls the judgement. The foreign observers who authenticated the 1990 election came from many democratic countries—not just from the United States—and it may therefore be that in 1996 the Sandinista electoral opposition will benefit from the same international guarantees that served their opponents in 1990. But the result of the conflict of the past decade has been that many thousands of lives have been lost and the Nicaraguan economy has been ruined. Clearly this does not assist the promotion of democracy, and it seems unlikely that Washington will devote as many resources to reconstruction in the 1990s as it did to destruction in the 1980s.

However, defenders of the Reagan Administration will argue that there was no other way to 'save Nicaragua for democracy'. It could be that intimidation was the surest way to break Nicaragua's ties with Moscow and Havana, and with the Salvadorean guerrillas (although the Contadora and Esquipulas initiatives suggest that alternative approaches merited more attention than Washington was willing to concede). But on the question of democracy, the centre-piece of Reagan's strategy was the claim that since the Sandinistas were Marxists–Leninists, by definition any political concession they gave was just a stratagem to buy time. This was the argument for seeking to discredit the 1984 election, and for rebuffing all subsequent Sandinista proposals for a political settlement.

In view of their scrupulous conduct of the February 1990 election, and of their disciplined acceptance of an unexpectedly adverse result, it remains a serious question whether the Sandinistas were previously as intransigent and anti-democratic as they have been portrayed. The obvious alternative way to promote Nicaraguan democracy would have been to support and reinforce the electoral process of 1984, and to encourage and reward subsequent compliance with the pluralist provisions of the 1987 constitution. Arguably, then, intimidation was not the only possible form of democracy promotion available to the United States in the 1980s.

Intimidation was, however, the only form considered, and in the end the Sandinistas were evicted from office by the Nicaraguan electorate. So the policy worked, which on one view is what really matters. As in the discussion of Panama, this chapter does not dismiss that view out of hand but only argues for caution. The legacy of the past will continue to darken the prospects for an authentic and durable democratization of Nicaragua in the 1990s. Since their election defeat in 1990 the Sandinistas have remained a major political force in Nicaragua, to some extent opposing President Chamorro's administration, but also to some extent underpinning it. The US Congress has taken a dim view of General Ortega's continued presence as head of the armed forces (even though his record in demobilizing the military and in promoting national reconciliation could be said to compare favourably with that of, for example, General Pinochet in Chile), and the US Republican Party's capture of majorities in both Houses of Congress in the November 1994 elections seems to bode ill for relations between Washington and Managua in the run-up to the crucial 1996 Nicaraguan presidential contest. On their side, the Sandinistas have not found the transition to the status of a democratic opposition an easy one. By distributing state-held property to party favourites on the eve of their departure from office (the so-called *piñata sandinista*) they undermined their moral authority and created internal divisions which now threaten to block the prospects of a conventional system of party alternation. Thus the forthcoming 1996 elections pose a series of doubts about the nature of the representative system emerging in Nicaragua after so many years of US pressure to democratize. After so much harassment and political warfare against the Sandinistas it is hard for political observers of any tendency to believe that henceforth Washington will act as a staunch defender of procedural democracy in Nicaragua, regardless of the electoral outcome. (Certainly Senator Jesse Helms, the incoming Chairman of the Foreign Relations Committee, seems an unlikely bearer of such a message.) One of the greatest dangers of resorting to a policy of intimidation is that it is so difficult to find a clear rationale for stopping. And as the English discovered when they finally stopped coercing the Irish, it is even more difficult to convince the other side that you really have stopped.

5. Conclusion

The three instances of democracy imposition reviewed here are extreme, not typical. Here we have selected those cases where the US track-record is longest; where the scale of American involvement in shaping the political affairs of its Latin neighbours has been greatest; and where the underlying inequality of power and resources maximizes the likelihood that Washington can have its way. After applying these restrictive criteria, one might expect to find three highly successful cases of democracy promotion, but in fact the results are very mixed. They are also startlingly diverse, with US power being deployed in markedly different ways in each instance. Incorporation, invasion, and intimidation are quite varied methods for imposing democracy on other countries; when such contrasting methods are used it is perhaps hardly surprising that the outcomes are also various.

The incorporation of Puerto Rico produced the best results. By most normal criteria the islanders live in a well-consolidated political democracy that has received massive and sustained US support over several generations. Even here, however, certain qualifications are called for. Almost a century has elapsed since the United States began reshaping Puerto Rican politics, perhaps half a century since serious democracy promotion began. Yet the process is still incomplete, in that the islanders remain in an international limbo, and viewed from within the US system they are still second-class citizens. Full incorporation and definitive democratization may well occur in the next few years. But in the mean time Puerto Rico's half-way-house status requires indefinite transfusions of federal funds, which typically account for around one-quarter of the island's domestic product. Even for those who think that the gain in democracy and prosperity justifies the surrender of sovereignty, the Puerto Rican example hardly constitutes a model, since neither the US government nor the population of any other Latin American nation expect this pattern of democracy promotion through incorporation to be repeated elsewhere.

The invasion of Panama reinstated the authorities chosen in the frustrated election of 1989 and destroyed a tyrannical government. Taken out of context, these two accomplishments can be presented as another major success for democracy promotion. But on a longer view the contribution of the United States to the democratization of Panama is little cause for congratulation. The first eighty-seven years present a fairly sorry record, and the best that can be claimed is that the invasion could mark a new beginning. The Grenada operation of 1983 offers some encouragement for this view, but the differences should also be kept in mind. In Panama the United States was protecting its long-established vested interests, whereas the population of Grenada viewed the 'rescue mission' as an act of altruism by a country with no prior record of intervention there. In Panama the United States acted without the endorsement of neighbouring democracies, and against a ruler whose power it had previously built up; its credibility as a disinterested protector of the popular will was accordingly reduced. In Grenada it was possible for the United States to withdraw rapidly and comprehensively leaving a fairly broad-based multi-party democracy to function on its own. Such an outcome is likely to prove far more problematic in Panama. If comparisons are to be made with other instances of democracy imposition through invasion, the Panamanian experience may more realistically be compared with the Dominican intervention of 1965. But in that case twelve years had to elapse before the outcome of the invasion could be subjected to genuine democratic control, and even in 1978 the transition to pluralist democracy remained precarious and unsatisfactory. In view of the continuing US interest in the Canal and the nationalist reactions this is still likely to generate, not even the distinctly qualified success of the Dominican democratization-through-invasion can be taken for granted in Panama.

The intimidation of the Sandinistas forced them to accept an unprecedently high degree of international supervision of the 1990 elections due under the constitution they wrote in 1987. For most of the 1980s they had derived political support from their role as defenders of national sovereignty against US provocations, but by 1990 this mechanism no longer worked in their favour. The voters preferred a compromise settlement that would end US harassment, permit national reconciliation, and open the way to economic reconstruction. The Nicaraguan electorate made a democratic choice (albeit constrained from without). Indeed the 1990 result has the potential to trigger a cumulative process of democratization as rival power contenders are forced to recognize that they must work together within an agreed political framework, since none is strong enough to rule alone. However, the election outcome did not signify a general willingness to compromise Nicaraguan sovereignty, nor to abandon all the changes brought in by eleven years of Sandinista government, and the Sandinista army was not defeated by the Contras. The election has given Washington an unexpectedly easy opportunity to reinforce the democratization process in Nicaragua by ceasing all acts of intimidation and by respecting the new political framework. But this requires a clear US understanding of all the implications of the 1990 vote. The main test of democracy promotion through intimidation is whether interventionist methods can be convincingly and lastingly forsworn once the democratic transition is under way. In Nicaragua that test has yet to come.

Although the three examples considered here are all extreme, they are unlikely to be unique. Indeed in the 1990s we have been witnessing not only further evidence of the fruits of these three democracy-promotion strategies in the countries studied, but also greater tests of the US capacity for democracy promotion in other parts of the Caribbean Basin. Despite their importance, the difficult cases of El Salvador, Haiti, Guatemala, and even Mexico cannot be considered here, but some mention must be made of the largest imponderable, namely Washington's posture towards a prospective post-Castro Cuba.

As is well known, after 1898 the policy of incorporation applied to Puerto Rico was not extended to Cuba, and after the failure of the Bay of Pigs invasion attempt in 1961, Washington also dropped the policy of invasion. Instead, for over thirty years Castro's Cuba has been subjected to an unbroken policy of isolation and intimidation, more comprehensive and sustained than that which brought the Sandinista revolution to a halt. Yet Cuba's personalist brand of Communism succeeded in resisting all such pressure, in part because of large-scale Soviet assistance, in part because of Castro's own achievements and determination, and in part because of his success in promoting an anti-United States definition of Cuban nationalism. Following the collapse of Communism throughout Eastern Europe in 1989–90, a widespread impression developed that at long last the US policy of intimidation might be about to pay a massive dividend, in the form of a spectacular collapse of the Castro regime. If this were to occur, it would overshadow all the three cases considered here; indeed, if the outcome were to be the installation of a conventional pluralist democracy in Cuba, then no amount of academic reservations about the past history of US democracy promotion through intervention would dent the surge of American self-confidence. Nevertheless, without foreknowledge of Cuba's route beyond Castroism, an attempt can be made to extend the logic of the preceding analysis to the Cuban case.

The Cuban armed forces have not been, and probably will not be, defeated. Unlike Nicaragua the Cuban people have not been, and probably will not be, offered an internationally supervised electoral forum within which to choose their preferred future. Under Gorbachev's leadership the USSR proved either unwilling or unable to bring about a regime change either in Cuba or in China. It was only in those East European countries where Communism had been installed by the Red Army that Moscow had the capacity to dismantle it. Instead, between 1990 and 1992, first the Soviet bloc and later the successor post-Communist states simply and abruptly withdrew virtually all their economic as well as political and military support to the island. Then, in late 1992, under challenge from candidate Clinton, President Bush signed into law the Cuban Democracy Act, which had the effect of tightening the US economic embargo, ostensibly to force Cuba to convoke open multiparty elections. Castro responded by reaffirming the Cuban Communist Party's political monopoly, and then by introducing a succession of incremental economic and even some political reforms aimed at keeping his revolution afloat despite its international isolation. The US embargo (further reinforced by President Clinton in August 1994) is a unilateral measure lacking in international support. Indeed the UN General Assembly voted to disapprove it by 101 to 2 in October 1994. It is unwelcome to Washington's closest allies (including impeccably democratic Canada and the European Community as well as the whole of Latin America), not least because it attempts to extend US jurisdiction extra-territorially, and thus is in violation of a basic democratic principle. So there is a real question whether these further reinforcements and intensifications of Washington's long-standing policy of intimidation is likely to prove an effective instrument of democracy promotion in Cuba. The suggested limitations to this method are that it is too blunt (and may therefore damage rather than build up the social supports for democracy); that it seeks to grind down rather than immediately to destroy (therefore leaving the target regime with a possibility of retaliation, albeit at a disproportionate cost to itself); that it is in its own terms contrary to the spirit of democratic accommodation (and therefore potentially harmful to the democratic processes of the country that employs it, and damaging to a nation's democratic credibility); and that great self-control is required to halt practices of intimidation once a democratic transition has begun. These are the reasons for fearing, in advance of the fact, that the long-standing US policy of intimidation may not even now very well serve the cause of democracy promotion in Cuba.

It should not be too readily assumed that the collapse of Communism in Eastern Europe vindicates the US approach to democracy promotion in Cuba. After all, the Federal German constitution of 1949 offered the East Germans the unqualified prospect of reunification whenever they chose to apply for it; this was voluntary incorporation rather than imposition. West Germany also relied heavily on incentives rather than sanctions to win the East Germans round. As for the rest of Eastern Europe (and previously in relation to southern Europe), the Treaty of Rome offered the permanent incentive of a right to apply for admission to the European Community to any neighbouring state that adopted the required standards of political democracy and market liberalization. In contrast to these European incentives to voluntary reform, Washington appears to seek the national prostration of Cuba, in return for which the United States offers neither full admission to the union nor any assurance that an independent democratic Cuba would be allowed to exercise its sovereignty. (However, as discussed in Chapter 14 below, the EU's method of reform promotion within the constituent parts of what used to be Yugoslavia has helped to produce more catastrophic results than anything the US has recently done in the Caribbean.)

Thus, however events in Cuba may unfold, this discussion raises an important theoretical issue related to the nature of the democratic outcome being sought or promoted. The traditional view to which most Latin American (and for that matter most European) democrats would probably adhere is that the consolidation of national sovereignty is a pre-condition for the implantation of a representative democracy. For a government to be securely democratic—answerable to the citizenry through the test of competitive elections—it must establish its authority and policy effectiveness throughout the national territory, and must secure international acceptance of that authority. If extra-territorial authorities not accountable to the local electorate were to exercise decisive power, then according to this view the quality of that particular democracy would be drastically impaired. By this test Puerto Rican democracy falls short, in that San Juan has no say over such critical issues as the waging of war; Panamanian democracy depends on the acquiescence of an occupation force whose first loyalty is to Washington, and whose second priority is the security of the Canal; only Nicaraguan democracy appears more or less sovereign. What US efforts at democracy promotion in the Caribbean Basin seem to assume is that democratization can be a substitute for what Washington regards as unacceptable or impractical assertions of national sovereignty. Given the overwhelming inequalities of power involved, and the wide range of strategic, economic, and political interests Washington is expected to promote there, such a redefinition of the concept of democracy may be understandable. But from the standpoint of democratic theory it would only be tenable if the relinquishment of sovereignty were to be offset by full incorporation into the American political union. The peculiarity of the form of democracy promotion practised by the United States in the region where it has the greatest influence is that neither full incorporation nor full democratic sovereignty is consistently envisaged. This peculiarity goes far to explain the apparent paradox presented at the outset of this chapter—why in such favourable conditions such a powerful country, with such a long commitment to democracy promotion, has achieved such modest results. The policy-making process within the United States largely accounts for this peculiarity, in that the American public demands a strong rationale for foreign policy initiatives (democracy promotion), while the Constitution erects formidable barriers against the incorporation of new states, and specific lobbies have frequently induced Washington to exert its power whenever the assertion of sovereignty by small Caribbean states (even the most democratic) seemed likely to clash with their interests.

With the ending of the Cold War and the rapid extension of economic and political liberalism, it becomes even more important than before to determine whether (or in what circumstances) democratization involves a trade-off in sovereignty, or whether a new phase of democracy promotion can now begin, with more respect for non-intervention and the formal equality of all democratic states, however large or small.

The three methods of democracy promotion discussed in this chapter (incorporation, invasion, and intimidation) all have one thing in common—they express a radical inequality between the power and rights of the country acting and the country acted upon. They involve unilateral acts of imposition. This radical inequality has deep roots in US history[14] and is a particularly celebrated feature of the US presence in the Caribbean Basin throughout the current century. The US military proclamation of July 1898, already quoted, expresses the central idea common to all forms of democracy promotion by imposition. This is the assumption that one's own domestic political arrangements are secure and beyond reproach. From this starting-point it follows that democracy promotion involves a unilateral transfer that will be best facilitated by maximizing the power and control of the giver, and by minimizing the scope for resistance or modification by the receiver. For this reason the imposition of democracy abroad is likely to prove highly affirming to the status quo at home.

However this is not the only possible model of democracy promotion, as the European Union has recently demonstrated in southern and Eastern Europe. It is not even the only model of democracy promotion in the Caribbean, as both the decolonization of the British and Dutch West Indies and the incorporation of the French overseas territories in their different ways attest. The broad alternative to democracy promotion by unilateral imposition is democracy promotion by mutual accommodation. In this case the giver may well recognize the imperfection or vulnerability of the home democracy, which may be strengthened by external reinforcement. (This certainly helps explain why the recently restored democracies of Europe engage in democracy promotion.) In this case democracy promotion will involve strengthening the authority of political forces in the receiving democracy (usually this includes enhanced respect for its sovereignty), and may well require some demotion of the agencies of control in the countries engaged in democracy promotion. (For example, European decolonization required a dismantling of imperial institutions, which was often unsettling to the status quo at home but which, once achieved, contributed to the quality of Western European democracy.)

Probably the most interesting of these alternatives to the historical US approach is the partial pooling of sovereignty in an enlarged community of democratic nations, as currently envisaged in Europe. This is not an easy alternative for the United States to pursue, in part because the objective inequalities of wealth and power are so much greater than between the European states, in part because it runs counter to strong historical traditions, and in particular because both the US legal system and the policy process would have such difficulty in adapting to any form of supranational constraints. However, as noted at the beginning of this chapter, the republics of the Americas share a number of common liberal features and traditions—more so than the Europeans— that ought to facilitate the establishment of a democratic community of nations, provided that nineteenth-century traditions of unilateralism and imposition can be overcome.

Thus, it may be appropriate to end this chapter on a mildly positive note. Perhaps the December 1994 Summit of the Americas will reinforce the potential for a more democratic approach to democracy promotion in the Western hemisphere. At any rate, the thirty-four elected leaders attending the Summit undertook to co-operate in making their governments more transparent and accountable, as part of a specific and comprehensive continent-wide programme of trade liberalization. They also scheduled a series of follow-up meetings on specific topics, including measures to build confidence in democracy, and proposals to enhance the role of the Organization of American States in the field of democracy promotion. However, their main focus was on trade liberalization rather than on the broader issues of economic (and therefore ultimately political) integration which preoccupy the European Union. In consequence, the prospective Free Trade Area of the Americas, to be created by 2005, may operate with a less demanding standard of democratic performance than would have to be required of, for example, a new member of the European Union.[15]

Nevertheless, the Miami formula does appear to include some explicit element of democratic conditionality, which will require clarification in due course. On the one hand, the benefits of trade liberalization could well induce some powerful groups and interests to accept democratizing reforms that would not otherwise receive their approval. In this case the Free Trade Area of the Americas could serve to ratchet up standards of democratic performance across the hemisphere. On the other hand, it should not be forgotten that ratchets can also operate in reverse. Are the elected leaders of the Americas really resolved to suspend the benefits of trade liberalization in response to the breakdown of any democratic regime in the region? Through what process of collective (or unilateral) deliberation would such a serious decision be taken? Could it be effectively implemented in particular against a country with economic leverage? (Even in the Haitian case economic sanctions imposed following the September 1991 coup remained in place for almost three years, without achieving the restoration of the elected President. Enforcement was always uneven, and the poor of Haiti bore most of the costs.) Given the region's long history of democratizations followed by partial reversals, it would be imprudent to assume that such tests of the new strategy will never again arise. On the strength of the evidence presented in this chapter it must remain an open question whether such a prospective challenge to the current ascendancy of democracy in the Americas would be countered by consensual and multilateral means, or whether the embedded reflexes of unilateralism and impositionism would reassert themselves.

Notes

1. To circumvent Article 2, paragraph 7 of the Charter (which bars the UN from intervening in matters which are essentially within the domestic jurisdiction of any state), it was necessary to pretend that the Cedras dictatorship was posing a threat to international peace.
2. In Spanish *Estado Libre Asociado*, but the literal English translation, 'free associated state' has connotations unacceptable to US constitutionalists.
3. L. Whitehead, 'The Consolidation of Fragile Democracies: A Discussion with Illustrations', in R. A. Pastor (ed.), *Democracy in the Americas: Stopping the Pendulum* (New York: Holmes & Meier, 1989), 76–95.
4. For a detailed account, see F. Bayrón Toro, *Las Elecciones de 1980* (Mayagüez, Puerto Rico: Editorial Isla, 1982). The statistics on turnout are from p. 33.
5. R. D. Gastil, *Freedom in the World 1985–6* (New York: Freedom House, 1986), 32–40. By 1989–90, however, 29 sovereign states and 33 non-sovereign territories were ranked by the same institution as enjoying full civil liberties.
6. Quoted in R. L. Lael, *Arrogant Diplomacy: US Policy towards Colombia, 1903–22* (Wilmington, Del.: Scholarly Resources, 1987), 18–19. The following headlines from the *New York Times* give the flavour of the period: 'Elections in Panama must be OK'd by Taft' (11 May 1906); 'Panama must Make its Election Fair' (12 June 1908); 'Want US to Intervene: Panama Parties would Insure Fair Play at Coming Elections, Says Former President' (28 May 1916).
7. L. D. Langley, *The United States and the Caribbean in the Twentieth Century* (Athens, Ga.: University of Georgia Press, 1980), 139.
8. 'While we will not permit conditions to reach a stage that could produce another Bogotá, we will not pull anyone's chestnuts out of the fire to maintain a government in power' was how Chargé Hall summarized the conversation with Marshall, in *Foreign Relations of the United States (FRUS), 1948*, ix (Washington DC: US Government Printing Office, 1972), 667.
9. W. LaFeber, *The Panama Canal* (Oxford: Oxford University Press, 1978), 111.
10. Ambassador Davis to Secretary of State Marshall, 25 November 1949, printed in *Foreign Relations of the United States (FRUS), 1949*, ii (Washington DC: US Government Printing Office, 1974), 725–6.
11. Ibid. 729. Subsequently, in May 1951, President Arias dissolved the National Assembly and abolished the 1946 constitution in an attempt to extend his power. Colonel Remón thereupon overthrew him, and had

himself elected President in 1952. Ambassador Wiley wrote to Secretary of State Acheson in December 1951 that 'the American eggs all seem to be in one basket, that of Colonel Remón, since he is the sole anti-Communist leader in the entire political panorama. Though the basket, as the Department is well aware, is far from commendable, Colonel Remón still remains an irreplaceable *faut de mieux*': *Foreign Relations of the United States (FRUS), 1951*, ii (Washington DC: US Government Printing Office, 1979), 1567. In January 1955 President Remón was assassinated, apparently in a dispute with the Mafia over control of Panama's narcotics traffic: LaFeber, *Panama Canal*, 120.
12. 'Panama and the Path to Democracy', a speech by Assistant Secretary of State Elliott Abrams, 30 June 1987.
13. Ibid.
14. See, for example, A. K. Weinberg, *Manifest Destiny: A Study of Nationalist Expansion in American History* (Baltimore: Johns Hopkins University Press, 1935).
15. See also L. Whitehead, 'The Requisites for Admission', in P. H. Smith (ed.), *The Challenge of Integration: Europe and the Americas* (New Brunswick: Transaction, 1993).

4

The Effectiveness of US Human Rights Policy, 1973–1980

KATHRYN SIKKINK

While US human rights policy has been the object of intense debate and discussion, few serious attempts have been made to assess and explain the effectiveness of US human rights policy towards Latin America. An assessment of the influence of US policy is essential, not only as a guide to future policy-making, but as a means of strengthening our understanding of the causes of and remedies for repression in the hemisphere. This chapter presents a preliminary analysis of the influence of US human rights policy on human rights practices and democratization in Argentina, Guatemala, and Uruguay in the 1970s and early 1980s, primarily focusing on the Carter period.[1] In each of these cases, the United States attempted to influence the domestic human rights situation through linking the improvement of human rights practices to the provision of military or economic aid. But the nature of the pressures applied and the responses to human rights pressures were quite different in the three countries.

The Carter Administration human rights policy has been criticized as ineffective and inconsistent.[2] Yet many analyses of human rights policies fail to explore the precise linkages between the implementation of policy and the changing human rights practices in specific countries. This requires careful case-by-case research not possible in large quantitative studies or studies that focus only on the US policy-making process without examining the response to US policy in target countries. Secondly, most discussions of the effectiveness of US human rights policy look only at the short-term impact of the policy on repressive practices. Although the short-term impact of a human rights policy is important, it is equally essential to evaluate the longer-term impact of human rights policies, especially the impact on democratization. In the midst of the current concern with supporting democracy, the effectiveness of the Carter human rights policy deserves a re-evaluation.

Using the case-study approach and looking at both policy implementation and the response in selected countries, I conclude that US human rights policy was neither as disastrous as its critics alleged nor as successful as initially promised. I argue that the Carter policy was partially effective in both the short term and the long term in Argentina and Uruguay, but to different degrees, and in different ways. In the short term, the policy helped to limit direct human rights abuses, but also, by helping to isolate military regimes from a traditional ally by removing symbolic and material support, the US human rights policy indirectly contributed to the transition to democracy. In Guatemala, where a true transition to democracy has yet to occur, US policy failed to make a contribution to respect for human rights in either the short term or the long term. The purpose of this study is to examine the conditions under which a human rights policy can be effective.

1. Defining Effectiveness

The first task is to define what we mean by a successful or effective human rights policy. In the first instance, a successful human rights policy is one that has an immediate impact on the victims of human rights abuses: that saves live, stops torture, and helps get political prisoners released from prison. This is a central goal of any effective policy, and must be taken into account in any discussion of success. This is what is referred to here as the short-term impact of human rights policy.

But we cannot limit our definition of success only to the direct impact on victims of repression. As important as it is to help victims, human rights policy has broader objectives in addition to direct assistance.[3] In particular, I am interested in looking at the impact of human rights policy on:

(1) the strengthening of regional and international human rights organizations;
(2) destabilizing and delegitimizing authoritarian governments, and contributing to redemocratization;
(3) influencing the linkages between the political opposition in Latin America and US policy-makers; and
(4) reinforcing transnational linkages between human rights

groups in Latin America and policy-makers and NGOs in the United States.[4]

This is what I refer to as the long-term impact of human rights policy. In a broad sense, changes in each of these dimensions could make a contribution to the democratization process in Latin America.

As a starting-point for this discussion, it is first necessary to relax the unitary actor assumption inherent in much research on foreign policy. As the disputes within the US government between the newly formed Bureau for Human Rights and Humanitarian Affairs (HA) and the American Regions Area (ARA) in the State Department during the Carter Administration made clear, the US government did not speak with a single voice on human rights policy towards Latin America, and the outcome of policy often depended on which side won out in a particular internal debate. In the United States, the primary relevant actors in making human rights policy include Congress, the different parts of the executive branch, and the US human rights lobby, as well as domestic business groups who were potentially affected by human rights legislation.

In authoritarian regimes the number of actors making policy is much smaller, since the influence of political parties and some interest-groups is diminished. Nevertheless, common to the literature on military regimes in Latin America is the distinction between the soft-liners (*blandos*) and the hard-liners (*duros*) among the military. Military leaders must negotiate with other branches of the armed forces, as well as with hard-liners or soft-liners within their own force. The concerns of some interest-groups, such as business organizations, may also play a role within the domestic game in military regimes. The outcome of human rights policy depended on the ways in which the external pressures interacted with the internal negotiations within the authoritarian regime.

In a chapter that focuses on US policy, it is important to remember that US human rights policies are only one part of a broader process of international human rights pressures involving international and regional organizations, non-governmental organizations, and other governments. To study the influence of human rights policy in Latin America we must understand the ways US policy fit within the wider international context of human rights pressures. More than any other issue area, the human rights area presages the possibility of positive international humanitarian linkages, binding together the effort of non-governmental organizations interacting with government policies and international organizations to promote positive change.

Any examination of US human rights policy cannot ignore the earlier role of the United States in contributing to the rise of the very regimes responsible for human rights abuses. Such historical responsibility is the result of both direct and indirect actions, including military interventions, diplomatic manœuvres, the US contribution to military training in National Security Doctrine, direct police training through the office of Public Safety, and the ongoing covert activities of the CIA operatives in these countries. The recognition of historical US responsibility in contributing to the emergence of authoritarian regimes, however, does not invalidate the importance of evaluating the effectiveness of US human rights policy during the Carter Administration. In fact, past responsibility points more urgently to the need to develop and evaluate alternative policy goals and means that can build a more constructive relationship between the USA and the region. I believe that human rights policy offers this potential.

2. Background

In the seven-year period from 1973 to 1980, the United States substantially altered its external policy by explicitly incorporating human rights criteria into the foreign policy calculus.[5] To say that a country has a human rights policy does not imply that human rights considerations are taken into account in all bilateral relations, but rather that there are explicit mechanisms for integrating human rights concerns into foreign policy, and that these have modified foreign policy decisions in some cases. Although human rights policy is usually associated with the Carter Administration, it actually began in the Congress well before Carter was elected.

When Carter took office, virtually all of the essential human rights legislation was already in place. In addition to the standard array of diplomatic tools, the new human rights legislation led to the adoption of new policies, including the annual Country Reports on Human Rights; the diplomatic initiatives of the newly created Bureau for Humanitarian Affairs and Human Rights or of human rights officers in embassies; cut-offs of bilateral military assistance and sales and of bilateral economic aid; no-votes or abstentions on multilateral loans in the international financial institutions; and the denial of export financing through the Export–Import Bank.

During the Carter Administration the human rights concerns that the Congress initiated were strongly endorsed by the executive, and incorporated as a crucial component of the administration's foreign policy, although the administration opposed human rights legislation that appeared to place limits on Executive discretion in foreign policy-making. The cases of US human rights policy towards Argentina, Guatemala, and Uruguay illustrate the range of new and old policy tools available to policy-makers and the degree of Executive discretion as to how forcefully policy was implemented.

Argentina

The military coup that brought General Jorge Videla to power in 1976 was preceded by an upsurge in activities by right-wing death squads and by left-wing guerrilla movements. Once in power, the military government initiated a programme of brutal repression of the opposition, including mass kidnappings, imprisonment without charge, torture, and murder.[6]

Early in the Carter Administration, Argentina was chosen as one of three human rights target countries, along with Ethiopia and Uruguay. According to one State Department official, no human rights situation created greater concern in Washington than that of Argentina in the 1970s.[7] In 1977 the Carter Administration reduced the planned level of military aid for Argentina due to human rights abuses.[8] In July 1977 Congress passed a bill eliminating all military assistance to Argentina, which went into effect on 30 September 1978.[9] A number of high-level delegations met with the junta members during this period to discuss human rights, including a delegation to Argentina led by Secretary of State Cyrus Vance. Vance carried with him on this visit a list of approximately 7,000 disappeared people in Argentina, which was presented to Argentine authorities.[10]

In the multilateral financial institutions, the United States voted against or abstained on 23 of 25 Argentine loan applications, although no loan was denied because of a US 'no' vote. During meetings of President Videla of Argentina with both President Carter and Vice-President Mondale, the US requested that Videla invite the Inter-American Commission on Human Rights (IACHR) for a visit to Argentina as a means of improving US–Argentine relations.[11] In exchange the USA offered to release Export–Import Bank funds to Argentina that had been blocked because of Argentine human rights abuses.[12] In December of 1978 the Argentine government invited the IACHR to conduct an on-site investigation. Although human rights pressures were relaxed in 1980 as the United States tried to gain Argentine co-operation with the grain embargo to the Soviet Union, the ban on arms sales continued until 1983.

Guatemala

During the period 1954–76, Guatemala was a major recipient of US military and economic assistance, including substantial training and equipment for military and police officers.[13] In Guatemala police brutality and military repression against civilians has been commonplace since the late 1960s, when the military was joined by private death squads organized under the patronage and approval of the government and army. Within this general framework of repression, however, the human rights situation deteriorated in the period from 1978 to 1982. In 1980 evidence surfaced of a specialized agency, under the control of President Lucas García and located in an annexe to the National Palace, that co-ordinated the actions of various private death squads and regular army and policy units.[14]

Although Congress eliminated all military aid to Guatemala for the period from 1978 to 1983, military supplies already in the pipeline continued to flow, and the administration continued shipments of some military supplies by reclassifying them as non-military items.[15] The primary means Guatemala used during this period to obtain military equipment and technology from the United States was commercial sales made by US companies to the Guatemalan government and private businesses but licensed by the US government.[16] Continued military sales during this period indicate the Executive's lack of commitment to implement fully the human rights policy in Guatemala. Neither the administration nor Congress took any steps toward cutting economic aid or imposing trade sanctions as they did to Argentina and Uruguay. The United States opposed two multilateral development bank loans to Guatemala on human rights grounds, but approved five others during this period.[17] US human rights policy towards Guatemala became even more compromised after the Sandinista revolution in Nicaragua in 1979, when policy towards Central America became dominated by the perceived threat of revolution throughout the region.

Uruguay

Because the military took power in a more gradual three-stage coup in 1973, maintaining the civilian president in power, and because the coup in Uruguay was overshadowed by the more dramatic coup in Chile three months later, it took longer for international public opinion to understand the profoundly repressive nature of the new Uruguayan regime. Repression in Uruguay was not characterized by massacres and death squads, as in Guatemala, or by legions of disappeared people, as in Argentina. Instead the military implemented a programme of far-reaching arrests, routine torture of prisoners, and complete surveillance of the population. In 1976 Amnesty International estimated that 60,000 people had been arrested and detained in Uruguay; one out of fifty Uruguayans had been through some period of imprisonment since the coup. Seventy-eight prisoners died in prison, many as a result of torture.[18] With its 1976 report detailing extensive human rights abuses, Amnesty International brought the human rights situation in Uruguay to the attention of Congressman Edward Koch, who led the movement to ban military aid. The Koch amendment was one of the earliest country-specific cut-offs of military aid motivated by human rights concerns. Early US human rights policy to Uruguay sent mixed messages because of differences between Congress and the Executive branch,[19] but under the Carter Administration US human rights policy towards Uruguay from 1977 to 1980 was one of the most coherent and consistent of all the bilateral human rights policies. In 1977 Secretary of State Vance announced that the United States would reduce economic aid to Uruguay, making it a test case of the new administration's commitment to take human rights into consideration in the granting of economic aid. The USA also opposed 12 of 13 loan requests from Uruguay in international financial institutions during the period 1977–80.[20]

Although the United States kept a lower profile with Uruguay on the human rights issue than in the case of Argentina, under the guidance of Ambassador Lawrence Pezzullo, it maintained strong and consistent pressure on the Uruguayan military.[21] Early in 1980, however, the Carter Administration approved the sale of three search-and-rescue aircraft, apparently as a means of encouraging the move towards the plebiscite that year. The Uruguayan people's dramatic defeat of the military constitutional draft is generally considered the turning-point for the transition to democracy and the eventual improvement of human rights practices.

This simple recounting of bilateral relations between the United States and the three countries, however, does not give adequate attention to the very substantial behind-the-scene role played by non-governmental human rights organizations during this period. Non-governmental human rights groups provided the information to US policy-makers about human rights abuses that served as a basis for human rights policy. Human rights organizations presented information on human rights abuses and recommended contacts to give testimony at hearings that provided the basis for Congressional decision-making on Guatemala, Uruguay, and Argentina.

3. Judging the Effectiveness of Human Rights Policy

Direct Impact on Victims of Repression

US human rights policy had very different impact on the victims of human rights abuses in the three countries. In Argentina it appears that US human rights policy contributed to limiting the practice of disappearances. In Guatemala, however, there was no immediate discernible impact on the victims of repression; to the contrary, human rights abuses actually escalated during the period 1976–80, compared with the previous four-year period. In Uruguay US pressure appears to have contributed to the release of a considerable number of political prisoners.

In the cases of Argentina and Uruguay I do not argue that external pressures, in and of themselves, led to changing human rights practices. Rather, external pressures influenced internal negotiations within the military governments, lending crucial weight to the positions of soft-liners within these regimes. The external influence is necessary but not sufficient to explain the changes, since to function it must coincide with the agendas of internal actors. The following section will summarize the evidence that leads to these conclusions.

Estimates of the total number of the disappeared in Argentina vary from 6,000 to 30,000. The National Commission on Disappeared People (CONADEP) received 8,960 documented cases of disappeared individuals whose whereabouts is still unknown. The great bulk of these disappearances occurred during the two-year period 1976–8: by 1979 the number of disappearances was much lower, and after 1980 the practice was no longer used.[22] At the same time, over 10,000 people were illegally detained and imprisoned; many others were threatened, robbed, and removed from their jobs.[23]

Although it is difficult to chart the exact causes for the changing patterns of disappearances and imprisonment in Argentina, there is evidence that the decline in the use of the practice of disappearances followed a period of intense international scrutiny, and the convergence of strong US pressures on the Videla–Viola regime. In the period that followed the decision to invite the IACHR, the human rights situation in Argentina improved significantly; especially noteworthy was the decline in the practice of involuntary disappearance for which the Argentine regime had gained international notoriety.[24] The decline in the practice of disappearance is particularly noticeable in the period following September 1978. At this point, the Congressional arms embargo went into effect, the Ex-Import Bank loan to Argentina was still being withheld, and at high-level meetings, US officials had stressed the importance of improving human rights practices and the invitation to the IACHR as a pre-condition for improved bilateral relations.[25] This analysis of the impact of US policy is reinforced by the testimony of a number of victims and some interviews with Argentine policy-makers during the military regime.[26]

The counterfactual argument that one has to confront here is that the changes in levels of repression were due to an internal dynamic in Argentina that happened to coincide with external pressure, but was not related. What this fails to take into account are the divisions within the Argentine military about the definitions of 'the enemy' and the necessary extent of the dirty war. One faction was led by Admiral Massera, a right-wing populist, another by Generals Carlos Suárez Masón and Luciano Menendez, who supported indefinite military dictatorship and unrelenting war against the left, and a third, led by Generals Videla and Viola, who hoped for eventual political liberalization under a military president.[27]

It is of crucial importance which one of these factions prevailed, and in particular, the way in which international pressures influenced the internal negotiating process within the Argentine military.[28] By 1978, when the Videla–Viola faction had emerged supreme within the junta, US–Argentine relations, and to a lesser extent Argentine relations with European countries, had deteriorated over the human rights issue. Meanwhile, the conflict with Chile over the Beagle Canal had intensified in mid-1978, while relations with Brazil remained troubled.[29]

Videla and Viola understood that in order to improve their international image, as part of the process of military-led political liberalization they were advocating, some kind of explanation of past repression would have to be provided. It appears that they saw the visit of the IACHR and its report as a potential means of whitewashing or drawing a curtain over the past by providing a minimal explanation of abuses, while placing emphasis on the limited process of liberalization they were initiating.[30] Thus the international pressures played into the internal conflicts within the Argentine military, adding strength to the argument that something had to be done to change repressive patterns and improve external relations.[31] The strengthening of Videla's position in the autumn of 1978, and the problems Argentina faced in the foreign policy realm, combined with US pressure, helps to explain Videla's willingness to deliver on his promise to invite the IACHR to visit Argentina.

In the Guatemalan case, the situation was quite different. Although the United States had linked military assistance and sales to the improvement of domestic human rights practices, US human rights policy towards Guatemala was less comprehensive and forceful than its policy towards Argentina. The period following the cut-off of US assistance witnessed not a decline in human rights abuses, but an escalation in outright killings and disappearances. While estimates of human rights abuses differ for the period, there is agreement that 1978 marked the beginning of an escalation of repression which continued for the next five years, during the administrations of General Lucas García and General Rios Montt.[32]

US policy was less effective in Guatemala because it was ambiguous and less forceful, and also because there was no internal faction inside the military willing to respond. Contrary to the situation in Argentina, where many commentators spoke of 'moderates' (albeit murderous ones) within the military, by the 1970s in Guatemala, the reformist groups within the Guatemalan military had been virtually eliminated.[33] The Guatemalan military had received substantial US assistance and training over twenty years. In many ways, past US influence (especially during the coup of 1954, and the counter-insurgency campaign of 1966–8) contributed to the structure of the Guatemalan military that later blocked US human rights pressures.[34]

In Guatemala the revolutionary forces were gaining strength during the period 1975–80. It is estimated that by 1979 the guerrillas had at least 1,800 armed men, and substantial civilian support.[35] The upsurge in the rural insurgency in Guatemala in the late 1970s served to unify the military ideologically and to focus them on the shared task of counter-insurgency. In this context, the military viewed US human rights policy as interventionist, divisive to the military as an institution, and an interference in the strategy of counter-insurgency.

In Uruguay, US and international human rights pressures contributed to the release of political prisoners. In the two years that corresponded to the most intense human rights pressures, 1977–9, the number of political prisoners dropped from around 4,300–5,000 to between 1,000 and 2,500.[36] US human rights pressure focused on the problem of political prisoners, with the embassy playing an active role in urging the release of prisoners.[37] Although it is impossible to discover the exact cause of the release of each prisoner, US pressure appears to have contributed to this reduction in the number of prisoners.

Other Measures of Effectiveness

The discussion above mainly focuses on the short-term impact or lack of impact of US human rights policy on the victims of repression. It is more difficult to judge the long-term effectiveness of a human rights policy, because there is no clear yardstick to use to measure success. Nevertheless, it is essential to attempt to evaluate these other criteria because the long-term impact of a human rights policy may be more important than the short-term impact. The following discussion represents a first attempt to consider the longer-term effect of human rights policy in the three case countries.

Strengthening regional and international human rights organizations. If US human rights policy contributed to strengthening regional and international human rights organizations, then it is more likely to have had a long-term effect on human rights practices. Indirectly, these human rights organizations worked together with US human rights policy to magnify the effect of bilateral pressures, and they continued to function even after Carter left office, providing ongoing monitoring and reporting on human rights situations in Latin America.

In the case of Argentina, there is evidence that the Carter Administration human rights policy towards Argentina contributed to strengthening regional and international human rights organizations, especially the IACHR. The Carter Administration worked to strengthen the human rights activities of the OAS: it increased the US financial support of the IACHR fourfold during its administration, signed the Inter-American Convention on Human Rights, and encouraged Latin American nations to do the same.[38]

The request for the visit of the Inter-American Commission on Human Rights was not a unique feature in the Argentine case, but a request that the Carter Administration officials made to the officials of many repressive regimes in Latin America. A side-effect of this policy was the fortifying of the regional organization. In the Argentine case the routine request to invite the IACHR became a key linchpin in the negotiations. The Carter Administration may have hit upon one of the few face-saving alternatives that allowed the Videla administration to respond to human rights pressures. A report by a regional organization was more legitimate in the eyes of the Argentine government and public, and less compromising to the government than direct interference from the US government. It was not until the IACHR report was written after the visit that Videla and Viola realized that they had seriously misjudged the Commission. In the words of one observer, the Commission's report 'boomeranged' on Videla.

The Argentine case also had very important repercussions on the main UN human rights body, the Human Rights Commission.

In a well-documented book on this topic, Iain Guest shows 'how, after seizing power in 1976, Argentina's military rulers set out to cripple the UN's human rights machinery in an effort to muzzle international protest, and how—with the support and encouragement from the Carter Administration—the UN fought back. This fight rejuvenated the UN's ponderous human rights machinery.'[39] The very able diplomacy of the Argentine foreign service, with the support of the Soviet Union, with which the Argentine military regime had developed a close trading relationship, initially blocked consideration of the Argentine human rights situation at the UN. The creation of the UN Working Group on Disappearances in 1980, with strong US support, allowed the UN a less politicized forum to draw attention to the practice of disappearances in Argentina and elsewhere in the world. Jerome Shestack, Carter's delegate to the UN Human Rights Commission's 1980 session, and former president of the International League for Human Rights, played a central role in the creation of the Working Group on Disappearances. The UN policies during the Reagan Administration, however, undermined many of the advances in the human rights machinery at the UN made during the 1970s.

The Carter Administration also attempted to interpose regional and international organizations in the case of Guatemala, but with much less success. During this period, the Guatemalan government refused to permit an on-site visit by the Inter-American Commission on Human Rights, or to co-operate with any international or regional human rights organization. The Guatemalan government effectively stonewalled the IACHR by extending a formal invitation for a visit, but then never agreeing to set a date for the visit.[40] The IACHR still issued a report on human rights in Guatemala, but without an on-site visit the report was less forceful, and there was no possibility for the visit of the Commission to have an impact on domestic public opinion as in the case of Argentina. The effectiveness of UN action on Guatemala was also limited. During the height of repression, 1978–82, the Guatemalan government avoided UN investigation. When a special UN human rights investigator was appointed in 1983, he became what one author referred to as 'a full-blooded apologist for the Guatemalan government and the most "politicized" human rights investigator ever appointed in the UN'.[41]

The Uruguayan government also refused to permit the IACHR an on-site visit to prepare its 1978 report on the human rights situation in Uruguay. Nevertheless, the IACHR issued reports in 1978, 1979, and 1980 outlining abuses of human rights in Uruguay, reports that were later adopted by the OAS General Assembly. As a result of this human rights record, and lobbying by Venezuela and the USA, the OAS permanent council rejected the Uruguayan government's offer to host the meeting of the General Assembly in 1978.[42]

Aside from the OAS, the international body most active on Uruguay was the UN Human Rights Committee, generally considered the most forceful part of the UN human rights machinery. Prior to the dictatorship, Uruguay had signed the optional protocol of the Covenant on Civil and Political Rights, which permitted individual citizens to bring claims against Uruguay in the UN Human Rights Committee. Under this provision, the Committee considered a number of individual cases of violations of human rights in Uruguay, and found the government responsible for diverse human rights abuses, including torture and arbitrary detention. The committee published its findings in press releases, and called upon the Uruguayan government to release the prisoners and provide compensation.[43] Because of the legal legacy of Uruguayan ratification of the optional protocol, the UN human rights activity was more effective in Uruguay than in Argentina and Guatemala. US human rights policy, however, was less responsible for UN action on Uruguay, since the UN Human Rights Committee is made up of members who serve in their individual capacity.

Destabilizing and delegitimizing authoritarian governments, and contributing to redemocratization. The human rights policy designed by Congress and endorsed by the Carter Administration was focused on a relatively limited number of gross violations of basic rights, including torture, summary execution, and prolonged detention without trial. In this sense, it was not designed to promote democracy.[44] Nevertheless, it is useful to ask if one of the indirect effects of US human rights policy under Carter was to contribute to redemocratization in Latin America. If this is the case, the long-term effects of the bilateral policy are enhanced, since democratic government's human rights practices are far superior to the records of non-democratic regimes.

One of the clearest examples of Carter human rights policy making a direct contribution to redemocratization is in the Dominican Republic in 1978. After twelve years of authoritarian rule under Joaquín Balaguer, the 1978 elections represented the possibility of a transition to a more democratic regime. When it became evident that the opposition party was winning, however, a group of military officers stopped the vote count. International and domestic protest was massive and immediate. According to Jonathan Hartlyn, however, 'the most important actions came from the United States. This included visits by embassy staff and military attachés, strong statements by Secretary of State Vance and President Carter . . . and a phone call to the Dominican military from General McAuliffe, the commander in chief of the Southern Command in Panama.'[45] As a result of this external and internal protest, the opposition candidate, S. Antonio Guzmán, was allowed to take office.

None of the cases considered in detail here offer such a clear case of a direct contribution to redemocratization. The causes of redemocratization in Argentina are usually traced to the impact of the defeat in the Falklands–Malvinas war on the military and the pressures of domestic societal groups for change. While the United States did not play an important role in the immediate transition to democracy in Argentina and Uruguay, however, it had an influence in both countries at a crucial turning-point in the decision to initiate a process of liberalization.

In Uruguay, US pressure appeared to have contributed to pushing the military towards adopting a timetable for a transition to democracy. Some authors agree that the adoption of the so-called *cronograma* (timetable) for transition was in part the result of pressure from the Carter Administration.[46] Just as in the case of Argentina, external pressures influenced the internal negotiations among the military, strengthening the position of the soft-liners. According to Charles Gillespie, 'partly as a result of pressure from the Carter Administration, the power struggle in the army resulted in a complex victory for the proponents of what was called the "cronograma"'.[47] Other authors minimize the role of external pressures in the process of redemocratization, stressing instead the pressure of internal political groups, especially political parties, and the democratic tradition within the Uruguayan armed forces.[48] After the plebiscite in 1980, the dynamic of redemocratization was clearly internal, but during the more repressive period in Uruguay from 1976 to 1979, internal political groups were barely permitted to function. It is at this point that a stronger case can be made for the importance of external factors. It appears true that a stronger democratic tradition existed in the Uruguayan military than in the other military forces in the Southern Cone. For example, the number of military officers in Uruguay forced to retire early because of their apparent support for political opening is much higher than in either Argentina or Guatemala. For example, in 1977 alone, over 75 officers were forced into retirement.[49] Yet, the purges themselves indicate that the pro-democracy officers were a minority and the hard-liners continued to have the upper hand. In this situation, international pressures helped to throw new weight behind the arguments of the soft-liners.

Yet, perhaps the most important impact of US human rights policy on the process of redemocratization was the removal of symbolic support for the military regime, which in turn contributed to delegitimization of the regime. It is extremely difficult to document the impact of these symbolic gestures, but they should not be underestimated.

For example, in February 1977 Robert White, the US ambassador to the OAS, addressed the opening session of the seventh meeting of the Inter American Council on Education, Science and Culture in Montevideo, saying 'culture cannot enrich the lives of our citizens unless the state protects certain rights . . . the right of assembly, freedom of expression, protection against arbitrary arrest and punishment'. White's speech was published in full by two daily newspapers in Uruguay, but the military denounced it as a 'veiled but direct attack on the country'. The military banned further diffusion of the speech, and prohibited journalists from either commenting on the text or interviewing White.

Another key symbolic moment in Uruguay came in September 1976, when Uruguayans were surprised to find in their normally highly censored daily newspapers a partial transcript of hearings in the US Congress on human rights abuses in Uruguay. The rumour circulated that the US embassy in Montevideo had pressured the Uruguayan government to allow publication of the transcript. This is almost certainly not true, since Ambassador Siracusa had made clear his opposition to the attempts by the Congress to cut off aid. President Aparicio Mendez of Uruguay was so outraged by the debate that he later made remarks to the press accusing Senator Edward Kennedy of being linked to sedition and a supporter of Fidel Castro. This in turn led to the unexpected result that the government closed a newspaper, *La Mañana*, for one day for having quoted remarks made by the President of Uruguay.

In Guatemala, eventually the extreme corruption of the Lucas García government and the sense of increasing international isolation led to the ousting of that government in March 1982. US military aid cut-backs were among the multiple factors that contributed to the coup against the Lucas García regime. As government reserves declined, junior officers became increasingly concerned about the lack of adequate supplies, and some even called for a reduced level of human rights violations to improve the military's image.[50] This regime change, with General Rios Montt taking power in a coup, did not lead to an improvement in human rights practices. Later, in 1985, Guatemala did experience a transition to the civilian regime of Cerezo, but not to full democracy, since the military retained extraordinary power and human rights abuses continued at very high levels. In one sense, US human rights policy has contributed to crude forms of redemocratization in Guatemala by encouraging Guatemalan élites to move towards civilian-led governments. But instead of serving to promote respect for human rights, these tenuous civilian regimes served to diminish international awareness of human rights abuses in Guatemala and legitimize continued military aid in spite of ongoing human rights abuses.

Influencing the linkages between the political opposition in Latin America and US policy-makers. Some authors have suggested that one of the main effects of US human rights policy was to win friends among democratic opposition parties.[51] This pattern was far from uniform, however, and varied significantly from country to country. In Argentina Carter's human rights policy did not lead to the development of strong linkages between the opposition political parties and US policy-makers. The greater success of the military government in mobilizing Argentine nationalism against international human rights pressures led Argentine political parties to be extremely cautious in avoiding association with the human rights policy and the Carter Administration. Even human rights organizations were initially very reluctant about developing contacts with US policy-makers, because of the general assumption that it was anti-national to denounce the actions of your government to representatives of the United States.[52]

In terms of its influence on political parties in Argentina, at most US human rights pressure can be said to have contributed indirectly to changing the terms of political discourse used by political parties and other societal groups, including the Catholic Church, to talk about repression. In Argentina the great majority of the military believed that they were fighting (and winning) an irregular war against international subversion, and that they should be thanked, not condemned, by domestic and international groups. The military has never retreated from this discursive position. But domestic and international human rights pressures may have had an impact on civilian and public understanding about the nature of the conflict in Argentina. Initially, the military were able to use international human rights pressures to their advantage. In the late 1970s a large number of Argentine citizens accepted the government line that international human rights activity was part of an international anti-Argentine campaign to discredit their country. International human rights pressures initially sparked a nationalist backlash that galvanized support for the military government.

The major political parties in Argentina during this period adopted an ambivalent position on the issue of human rights. Some sectors of the political parties adopted the government's discourse and definition of the situation as one of 'war against subversion' rather than as a problem of human rights abuses. Political party leaders, with a few notable exceptions, were unwilling to participate in the activities of human rights organizations or to endorse their definition of the Argentine situation as one of massive human rights violations initiated by the highest levels of the armed forces. The first time that an Argentine political party denounced human rights violations before an international body was in September 1979. After meeting with the delegates of the IACHR during their visit to Argentina, the leader of the Peronist party issued a public statement denouncing the 'death and/or disappearance of thousands of citizens'.[53]

One of the important indirect results of the visit of the Inter-American Commission on Human Rights was that it began to transform the way in which societal groups such as political parties thought and talked about the issue of repression. The IACHR report provided the most in-depth, well-researched information on the human rights situation in Argentina, documenting that the Argentine government had engaged in a systematic government campaign of gross abuses of human rights.[54] The visit of the IACHR to Argentina and its report provided a turning-point in the Argentine human rights situation. It helped to create more general awareness in Argentina about the nature of the abuses that had occurred. This awareness was deepened and solidified during the 1985 trials of the military juntas for human rights abuses.

In Uruguay, on the other hand, Carter's human rights policy did lead to the development of closer relationships between the political opposition and US policy-makers. In Uruguay, one of the explicit practices of the embassy during the Carter Administration was to invite opposition politicians to embassy receptions and dinners for visiting US policy-makers. During his visit to Montevideo in 1977, Assistant Secretary of State for Inter-American Affairs Terrance Toddman met with a handful of politicians from the traditional parties. During a similar visit by Sam Eaton in 1980, including a sit-down dinner with politicians from the Blanco, Colorado, and the Christian Democratic parties, Eaton was snubbed by military commanders who failed to turn up at the dinner to protest about his decision to meet with opposition politicians. Although it alienated the military, this practice helped to maintain positive relations between the US government and opposition politicians.

In February 1977 a spokesman for the joint commission of opposition party leaders of Blanco and Colorado parties called upon the Carter Administration to show its concern for human rights in Uruguay by withdrawing Ambassador Siracusa, who had expressed his clear opposition to the Koch amendment. Carter Administration officials indirectly responded to this concern in June 1977, when Vance wrote to Congressman Koch to assure him that Siracusa was retiring, and the new ambassador 'possesses the deep respect for human rights'.[55]

In addition to the contacts formed by members of the administration, some members of the US Congress also developed relations with members of the Uruguayan opposition parties. Senator Wilson Ferreira Aldunate of the Blanco party, who testified in Congressional hearings in favour of the Koch amendment cutting off military aid to Uruguay, maintained good relations with a number of Congressional offices while he was in exile.

In Guatemala, the possibilities for these kinds of contacts between US policy-makers and opposition politicians were limited because of a concerted repressive policy of murdering centrist politicians. The 1979 murders of Alberto Fuentes Mohr and Manuel Colóm Argueta, 'two of the most prominent genuinely reformist politicians', were examples of attacks on centrist parties. The Christian Democrats alone suffered 120 assassinations from mid-1980 to mid-1981.[56] In such an atmosphere of violence, strong links with opposition political party figures were not developed.

Reinforcing transnational linkages between human rights groups and the US government, and between human rights groups in the USA and in Latin America. The most important way in which human rights policy was institutionalized in US foreign policy was through the formation of the Bureau for Human Rights and Humanitarian Affairs of the State Department, and the requirement that the State Department issue country human rights reports every year. This requirement in turn altered the job requirements of foreign service officers around the globe, who for the first time were instructed to gather information on human rights abuses. In some embassies, this led newly appointed human rights officers to form direct and enduring contacts with local human rights organizations. These domestic human rights organizations learned that they could indirectly pressure their governments to change practices by providing information on human rights abuses for inclusion in the annual country reports. At the same time, the sub-committees of Congress responsible for human rights also developed links with human rights organizations in Latin America.

Human rights policies were promoted by existing non-governmental organizations, and in turn led to the formation of new human rights groups. Important interest-groups grew up around the issue of human rights. Some, like Amnesty International, existed prior to the adoption of US human rights policy and contributed to the emergence of the policy. But many organizations were set up together with or as a reaction to the adoption of the human rights policy. Once established, they created an important lobby in favour of continuing the human rights policy. In turn, these human rights organizations developed strong links to domestic human rights organizations in countries experiencing human rights violations.

The influence of these human rights organizations is unlike most types of influence studied in international relations. They were not numerically strong nor economically powerful; they were not able to contribute money to re-election campaigns, and rarely able to mobilize constituents to vote. The influence they wielded was the direct result of the reliability of their information and the resonance of their arguments with the moral concerns of policy-makers. But in order to ensure the reliability of their information, they developed strong transnational networks with other groups, sharing and disseminating the latest information on human rights abuses.

Some of the linkages among human rights organizations in the Unites States and Latin America were formed in the mid- to late 1970s, as part of the process of providing information and testimony for US policy-makers about US human rights policy. This was most effective in Argentina, where a strong community of human rights organizations already existed. One important reason for international awareness of Argentine human rights abuses was the presence, by 1977–8, of a wide range of domestic human rights organizations with significant external contacts. Thus, organizations like the Mothers of the Plaza de Mayo, the Grandmothers of the Plaza de Mayo, the Center for Legal and Social Studies, the Permanent Assembly for Human Rights, the Commission of the Family Members of the Disappeared and Detained, the League for Human Rights, the Service for Peace and Justice, and the Ecumenical Commission for Human Rights worked to document and publicize the abuses of human rights in Argentina. It is not clear whether these groups eventually had a direct impact on the decision-making of the Argentine military. They were often the target of abuse: their members were disappeared, their offices sacked, and their documents confiscated. These transnational linkages also served to help protect domestic human rights organizations. These groups sought external contacts to publicize the human rights situations, and to help protect themselves against further repression by their government. They were a crucial link in providing documentation and information to spur the interests and concern of US policy-makers.[57]

If we examine some key events that served to keep the case of Argentine human rights in the minds of US policy-makers, the impact of these transnational linkages on policy becomes apparent. In 1979 the Argentine authorities released Jacobo Timmerman, whose powerful memoir detailing his disappearance and torture by the Argentine military made an important impact in US policy circles.[58] Timmerman's release was largely due to US government pressure, which had made it a key case in bilateral relations. Patricia Derian enquired specifically about Timmerman during her visits to Argentina. But it was societal groups who first brought Timmerman's case to the attention of US policy-makers. Human rights organizations, members of the US Jewish community, and US journalists helped make Timmerman's case a *cause célèbre* in US policy circles.

In 1980 the Nobel Peace Prize was awarded to Argentine human rights activist Adolfo Pérez Esquivel. Peace and human rights groups in the USA helped sponsor Pérez Esquivel's speaking tour to the United States at exactly the same time that the OAS was considering the IACHR report on Argentina, and the Congress was considering lifting the arms embargo to Argentina. He used his public position, including a group meeting with members of the House Foreign Relations Committee, to speak out against the continuing human rights abuses in Argentina and to urge Congress to maintain the arms embargo.

A third example of the power of transnational linkages is the role of the Mothers of the Plaza de Mayo in creating international awareness of the human rights situation in Argentina. These women, many of whom did not speak any foreign languages and had never travelled abroad before, launched an impressive international lobbying campaign with the help of the network of human rights organizations in the USA and Europe. They met with parliamentarians and with the press. During the meetings of the UN

Human Rights Commission or the OAS, the vigil of the women in the white headscarves helped undermine the Argentine diplomatic strategy of burying human rights issues.

In Guatemala the absence of human rights organizations, and the explicit government policy of eliminating leading members of the political parties, made the formation of transnational linkages difficult. Domestic human rights groups were formed for the first time in the 1980s in Guatemala, but they continue to face profound repression and have not been supported by the US government.[59] Indeed, by reinstating military aid to Guatemala in 1983 in the presence of continuing gross violations of human rights, the US Congress signalled that it was prepared to disregard and de-emphasize human rights violations.

Since 1986 the government has formed three governmental human rights offices—the Human Rights Attorney's Office, a Congressional Human Rights Commission, and a Presidential Advisory Commission on Human Rights.[60] These groups may in the future begin to operate as true human rights organizations, but they have not yet been able to address government human rights abuses. In particular, they have not even played an active role in protecting non-governmental human rights monitors.[61]

The presence of non-governmental human rights organizations suggests that the seeds of improved human rights practices exist in Guatemala today, but they have not yet started to bear fruit. Such institutional features as a new constitution enshrining respect for human rights, and organizations with a mandate to protect human rights, are not insignificant, but for them to be translated into improved human rights practices will take major changes within Guatemala, supported by concerted international efforts. To date, US human rights policy has failed to support and promote respect for human rights in Guatemala.

The US government also co-operated with some NGOs as regards human rights in Uruguay. In particular, it encouraged a visit by a delegation from the US American Bar Association in May 1978 that led to some apparent changes in government policy on human rights. Perhaps most significant was that the ABA mission received collaboration from the military regime, largely, it appears, because the leader of the soft-line faction, General Alvarez, believed that progress on the human rights front could help him in this internal power struggles with other members of the military and with his future presidential ambitions. Once again, the pattern of influence is similar to that in Argentina: policy is effective because it overlaps with the goals of a faction of the armed forces who believe that they can use external human rights pressures to strengthen their internal position.

The role of internal human rights organizations was minimal in Uruguay as compared to Argentina. Until 1981, when a Uruguayan branch of SERPAJ was set up, no human rights organization existed in Uruguay. As a result, whatever human rights documentation work there was in Uruguay was done by people connected to political parties rather than by non-partisan human rights organizations. Internationally, however, quite a number of groups devoted their energies to the cause of human rights in Uruguay. Of these, Amnesty International played the most crucial role throughout the period of the dictatorship by denouncing and documenting human rights violations.

4. Conclusions: Why and When is US Human Rights Policy Effective?

Can a human rights policy contribute to democratization? In Argentina and Uruguay, in the later stages of transition to democracy, domestic groups were key actors in pressing for change. But many theorists of transition to democracy assert that transitions always begin as a direct or indirect result of important divisions within the authoritarian regime itself, principally between hard-liners and soft-liners.[62] I argue that it is at exactly this point of decision within the authoritarian regime, when civil society is still severely repressed and not yet actively able to mobilize, that international human rights efforts may help to affect the calculations of actors internal to the regime, giving weight to arguments that the soft-liners are making in favour of liberalization. In this sense, this argument fits in between what Whitehead refers to (in Chapter 1 above) as the 'control' and the 'consent' perspectives for analysing democratizations. Direct US pressure during a very authoritarian phase contributed to initial liberalization, which in turn opened space for more active participation by domestic groups during the transition phase.

The argument presented here is that US human rights policy towards Argentina was effective because:

1. it was applied in a comprehensive and forceful manner—a clear message was sent through multiple channels that the USA was serious about human rights policy and that bilateral relations would suffer until changes were made;

2. it worked through both bilateral and multilateral channels,

thus reinforcing bilateral pressures with actions from regional and international organizations;

3. a faction existed within the Argentine military government, the so-called soft-liners associated with Videla and Viola, that by 1978 decided to try to use US and international pressure to pursue their own internal policy;

4. it was supported by the work of strong domestic human rights organizations within Argentina with links abroad, which facilitated the gathering and dissemination of information on the Argentine human rights situation. In Argentina, however, US policy did not lead to the furthering of links between US policy-makers and opposition political parties.

The effects of US policy in Uruguay were also meaningful. As compared with Argentina, the policy was applied comprehensively but less forcefully towards Uruguay. Few public statements were made, policy was handled by lower-level officials, and maximum sanctions, such as an Eximbank cut-off, were never applied. Similarly to the situation in Argentina, the policy worked through both multilateral and bilateral channels, and a faction also existed within the Uruguayan military which was willing to use external pressure to pursue its internal policy. One important difference between Argentina and Uruguay, however, was that until 1981 no domestic human rights groups existed in Uruguay to work together with international groups. Instead, US human rights policy seemed to be more effective in developing links between US policy-makers and opposition politicians than was the case in Argentina.

What made the Guatemalan situation different from the situation in Argentina and Uruguay? Five conditions seem to be important:

1. US human rights policy towards Guatemala was much less forceful and comprehensive. The priority of counter-insurgency goals led to a de-emphasis on human rights issues.

2. No powerful group existed within the Guatemalan military that could perceive a tactical advantage in responding to US human rights pressures.

3. The late 1970s witnessed a dramatic upsurge in the size and success of the rural armed insurgent movement.

4. No domestic human rights organizations existed to document human rights abuses and establish transnational linkages with international human rights organizations.

5. Opposition political parties were targeted as victims of governmental repression, thus eliminating any interlocutors for human rights policy, and narrowing political alternatives.

I shall briefly examine some of these factors separately.

A Forceful and Comprehensive Policy

The case of Argentina suggests that the combination of very severe pressure (military and economic aid cut-offs, 'no' votes in international financial institutions, and the denial of Eximbank loans) plus the willingness to bargain on one important sanction (the Eximbank funds) contributed to change. This suggests that if the United States had made human rights a higher priority in its bilateral relations with Guatemala and brought more pressure to bear, the chances of success might have been greater, but instead the pressures were much less forceful in the Guatemalan case. Congress never threatened to reduce economic aid or impose any kind of trade sanctions, except denial of military assistance.

This kind of forceful and comprehensive human rights policy is most likely to be applied in countries where the USA has few competing policy goals. The Argentinian academic Carlos Escudé puts it more harshly, arguing that US moral imperialism will only be applied in marginal countries.[63] The Argentine case, however, was not without cost to the US government, since it involved alienating a potentially valuable ally. But even extremely forceful human rights pressures cannot guarantee success unless other necessary pre-conditions exist within the repressive country to allow negotiations to succeed.

A Faction in the Target Government is Willing to Negotiate on Human Rights Issues

Forceful policy would have been insufficient to bring about changes in Argentina and Uruguay if no faction had existed which was prepared to negotiate on the human rights issue. Soft-liners in both Argentina and Uruguay attempted to use the international pressure in order to pursue an internal political strategy *vis-à-vis* other sectors of the military.[64] And in both cases, the strategy of controlled opening backfired on the military. In the case of Argentina, the IACHR report was much more damning than the military had anticipated. In Uruguay the defeat of the plebiscite undermined the military's plans and reinvigorated domestic political dissent. But by the time the strategy had backfired it had gained a momentum of its own that made it difficult for the military to backtrack.

The soft-liner argument is often misused by opponents of a human rights policy. The argument is frequently made that strong human rights pressures fortify the positions of the hard-liners and undermine soft-liners. But the evidence from the Argentine and Uruguayan cases does not support this argument. Rather, it was the existence of very strong pressures, the most consistent and forceful pressures in all the human rights cases, pressures that were denounced and criticized by the soft-liners, that nevertheless eventually led to an improvement in the human rights situation. Since the soft-liners use international pressures to fortify their positions *vis-à-vis* hard-liners, more forceful pressures create more leverage in internal negotiations.

In Guatemala in the 1970s and 1980s there were no factions within the Guatemalan regime looking for an excuse to bring the death squads under control, and, as a result, US human rights policy failed there. An analysis of current policy, however, neglects the historical reasons why there is no progressive coalition within the Guatemalan military. To a large degree the absence of a progressive faction within the military interested in responding to US human rights policy was the result of past US interventions, such as the CIA-supported coup in 1954 against the government of Jacobo Arbenz, exactly the kind of reform-minded government that the Carter Administration was seeking. Since then the United States has trained over 3,000 Guatemalan officers in US military academies. To include history in the game, we see that the United States contributed to creating the kind of military that has committed the current abuses. The human rights policy found no resonance from within the government. 'If only we had an Arbenz now,' a State department official under Carter lamented. 'We are going to have to invent one, but all the candidates are dead.'[65]

Support for International, Regional, and Domestic Human Rights Organizations

The single most successful element of the US policy towards Argentina was the reiterated emphasis on the importance of an invitation for an on-site visit by the Inter-American Commission on Human Rights. By integrating its bilateral pressures within a multilateral strategy, the US both strengthened multilateral human rights institutions and was more effective. Secondly, combining bilateral and regional activities with the actions of non-governmental human rights organizations led to especially effective human rights pressures.[66] In Uruguay US bilateral policy was reinforced by multilateral actions by the OAS and the UN, but the absence of domestic human rights groups weakened the potential for positive international linkages.

These cases suggests the importance of transnational linkages in influencing human rights practices. The activities of domestic and international human rights organizations provided the essential information that led to the emergence of the issue and permitted monitoring of change.[67] Because few powerful domestic interest-groups competed for influence, relatively small non-governmental organizations armed with information were able to have a substantial effect on policy.

Notes

1. Although this chapter has a different focus, it draws upon an earlier co-authored work: L. Martin and K. Sikkink, 'US Policy and Human Rights in Guatemala and Argentina', in P. Evans, H. Jacobson, and R. Putnam (eds.), *International Bargaining and Domestic Politics: An Interactive Approach* (Berkeley: University of California Press, 1992). I wish to recognize the contribution of Lisa Martin to the overall project, and thank her for permission to use some of the material from that chapter here.
2. See, for example, M. Stohl, D. Carleton, and S. E. Johnson, 'Human Rights and US Foreign Assistance from Nixon to Carter', *Journal of Peace Research*, 21/2 (1984), and C. Escudé, 'Argentina: The Costs of Contradiction', in A. F. Lowenthal (ed.), *Exporting Democracy: The United States and Latin America: Case Studies* (Baltimore: Johns Hopkins University Press, 1991).
3. S. Hoffman discusses four possible goals of a human rights policy: (1) to help victims; (2) to raise consciousness; (3) to advance the national interest; (4) to change regimes: *Duties Beyond Borders* (Syracuse: Syracuse University Press, 1981), 113–14.
4. As regards some of the ideas presented in this paragraph as to how to define the success of US human rights policy, I am indebted to comments by Marcelo Cavarozzi, Catalina Smulovitz, and Carlos Acuña in response to a presentation of an early study at CEDES in Buenos Aires.
5. For an excellent overview of US human rights policy towards Latin America, see L. Schoultz, *Human Rights and United States Policy toward Latin America* (Princeton, NJ: Princeton University Press, 1981).
6. Amnesty International, *Report of an Amnesty International Mission to Argentina* (London: Amnesty International Publications, 1977). Most of the disappeared were eventually murdered, and their bodies were buried in unmarked mass graves, incinerated, or thrown into the sea:

Nunca Mas: The Report of the Argentina National Commission on the Disappeared (New York: Farrar Straus Giroux, 1986), 209–34.

7. P. J. Flood, 'US Human Rights Initiatives Concerning Argentina', in D. D. Newsom (ed.), *The Diplomacy of Human Rights* (New York: University Press of America, 1986), 129.

8. *New York Times*, 25 February 1977, 1; 2 March 1977, 10.

9. Congressional Research Service, Foreign Affairs and National Defense Division, *Human Rights and US Foreign Assistance: Experiences and Issues in Policy Implementation (1977–1978)*, Report prepared for US Senate Committee on Foreign Relations, November 1979, 106.

10. In addition, in two years the US embassy made more than 1,200 representations to the Argentine government on cases of human rights abuse. Americas Watch, *With Friends Like These: The American Watch Report on Human Rights and US Policy in Latin America* (New York: Pantheon Books, 1985), 99–100.

11. Interview with Robert Pastor, 28 June 1990, Wianno, Massachusetts.

12. Interview with Walter Mondale, Minneapolis, 20 June 1989.

13. From 1950 to 1980, 3,360 Guatemalan military officers were trained by the USA as a part of the International Education and Training Program (IMET). United States Department of Defense, *Foreign Military Sales, Foreign Military Construction Sales and Military Assistance Facts as of September 30, 1984*. A large number of police officers were also trained in the Office for Public Safety Program, under the aegis of the Agency for International Development.

14. Amnesty International, *Guatemala: A Government Program of Murder* (London: Amnesty International, 1981), 7. It is even more difficult to chart the pattern of human rights abuses in Guatemala than it is in Argentina. This is partly the result of an apparently deliberate government policy to eliminate evidence. One Guatemalan colonel told a US journalist, 'In Argentina there are witnesses, there are books, there are films, there is proof. Here in Guatemala there is none of that. Here there are no survivors': A. Nairn and J. M. Simon, 'Bureaucracy of Death', *New Republic*, 30 June 1986, 14.

15. Congress prohibited FMS credits to Guatemala in the Foreign Assistance Appropriations Act for 1978, but the deliveries never ceased and other types of economic and military aid continued. In fiscal years 1978, 1979, and 1980—the three years for which the Carter Administration can be held wholly responsible—the USA delivered $8.5m. in military assistance, mostly FMS credit sales, and it issued export licences for commercial arms sales worth $1.8m., a rate that does not differ much from that of the Nixon–Ford Administrations: testimony by L. Schoultz, 'Human Rights in Guatemala', Hearings, 30 July 1981, 98.

16. United States General Accounting Office, 'Military Sales: The United States Continuing Munitions Supply Relationship with Guatemala', 4. Approval of export licences to Guatemala varied over this period: the State Department disapproved of 2.1 per cent of licences in 1979, 68

per cent in 1980, 62 per cent in 1981, 57 per cent in 1982, and 13.3 per cent in 1983; 21.

17. Schoultz, 'Guatemala', 187.
18. M. Weinstein, *Uruguay: Democracy at the Crossroads* (Boulder, Colo.: Westview Press, 1988), 53; Servicio Paz y Justicia Uruguay, *Uruguay Nunca Más: Informe sobre la violación a los derechos humanos (1972– 1985)* (Montevideo: Altamira, 1989), 417–30.
19. *Latin American Regional Report: Southern Cone*, 13 May 1977, xi (18), and *Latin America*, 22 October 1976, x (41).
20. Schoultz, *Human Rights and United States Policy*, 295.
21. *Latin American Political Report*, 17 June 1977, xi (23); interview with Lawrence Pezzullo, 29 August 1991, Baltimore, Md.
22. United Nations Working Group on Enforced or Involuntary Disappearances, UN Doc. E/CN.4/1986/18 (1986), 21; reported in D. Weissbrodt and M. L. Bartolomei, 'The Effectiveness of International Human Rights Pressures: The Case of Argentina, 1976–1983', *Minnesota Law Review*, 75 (Feb. 1991).
23. The substantial documentation provided by the military themselves and uncovered by the judiciary in the trials of the military juntas demonstrates that the decisions to engage in repression were made at the highest levels of the Argentine government. Thus, the eventual decision to diminish that repression was also made by top-level government officials. See, for example, 'La Sentencia', *Diario del Juicio*, 11 December 1985.
24. See Asamblea Permanente por los Derechos Humanos, *Las Cifras de la Guerra Sucia* (Buenos Aires, 1988), 26–31.
25. This interpretation differs from that of Carlos Escudé, who claims that US human rights policy was unsuccessful in Argentina. Although Escudé is correct that US human rights policy was sometimes applied in a contradictory fashion in Argentina, he does not discuss the fact that it was applied more consistently in the case of Argentina than in any other country except Uruguay. Second, he does not discuss the granting of blocked Eximbank credits in exchange for the Argentine invitation of the IACHR, which is key to the argument here. Third, Escudé underestimates the importance of diplomatic pressures on the Argentine military government. While it is true that initially the Argentine government reacted nationalistically against the campaigns, by 1978 they were profoundly concerned about the international isolation of the military regime: C. Escudé, 'Argentina: The Costs of Contradiction', in *Exporting Democracy*.
26. See, for example, J. Timmerman, *Washington Post*, 22 May 1981, and interviews conducted in Buenos Aires, July–August 1990.
27. D. Rock, 370–1. This understanding of divisions within the military is reinforced by other observers, including victims of repression who saw the functioning of concentration camps from the inside, such as J. Timmerman, *Prisoner Without a Name, Cell Without a Number* (New York: Vintage Books, 1982), 147, 163.

28. The only significant civilian allies of the Argentine government whose opinions could have contributed to the process of military decision-making were the civilian technocrats, especially the economic policy-makers, and key business groups. The economic programme of the military regime constituted one of the two main goals of the government: the re-establishment of order and the reinvigoration of the economy through a programme of liberalization, expansion of exports, and foreign assistance and investment. The civilian technocrats and their closest allies in the military, the Videla–Viola faction, were concerned with the international image of Argentina, and the damage done to that image by the widespread reports of human rights violations. Nevertheless, neither the economic policy team, nor domestic entrepreneurs advocated changing human rights practices, in part because the topic of the repression was perceived as taboo by civilian allies of the military: interview with a high-level official in the Ministry of Economics, Buenos Aires, 31 July 1990. Also, because businessmen and members of the economic team had been targets of left-wing kidnapping and assassination attempts, they tended to support the repressive measures of the military: interview with Jose A. Martínez de Hoz, Minister of Economics during the Videla administration, 6 August 1990, Buenos Aires.
29. *Carta Politica*, no. 59 (October 1978).
30. Interview with Tom J. Farer, member of the Special Commission of IACHR that conducted the on-site observation in Argentina in September 1979, 13 May 1990; and with Ambassador Arnoldo Listre, Buenos Aires, 20 July 1990.
31. Interview with Ambassador Arnoldo Listre, Buenos Aires, 20 July 1990.
32. Amnesty International, *Guatemala: The Human Rights Record*, 7. See Amnesty International, *Guatemala: A Government Program of Political Murder* (London: Amnesty International, 1981); Americas Watch, *Human Rights in Guatemala: No Neutrals Allowed* (New York: Americas Watch, 1982).
33. G. Aguilera Peralta, 'El Proceso de Militarizacion en el Estado Guatemalteco', *Polemica*, 1 (September–October 1981), 39. M. Simons, 'Guatemala: The Coming Danger', *Foreign Policy*, 43 (1981), 103.
34. See S. Jonas, *The Battle for Guatemala: Rebels, Death Squads, and US Power* (Boulder, Colo.: Westview Press, 1991).
35. Peralta, 'El Proceso de Militarización', 35.
36. *Latin America*, 11 February 1977, xi (6); and Schoultz, *Human Rights*, 350.
37. Interview with Lawrence Pezzullo, 29 August 1991, Baltimore, Md.
38. Interview with Robert Pastor, 28 June 1990, Wianno, Mass. See also *Latin American Political Report*, 24 January 1977, xi (24).
39. I. Guest, *Behind the Disappearances: Argentina's Dirty War Against Human Rights and the United Nations* (Philadelphia: University of Pennsylvania Press, 1990), p. xiii.

40. T. Buergenthal, R. Noms, and D. Shelton, *Protecting Human Rights in the America: Selected Problems* (Strasbourg: N. P. Engel, 1986), 157–62.
41. I. Guest, *Behind the Disappearances*, 375.
42. *Latin American Political Report*, 10 February 1978, xii (6).
43. N. Macdermot, 'Uruguay in the International Organization for the Protection of Human Rights,' paper presented at the Colloquium on the Policy of Institutionalization of the State of Exception and its Rejection by the Uruguayan People, Geneva, 27–8 February 1981, 91.
44. For a discussion of efforts to promote democracy by the US government through AID and the National Endowment for Democracy, see Chapter 5 below.
45. J. Hartlyn, 'The Dominican Republic: The Legacy of Intermittent Engagement', in *Exporting Democracy*, 82.
46. L. Weschler, *A Miracle, A Universe: Settling Accounts with Torturers* (New York: Pantheon, 1990).
47. C. Gillespie, 'From Suspended Animation to Animated Suspension: Political Parties and the Reconstruction of Democracy in Uruguay', unpublished paper, Yale University, 12 January 1984, 32.
48. See, for example, G. Rama, *La Democracia en Uruguay* (Buenos Aires: Grupo Editor Latinoamericano, 1987), 200. Rama argues in passing that diplomatic pressures from the USA and Europe were not significant in the process of redemocratization, but does not present any material to back up this argument.
49. *Latin American Political Report*, 23 and 30 September 1977, xi (37–8).
50. J. Handy, *Gift of the Devil: A History of Guatemala* (Toronto: 1984), 182.
51. In Chapter 7, below, Alan Angell quotes Susan Kaufman Purcell, who argues that the main effect of US human rights policy in Chile was that it 'won friends for the Unites States among the democratic opposition parties of the center and center left'. Angell clarifies, however, that there were no direct party links between US parties and Chilean parties of the kind that existed between European and Chilean parties, and there was still considerable suspicion towards the US government on the part of many Chilean politicians.
52. Interview with Dr Jose Federico Westerkamp, 20 August 1989, Buenos Aires.
53. I. Gonzáles Bombal, 'El Diálogo Político: La transición que no fue', CEDES, August 1990 (mimeo), 65–6.
54. Organization of American States, Inter-American Commission on Human Rights, *Report on the Situation of Human Rights in Argentina* (Washington DC: General Secretariat, Organization of American States, 1980), 134.
55. *Latin American Political Report*, 4 February 1977, xi (5); 17 June 1977, xi (23).
56. Jonas, *Battle for Guatemala*, 125.

57. Members of these organizations frequently travelled to the USA and to Europe, where they met with human rights organizations, talked to the press, testified before Congress, and met with Members of Congress and their staff, and with State Department Officials. One key human rights advocate, Emilio Mignone, talks of the threats that he and his family suffered, and affirms, 'I think the openness of our activity and the international recognition it began to receive helped save our lives': *Derechos Humanos y Transicion Democratica en la Sociedad Argentina* (Buenos Aires: Ediciones del Pensamiento Nacional, 1991), 94.

58. Timmerman, *Prisoner Without a Name.*

59. Guatemala now has three non-governmental human rights organizations, two formed since President Cerezo came to office. Two have lost members to government violence. All receive threats and harassment. See, Americas Watch, *Persecuting Human Rights Monitors: The CERJ in Guatemala* (May 1989), 43.

60. Interview with Jorge Arturo Roche Tobar of the Human Rights Attorney's Office, and Ana Carolina Reyes Riveiro, Assistant to the Congressional Commission on Human Rights, Minneapolis, Minnesota, March 1990.

61. Americas Watch, *Persecuting Human Rights Monitors* (New York: Human Rights Watch, 1989), 54.

62. G. O'Donnell and P. Schmitter, *Transitions from Authoritarian Rule: Tentative Conclusions about Uncertain Democracies* (Baltimore: Johns Hopkins University Press, 1986), 19.

63. C. Escudé, *La Argentina: Paria internacional?* (Buenos Aires: Editorial Belgrano, 1984), 26.

64. On Argentina, interviews with Ambassador Arnoldo Listre, 20 July 1990, Buenos Aires, and with Dr Ricardo Yofre, 1 August 1990, Buenos Aires.

65. Simons, 'Guatemala: Coming Danger', 103.

66. For example, it is unlikely that the IACHR would have been able to do such well-documented work in so short a time if it had not been for the collaboration of domestic human rights groups. In anticipation of the IACHR visit, DELS select 300 of the strongest cases from over 4,000 cases, which became the cases analysed and presented in detail in the Commission's report: E. Mignone, 'Derechos Humanos y Transición Democrática en la Sociedad Argentina', paper presented at a Seminar on Transition to Democracy in Argentina, Yale University, New Haven, 4–8 March 1990, 117.

67. The importance of human rights organizations is reflected in the opening statement of Representative Bonkers in the hearings considering the reinstatement of military aid to Argentina in 1981: 'If Reagan Administration officials . . . had read the reports on Argentina by Nobel prize winning organization Amnesty International, if they had read the report of the United Nations Human Rights Commission working group on disappearances; if they had read the 266 page report on

Argentina by the Organization of American States' Inter-American Commission on Human Rights, a Commission that has distinguished itself in the hemisphere by its objectivity and fairness in advancing human rights; and if they read the reports on Argentina by the International Commission of Jurists; they would not be making silly statements such as "We want good relations with Argentina"': 'Review of United States Policy on Military Assistance to Argentina', Hearing before the Subcommittees on Human Rights and International Organization and on Inter-American Affairs of the Committee on Foreign Affairs, House of Representatives, 1 April 1981 (Washington DC: US Government Printing Office, 1981), 3.

5

The Resurgence of United States Political Development Assistance to Latin America in the 1980s

THOMAS CAROTHERS

1. Background

The United States first gave substantial political development assistance to Latin America in the late 1960s, pursuant to Title IX of the Foreign Assistance Act. Title IX directed the Agency for International Development (AID) to assure 'maximum participation in the task of economic development on the part of the people of developing countries, through the encouragement of democratic private and local governmental institutions'.[1] It reflected a concern among some US Congressmen that economic growth in many developing countries was benefiting only traditional élites and that the only way to ensure equitable economic growth was to promote wider political participation.[2] In Latin America, AID translated the Title IX mandate into programmes emphasizing civic education, leadership training, and strengthening local government and national legislatures.

AID's early venture into political development assistance was not a happy one. It had no experience or expertise in political

Much of this chapter is based on the author's interviews with US officials at the Agency for International Development, the State Department, the White House, the United States Information Agency, the Justice Department, and the National Endowment for Democracy responsible for US political development assistance to Latin America in the 1980s. The chapter also reflects the author's personal experience as a staff attorney in the Office of Administration of Justice and Democratic Development in the Bureau for Latin America and the Caribbean of the Agency for International Development from 1986 to 1987.

development and felt that such programmes were a distraction from its core economic work. Furthermore, the effort to develop democracy assistance programmes in Latin America clashed with the dominant political trends of the region at the time. In the late 1960s much of Latin America was experiencing a resurgence of authoritarian rule, a resurgence the US government was openly condoning in many cases, undermining its own political development assistance efforts.

US political development assistance to Latin America was essentially abandoned in 1973, when AID shifted from an emphasis on promoting economic growth in the developing world to a 'basic human needs' strategy. Political development assistance resurfaced in a minor way towards the end of the decade as part of the emerging emphasis on human rights in US foreign policy. In 1978 Congress added Section 116(e) to the Foreign Assistance Act, which, among other things, authorized AID to carry out development programmes to enhance political and civil rights abroad. In 1979 and 1980 AID spent around $1 million per year in Latin America on human rights programmes.

When the Reagan Administration came into power in 1981, few observers expected it would show any interest in political development assistance. The early Reagan team was preoccupied by what it saw as the global expansion of Soviet influence and appeared determined to pursue purely security-oriented policies. Yet the Reagan Administration ended up initiating a large, varied set of political development programmes in Latin America, eclipsing the efforts of the 1960s in both size and scope. These programmes included an extensive judicial assistance programme, a number of major election assistance projects, and numerous democratic participation projects involving community groups, journalists, national legislatures, municipal governments, and civil–military relations. US government political development assistance to Latin America grew to over $20 million per year by the late 1980s, and totalled approximately $100 million during the Reagan years.[3]

The National Endowment for Democracy (NED) also carried out democratic development programmes in Latin America in the 1980s. The National Endowment, a private, non-profit organization funded by the US government, was created by the Reagan Administration and Congress in 1983 for the purpose of promoting democracy abroad. The Endowment, through its component organizations representing US business, labour, and the Democratic and Republican Parties, initiated a range of democracy development programmes in Latin America involving assistance to political parties, trade unions, economic policy institutes, and non-profit organizations. NED's activities in Latin America were much smaller than the US government political development programmes, totalling approximately $25 million for the 1983–8 period.[4]

A number of questions can be asked about this surprisingly large and varied set of political development assistance programmes. First, what did the many different programmes actually consist of? Second, what methods did the programmes employ? Third, what was the relation between the democracy assistance programmes of the 1980s and the Reagan Administration's overall Latin America policy? Fourth, what were the results of the policies; did they contribute significantly to the democratic trend in Latin America?

2. President Reagan's 'Project Democracy'

To understand US political development assistance to Latin America in the 1980s, it is necessary to look briefly at the Reagan Administration's 'Project Democracy'. Project Democracy has been the subject of considerable confusion among observers, both because the rhetorical dimensions of the project so greatly exceeded its real dimensions and because the project subsumed two similar-sounding but separate initiatives—an effort by a group of US officials in the early Reagan Administration to create a centralized US government programme of democracy assistance, and a project by a group of eminent private citizens (with some Congressional participation) to create a semi-autonomous democracy foundation to promote democracy abroad.

The idea for a centralized US government programme of democracy assistance was developed by a small group of officials in the White House and the United States Information Agency (USIA) in 1981 and 1982. They were concerned that the United States might not only be slipping behind the Soviet Union militarily, but also be losing the 'war of ideas'—that the United States was doing too little to promote the idea of democracy in the face of the Soviet Union's international propaganda offensive to spread the gospel of Marxism–Leninism. They decided to create a centralized democracy programme which would be based at USIA but would involve projects carried out by a variety of federal agencies, including the State Department and AID. USIA was chosen as the base of the programme both because of the close relationship between USIA director Charles Wick and President Reagan and because USIA is responsible for disseminating ideas and information about the

United States abroad and thus seemed to be the logical centre for an idea-oriented democracy campaign.

At the same time that the early Reagan Administration was moving to create Project Democracy, planning was also going on in Washington among a group of interested persons for the creation of a semi-autonomous democracy foundation to promote democracy abroad. The idea for such a foundation had been floating around for years and had begun to gain momentum in the late 1970s with the backing of an influential assortment of people including Representative Dante Fascell, Lane Kirkland (from the AFL–CIO), William Brock (of the Republican National Committee), Charles Manatt (of the Democratic National Committee), Michael Samuels (from the US Chamber of Commerce), George Agree (a political scientist), Allen Weinstein (a historian), and others. The idea for such a foundation was based in part on the West German party foundations, whose active role in the transitions to democracy in Spain and Portugal had impressed American observers. Impetus also came from the main US labour federation, the AFL–CIO, which had been looking for a new source of funds for its international outreach work ever since losing its CIA funding in the late 1960s.

William Brock, Charles Manatt, and George Agree formed the American Political Foundation in 1979 to explore the idea seriously. Over the next several years they promoted the project in Washington and began to build a base of bipartisan support in Congress. The early Reagan Administration was sympathetic to the project and the American Political Foundation (APF) received a $400,000 grant from the Administration to draw up specific plans. The APF initiated its formal planning in November 1982 under the name of 'the Democracy Programme'.[5]

Although these two initiatives were intended to be complementary, they ended up as rivals for Congressional support. The Administration presented its Project Democracy plan to Congress in February 1983 in the form of a $65 million request for forty-four ongoing or proposed US government democracy assistance projects. Project Democracy did not fare well before Congress.[6] Congress found many of the proposed projects to be simplistic efforts to expose the evils of Communism and boost US-style democracy; Congress questioned whether the whole programme would not simply be 'a multimillion dollar American propaganda effort'.[7] Congress also had trouble determining whether Project Democracy was a repackaging of existing projects under a USIA umbrella or a genuinely new initiative.

Two months after the Administration sent the Project Democracy proposal to Congress, the APF's Democracy Programme issued a report calling for the establishment of a National Endowment for Democracy (NED) that would be funded by the US government but would operate independently from the government. Congress considered this proposal alongside the Administration's Project Democracy request and ended up rejecting most of Project Democracy but funding the National Endowment. The National Endowment's initial funding was less than the Endowment's backers had hoped for ($18 million for 1984), but it was enough to get NED going. The Endowment was formally inaugurated in December 1983 and began operation in 1984. Project Democracy, having failed to gain significant Congressional support, was essentially still-born. The specific democracy assistance projects that were already under way continued, but no centralized US government programme of democracy assistance was established.[8]

3. US Government Political Development Assistance to Latin America

Although the Reagan Administration's attempt to create a centralized democracy assistance programme failed, it did contribute to the development of democracy assistance programmes in Latin America. The planning process for Project Democracy brought together officials responsible for Latin American affairs from all the relevant US agencies and encouraged them to think of ways the US government could promote democracy in the region. After the demise of Project Democracy in 1983, many of these officials kept meeting and set in motion plans for Latin American projects. Long after Project Democracy faded from sight, they invoked the initiative, or the spirit of the initiative, to convince reluctant colleagues to support democracy assistance programmes.

The US government democracy assistance programmes in Latin America developed as a complex cluster of overlapping activities carried out by a relatively small set of officials, primarily at the State Department, AID, and USIA. Planning for most of the programmes took place in 1983 and 1984, and they became operational during the second Reagan Administration. At the risk of some oversimplification, the programmes can be divided into three categories —programmes to promote human rights and democratic participation, elections assistance, and judicial assistance.

Human Rights and Democratic Participation

As mentioned above, in the late 1970s AID carried out a small set of human rights projects in Latin America pursuant to Section 116(e) of the Foreign Assistance Act. Most of these projects consisted of support for local legal service or legal aid organizations. The incoming Reagan Administration team in AID was unfriendly towards human rights projects generally and flatly opposed to legal aid projects, which they saw as left-wing activism cloaked in legalistic garb. The legal aid projects were quickly shut down and AID's Section 116(e) expenditures in Latin America shrunk from $1,028,000 in 1979 and $813,000 in 1980 to $631,000 in 1981 and $408,000 in 1982 ($200,000 of which was for an election observer mission to El Salvador).[9] The handful of career AID officers interested in human rights assistance to Latin America feared that the Reagan Administration would halt human rights assistance altogether and looked for ways to prevent that from happening. As the high-level planning for Project Democracy got under way, they saw that while the human rights theme was in decline in US policy, the democracy theme was ascendant, and that many of the same activities which had been carried out in human rights projects could be pursued under the heading of promoting democracy.

Beginning in 1983, these AID officials developed a new set of Latin American projects which formally emphasized promoting democratic participation rather than human rights, utilizing the Section 116(e) funds along with new aid funds that became available for Central America starting in 1984. 'Democratic participation' was interpreted fairly broadly; most of the programmes were civic education and community action projects, such as a programme of training for community groups in Latin America by OEF International (a private, non-profit US organization) and an exchange programme between local groups in Central America (community organizations, youth groups, and public service agencies) and counterpart groups in the United States, organized by Partners of the Americas. Some projects dealt with specific issues considered to be relevant to democratic development, such as training journalists, strengthening national legislatures, and improving civil–military relations.

Overall, AID spent close to $20 million for human rights and democratic participation programmes between 1983 and 1988. Almost all of it went to projects in Central America, reflecting the greater availability of aid funds for that region than for South America, and the high level of US interest in that region.

Elections Assistance

AID carried out a number of major elections assistance projects in Latin America in the 1980s. Elections assistance was a new activity for AID; it had previously stayed away from such work out of a desire to avoid overtly political assistance projects. The door to elections assistance was opened in El Salvador when, at the State Department's insistence, AID provided $200,000 to fund an international observer mission for the 1982 elections. After the elections, the Salvadorean government requested assistance from the United States to develop a computerized voter registry. AID and the State Department hesitated, being sceptical of El Salvador's need for a relatively high-technology registry. The Salvadoreans, who were aware of the importance of elections to the Reagan Administration's El Salvador policy, 'told us [the US government] that if they didn't get the assistance for a registry there would be no more elections'.[10] The aid was duly provided, involving the US AID mission in El Salvador in a long, difficult relationship with the highly politicized Salvadorean electoral commission.

The growing assistance to the Salvadorean electoral process increased dramatically in the 1984 presidential elections. AID mounted a major technical assistance project as one part of the Reagan Administration's intensive effort to ensure the technical credibility of the Salvadorean elections and the victory of the moderate Christian Democrat José Napoleón Duarte. AID provided several millions of dollars worth of local currency assistance for the purchase of electoral supplies such as ballot paper and indelible ink, and supplied the Salvadorean government with computers to be used for electoral registries and vote-counting.[11] AID and State Department officials in the US Embassy in San Salvador were closely involved in the mechanics of the elections, trying to hold together a very shaky technical process. The embassy's involvement reached extraordinary levels at the time of the elections. At one point, for example, voter lists were printed out on the US Embassy's computers after the Salvadoreans' computers failed.[12]

AID got involved in similar fashion in the Honduran presidential elections of 1985. Credible elections in Honduras were a critical aspect of the Reagan Administration's anti-Sandinista policy in Nicaragua—the Reagan Administration was able to secure Congressional approval for massive military aid to Honduras (which was a crucial quid pro quo for Honduras's tolerance of the Contras) only as long as Honduras had a democratically elected government. At the State Department's prodding, AID gave a very large quantity of assistance (around $6 million of local currency funds as well as $680,000 of dollar funds from Washington[13]) for electoral materials and equipment for the 1985 elections. And as in El Salvador the year before, AID and State Department officials in the US Embassy in Tegucigalpa, Honduras were deeply involved in the mechanics of the elections, even to the point of assembling ballot boxes in their offices and assuring the distribution of boxes to polling stations.[14]

A smaller but still significant assistance effort was directed at the 1985 Guatemalan presidential elections. AID gave $234,000 to the Guatemalan electoral tribunal for the purchase of ballot paper and $321,260 for a training programme for poll-workers and poll-watchers. The small size of the Guatemala project compared to the El Salvador and Honduras projects reflected the perception within the US government that the Guatemalan electoral tribunal was relatively well organized and unlikely to fumble away the elections through simple disorganization. It also resulted from the unwillingness of the US aid mission in Guatemala to have any extensive involvement in an election process it was deeply sceptical of.

AID also supported elections in Latin America through the Inter-American Centre for Electoral Promotion and Assistance (CAPEL), a Costa Rica-based organization affiliated with the Inter-American Institute of Human Rights. CAPEL was founded in 1983, primarily by some Costa Ricans who believed that with the spread of electoral transitions in the region there was a growing need for a Latin American electoral assistance organization. Their project was nurtured by AID human rights and democracy officers in Washington, who hoped to channel the Administration's strong desire to promote elections in Central America away from unilateral, interventionist efforts into a Latin American organization. AID funded CAPEL from its inception and by the end of 1988 had provided more than $4 million of assistance, which represented almost all of CAPEL's budget. CAPEL carried out many different activities, in South America as well as Central America, including technical assistance to electoral tribunals, conferences for electoral officials, training courses in electoral processes, electoral research, and election observer missions.

AID undertook two elections assistance programmes outside Central America, in Haiti in 1987 and Chile in 1988. US policy in post-Duvalier Haiti was aimed at encouraging the interim government to hold presidential elections. Faced with the interim government's inexperience in elections and the general lack of a democratic tradition in Haitian society, AID and the State Department put together an ambitious elections assistance project which consisted of civic education concerning basic democratic norms and practices as well as financial and technical assistance to the Haitian government for electoral planning. In Chile AID contributed to the multi-faceted US effort to promote the 1988 plebiscite on Pinochet's continued rule by giving CAPEL $1.28 million to be used for an election registration project carried out in conjunction with Civitas, a non-partisan, pro-democracy Chilean organization.

The Administration of Justice Programme

The third area of US government democracy assistance to Latin America in the 1980s, and by far the largest, was the Administration of Justice Programme, a programme of judicial assistance to Latin America carried out by AID, the State Department, the Justice Department, and USIA. The main emphasis of this programme was not on legal aid projects, as previous US legal assistance to Latin America had been, but on assistance to Latin American courts, judges, prosecutors, bar associations, and law commissions to improve the administration of justice, particularly criminal justice. A secondary component was assistance to police forces in Latin America, to assist them in developing their criminal investigative skills. Planning for the Administration of Justice Programme got under way in 1983, the first project was initiated in 1984, and by 1988 the programme had grown to $20 million per year and included projects throughout Central America and the Caribbean, as well as in a number of South American countries.

The Administration of Justice Programme developed as a response to the right-wing political violence in El Salvador. In the early 1980s Democrats in the US Congress pushed the Reagan Administration hard on the Salvadorean government's lack of progress in bringing to justice the perpetrators of the 1980 murder of four US churchwomen and the 1981 murder of two US land-reform advisers. The State Department officials working on the cases were amazed by the incompetence of the Salvadorean judicial system and concluded that the lack of effective justice was an important cause of the uncontrolled right-wing violence in El Salvador. As Congress continued to press the Administration to do something about the high-profile murder cases and the general problem of right-wing violence, the State Department settled on the idea of creating an assistance programme for the Salvadorean judiciary.

In 1983 the State Department formed an inter-agency working group on the administration of justice in Latin America, bringing together representatives of AID, USIA, the Justice Department, and the State Department to plan a judicial assistance project for El Salvador. The working group also began to develop plans for judicial assistance programmes in other Central American countries, acting on a general pro-democracy rationale: the US officials believed that since independent judicial systems are an integral part of a working democracy, a natural element of promoting democracy in countries with nascent democratic governments is helping those countries to improve the independence and competence of their judicial systems.

The inter-agency working group studied the previous US government legal assistance programme to Latin America, the Law and Development Programme of the late 1960s and early 1970s, to avoid repeating the mistakes of the past.[15] Based on this examination, the group established a set of clear operational principles: not to export US legal models; to support existing local institutions rather than create new institutions; to focus on practical, incremental goals; and to work only with democratic governments.

The first project, the El Salvador Judicial Reform Project, was established in 1984 as a five-year, $9.2 million effort. The El Salvador project mixed the immediate concern over obtaining progress in high-profile murder cases with a more long-term interest in structural improvements in the judicial system. Two of the project's four components—the creation of an investigative commission for politically sensitive crimes and a judicial protection unit to protect participants in sensitive trials—aimed at the former goal. The other two components—a law reform commission and a judicial training programme—were aimed at long-term structural improvements in the judicial system.

With the El Salvador project launched, the Administration of Justice Programme was quickly broadened into a region-wide initiative. The State Department persuaded Congress to establish a legislative foundation for judicial assistance to Latin America in 1985, and leaned on AID to allocate some funds for the programme. AID created an administration of justice office in its Latin America bureau and folded into it the other democracy assistance programmes, centralizing all democracy programmes for Latin America in one office.

In 1985 AID established the Regional Administration of Justice Project, a Central American regional programme based in Costa Rica at the United Nations Institute for the Prevention of Crime and Treatment of Offenders (ILANUD). Under this programme ILANUD offers a range of assistance to judicial systems in Central

America, including training courses for judges, prosecutors, and other legal personnel, and technical assistance on many judicial issues such as case management and legal databases. The regional project was originally budgeted at $9.6 million but grew to over $12 million within a few years. A $10 million Caribbean regional project was initiated in 1986, based at the University of West Indies in Barbados. From 1986 to 1988 single country projects were established in Costa Rica, Guatemala, Honduras, Peru, Bolivia, and Colombia, ranging in size from $1 million to $5 million.

The Administration of Justice Programme also included assistance to police forces. In the early 1980s State Department officials working on El Salvador were struck not only by the infirmity of the Salvadorean courts and prosecutors but also by the Salvadorean police's almost complete lack of investigative skills. The working group on the administration of justice decided that any effort to improve criminal justice in El Salvador must include investigative training for police. Like judicial assistance, investigative training for police was soon transformed into a region-wide initiative.

In planning police assistance, the working group drew a line between investigative skills, such as fingerprinting or evidence preservation, and operational skills, such as crowd control or arrest methods, and held that only training of investigative skills would be funded. This emphasis on investigative training reflected the recognition that obtaining Congressional approval would be easier if police assistance were focused on the investigative domain. After some skilful lobbying, the State Department was able to persuade Congress to include in its authorization for an Administration of Justice Programme a provision for 'programs to enhance investigative capabilities conducted under judicial or prosecutorial control'.[16] This provision artfully established an authorization for police assistance without actually using the word 'police'.

With this authorization obtained, the International Criminal Investigative Training Assistance Programme (ICITAP) was created at the Department of Justice in 1985. ICITAP very rapidly built up an extensive programme of training courses for police officers in Central America and the Caribbean in basic investigative skills, such as crime-scene search, collection and preservation of evidence, fingerprinting, and interviewing. The training in specific skills was grounded in a general emphasis on attempting to solve criminal cases through scientific procedures and physical evidence rather than the forcible extraction of confessions.

ICITAP was not the only police training programme the US government carried out in Latin America during the 1980s. The State

Department, Defense Department, and Drug Enforcement Agency trained Latin American police in a variety of counter-terrorism, military, and drug-enforcement programmes. But ICITAP was the only police training programme that was part of the democracy assistance effort, and the only programme to try to change the conception Latin American police have of their socio-political role rather than simply to increase their operational skills.

4. The National Endowment for Democracy

During its first five years of operation, the National Endowment for Democracy devoted a significant part of its funds to Latin America, between $4 million and $6 million per year, out of annual budgets ranging from $15 million to $21 million. None the less, the total funds disbursed for Latin America, approximately $25 million, were small, at least compared to the approximately $100 million of US government democracy assistance in the same years.[17]

The National Endowment consists of a core organization (the Endowment itself) and four component organizations representing the US business community, US labour, the Republican Party, and the Democratic Party: respectively, the Center for International Private Enterprise, the Free Trade Union Institute, the National Republican Institute for International Affairs, and the National Democratic Institute for International Affairs. The Endowment receives a governmental funding allocation each year and gives lump-sum grants to each of the component organizations. The Endowment and the four component organizations each has its own Board of Directors and staff and pursues its own programmes.

The Center for International Private Enterprise (CIPE), a private, non-profit organization affiliated to the US Chamber of Commerce, funds projects throughout Latin America to promote public understanding of the benefits of private enterprise and free markets. Most of these projects consist of short courses or seminars, organized by private Latin American business or economic institutes. The pro-democracy rationale of CIPE's economically oriented approach is the idea that 'economic freedom' (i.e. free-market policies) and political freedom go hand in hand, and that, therefore, promoting free enterprise is a means of promoting democracy.

The Free Trade Union Institute (FTUI), a private, non-profit corporation affiliated to the AFL–CIO, supports projects to strengthen Latin American labour unions. These projects consist primarily of union-organizing activities and also include some public education efforts on the role of labour unions in democratic societies. FTUI's projects in Latin America in the 1980s were carried out by the American Institute for Free Labour Development and were basically a continuation of the AFL–CIO's work in Latin America of the 1960s and 1970s. The AFL–CIO's labour-organizing work abroad has traditionally had a strong anti-Communist orientation. The goal is not simply to strengthen unions but to combat leftist influences in unions. The pro-democracy rationale of this work is that Marxist-dominated unions are anti-democratic and that, therefore, promoting non-Marxist unions is a means of promoting democracy.

The two political party institutes, the National Republican Institute for International Affairs and the National Democratic Institute for International Affairs, both work with political parties in Latin America but in quite different fashions.[18] The Republican Institute supports what it calls 'like-minded' Latin American political parties and institutes, that is to say, ones that espouse a clearly defined set of conservative political and economic values. For example, in Argentina it has given funds to an institution affiliated with the Unión del Centro Democrático (UCD), a small conservative party known for its advocacy of free-market economic policies, to assist in grass-roots organizing and general party-building.

The National Democratic Institute (NDI), in contrast, pursues what it considers to be a non-partisan approach. Rather than supporting political parties representing a particular ideology, it seeks to foster democratic political processes by supporting multi-party coalitions struggling against undemocratic regimes. For example, in both Haiti and Chile, the NDI assisted multi-party coalitions in their efforts to forge viable electoral processes. The NDI has also sponsored a number of election observer missions to monitor key transitional elections or plebiscites—such as in Chile in 1988, Paraguay in 1989, and Panama in 1989—and projects on democratic governance issues related to the consolidation of democracy such as the budget process, constitutional reform, and civil–military relations.

The pro-democracy rationale of the Republican Institute's approach is somewhat indirect. The Republican Institute's projects aim to strengthen the conservative side of the political spectrum in countries that already have democratically elected governments. Its projects can be considered pro-democratic as opposed to just pro-conservative in the limited sense that they help strengthen at least one part of the formal democratic infrastructure of the target countries and contribute to democratic civic education. The pro-democratic rationale of NDI's approach is clearer. The assistance projects involving multi-party opposition coalitions are explicitly designed to help those coalitions campaign against non-democratic governments. And the election observer missions aim to enhance the fairness of elections or plebiscites that seek to move countries away from non-democratic rule.

Finally, the Endowment itself funds some projects directly, rather than through its component organizations. Not being related to any one social sector (such as business or labour) or political party in the United States, the Endowment has no obvious counterpart recipient groups in Latin America. The Endowment has taken the approach of funding democratic civic education projects carried out by Latin American citizen groups, such as Conciencia, an Argentine women's organization. The Endowment has also funded US educational institutions to carry out seminars or conferences with Latin American counterparts.

Although the National Endowment for Democracy and its component organizations are concerned with promoting democracy abroad, they have devoted little time or effort to articulating what notion of democracy they adhere to. All appear to embrace a simple operative conception of democracy as US-style democracy, that is to say, a strong emphasis on elections, as well as on the principles of popular representation and political rights. For the most part the Endowment and its component organizations take that definition of democracy as given and concentrate on developing and implementing programmes which concern issues or groups of special interest to them, such as trade unions, liberal economic policy organizations, political parties, or non-partisan civic action groups.

5. Democracy Assistance and Foreign Policy

Of the various strands of US government democracy assistance programmes in Latin America, the election assistance was most closely connected to the Reagan Administration's wider policies in the region. Promoting transitions to elected, civilian governments was an important part of the administration's Latin American policy, particularly in Central America. The elections assistance projects were an integral part of that effort. The other democracy assistance programmes were less closely related to the wider policies. Both the democracy participation projects and the Administration of Justice Programme were the work of a relatively small group of mid- to low-level US career officials interested in long-term, democratic change in Latin America. They perceived that the high-level officials in the Reagan Administration were primarily interested in Nicaragua and that what concern the high-level officials had for democracy in the rest of Latin America was largely a superficial interest in fostering elected governments. They also saw, however, that the stated emphasis on democracy was a useful rhetorical umbrella under which they could develop programmes to foster more substantive processes of democratization.

Thus, these democracy assistance programmes had an ambiguous relation to the larger policies. On the one hand they were connected to the larger policies in that they shared the same stated goal of promoting democracy and in some ways grew out of the Reagan Administration's frequent use of the democracy theme. On the other hand, they were separate from the larger policies in that they treated democratization in a more substantive way than the election-oriented focus of the overall policy and were carried out with little interest or support from the higher-level officials. This ambiguous relationship demonstrated both the multi-layered nature of the policy bureaucracy, in particular the division between high-level political appointees and mid- to low-level career officials, and the ways in which policy rhetoric, such as the Reagan Administration's democracy theme in Latin America, ends up creating substantive policy measures.

The relationship between the National Endowment for Democracy's programmes and US policy in Latin America was and continues to be one of informal concordance. The Endowment receives nearly all its funds from the US government; none the less, the Endowment and its components organizations design and implement their programmes with relative independence. Although each project must be cleared by the State Department before being initiated, in practice this is a pro forma step which largely serves to notify the State Department of the Endowment's activities. The Endowment's programmes tend to correspond to the general policies followed by the US government, less because of any direct methods of government control than because of the fact that NED is a mainstream Washington organization whose directors and staff tend to share the same basic assumptions as government officials do about US interests abroad. To the extent that the US government influences NED directly, Congress is a much more important actor than the executive branch. NED depends on Congress for its funding and is extremely careful to avoid offending Congress. Congress monitors the Endowment closely and in some cases directs it to spend money in certain countries, such as in Chile for the 1988 plebiscite and in Nicaragua for the 1990 elections.

6. Democratic Methodology

Two contrasting methodologies have dominated US democracy assistance programmes in Latin America in the past several decades: the 'bottom-up' approach, which consists of assisting local nongovernmental organizations that educate, organize, and train people in democratic ideas and practices, reflecting the view that democracy develops out of the activities and beliefs of the population as a whole; and the 'top-down' approach, which consists of working directly with governing institutions to encourage or train them to adopt democratic norms and practices, reflecting the view that democracy develops when ruling institutions and élites adhere to democratic norms.

In the 1960s the bottom-up approach was dominant. With its emphasis on increasing mass participation in political processes, Title IX embodied the bottom-up approach. In the 1980s the emphasis was reversed. The two largest areas of democracy assistance to Latin America, the Administration of Justice Programme and the elections assistance programmes, involved assistance to governmental institutions to improve their adherence to democratic norms and practices. The human rights and democracy participation programmes followed the bottom-up approach, but they were the smallest of the three strands of US government democracy assistance and the one least supported by the State Department and the higher levels of AID.

The reversal of emphasis between the 1960s and the 1980s was primarily due to the differing origins of the programmes. The political development assistance of the 1960s was the result of an initiative by some Congressional Democrats who believed that the United States must assure a harmonious correspondence between economic and political development in the developing world by politically empowering 'the masses'. The US government political development assistance of the 1980s was largely a State Department initiative (except for the human rights and democratic participation programmes) and reflected the tendency of State Department officials to conceive of democracy assistance as an effort to train foreign governments to meet certain standards of behaviour.

An integral feature of the 1980s top-down approach was an emphasis on helping Latin American governments keep order. Of all the sectors of Latin American societies that a democratic development effort might focus on, it is notable that the bulk of US government democratic assistance in the 1980s was directed towards the law-enforcement sector, i.e. the courts and police. This emphasis exemplified the close connection between order-keeping and democracy promotion that has long marked US Latin American policy. For generations the US government has espoused an interest in promoting democracy in Latin America while having as its main concern helping Latin American governments to maintain order, in particular, preventing the rise of leftist revolutionary movements.

A clear methodological difference existed between the National Endowment for Democracy's programmes and the US government democracy assistance programmes. Instead of the top-down approach of the US government programmes, the National Endowment pursued a bottom-up approach—NED's projects focused on non-governmental organizations and were designed to promote democracy by changing the ideas and attitudes of the general population and strengthening civil society.

One explanation for this difference in approach was that NED was created to spread the idea of democracy around the world, whereas the US government programmes were developed by officials hoping to get Latin American governments to behave in more acceptable, democratic ways. Thus the NED has remained oriented towards disseminating the idea of democracy among all different sectors of target countries, whereas the US government development programmes have focused on technical assistance to governments. Another explanation is that in the political development field, donors tend to fund persons or institutions who resemble themselves—US labour unions give to Latin American labour unions; US businessmen fund projects for Latin American businessmen; US conservatives give money to Latin American conservatives; and US government officials aid Latin American government officials. The only exception to this rule is US liberals (the National Democratic Institute), who have taken a relatively non-partisan approach.

7. Results

The results of US democracy assistance in the 1980s cannot be conclusively evaluated without a large-scale empirical study, which is well beyond the scope of this chapter. At the level of general impressions, it can be said that such assistance was a positive initiative. The assistance was a genuine attempt to contribute to the socio-political good of Latin America by persons who for the most part had some working familiarity with Latin American and were sincerely interested in promoting democracy. The programmes had some limited positive effects. The human rights and democratic participation programmes raised awareness in Central America about human rights issues and strengthened local human rights groups. The elections assistance programmes did manage to improve the technical quality of elections in the target countries. The Administration of Justice Programme trained judges and police, improved the technical facilities of judicial systems, and raised the profile of long-ignored judicial systems. And the NED's programmes strengthened civic education groups, improved elections, strengthened political parties and private economic institutes, and bolstered labour unions.

Despite these limited positive achievements, there is no significant evidence, however, that the US democracy assistance programmes had or are having a profound effect on any Latin American societies. In the 1980s, just as in the 1960s, the United States invested its political development assistance to Latin America with unrealistically high expectations. The assistance was publicly characterized as a major initiative that, if successful, would have far-reaching effects on Latin American political systems. This characterization, however, was specious. The magnitude of the task of political development in Latin America was so much greater than the scale of the problems addressed that even if the programmes had been flawlessly executed, they would not have had profound effects. Problems in Latin America—such as political violence, the weak rule of law, and the absence of real democratic norms—obviously represent deep-seated economic, political, and social structures. The notion inherent in US democracy programmes that some modest quantity of training seminars, exchange programmes, and technical assistance can solve these problems has no empirical foundation.

It is worth considering why Americans so readily embrace the idea of political development assistance to Latin America and invest that assistance with high expectations. At work are a number of cultural attitudes about US–Latin American relations and about democracy itself. One cause is the common belief among Americans involved in Latin America affairs that the United States has the capability of exerting powerful influence on the domestic political evolution of Latin America. This view is held in spite of the fact that US influence in Latin American has obviously declined greatly in the past twenty years and that even when the United States did exert a powerful influence it was more to topple governments or suppress movements it did not like than to bring about long-term positive political evolution.

Another cause was the fact that when Americans involve themselves in other societies, they usually work from an ahistorical point of view, reflecting their lack of knowledge about the other society and with a culturally ingrained attitude regarding the impotence of history to bind the present. They tend to assume that people, institutions, and societies can change relatively easily if a conscious, rational effort is made to do so. Training is the key operational element in this outlook and US political development programmes in Latin America and elsewhere almost always emphasize training programmes in the apparent belief that occasional or even repeated one-week courses and seminars can quickly reverse the most deeply entrenched attitudes and practices. Thus, the approach taken to a generations-old problem such as the staggering political violence committed by the Salvadorean security forces is a series of short courses for military personnel on the importance of human rights and general 'professionalization'. The repeated failures of such training efforts in the past, in particular the large training programmes with the Guatemalan and Salvadorean police in the late 1960s and early 1970s, are ignored or simply dismissed as irrelevant.

Finally, American attitudes towards democracy itself also foster an unrealistic faith in political development assistance. Americans tend to view democracy as a natural political state; non-democratic systems are aberrations from a norm. This view of democracy leads to a view of political development (defined by Americans as progress towards US-style democracy) as a relatively easy process. Americans confronting a non-democratic country such as Honduras or El Salvador tend not to ask 'I wonder whether this country might ever become democratic?' but rather 'I wonder why democracy hasn't succeeded?' with the implicit assumption that democracy should naturally succeed and success is just a question of making the right adjustments. Political development assistance programmes are thus seen more as attempts to adjust something that has gone wrong or to remove obstacles in an already defined path than to build something from scratch or fundamentally alter the existing state of affairs.

Notes

1. Section 281(*a*) of the Foreign Assistance Act of 1961, as amended (superseded by the Foreign Assistance Act of 1973).

2. *A Retrospective of AID's Experience in Strengthening Democratic Institutions in Latin America 1961–1981*, a report produced for AID by Creative Associates International, September 1987; R. Packenham, *Liberal America and the Third World* (Princeton, NJ: Princeton University Press, 1973), 98–110.

3. The $100m. figure represents the sum of the approximately $20m. spent on human rights and democratic participation programmes, $60m. spent on the Administration of Justice Programme, and the $15m. to $20m. spent on electoral assistance. The figures for those programmes were drawn from AID budget documents, such as those included in the annual AID Congressional Presentation and from information about the programmes gained through interviews with AID officials.

4. NED's budgets are set out in its Annual Reports. The $25m. figure is a summation of all Latin American programmes listed in those reports.

5. On the planning process for the National Endowment for Democracy see, 'Events Leading to the Establishment of the National Endowment for Democracy', Report to Senator Malcolm Wallop, US General Accounting Office, 6 July 1984. See also C. Madison, 'Selling Democracy', *National Journal*, 28 June 1986, 1603–8.

6. Secretary of State Shultz, USIA Director Wick, and some other USIA officials testified on Project Democracy in early 1983. The hearings reveal some of Congress's doubts about the project. See 'Authorizing Appropriations for Fiscal Years 1984–85 for the Department of State, the US Information Agency, the Board for International Broadcasting, the Inter-American Foundation, the Asia Foundation, to Establish the National Endowment for Democracy', Hearings and Markup before the Committee on Foreign Affairs and its Subcommittee on International Operations, House of Representatives, 98th Congress, 1st Session on HR 2915 (Washington DC: US Government Printing Office, 1984).

7. Rep. Kostameyer used that phrase to describe Project Democracy in the hearings on the Project: ibid. 41.

8. Several years after Project Democracy went down to defeat in Congress the term 'Project Democracy' reappeared. Oliver North nicknamed the secret NSC–CIA Contra supply operation 'Project Democracy', and during the Iran–Contra investigations in 1987 this fact emerged, prompting speculation of links between the illicit Iran–Contra activities and the original Project Democracy initiative. The only actual such link was in the public diplomacy realm—the secret NSC–CIA Contra supply operation had some ties to the US government's anti-Sandinista public diplomacy operation, which had been created by some of the same people involved in the original Project Democracy proposal.

9. These figures are drawn from AID's annual reports on Section 116(e) programmes.

10. Author interview with AID official involved in elections assistance to Latin America.

11. Local currency assistance consists of the following: when AID gives dollar grants to be used for balance-of-payment support, it requires the Central Bank of the recipient country to generate one dollar's worth of local currency for every dollar of balance-of-payment support funds. This local currency is to be used for development purposes and is referred to as 'local currency assistance'. Exact figures for local currency expenditures, such as those going to the 1984 Salvadorean election, are hard to obtain because local currency expenditures are not reported by AID (since local currency assistance is technically considered funds of the recipient country, only the original dollar grants of balance-of-payment support funds are reported).

12. Author interview with US official who worked on the electoral assistance programme in El Salvador.

13. The $6 million figure for the local currency assistance to the Honduran electoral tribunal is only an approximation. As discussed in n. 11, no public reporting of local currency assistance is made. AID officials involved in the Honduran election assistance programme have differing memories as to the total amount of aid that went to the electoral tribunal, with estimates ranging from $5m. to $15m.

14. Author interview with State Department official who worked in the US Embassy in Tegucigalpa during the mid-1980s.

15. The inter-agency working group made considerable use of James Gardner's study of the Law and Development Programme, *Legal Imperialism: American Lawyers and Foreign Aid in Latin America* (Madison, Wis.: University of Wisconsin Press, 1980).

16. Section 712 of the 1985 International Security and Development Cooperation Act.

17. See n. 4.

18. A good description of the contrasting methodologies of the political party institutes is given in J. Muravchik, 'US Political Parties Abroad', *Washington Quarterly* (summer 1989), 91–100.

6

The International Dimensions of Democratization in Latin America: The Case of Brazil

ANDREW HURRELL

There is a paradoxical quality to the international aspects of democratic transition and consolidation in Brazil. On the one hand, the extent of direct external involvement in the processes of transition and consolidation and the scope for direct external influence have been limited and are probably less than in any other major Latin American country. Viewed in terms of direct influence, the case of Brazil reinforces one of the central conclusions of the literature on democratization, namely that external factors are of secondary, or even marginal, importance in shaping domestic political outcomes in Latin America. Yet on the other hand, it is difficult to understand the gradual transition towards civilian rule, the shape and character of the process of democratic consolidation, and the dilemmas facing Brazil without considering the broader international political and economic context and the ways in which this context has shaped the options available to policy-makers and politicians in Brazil.

This contrast between the overall importance of the international context and the relative absence of specific linkages highlights the general difficulty of conceptualizing the relationship between the international system and national political systems.[1] It also poses a serious dilemma as to how international support for political democracy in Brazil may best be examined. The primary objective of this chapter is to bring together, categorize, and assess the various ways in which both specific external actors and the broader international context have influenced domestic political outcomes in Brazil. For purposes of analysis it is necessary to disaggregrate the various categories or classes of interaction between

Brazil and the international system, and in this chapter four such categories will be considered. This necessarily involves a degree of over-simplification and a fuller account would need to pay greater attention to the relationship between these various categories and the ways in which they may reinforce or work against each other.

In the first place we might look for examples of direct external political involvement where specific external actors form close ties with major domestic political players operating at the heart of the Brazilian political system—for example, within the presidency, the military, the Congress, or the state bureaucracy. Second, there are forms of indirect external political involvement whereby external actors—both states but, very importantly, non-state transnational actors—seek to influence the character and direction of political activity of groups within civil society in Brazil. The focus here is on transnational contacts or networks involving, for example, church groups, trade unions, human rights organizations, or grass-roots social movements.

Third, there are the various ways in which the international political system can influence domestic political outcomes. Four (often interrelated) varieties of interaction need to be noted: first, the extent to which the power-political and ideological competition between the major states presses them to intervene in the internal affairs of weaker states and to make 'democracy' both a means and an objective of policy; second, the ways in which smaller powers use this concern both as a vehicle for external support and as a basis of domestic political legitimacy; third, the ways in which democratic values and preferences can be diffused through the international system, unmediated by specific government policies; and lastly, the extent to which democratic values may be incorporated into the institutions of international society and come to form a principle of international legitimacy.

The fourth, and most contested, level of interaction arises from the dynamics and constraints of involvement in an increasingly globalized world economy. Again, various broad categories of impact can be noted. First, as has been widely argued, increasing integration undermines the autonomy of national decision-makers as growing economic interdependence erodes the separateness of national markets and leads to increased vulnerability to changing external conditions. Second, a negative international economic environment may compound domestic economic problems, thereby limiting a government's freedom of manœuvre at precisely the time when popular expectations are high and the political bases for making hard choices are very limted. Third, domestic economic policies may be strongly influenced by the preferences of major economic powers, by international economic institutions, and by dominant sets of ideas about the 'correct' approach to development. Lastly, shifting patterns of global production and finance and the increased rate of technological change may severely narrow the range of economic development options, thereby influencing the character of the domestic political and social system within which democratization takes place.

1. Direct External Political Involvement

At the first level it is necessary to consider those categories of external involvement and international links which have had, or might have, a direct impact on Brazilian politics and the promotion of democracy. In the case of Brazil, two groups stand out as potentially important: the military and the political parties. In the post-war period it has been the Brazilian military that has most consistently looked abroad for external support—above all to the United States. The origins and nature of the relationship between the Brazilian military and the United States are well known and can be summarized briefly. The close personal relationships developed by many Brazilian military officers (above all the *castellista* faction) in the course of training in the United States and fighting during the Second World War in Italy were an important factor. The position of the United States as the dominant supplier of weapons, training, and military doctrine enhanced the relationship as did the close and very extensive network of bilateral military ties which grew up in the post-war period. The Brazilian military and the US government shared a common ideological stance, fostered by the Escola Superior de Guerra, on both attitudes to the Soviet Union and the danger of communist subversion within the region. Finally ideological ties between the two were buttressed by the belief in influential parts of the military that the country's economic development would best be served by promoting close ties with the United States. Equally well known is the role that these ties and beliefs came to play in the military coup of 1964.[2] Whatever the precise extent of US involvement in the immediate lead-up to the coup and the actual overthrow of Brazil's democratic government, Washington's support for the new military government was evident. Under Castello Branco the Brazilian military saw both international alignment with the United States and increased direct assistance from the United States as a central source of support and international legitimacy.

Yet these ties and this channel of external influence have declined very significantly over the past twenty-five years. The origins of the shift in military attitudes to the United States can be traced to the late 1960s: to the relative decline in the overall economic salience of the United States; to the belief that the benefits of the policy of 'automatic alignment' were too small to warrant such self-imposed limits on the country's foreign policy; to military irritation that Washington appeared unwilling to help Brazil in such areas as supplying modern weapons and providing nuclear technology; and to the loss of influence of the *castellista* group under Costa e Silva and Médici.

The growing divergence between Washington and Brasilia grew more marked as a result of the controversies of the Carter years and the disputes over human rights and nuclear proliferation. But more significant was the extent to which the Brazilian military refused to be drawn back into a close relationship in the early 1980s despite clear ideological affinities and intensive lobbying by the Reagan Administration.[3] Some outward progress was indeed visible. Thus Brazil accepted the US proposal, made during President Reagan's visit to Brazil in December 1982, to establish five joint working groups to discuss future co-operation between the two countries; there were an increased number of high-level military visits; and in February 1984, during the visit of George Shultz, a memorandum of understanding on renewed military co-operation was signed. Yet practical co-operation proved to be limited. On the one hand, there were significant differences between Brazil and the United States over both the relative priority to be accorded to security issues and the meaning and definition of security (see, for example, the divergence of attitudes towards the conflict in Central America). On the other hand, there was a growing feeling that the United States could no longer be counted upon to assist Brazil in the areas that were of most direct importance—above all in the economic field and in terms of foreign debt.[4] Indeed, the military found themselves in direct opposition to the United States over a number of the controversies that dogged US–Brazilian relations during the Sarney years from 1985 to 1989, including the informatics dispute, the question of nuclear proliferation and arms exports, and Brazil's Amazon policy.

The arrival of President Collor in March 1990 saw a determined attempt to improve relations with Washington. The Collor government sought to end the outstanding trade disputes, particularly over market reserve policies and intellectual property rights. Significant changes were announced in Brazilian environmental policies with the clear objective of preventing the issue of rainforest destruction from clouding relations. And there were also important modifications of policy on nuclear proliferation and the elaboration of a US-inspired control regime for weapons exports. Such moves were undertaken as part of a broader project of economic reform and modernization. Yet the military do not appear to have been central players in Collor's *rapprochement* with the United States and, whilst co-operation over some practical matters was certainly welcomed by the military (for instance the ending of the US embargo on super-computer technology), there was little sign of any desire to revive a special relationship with anything like the explicitly political dimension that had previously characterized ties. Under Collor's successor, Itamar Franco, relations with Washington once more assumed their ambivalent character in the light of Washington's heavy concentration on relations with Mexico as well as its barely concealed dismay and frustration at Brazil's still fitful and hesitant progress with economic liberalization.

None of this is to deny that close personal relationships continue to exist at an individual level. Nor is it to discount the possibility that political polarization or a radical breakdown of social order in Brazil might force the military to rethink their attitudes to the United States. Nor, finally, is it to argue that, faced with a possible retrogression to military rule, Washington would have no cards to play in warning the military of the possible consequences of such a step. The point, however, is to emphasize that this channel of external influence has changed enormously over the past twenty-five years and that the degree of external influence in this area has been very significantly reduced.

Although it does not in itself prove a decline of influence, it is certainly worth noting the marginal role played by the United States in the transition to civilian rule. This is true both of the original decision taken by Golbery and Geisel in the early 1970s to launch *abertura* (political liberalization), and the manner in which the final stage of the transition was handled (or perhaps mishandled) in 1984–5. If one leaves aside the impact of US economic policy (to be discussed below), there is little reason to quarrel with Langhorne Motley's statement:

The United States played no role in *abertura*. In the period of time that I was in Brazil, 1981 through 1984, I always counseled Washington, and for once they took my advice, that *abertura* was made in Brazil, and both from a public and private posture the United States was better off staying out of it. The Brazilians defined what *abertura* was and what the timetable was to be. All we did was applaud the process. There was no secret agenda of US involvement either. We stayed out of *abertura* because the dumbest thing we could have done was to have been in the middle of it, although we did insist on the right to talk to opposition groups and to deal with all factions of society, including the church.[5]

The other set of political actors to be considered under this heading are the political parties. The central point here is the relatively limited extent of international contacts and support and the overall degree of introspection that continues to characterize the Brazilian political system. On the one hand, Brazilian parties have not in general looked abroad for either material or ideological support. On the other, Brazil has not been a major target of external political parties or political groups anxious to build up political ties within the region. The only official links involve the PDT (Partido Democrático Trabalhista), which is a consultative member of the Socialist International (SI) and the PFL (Partido da Frente Liberal) which has been an observer member of the Liberal International since 1985. In addition, although some ties exist, the German party foundations have been less directly involved in building up party links than elsewhere in the region. Thus, the German liberal party foundation (the Friedrich Naumann Stiftung) has consistently sought to support the creation of a European-style liberal party, first the PP (Partido Popular) founded in 1980 and then the PL (Partido Liberal) founded in 1985. There has also been an increase in the number of contacts and agreements between the Partido dos Trabalhadores (PT) and various European political groups, especially in Italy. There have also been reports of Christian Democratic parties in Europe seeking to build up party links in Brazil.

Yet the overall picture is one in which party and electoral politics in Brazil have remained substantially isolated from the outside world. Various factors help to explain this. In the first place, the absence of 'exile politics' of the Chilean variety (see Chapter 7 below) reduced the opportunities for, and indeed the necessity of, building up a range of international contacts. The fact that party politics and elections, albeit often manipulated, continued throughout the period of military rule kept the focus of the leading political groups firmly within the country. The Brazilian military sought to maintain the major institutions of the previous political system (elections, the Congress, and even, to a certain extent, the parties) whilst intervening heavily when necessary (closing Congress, constantly manipulating election rules, etc.) and subjecting all political activity to the broader control of national security legislation. This pattern reinforced the introspection of the major political groups and the continuity of both leading personalities and party traditions that has been one of the most notable features of the so-called New Republic.

It is true that Leonel Brizola's period in Portugal and his role within the Socialist International, both in exile and following his return to Brazil in 1979, represented a partial exception. He was, for example, an active participant of the 1984 meeting of the Socialist International in Rio de Janeiro and in the disputes over SI support for the Sandinistas. Yet Brizola was forced to adapt himself to the political structure and political groupings that had grown up in his absence. Moreover, although he often spoke of his party (the PDT) in terms of European social democracy, much of his own appeal has been based on his own past achievements and on the quintessentially Brazilian tradition of Vargas and the historic PTB.

A second factor weakening international links arises from the fact that ideological affinities between European and Latin American parties are often problematic. As Wolf Grabendorff's chapter (Chapter 8 below) explains, identifying and establishing the 'political families' that link Western Europe and Brazil is certainly far from easy. The weakness of party structures and the high degree of institutional plasticity, the common absence of a clear ideological direction or programme, the strength of clientelist relations, and the dominance of individual personalities are all relevant factors here (although they vary from party to party and are hardly unknown elsewhere in the region). Thus, for example, the range of political currents within the PMDB (reduced somewhat since the schisms of July 1988) makes it unclear with whom it could or should ally internationally. Similarly, the absence of a strong Christian Democratic tradition has hampered the role of the Christian Democratic International and the Konrad Adenauer Stiftung. Moreover, the influence of the internationals has often rested as much on personal relations as on formal institutional structures and, in the case of Brazil, there have been few leading politicians who have viewed the cultivation of these kinds of contacts as a major priority—a phenomenon common to other continental-sized states.

Third, looked at from the European perspective, Brazil does not occupy anything like the same position in public opinion, the media, and the international interests of the major political parties as Chile or, at least in the Reagan years, Central America. This is very clearly illustrated by the marginal press and media coverage in Western Europe of the often dramatic developments in recent Brazilian political history. Finally, there have been strong practical reasons for the party internationals to focus on those (usually small) countries where their limited resources and influence would be most effective and could make a real difference. Thus in the critical period of transition from 1983 to 1988 combined expenditures of the party foundations in Brazil (DM32.2 million) were lower than Costa Rica (DM33.4 million), and below those in Venezuela, Peru, Argentina, and Chile.[6]

2. Indirect External Political Involvement

This section examines instances of indirect external involvement, covering those external links which usually operate outside the immediate arena of central government and which have a more diffuse impact on the political system. Of central concern here are the contacts and networks that have developed within what some have called 'international civil society', or 'global civil society' and that constitute 'a parallel arrangement of political interaction . . . focused on the self-conscious construction of networks of knowledge and action, by decentred, local actors'.[7] For many writers the growth of such networks has been stimulated by economic globalization and by new information technologies which create the material conditions both for the diffusion or 'contagion' of democratic values and for effective transnational political activity and the empowerment of citizens and citizen movements.[8] The strength of such groups rests partially on the mobilization of material resources, but far more on their ability to articulate a powerful set of human values, to harness the growing sense of a cosmopolitan moral awareness, and to respond to the multiple failures of the state system, both locally and globally.[9]

During the process of transition, the most important linkages of this kind involved the churches, and particularly the Catholic Church. The Catholic Church in Brazil played a central role in what O'Donnell called the 'resurrection of civil society' in the 1970s and the growth of popular opposition to military rule. Similarly, the rapid expansion of the CEBs (*communidades eclesiais de base*) has been the most frequently cited example of the emergence of so-called 'new social movements' in Brazil. Although the transition process cannot be seen solely, or even predominantly, in terms of growing social protest and popular resistance, such protest did undoubtedly affect the calculations of the military by raising the costs of continued authoritarian rule in general, and of direct coercion in particular.

However, even here, a degree of caution is in order. First, there is still very little detailed research on the specifically international aspects of this process.[10] We know, for instance, little about the exact amounts and sources of foreign assistance and the precise ways in which this money has been used. Without more detailed empirical studies, it is extremely difficult to judge what kind of political impact the myriad of externally supported church social projects have had and how much of that impact would have occurred without external finance or support. Second, the fact that the Catholic Church is a transnational actor does not mean that international influences are necessarily particularly important. After all, both the shift in the attitude of the Catholic hierarchy within Brazil in the late 1960s in response to growing repression and the broadening grass-roots participation and organization were to a significant extent the result of domestic factors. Similarly, the creation and expanded role of the CNBB (National Conference of Brazilian Bishops) represented a broader trend within the Church towards increased national autonomy.

Nevertheless, external links certainly played a part and several significant examples can be noted—for example, the dependence of the Brazilian Catholic Church on foreign priests and the role of these priests in the radicalization of the Church in the 1970s; or the determination of the Vatican in the 1980s to curb the influence of liberation theology at both the doctrinal and the organizational levels (for example the disciplining of Leonardo Boff, and the breaking up of the archdiocese of São Paulo in order to reduce the power of Cardinal Arns). It is also worth noting that the salience of Brazil in the overseas activities of European church groups is much higher than it is for either the party internationals or the German party foundations. In the period 1962 to 1977, for example, Brazil was the most important recipient of financial assistance from the German churches (DM94.1 million spread over 320 projects), ahead of Chile (DM42.6 million for 72 projects) and Argentina (DM28.8 million for 86 projects). Both Catholic and Protestant churches concentrated their efforts in Brazil with DM57.2 million coming from the Protestant churches and DM36.9 million from the Catholic Church.[11]

Moreover, during the long process of *abertura* one could list a variety of other politically significant foreign influences under this heading. There was the role of human rights groups (Amnesty International, the International Commission of Jurists, and Civilità Cattolica) in drawing attention to torture and repression in Brazil. The impact of this publicity is unclear. It may have been a factor in helping to convince the military of the lack of viability of long-term military rule. It may also have helped to sustain the emergence of domestic protest to human rights abuses. It certainly did have a significant impact in changing US Congressional attitudes to Brazil in the early 1970s, leading to pressure on the US government to distance itself from the Brazilian military. One might also point to the decisions of several leading foreign companies (particularly Volkswagen and General Motors) in the 1979–82 period to accept directly negotiated agreements with the new trade unions, thereby undermining the government's attempts at repression. Connected with this was the broader expansion of contacts and support between the metalworkers' unions in Brazil and their counterparts abroad, especially in West Germany. The links between the metalworkers and the Catholic Church within Brazil on the one hand and the network of international support on the other made it at least marginally harder for the Figueiredo government to control the wave of strikes and demonstrations in this period and served to increase the costs of coercion.[12]

Foreign involvement at this level has certainly continued in the post-1985 period. The number of externally funded church projects continued to develop above all in the areas of health, education, and local community projects. Similarly the German party foundations continued to fund a wide range of projects: journalists' associations; radio and television centres; women's organizations (for example the Konrad Adenauer Stiftung); co-operative associations at both a regional and national level (such as the Friedrich Naumann Stiftung); and trade union, media, and political education projects (such as the Friedrich Ebert Stiftung).[13] Moreover, it is likely that this area of external involvement will increase as donor countries seek to make their aid more conditional on both political democracy and good governance, and increasingly turn to NGOs as a conduit for aid and assistance. In many OECD countries moves to encourage wider political participation and strengthen grass-roots organizations have already become an increasingly important element of official aid policies.[14]

During the military period such groups were most directly influential as a focus for political protest, and foreign support was effective in so far as it assisted that protest. During the 1970s union mobilization, church opposition amongst both the hierarchy and the base communities, and the protests of human rights groups and professional associations helped to maintain pressure on the military government from below. They did not act as 'bridging institutions' in the sense described by Laurence Whitehead in Chapter

10, and played only an indirect part in the pacts and negotiations that accompanied the final (formal) exit of the military. In the post-1985 period, influence is harder to trace, partly because of the absence of a clear target for protest, but partly also because of the lack of effective articulation between the the density of civil society and the sophistication of many groups acting within it on the one hand, and the narrow structures of traditional political power on the other. External involvement of this kind may therefore have failed to achieve direct political results but still played an important diffuse and longer-term role, helping to strengthen different forms of social movements, to promote different kinds of political values, and to broaden the degree of political participation.

Nevertheless, there have been occasions when indirect external involvement achieved a measure of success in the post-1985 period. One example relates to the dramatic increase in the number of transnational environmental pressure groups, concerned both with narrowly 'ecological' issues, but increasingly with the linkages between human rights, democracy, and sustainability.[15] International NGO pressures in the late 1980s undoubtedly contributed to the changes that have taken place in Brazilian policy towards the Amazon and the protection of indigenous peoples, although the limits to change need to be noted, as does the extent to which success was dependent on a rather specific set of factors. These include: a degree of public concern in the North with environmental issues that has diminished dramatically over the past year and a half; the linking of the human rights of particular groups to ecological concerns that directly affect people in the North; the targeting of protest around specific and clearly identifiable large-scale externally funded projects; and the visibility of environmental issues at high-level gatherings (such as G7 summits).[16]

International pressure has also grown in response to Brazil's deteriorating record on human rights, visible in: the failure (despite the policy changes initiated by Collor) to offer adequate protection to indigenous peoples; the failure of the government to stem the tide of extra-judicial killings of criminals and suspects by members of the police forces or by groups tolerated by them; the failure to stem the tide of the deaths of Brazil's street children; and the failure to control rural violence and violent struggles for land and rights to land. For many NGOs the continued violations of human rights demonstrate the extent to which formal democracy has made little real difference to the security and, in some cases, survival of large numbers of impoverished people. Specific examples of protest include the Candelária and Vigário Geral murders of street children and the suppression of the Carandiru prison riot in São Paulo. Although very far from solving the problem, this pressure has been effective in two senses. First, as in the case of the environment, it has forced the Brazilian government to move away from its previously rigid insistence on its sovereign rights and the norm of non-intervention. Secondly, it has induced some change in policy, for example moves to pass a law making the state military police punishable in civilian courts, and increased federal pressure on state governments to reform the role of the military police. Perhaps more importantly, international pressure has helped to stimulate a wave of domestic concern over the issue in the press, in congress, and in the Brazilian NGO movement.[17]

Brazil's failures in the area of human rights matter in their own right. But they also provide an important reminder that political democracy offers no automatic guarantee of human rights, particularly in a society beset by the degree of social inequality long evident in Brazil. The human rights debate therefore helps focus international attention on the limits of excessively narrow procedural conceptions of democracy that stress free elections and political contestation. The human rights debate also draws attention to the social corrosion of democracy from below that is occurring in many parts of Brazil, as social order in many parts of the country is eroded, as the social crisis leads to the construction of networks of power and authority outside the control of the state (by both the rich and the poor), and as the capacity of the state to make and enforce laws is undermined. Indeed the international human rights agenda can help develop—both definitionally and practically—the critical space between an excessively narrow emphasis on the constitution of democratic regimes on the one hand and an excessively broad concern for substantive economic democracy on the other.

3. The International Political System

Shifts to and from political democracy in Brazil have historically been significantly influenced by wider power-political and ideological developments in the international political system. Thus the Second World War played a major role in the return to constitutional government in December 1945, with the defeat of the Axis powers and the dominance of the United States increasing the attractions of democratic government, particularly within the military, and helping to undermine the legitimacy of the Estado Novo. Equally, the spreading of the Cold War to Latin America played a major role in helping to shape the balance of political forces within the newly re-established constitutional system.[18] In the early 1960s the attitudes of the Brazilian military (and, of course, to a still greater extent of the US government) were significantly influenced by the broader evolution of the Cold War and especially by the Cuban Revolution. The military perceived a clear link between domestic and foreign policy. Domestically, the coup was seen as a necessary pre-emptive move against the spread of Communist influence, actively encouraged by Goulart for his own populist purposes, whilst anti-Communism provided one of the principal bases on which the military regime sought to establish its legitimacy and credibility. Internationally, anti-Communism provided the orienting principle of foreign policy and underpinned the re-establishment of the special relationship with the United States.

In the period from the late 1960s to the mid-1980s, however, Brazil appeared to be far more insulated from broader developments in the international political system. Thus the breakdown of *détente* and the increase in superpower confrontation in many parts of the Third World played no part at all in the transition to civilian rule in the late 1970s and early 1980s. This degree of insulation reflected the broader changes that had taken place in Brazilian foreign policy since the 1960s and the emergence of a consensus that rejected the idea of any kind of special relationship with Washington, accepted Brazil's gradual move towards *de facto* non-alignment on East–West issues, and argued for an increasingly hard-headed approach to the pursuit of its political and, above all, economic interests.

Two partial exceptions to this trend can be noted. First, it is possible to argue that the military's self-identification with Western values was not wholly rhetorical and helped to reinforce the belief that Brazil should eventually return to some form of democracy. This in turn reinforced the military government's (albeit highly qualified) respect for legalism and for the maintenance of many of the forms of electoral and constitutional procedures. Second, as the region moved towards democracy in the early 1980s, the decreasing international legitimacy for authoritarian government may have reinforced the domestic legitimacy crisis facing Brazil's military government. As Charles Gillespie has argued, there was no international club for authoritarian regimes and hard-line authoritarianism risked acquiring pariah status within the region.[19]

More recently the degree of insulation between Brazil and broader developments in the international political system has once more become eroded. Cold War interventionist pressures may be in decline, but the role of democracy and human rights as principles of international legitimacy has grown more salient, and Western governments have once more made democracy part of the rhetoric of foreign policy.[20] In marked contrast with the 1980s, Western governments have become far more willing to concede linkages between economic assistance and democratization, and the promotion of democracy and good governance has become a more central criterion of both official aid policies and the lending policies of the multilateral funding institutions.[21] Participation in elections and political activity has become a more central element of international human rights law, and the international monitoring of elections has become more widespread and accepted. Attempts have been made to condemn challenges to democracy (Haiti, Peru), to criticize the lack of 'good governance' (Kenya, Malawi), and to try to make democracy and respect of human rights an element in recognition policy (as in policy towards the former Yugoslav republics). For some commentators, OAS policy towards Haiti and Peru has at last demonstrated the possibility of translating the Charter's formal commitment to democratic government into actual policy.[22] Finally, democratization and democratic conditionality have begun to emerge as issues in the expansion of regional economic arrangements, with talk of NAFTA forming the core of an expanding hemispheric community based on both economic and political liberalism.[23]

These important changes certainly reinforce the perceived 'naturalness' of political democracy and the illegitimacy of authoritarian alternatives and may help keep non-democratic options off the political agenda in Latin America. Nevertheless, the capacity of such trends in the international political system to provide effective support to political democracy in a large country such as Brazil should not be exaggerated. In the first place, the problematic relationship between consistency and credibility that plagued US human rights policies in the late 1970s is once more complicating international support for democratization. Much international action has been concentrated on weak and dependent states (for example, Zaïre, Kenya, Malawi, and Haiti) whilst human rights abuses in large and important states are overlooked (China and Indonesia most conspicuously). Secondly, the ability of external actors to influence specific domestic policies in major states should not be exaggerated. As Haiti illustrates, international action is far from unproblematic even in the case of one of the weakest states in the region. Moreover, although Brazilian attitudes towards sovereignty and external pressure may well have softened somewhat, it is important to remember that previous attempts at external pressure, most notably in the 1970s, unleashed a nationalist backlash. Indeed the ambiguity of the Brazilian government's response to recent pressure on human rights and indigenous peoples reflects awareness that nationalist resentment is very far from dead (not least in the Congress).

Thirdly, democratic backsliding is not always easy to define and identify, and different elements in the broad definition of 'democracy and good governance' may well come into conflict with each other—as in the contrast between Brazil's record of free elections and its human rights failures. Fourth, there are tensions and trade-offs between economic and political liberalization and there are already signs that Western policy may be moving back towards the privileging of economic reform over political democratization. Finally, Brazil's continued ambivalence towards the United States and towards the idea of the southern expansion of NAFTA must place a question mark over the likely effectiveness of making democracy a criterion for admission to such a grouping.[24]

What of international factors at the regional level? The absence of any equivalent event to the Falklands–Malvinas war is of course stressed in all accounts of the Brazilian transition. Yet it is possible to argue that regional international politics did play a role in the decision of the military to promote a return to civilian rule, albeit in an indirect way. Thus Alfred Stepan has described the debate within the Brazilian military in the 1970s over the nature of its role, and the growth of the idea that that role should be focused on the professional duties of external defence rather than on direct involvement in government.[25] This belief was strengthened by what many within the military saw as the increased militarization of the region in the early 1980s and the increased likelihood that historic disputes could spill over into armed conflict. Thus military spokesmen pointed to the increasing disparity between Brazilian arms spending and that of other states within the region, to the near clash between Chile and Argentina in December 1979, to the border skirmish between Peru and Ecuador in 1981, and, above all, to the Falklands–Malvinas war of 1982.[26] According to Stepan, the impact of the war was particularly important: 'The interest in increasing purely military professionalism in post-Malvinas Brazil is clearly much stronger than before, and has worked toward resolving the military-mission identity crisis.'[27]

Yet whatever the precise role of this kind of thinking within the military in the process of transition, it is important not to exaggerate its importance in the more recent period. While there have been some signs of a shift towards a more professional, defence-oriented role, the overall picture is mixed. In the first place, the grandiose plans for equipment modernization that were put forward in the mid-1980s have been radically pruned because of the impact of the debt crisis and financial stringency. Secondly, trends within the region have been mostly towards conflict management and the amelioration of many traditional conflicts and rivalries—for example between Brazil and Argentina, Argentina and Chile, Argentina and Britain, Peru and Bolivia. It is thus far from clear that the Brazilian military have succeeded in developing a viable professional role. The so-called 'structural unemployment' of the Brazilian military may well therefore have increased rather than diminished—with still unresolved domestic implications. This does not necessarily preclude the shift towards a more professional mission. Indeed the creation of a regional security system might, from the domestic political standpoint, provide a useful outlet for military activity and attention, just as participation in UN peacekeeping has become increasingly important to the self-image of the Argentinian military.

Thirdly, whilst the military formally handed over power in March 1985, their alleged 'new professionalism' did not prevent them from carving out an extremely central role in the politics of the New Republic, above all under Sarney. Their continued role could be seen in the provisions of the new constitution concerning the right to intervene to maintain social order, in the continued presence of four military ministers in the cabinet and the absence of a civilian defence minister, and in their still considerable power in the intelligence community, and the nuclear and arms industries. It is uncertain, then, that trends in international politics at a regional level have had the kind of beneficial spill-over into the domain of military behaviour that some predicted. The contrast with the Spanish case is evident. There the period after transition did see a genuine move towards professionalization, with an upgrading of the Spanish role within NATO and a significant modernization of Spanish military equipment.

There is one further aspect of the regional situation that needs to be considered briefly, namely the extent and scope of sub-regional support for democracy, particularly as part of the movement towards sub-regional economic co-operation. Certainly the rhetoric of democratization was a conspicuous feature of the *rapprochement* between Brazil and Argentina that gathered pace through the 1980s, and in the network of co-operation agreements that have been signed between the two countries since 1985, culminating in the creation of Mercosur[28] as a regional trading community which also includes Paraguay and Uruguay.

Rhetorical insistence on the importance of democracy within schemes for regional co-operation may play some role in supporting democracy in Latin America, but it remains a marginal one. Although trade within Mercosur has grown faster than many predicted, the difficulties that still beset the integration project and the uncertainty about the underlying political commitment to the relationship mean that there is still an enormous contrast with the situation in Western Europe, where the economic benefits of membership of the European Community are substantial enough to make a real difference to the behaviour of domestic political groups.

4. The Impact of the International Economic System

The relationship between the international economic system and domestic political outcomes has long been a contested issue. It lay at the heart of many of the old debates about dependency theory and about the links between the emergence of bureaucratic-authoritarian governments and particular stages in the evolution of peripheral capitalism. For some writers, the very fact that the move away from military governments occurred in Latin America at the very time when economic dependency and external economic vulnerability had increased dramatically as a result of the debt crisis totally debunked the notion of any kind of necessary relationship (or even an 'elective affinity') between authoritarian rule in Latin America and the dynamics of peripheral capitalism. It was clear evidence that dependency theory had exaggerated the importance of external factors, denied the specificity of local circumstances and particular histories, and underestimated the autonomy of political variables. As one writer put it: 'In the process [of democratization], creative and committed political actors have repeatedly underscored the centrality of national-level politics, countering deterministic expectations according to which national patterns are ineluctably set by the play of global or regional forces.'[29] On this view, then, the process of democratization should be explained primarily, or even exclusively, in terms of national-level factors and the autonomous role of domestic political variables.

It is certainly the case that much of the literature on democratic transitions in Latin America tended to argue against attributing a major role to macro-structural economic factors and the implications for democratic transition of external economic dependency.[30]

Such work laid great weight on political institutions, on the importance of leadership, and on the autonomy of political factors.[31] In its more extreme form, it became a central claim of the triumphalist liberal literature that democracy is not the exclusive preserve of Western industrialized states but can survive and flourish in states of varying cultures, religions, and levels of economic development.[32] Yet, especially as the focus shifts away from analysing discrete moments of transition towards the broader factors affecting the prospects for democratic consolidation, external contextual factors need to be brought back in. Whilst it is indeed impossible to argue that there is a necessary and predetermined link between developments in the international economy and the success of democratization, the powerful impact of international economic forces has played, and continues to play, a major role both in shaping the domestic political agenda and in limiting the range of options available to politicians within Brazil.

There is, however, a danger that the manifest difficulties facing the process of democratic consolidation in countries such as Brazil will push academic fashion back towards an over-emphasis on the external. In the radical camp, limited 'élite democracies' or 'authoritarain democracies' are already coming to be seen as a function of the changing dynamics of global capitalism. One recent study, for example, seeks to provide:

an alternative critical interpretation of the current drive towards democracy, viewed as an integral aspect of the economic and ideological restructuring accompanying a new stage of globalisation in the capitalist world economy, and as a consequence of a shift in US foreign policy after the onset of serious economic amd hegemonic crises. In this sense the new formal democratisation is the political corollary of economic liberalisation and internationalisation.[33]

How, then, might we reintegrate the importance of the external economic context without falling prey to the systemic reductionism of earlier accounts? There are three broad arguments about the impact of external economic structures on the process of democratization in Brazil.

The first concerns its impact on the transition process itself and on the erosion of authoritarian rule. Although international economic factors did not play a crucial role in the original decisions of the Brazilian military to launch the process of *abertura*, the growth of economic difficulties and the increasing international economic constraints certainly came to play a major role in foreclosing the options available to the military and in shaping the pattern of liberalization and the timetable for transition. The negative international economic environment therefore contributed to the gradual accumulation of pressures on the military government to relinquish power, a process which began at the height of the Brazilian 'miracle'. The initial reaction of the Geisel government to the international economic shocks of 1973–4 was to press ahead with a high-risk strategy of expanded import substitution based around the accumulation of high levels of foreign debt. It was precisely the unravelling of this strategy in the face of the second round of international economic shocks of 1979–80 that left the government with so little room for political manœuvre and, ultimately, led to a loss of control over the process of transition. In addition, the dramatically worsening economic situation of the early 1980s dispelled the myth of the military as guarantors of efficient and successful technocratic management of the economy, and transformed the image of the Brazilian state from being the efficient instrument of national development into that of a 'paralyzed Leviathan'.[34] Rising unemployment, high inflation, and spiralling indebtedness were major factors responsible for the desertion of many middle-class groups that had previously supported the military, and especially for the gradual shift in the attitudes of business groups. For many of these groups the perception also grew that economic development under the military had been obtained at an unacceptable cost in terms of income inequality, neglect of basic social services, environmental destruction, and corruption. Lastly, economic failures exposed the underlying tension between the constraints of an increasingly centralized and authoritarian political system on the one hand and the complexities of managing a huge and increasingly internationalized economy on the other.

A second, and very common, argument is that the harsh external economic environment of 1980s exercised a major influence over domestic political outcomes by compounding the difficulties of democratization. Indeed, for some, the steadfast refusal of the creditor governments to provide greater assistance to the newly re-established democracies of Latin America provided clear evidence of their disinterest in democracy.[35] Such claims are intuitively plausible. The severity of the economic crisis and Brazil's continued external economic vulnerability complicated the process of democratic consolidation under Sarney, Collor, and Franco. The legitimacy of post-1985 governments was consistently undermined by their continued failure to revive growth, to control inflation, and to expand employment opportunities. On the one hand, fiscal austerity, high inflation, and repeated efforts to achieve significant structural reform exacerbated distributional conflicts within society. On the other, failure to match the high expectations engendered by the end of military rule undermined the president's political support. Although perhaps obvious, it remains critical to recall the striking contrast between the severely negative external environment facing Latin America in the 1980s and the high levels of international economic support given to post-war Europe and Japan by the United States and the degree to which Washington was prepared to forgo short-term benefits and to make exceptions to favoured principles in the interests of political and economic reconstruction of important allies.

Yet there are two potential difficulties with the thesis that the harsh external situation has jeopardized the prospects of democratization. First, Brazil's economic difficulties cannot be ascribed solely, or perhaps even predominantly, to a negative external environment. A great deal of the explanation for Brazil's protracted economic crisis lies in the failure of Sarney, Collor, and Franco to institute and maintain a coherent set of economic policies. This has, in turn, been due to a complex set of domestic political factors: the death of Tancredo Neves; the inability of Sarney and Collor to create a viable base of support at the level of either the political parties or public opinion; the long and drawn-out struggle between the president and Congress over the length of Sarney's mandate and the balance between a presidential and parliamentary system; the protracted arguments over the detailed provisions of the new constitution; the weaknesses of the political parties and the problems created by Brazil's extremely permissive laws on electoral and party organization; the continued political role of the military; the re-emergence of the historically deep-rooted struggles between the federal government and the states; the widespread degree of corruption; the difficulties of meshing coherent economic policy with the constraints of an overburdened electoral timetable; and, finally, the extent to which the apparently endless zig-zagging of policy has threatened the coherence and credibility of policy-making and led to the fragmentation of what had previously been considered as a strong and purposive state. This formidable (and incomplete) list of domestic political problems underpins the growth of fears of ungovernability and suggests that the relative role of a harsh international economic environment should not be exaggerated.

Secondly, Brazil provides a graphic illustration of the complexity of the relationship between democratization and economic crisis. Despite frequent predictions, the period since 1985 has witnessed a good deal of deprivation but relatively little direct social protest. In many ways Brazil's fragile democracy has coped extraordinarily well with the enormous underlying social pressures that have been intensifed by the economic crisis. Despite the depth, severity, and persistence of the economic crisis, the achievements need to be noted: the peaceful transition from military rule; the apparent diffusion of democratic values through society and the broadening normative commitment to democracy;[36] the successful holding of the first presidential elections in twenty-nine years in 1989; the steady expansion in political participation; the successful containment of the political crisis sparked by the impeachment of Collor; and even the ability of the Congress to set up an investigation into corruption amongst its own members. Indeed, it has been argued that even very rickety democracies are better able to cope with economic stagnation than their military predecessors, because their legitimacy does not depend to the same extent on economic success. As Paul Drake puts it, they have 'political goods' such as freedom of speech and assembly as well as or instead of just 'economic goods' to distribute.[37]

There is clearly some force in these arguments, but they cannot be pushed too far. In the first place, arguments about the successful diffusion of democratic values have to be set against the current deep disenchantment with traditional parties and politicians and the degree to which the still very diffuse *mentalidade democrática* highlighted by opinion polls may rest more on the absence of viable alternatives than on irreversible and positive commitment. Moreover, given the extent to which support for democracy rests not just on normative commitment but on self-interest and instrumental calculations, the increasingly common perception of a trade-off between successful political democracy and governability (unsurprisingly defined in terms of minimally coherent economic policy) remains an important measure of the unconsolidated nature of Brazilian democracy.

For many groups within Brazilian society the economic benefits of accepting the rules of the democratic game have still to be realized and this calculus is particularly dispiriting when viewed against the background of the extent of the country's social problems and of the incompleteness of Brazil's transition to a modern society.[38] If the end of military rule was to a great extent 'managed from above', the longer-term success of democratic consolidation will depend crucially on finding new forms of collective action and democratic expression for the social forces unleashed in the course of the rapid modernization of Brazil in the post-war period. It will also depend on at least beginning to tackle the social debt that was accumulated during the twenty-one years of military rule. This is not to argue that political democracy is meaningless when viewed against the extremes of social and economic inequality in Brazil. Rather, it suggests that democratic consolidation will remain politically vulnerable unless some progress is made in the direction of tackling this legacy, of establishing more inclusive forms of political participation, and of stemming the social corrosion of democracy.

The third, and most important, argument is that the international economic environment has played a major role, not directly in stacking the cards either for or against democracy but rather in helping to shape the character of the process of democratization and the range of political and economic options available to policy-makers. Underlying much of the hesitancy and indecision of Brazilian government policy since 1985 has been a series of unresolved debates about the future shape of the country's political and economic development—'competing utopias', to use Bolívar Lamounier's phrase. Amongst the most fundamental issues has been the debate over the viability of the existing model of economic development based on import substitution, high tariffs, a large role for the state, and a heavy emphasis on national autonomy. Arguments in favour of reform began to be heard in the last year of military rule and were evident in the debates of the constituent assembly and in the arguments over the future of Brazil's informatics regime. But, although there was much discussion of reform under Sarney, the dominant picture was one of continuity, with little willingness or ability to institute structural reform. Since 1990, however, demands for more deep-rooted economic reform have gradually gained ground. It is certainly true that Brazil remains a laggard compared to other countries in the region. Whilst countries such as Chile and Mexico moved early and consistently towards economic liberalization, actual reform in Brazil has been fitful, and tentative beginnings have often been reversed. Nevertheless, a degree of economic reform has taken place, particularly in terms of trade liberalization and, more recently, the speed-up of privatization. More importantly, the economic agenda has been dominated by talk of trade liberalization, restructuring and a reduction in the role of the state, privatization, and the need for comprehensive tax reform.

Much of the impetus for these changes has come from domestic factors: from the defeat or discrediting of alternatives; from the repeated failure of post-transition governments to provide financial stability and restore economic growth; from the erosion of state capacity in the face of persistent and unsustainable fiscal crises. The acceptance of the need for structural reform came gradually, partly because of the legacy of past economic success and partly because of the belief that Brazil's size and undoubted economic strengths provided a range of alternatives unavailable to other states in the region. Indeed, for all the radical rhetoric, the first two years of Collor's economic policies demonstrated powerful elements of continuity. Yet the successive failures of the Cruzado Plan of 1986, the Bresser Plan of 1987–8, the Summer Plan of 1989, and the two Collor Plans of 1990 and 1991 undermined faith in heterodox stabilization plans and helped push Brazil towards orthodoxy: making peace with the IMF, implementing the long-delayed privatization programme, speeding up trade liberalization, and seeking congressional support for major fiscal policy reform. Such reform would include cutting back and rationalizing government expenditures, restructuring the tax system, and reducing the very extensive entrepreneurial roles of the Brazilian state. Domestic pressure for change appears to have been the result of general disenchantment with the existing system, rather than the emergence of any well-organized interest-groups.

It is, however, impossible to understand these developments without recognizing the role of external factors. Some of these pressures have been direct: the growth of different forms of economic conditionality; the sanctions applied by the United States during the trade disputes of the mid-1980s; and the narrowing of international alignments and the extent to which participation in regional economic arrangements is coming to depend on the adoption of a particular set of domestic economic policies. Yet the international dimension cannot be limited to these kinds of specific pressures. In the first place, there is the obvious impact of the debt crisis itself: in constraining overall growth, in intensifying governments' fiscal crises, and in placing such a high premium on successful export promotion. Secondly, the widely discussed trends towards increased globalization have led to the belief in Brazil that dynamic economies are internationalized economies and that growth depends on successful participation in the world economy.[39] Thirdly, there was a growing perception that economic interdependence was increasingly developing on a North–North rather than North–South axis and that there was a real threat of the formation of rival regional trading blocs (Europe, the United States, and Japan) from which Brazil would be excluded if policies were not altered. Fourthly, there has been the impact of the historic collapse of central planning in Eastern and Central Europe and the USSR. And finally, the adoption (in many cases successful) of broadly neo-liberal policies in other parts of Latin America has increased the pressure on Brazil to institute similar reforms, or else risk a further dent in its self-perception as the most successful and dynamic economy in the region.

This shift in ideas and policies has to be explained by the interplay of domestic and international factors. Although direct external pressure has played a role, the take-up of these new ideas and policies cannot be seen as a simple matter of external imposition. Their adoption is linked to domestic developments, but also to a specific constellation of power and interests within the international political system (especially the renewed centrality of the USA); to changes in global patterns of competition, production, and technological change; and to the diffusion of a specific set of ideas about the nature of economic development and the relationship between politics and economics. Yet they have already modified the character of the political debate inside Brazil and, even if only patchily implemented, represent a major change in the economic and political framework within which the process of democratic consolidation is taking place. The policies themselves do not either guarantee or undermine the success of democratization. But they highlight a number of basic questions that are increasingly dominating the political landscape of Brazil: What will replace the state in areas where its role has been cut back? What roles will the state still be able to perform? And what will be the relationship between greater reliance on market mechanisms and social inequality?

5. Conclusions

This chapter has sought to open up a series of broad perspectives on the various international factors that may have affected domestic political developments in Brazil. The existing literature on international aspects of democratization has tended to view external factors as being of secondary importance. As one study noted:

Those who assume that the source of Latin America's political turmoil and democratic failures is primarily external—US intervention and manipulation; economic dependence—may be disappointed with the historical analyses in this volume. Without exception, each of our authors attributes the course of political development and regime change primarily to internal structures and actions, while acknowledging the way structures have been shaped historically by international factors.[40]

This chapter has argued that, in the case of Brazil, such a conclusion is warranted if the focus is on specific external linkages and attempts at direct external influence. But it also suggests that the broader international context has played a much greater role than is often acknowledged and that this role has increased as the focus of academic enquiry has shifted away from the study of discrete processes of political transition and towards the analysis of the broad range of factors that affect the character of democratic consolidation. The limits to the power of the external remain significant and the Brazilian case provides evidence for the entirely plausible proposition that international influences—direct, indirect, and contextual—have less impact on very large, relatively closed societies than on smaller, more open, and more vulnerable states. Nevertheless, the international political and especially economic context remains important, not in determining the success or failure of democratization (as in the above quotation), but rather in shaping the character of the political and economic system within which democratization takes place, in helping to explain the outcomes of domestic distributional conflicts, and in setting the domestic political agenda and the range of issues which politicians in Brazil will have to address.

Notes

1. On this general problem see P. Gourevitch, 'The Second Image Reversed: The International Sources of Domestic Politics', *International Organization*, 32 (1978), 881–912; G. Almond, 'The International-National Connection', *British Journal of Political Science*, 19 (Apr. 1989), 237–59; D. Held, 'Democracy, the Nation-State and the Global System', in D. Held (ed.), *Political Theory Today* (Cambridge: Polity Press, 1991), 197–235; special issue of *Government and Opposition*, 28/2 (spring 1993); and J. Art Scholte, *International Relations of Social Change* (Buckingham: Open University Press, 1993).
2. On this subject see P. Parker, *Brazil and the Quiet Intervention* (Austin: University of Texas Press, 1979).
3. On the Reagan Administration's efforts at *rapprochement* see T. Carothers, *In the Name of Democracy: US Policy Toward Latin America in the Reagan Years* (Berkeley: University of California Press, 1991), 117–27.
4. On the strains in US–Brazilian relations in the mid-1980s see M. Hirst (ed.), *Brasil–Estados Unidos na Transição Democrática* (Rio de Janeiro: Paz e Terra, 1985).
5. L. A. Motley, 'Letting Off Steam', in H. Binnendijk (ed.), *Authoritarian Regimes in Transition* (Washington DC: Foreign Service Institute, 1987), 250.

6. M. Pinto-Duschinsky, 'Foreign Political Aid: The German Political Foundations and their US Counterparts', *International Affairs*, 67/1 (1991), 38.

7. R. D. Lipschutz, 'Reconstructing World Politics: The Emergence of Global Civil Society', *Millennium*, 21/3 (winter 1992), 390.

8. Academic attention to transnational politics developed in the early 1970s (see especially R. Keohane and J. Nye (eds.), *Transnational Relations and World Politics* (Cambridge, Mass.: Harvard University Press, 1971)) but then declined very markedly. For a survey of its gradual return to fashion see M. J. Peterson, 'Transnational Activity, International Society and World Politics', *Millennium*, 21/3 (winter 1993); and, more recently, P. Wapner, 'Politics beyond the State: Environmental Activism and World Civic Politics', *World Politics*, 47/3 (Apr. 1995), 311–40.

9. For general arguments along these lines see J. Rosenau, *Turbulence in World Politics: A Theory of Change and Continuity* (Princeton, NJ: Princeton University Press, 1990); E. Skolnikoff, *The Elusive Transformation: Science, Technology and the Evolution of International Politics* (Princeton, NJ: Princeton University Press, 1993); and J. Camillieri and J. Falk, *The End of Sovereignty? The Politics of a Shrinking and Fragmenting World* (London: Edward Elgar, 1992).

10. For an early study see I. Vallier, 'The Roman Catholic Church: A Transnational Actor', in Keohane and Nye, *Transnational Relations*. More recently, Eric Hanson (*The Catholic Church in World Politics* (Princeton, NJ: Princeton University Press, 1987)) describes the political impact of the Church in many countries, including Brazil, but tells us little about patterns of influence between different parts of the Church, particularly those not involving the Vatican.

11. Bundesministerium für wirtschaftliche Zusammenarbeit, *Entwicklungszusammenarbeit zwischen der Bundesregierung und den christlichen Kirchen* (Bonn, 1979), 24–5. Figures for the 1980s do not provide a breakdown of church activities by country, although their overall importance remains evident. In 1984, for example, church projects and relief work in the developing world totalled DM1,019 million (compared with some DM207 million for the party foundations), with DM202 million provided by the German government and DM817 million raised by the churches themselves. 33 per cent of Catholic Church projects and 18 per cent of Protestant Church projects were in Latin America. See Bundesministerium für wirtschaftliche Zusammenarbeit, *Die Entwicklungpolitische Zusammenarbeit zwischen autonomen nichtstaatlichen Organizationen und dem Bundesmisterium für wirtschaftliche Zusammenarbeit 1984* (Bonn, 1985).

12. See T. Skidmore, *The Politics of Military Rule in Brazil, 1964–1985* (Oxford: Oxford University Press, 1988), 214–15 and 224–5.

13. These examples are taken from the annual reports of the foundations, various years.

14. For a discussion of these trends see J. Nelson, *Encouraging Democracy:*

What Role for Conditioned Aid? (Washington DC: Overseas Development Council, 1992).

15. See Amnesty International, *Brazil: Authorised Violence in Rural Areas* (London: Amnesty International, 1988); *Brazil: Cases of Killings and Ill-Treatment of Indigenous People* (London: Amnesty International, 1988); and *Brazil: Torture and Extrajudicial Execution in Urban Brazil* (London: Amnesty International, 1990). On the linkages between the environmental and human rights movements in Brazil see E. Viola and J. W. Nickel, 'Integrating Environmentalism and Human Rights', *Environmental Ethics*, 16/3 (autumn 1994), 265–73.

16. See A. Hurrell, 'The International Politics of Amazonian Deforestation', in A. Hurrell and B. Kingsbury (eds.), *The International Politics of the Environment* (Oxford: Oxford University Press, 1992), 398–429.

17. For an illuminating discussion of the impact of human rights networks in Latin America see K. Sikkink, 'Human Rights Issue-Networks in Latin America', *International Organization*, 47/3 (summer 1993); see also Ch. 4, above.

18. See L. Bethell, 'From the Second World War to the Cold War: 1944–1954', in A. Lowenthal (ed.), *Exporting Democracy: The United States and Latin America* (Baltimore: Johns Hopkins University Press, 1991), 41–70.

19. C. G. Gillespie, 'Interstate and Insocietal Factors in the Democratization of Brazil and the Southern Cone', paper delivered at a conference on The Challenge of Transition, University of South Carolina, March 1987.

20. For a recent argument that democratic entitlement is moving from being a moral prescription to an international legal obligation see T. Franck, 'The Emerging Right to Democratic Governance', *American Journal of International Law*, 86/1 (1992), 46–91.

21. These changes are catalogued and analysed in Nelson, *Encouraging Democracy*, esp. 10–25.

22. Article 5 of the OAS Charter establishes the duty of members to promote 'the effective exercise of representative democracy' and the 5 June 1991 resolution on Haiti states that the principles of the organization 'require the political representation of [member] states to be based on the effective exercise of representative democracy'. See Franck, 'Emerging Right', 65–6 and T. Farer, 'The United States as Guarantor of Democracy in the Caribbean Basin: Is There a Legal Way?', *Human Rights Quarterly*, 10 (1988).

23. See A. Hurrell, 'Regionalism in the Americas', in A. F. Lowenthal and G. F. Treverton (eds.), *Latin America in a New World* (Boulder, Colo.: Westview, 1994), 167–90.

24. On this question see L. Whitehead, 'Requisites for Admission', in P. H. Smith (ed.), *The Challenge of Integration: Europe and the Americas* (New Brunswick: Transaction, 1993), 149–82.

25. A. Stepan, *Rethinking Military Politics: Brazil and the Southern Cone* (Princeton, NJ: Princeton University Press, 1988), chapters 5 and 6.

See also M. R. Soares de Lima, 'Contexto Internacional e Democratizaçaõ no Brasil', in F. Wanderley Reis and G. O'Donnell (eds.), *A Democracia no Brasil: Dilemas e perspectivas* (Saõ Paulo: Ediçoões Vertice, 1988).

26. For a detailed elaboration of this argument see A. Varas, *Militarization and the Arms Race in Latin America* (Boulder, Colo.: Westview, 1985).

27. Stepan, *Rethinking Military Politics*, 87.

28. For a discussion of this issue see P. Schmitter, 'Change in Regime Type and Progress in International Relations', in E. Adler and B. Crawford (eds.), *Progress in Postwar International Relations* (New York: Columbia University Press, 1991).

29. D. H. Levine, 'Paradigm Lost: Dependence to Democracy', *World Politics*, 40/3 (1988), 378. For a restatement of the old orthodoxy about the centrality of 'longer-run and structural influences of international capitalism on political change in Latin America', see A. MacEwan, 'Transitions from Authoritarian Rule', *Latin American Perspectives*, 15/3 (1988), esp. 128. See also the more recent attempt to analyse the impact of transnational structures of power on democratization as part of a broader analysis of the links between capitalist development and democracy in D. Rueschemeyer, E. Huber Stephens, and J. D. Stephens, *Capitalist Development and Democracy* (Cambridge, 1992), esp. 69–75, 219–22.

30. This is true of G. O'Donnell, P. Schmitter, and L. Whitehead (eds.), *Transitions from Authoritarian Rule: Prospects for Democracy* (Baltimore: Johns Hopkins University Press, 1986), and of L. Diamond, J. J. Linz, and S. M. Lipset, *Democracy in Developing Countries: Latin America* (Boulder, Colo.: Lynne Rienner, 1989).

31. For an analysis of the revelant literature see S. Mainwaring, 'Transitions to Democracy and Democratic Consolidation: Theoretical and Comparative Issues', in S. Mainwaring, G. O'Donnell, and J. S. Valenzuela (eds.), *Issues in Democratic Consolidation* (Notre Dame, Ind.: University of Notre Dame, 1992), esp. 326–9.

32. See, for example, J. Muravchik, *Exporting Democracy: Fulfilling America's Destiny* (Washington DC: AEI Press, 1991), esp. chapter 6; C. Gershamn, 'The World Democratic Revolution', in B. Roberts (ed.), *The New Democracies: Global Change and US Policy* (Cambridge, Mass.: MIT Press, 1990).

33. B. Gills, J. Rocamora, and R. Wilson, 'Low Intensity Democracy', in eid. (eds.), *Low Intensity Democracy: Political Power in the New World Order* (London: Pluto, 1993), 4.

34. See W. Guilherme dos Santos, 'Mitologias institucionais brasileiras: do Leviatã paralítico ao Estado de natureza', *Estudos Avançados*, 7/17 (1993), 101–16.

35. For a strident statement of this position see N. Chomsky, *Deterring Democracy* (London: Vintage, 1992), esp. 215–35.

36. See, for example, the chapters by J. Muszynski and A. M. Teixeira Mendes and by A. de Souza and B. Lamounier, in B. Lamounier (ed.),

De Geisel a Collor: O balanço da transição (São Paulo: Editora Sumaré, 1990).

37. P. Drake, 'Debt and Democracy in Latin America, 1920s–1980s', in B. Stallings and R. Kaufman (eds.), *Debt and Democracy in Latin America* (Boulder, Colo.: Westview, 1989), 54.

38. On this theme see E. Bacha and H. Klein (eds.), *Social Change in Brazil 1945–1985: The Incomplete Transition* (Albuquerque: University of New Mexico Press, 1989).

39. For a brief but fascinating discussion of the constraints that follow the globalization of capitalism see F. H. Cardoso, 'Alternativas Econômicas para a América Latina' (written in 1990), in F. H. Cardoso, *As Idéias e seu Lugar* (Petrópolis: Vozes, 1993).

40. L. Diamond and J. J. Linz, 'Introduction: Politics, Society, and Democracy in Latin America', in Diamond, Linz, and Lipset (eds.), *Latin America*, 47.

International Support for the Chilean Opposition, 1973–1989: Political Parties and the Role of Exiles

ALAN ANGELL

For ten years following the coup in September 1973 until the protest movements erupted in May 1983, political activity in Chile was limited to issues defined and controlled by a highly central-ized government. Opposition politics were conducted not in Chile, but abroad. The parties of the centre and moderate left were active in Europe, the United States, and a variety of Latin American countries. The parties of the Marxist left were based inside the Communist bloc.

The international dimension of Chilean politics, and not least the effect of exile, was of greater importance than in the other con-temporary military dictatorships of Latin America. After 1983 many exiles returned, but the links they forged with a variety of gov-ernments, parties, and non-governmental organizations (NGOs) played a fundamental role in the opposition to the Pinochet regime. Moreover, their ideas were profoundly reshaped by prolonged con-tact with the politics and parties of the host countries. Financial assistance to the opposition from a number of foreign sources was essential to keep the opposition alive and organized, not least in the enormous effort that was involved in defeating Pinochet in the plebiscite of 5 October 1988, and in securing electoral victory in December 1989.

I would like to thank former Ambassador Harry Barnes for his comments on this chapter, and the former British Ambassador Alan White for his com-ments and an extremely useful interview. It is more than usually necessary to stress that neither of them has any responsibility for this analysis. Esteban Tomic and Jose Antonio Viera Gallo offered me useful advice on the subject, and I am grateful to them.

1. The Opposition in Exile

Chile attracted great international attention during the Popular Unity government, and continued to attract interest after 1973. For a small, relatively uninfluential South American country, this degree of attention seems disproportionate to its real importance, though it reflects continuing international interest and activities in Chile at least from the early 1960s. The very similarity of Chilean politics and parties to those of some European countries attracted sympathy and understanding in a way that was not forthcoming for other Latin American countries. Christian Democrats, Socialists, Communists, and Radicals had links with parties abroad, followed their ideological developments closely, and benefited from financial support.

Both superpowers paid close attention to Chile, especially when the Marxist parties almost secured an electoral victory in 1958. The USA employed a variety of overt and covert means to try to block the progress of the left, and the story of US intervention in Chile following the election of Allende in 1970 is too well known to need repetition. However, it should be noted that the amount spent on covert operations by the USA in Chile from 1963 to 1973 was about $8 million, which is in real terms considerably more than was spent on aiding the opposition to the Pinochet government.[1]

Following the 1973 coup, party activity was banned in Chile, and parties were forced underground or abroad, with many leading politicians exiled. Exile was basic to the system of political control and repression of the Pinochet government, and it was employed on a scale without precedent in Chilean history. There had been waves of exile before—during the Ibáñez government in the late 1920s, during the González Videla government when he banned the Communist Party in 1948, and during the Allende period when many businessmen sought exile rather than try to survive in Chile. But the scale, extent, and arbitrariness of exile under Pinochet was of a totally different order. Indeed, the government justified exile on the grounds that a new political order could not be constructed in Chile unless there were expulsions of those considered to be enemies of the state.[2]

It is not known exactly how many Chileans suffered exile after 1973. In the mid-1980s, the Office of the UN High Commissioner for Refugees (UNHCR) estimated the number of exiles as 30,000, while the Comité Pro-Retorno in Chile suggested between 100,000 and 200,000.[3] The estimate of the Chilean Commission for Human Rights in its 1982 annual report was of 163,686 exiles. The government in mid-1986 published a list of 3,717 exiles who could now return, and implied that this was the great majority. Moreover, the government argued that most exiles had left Chile voluntarily and had little desire to return.

The coup of 11 September 1973 was brutal, and killings and torture were commonplace. Many Chileans sought asylum in foreign embassies. Both Catholic and Protestant churches attempted to help those being persecuted. The National Refugee Commission (CONAR), which was set up a few months after the coup by a group of leading church figures, often conducted people to asylum in foreign embassies at grave personal risk. At the time of the coup, there were many refugees in Chile from the military dictatorship in Brazil, and UP (Popular Unity) sympathizers from other Latin American countries. By March 1974, 3,400 foreigners, mostly refugees from other dictatorships, had been moved from Chile.

A special programme of assistance was established through ICEM (the Inter-governmental Committee on European Migration) to overcome UNHCR's procedural difficulties in dealing with those seeking asylum within their own country. By the end of 1974 a total of 6,700 people had been officially resettled. In December 1974 an agreement was signed between ICEM, the International Committee of the Red Cross, CONAR, and the Chilean government to allow for the transfer to exile of those detained without trial under the provisions of the State of Siege.

As well as those seeking asylum directly from Chile, there were many thousands who fled to neighbouring countries, and as early as 1974 there were estimated to be at least 15,000 Chilean refugees in Argentina and 1,500 in Peru. There was a continuous migratory flow from Chile to Argentina and many more undoubtedly fled across the border, particularly from country areas where repression was less well documented, and therefore were never registered formally with any official body. Within Argentina the political situation deteriorated throughout 1975, and with the 1976 military coup refugees were in real danger. The UNHCR appealed to member countries to grant asylum to Chilean refugees residing in Argentina and many obtained visas mainly for Europe, for other countries of Latin America, and for Australia. The UNHCR estimate for official resettlement was around 30,000 Chilean exiles. The difficulty in calculating numbers accurately lies in different governments' attitudes towards immigrants and refugees. In the UK, where controls are strict, the number of Chileans additional to the official figures was fairly small. In other countries the discrepancy was likely to be enormous.[4]

It is even more difficult to be precise about who exactly the refugees were. Exiles have been considered as two separate groups— those motivated by political reasons and those with a purely economic motivation—but circumstances were confused and motivations inevitably mixed. Nevertheless, exile from Chile was largely a political phenomenon. Most exiles were members of political parties that formed the UP alliance, and the MIR (Movement of the Revolutionary Left). There were a small number of prominent Christian Democrat (PDC) exiles. The major parties of the UP were the Socialist and Communist Parties, part of the Radical Party, and the much smaller MAPU (United Popular Action Movement), and the Christian Left. Although many politicians were killed in the coup, the general secretaries of the parties survived and went into exile; in the case of Luis Corvalán of the Communist Party (CP), this was only after long imprisonment and a much publicized East–West exchange.

There were attempts to establish central bodies internationally for the whole of the opposition. The Chilean Trade Union Congress (CUT), based in Paris, was a centre for a while, as was Chile Anti-Fascista, based in Berlin. None of these organizations was able to unify a disparate and still politically divided exile community. As in Chile itself, political identity abroad was defined essentially by membership of a specific political party rather than by membership of a broader alliance.

The majority of refugees were probably from the Socialist Party (PS), a party with a substantial mass membership in Chile but with little or no preparedness for illegal organization status. The Communist Party (CP) was probably under-represented among exiles because of its former experiences with underground operations (it had been banned from 1948 to 1958), and its greater ability to operate clandestinely. Of the smaller parties, MIR and MAPU were probably over-represented among exiles, the latter because of its high middle-class intellectual membership with easier access to contacts abroad. MIR members experienced very heavy repression because of their policy of armed resistance to the military junta.

Chileans were exiled in countries the world over. Sweden was outstanding in responding swiftly to urgent cases, and therefore may initially have received a higher proportion of MIR members in need of immediate assistance. The number of refugees in the USSR was small and probably all were Communists, though among the larger population of exiles in East Germany there were a substantial number of socialists, most notably Clodomiro Almeyda,

Allende's former Foreign Minister. Cuba was particularly sympathetic to MIR. Paris and Rome were seen by Chilean intellectuals as the cultural and political centres of Europe and they opted for these countries when they had a choice. Mexico and Venezuela were sympathetic to exiles from many parties.

Return

Even before the effective end to political exile in 1988, there was a continual process of return, especially when in the late 1970s the economy started to experience its short-lived boom. But many were refused entry and others objected as a matter of principle to submitting to procedures which gave the government complete discretion over whom to admit and whom to reject.

In October 1982 Pinochet convened a short-lived commission to examine the exile question. A list was issued in December 1982 of 125 people authorized to return, and subsequent lists included about 4,000 people. In September 1984 the policy changed and a list was issued of 4,942 people not allowed to return. During 1985 this list was revised and 1,347 names were removed. In February 1985 the government gave a formal guarantee that those not named on the lists would be allowed to return, but there was understandable apprehension on the part of exiles about trusting such statements. The overall number of exiles returning to Chile between 1976 and May 1985 was around 3,000. Most returned from 1983 onwards when the gradual liberalization in Chile and the growth of the opposition created sufficient confidence.

2. *Exile and the Political Parties*

Political parties play a dominant role in the organization of political life in Chile. Most social organizations, such as trade unions, have been closely linked to one or more parties and remain so in spite of all the attempts of the Pinochet government to destroy those links. On the evidence of the 1989 elections, parties still dominate the political landscape of Chile. One of the major aims, if not the major aim, of the dictatorship was to break the hold of parties over political life in Chile, and a principal method used was to exile leaders. Although this aim was clearly not achieved, nevertheless repression and exile did lead to changes in the parties.

It is hardly surprising that opposition parties turned to external support simply to survive. Only after 1983 could parties of the centre operate in Chile, and even then with many restrictions. Parties of the left had no alternative: their leaders were in exile. All parties had to rethink their basic political beliefs after 1973. Some 200,000 Chileans were scattered in countries all over the world. They were politically experienced and keenly aware of the major political debates taking place in their host countries. Their perceptions were bound to be influenced by a decade or more in exile, though not all in the same direction. Moderate socialists returning from Italy, France, or Spain may have abandoned Lenin in favour of Gramsci, but other socialists located in East Germany remained faithful to orthodox Marxist–Leninist ideas. Exile in Cuba for young Communists or members of the MIR meant training in guerrilla warfare, and it is not too fanciful to suppose that the group that attempted to assassinate Pinochet in September 1986 was a product of that training.

In France and Italy the debate on the lessons of Chile led to a rethinking of political strategies on the left, and Chilean exiles were, in turn, deeply affected by the political discussion around them. The debate over Eurocommunism helped to produce a more moderate and pragmatic Chilean left. The European left developed ideas on the desirability of the mixed economy and the need for co-operation between capital, labour, and the government that profoundly affected the Chilean exiles, especially those in the socialist parties. Chileans exiled in Venezuela also seem to have been persuaded of the virtues of political compromise as a means of consolidating a stable democracy. Exiles in countries which stressed the virtues of revolution rather than of democracy—such as Mexico, Cuba, or Nicaragua—seem to have maintained more firmly their beliefs in the essential correctness of the aims of the Popular Unity government.

The party most affected by exile and repression was the PS, the largest party on the left under Allende and always more divided and less cohesive than its major rival, the CP. In the words of one of the major leaders of the moderate Socialists, Ricardo Lagos,

How can a party exist when practically all of its leadership has been exiled, imprisoned or 'disappeared'? All the regional committees of La Serena, of Atacama, of Calama, of Antofagasta, of Iquique, died. In Chile, there are only two parties that managed to maintain a unified leadership in the period of dictatorship—the PDC and the Communist Party. The rest were incapable of overcoming the organic crisis created by the dictatorship, and we were no exception. This explains the diaspora of socialism.[5]

Chilean socialism after the coup was disorganized and confused.[6] Various exile groups claimed to be the authentic representative of the party, but links with the small underground movement in Chile were complicated and tenuous.[7] The party split in 1979, following a session of the central committee of the party in Algeria in 1978. It was a complicated event involving ideological differences, personal ambition, problems of communication, and, presumably, foreign influences on the major groups inside the party, not least through financial pressure, though details of that kind of activity are shrouded in mystery.

Chilean socialism after 1973 underwent a period of profound self-analysis, and produced two major rival interpretations of policies for the future—one towards a Eurosocialist tendency, the other towards closer alliance with the Communists. This debate took place largely in exile after the party in Chile was repressed, with these rival interpretations imported back into Chile as party activity of a subdued kind gradually became possible in the 1980s. The major difference was expressed in the choice of alliance partners. The moderate socialists allied with the Christian Democrats; the radical socialists, called after their leader Clodomiro Almeyda, preferred to ally with the Communists.

The moderate socialists, known by the name of their secretary general (first Carlos Briones, then Ricardo Núñez, and then Jorge Arrate), advocated a less utopian and less sectarian version of socialism. Ricardo Lagos, for example, stressed the necessity of constructive dialogue with the entrepreneurial sectors: 'this is the influence of European Socialism on Chilean Socialism today'.[8] He identified the influence of Gramsci, in the sense that socialism was not to be seen as a seizure of state power, but as the widespread diffusion of socialist values. This kind of analysis was reinforced by the entry into the Socialist Party of important sectors of the intelligentsia, once part of the MAPU. The Almeyda socialists' view of socialism, by contrast, was initially intransigent, and expressed its belief in the ideas of the Communist Manifesto, and in the need to seize state power and overthrow the Pinochet dictatorship. Their criticism of the moderate socialists was that they ran the risk of becoming a mere appendage of the Christian Democrats, and that their ideas were little more than thinly disguised social democracy. It was only with the unifying impulse from the formation of the coalition to confront Pinochet in the plebiscite and then to contest the elections of 1989 that the two wings of socialism came together to form a single party.

The CP lost many middle-level leaders in the repression following the coup, but several dominant figures were either abroad at the time of the coup (Volodia Teitelboim), or were released from

Chile (Luís Corvalán). The exiled leaders were firmly in control
with the backing of Moscow. The CP was able to maintain a limited underground existence in Chile. Exile did not mean loss of
funds, international support, and prestige, nor contradictory pressures leading to splits. But there was tension between the exiled
leadership—with its background in Congress or the union movement and adeptness in the Popular Front style of politics—and the
rank and file in Chile, increasingly drawn from the young and unemployed poor of the shanty towns, who were tempted to use violence
as a basic political tactic.

The CP changed policy in 1980, when it argued that violence
was a legitimate tactic in the struggle to overthrow Pinochet. This
change of tactic was partly a response to international pressure,
since the international Communist movement was anxious not to
be always last on to the revolutionary barricades, as happened in
the movement that overthrew Somoza in Nicaragua. But there
were also internal reasons for the change. The social base of the
party changed with the decline in the power of organized labour
and the rise of a radicalized and largely unemployed youth population in the shanty towns. Anxious to tap this potential source of
opposition to Pinochet, the party was prepared to change to political tactics more appropriate to those who could exercise influence
not by going on strike, but by organizing protest in the shanty
towns.

Exile did not have the same divisive effect on the CP as it had
on the PS. The CP had long been loyal to Moscow, and most
leaders were exiled in the USSR or Eastern Europe. Even more
than before, the CP depended upon Moscow for support, not least
for financial support. The decision to abandon the armed struggle
and work for the election of the opposition to the Presidency and
to Congress, taken reluctantly and too late to bring much credit to
the party, led to divisions and disagreements in the late 1980s.
And as this decision coincided with historic changes in Communism in Eastern Europe and the Soviet Union, it is hardly surprising that the famous monolithic unity of the Chilean Communist
Party began to look very shaky in the 1990s.

The PDC suffered from fewer traumas than the parties of the
left. There was little doubt that it was the major party opposing the government, both in terms of popular support, and in its
ability to maintain at least a minimal organization in operation.
The number of PDC exiles were far fewer and their period of exile
shorter, and the presence of such obviously moderate leaders as
Jaime Castillo in Venezuela and Andrés Zaldívar in Madrid (where

he was President of the Christian Democratic International) helped to improve the image of the PDC with foreign governments and to intensify the international isolation of the Pinochet government. Perhaps the party was able to maintain a high degree of internal unity because it suffered less repression than other parties, and its leaders were less subject to exile.

The effect of exile upon the Radical Party was broadly similar to that of the PS, but the Radicals were so badly divided before 1973 that loss of support and divisions in the party were only exacerbated, but not caused by exile. The Radical Party in Chile, led by Enrique Silva Cimma, formed an alliance with the PDC, and advocated policies similar to those of European social democracy. But the party in exile was dominated by one of its Vice-Presidents, Anselmo Sule, whose position was closer to that of the Almeyda Socialists and the CP, and whose power in the party was partly based upon control of the international funds that helped to keep the party alive—for example, money from the Socialist International, of which the Radical Party is a member.

After 1983 the exiles began to return, and opposition politics returned to Chile from abroad, but that did not mean a lessening of international interest in Chile. Large amounts of aid had been going to Chile for humanitarian purposes; Catholic organizations in Europe and the USA gave more than $67 million in humanitarian aid between 1974 and 1979. Another $20 million came to church groups from the US Congress and the West German government: only $4 million was raised locally.[9] The direction of aid after 1983 shifted to more political purposes, though not always openly. Exiles played key roles in obtaining and using this aid. Where did it come from and why? What effects did it have? Was it an unmixed blessing? What was the role of the USA?

3. The International Relations of the Pinochet Government

Few governments have been so universally condemned as that of the Pinochet government in Chile, above all for its systematic violation of human rights. Chile's human rights record was reviewed and condemned annually in the General Assembly of the United Nations after 1974. In 1974, 90 nations condemned Chile's abuse of human rights; 8 supported Chile and 26 abstained. The best year for Chile was 1981 when 81 nations criticized Chile, 20 supported her, and 40 abstained. By 1985 the relevant figures were 88 for condemnation, 11 against, and 47 abstentions.[10] Because the government was so widely condemned, the opposition was widely supported. Exile might have contributed to the short-term consolidation of the Pinochet regime in so far as it removed opposition politicians from Chile, but the long-term effects were adverse for the government. Exiled politicians became adept in mobilizing international support for their opposition to the Pinochet government, and the very fact of exile on such a massive scale dramatically underlined the abuse of human rights committed by the Pinochet regime.

The attitude of the Pinochet regime did not make for easy relations with any foreign government: it would accept only unconditional and uncritical support. The government ignored international reaction to incidents such as the arrests of opposition leaders in the 1980s, or the expulsion of French priests in 1986. The only countries of any international significance that consistently supported Pinochet's Chile were China, Israel, and South Africa. Pinochet's abortive attempt to visit Marcos showed that even dictators could not be counted upon to support his regime. China was clearly interested in occupying the space left by the Moscow Communists in Chile after 1973, wanted to keep Taiwan out of Chile, and hoped to secure an international ally against the USSR. Trade between the two countries rose from US$1 million in 1970 to $137 million in 1984, with a strong positive balance in favour of Chile. Chile's relations with the Republic of South Africa and Israel were similarly based upon the desire of unpopular countries to find allies, and Israel was an important supplier of arms to Chile.

However, if Chile was diplomatically isolated it was not economically isolated, and it enjoyed improving trade relations even with some of its sternest critics in the West. The Pinochet government was prepared to accept a loss of international prestige as a democracy for an increase in prestige as a rare example of a successful Third World economy. Nor did the government experience any difficulties in purchasing arms from abroad. Even in the period 1982–6, when the government was heavily criticized for the way it repressed the protest movements, 90 per cent of its arms purchases came from its European critics.

Relations with the USA

The major foreign policy concern of the Pinochet government was to establish good relations with the United States. This was difficult over the long term, partly because both Congress and the liberal press in the USA continuously condemned the violation of human rights in a country long admired for its democratic tradition; partly because of the assassination of the exiled socialist leader Orlando Letelier in the centre of Washington in 1976; partly because of incessant campaigning by the Chilean opposition in the USA; partly because the human rights lobby in the USA attached a symbolic importance to Chile; and partly because the Reagan government found that condemnation of Chile was a useful counterpoint to condemnation of the Sandinista government.[11]

US policy towards Chile had not been consistent over time, nor uniform between the various agencies of the government. Relations were good immediately after the coup. Chile received from the USA, in direct bilateral aid and loans, and also from the World Bank and the Inter-American Development Bank, a total of US$628.1 million between 1974 and 1976. This compares with only $67.3 million received during the Allende years. With the election of Carter there was an abrupt change of policy. In an attempt to isolate the regime, the US government voted against loans to Chile from the multilateral banks, condemned the Chilean government's human rights record in the UN debates, forbade new Export–Import Bank loans, and did not invite Chile to participate in naval exercises. However, in the words of Susan Kaufman Purcell, these actions

produced more of an impact in the United States than in Chile. They allowed the US government and the American people to feel good again about US foreign policy in the aftermath of the Vietnam war . . . In Chile while the policy won friends for the United States among the democratic opposition parties of the center and center left, its impact was otherwise minimal.[12]

This was so, not least of all, because Chile was about to enter a short-lived economic boom from 1977 to 1981 when foreign loans were easy to obtain.

After Carter, policy shifted towards more cordial relations until 1985, when increasing repression in Chile and the renewal of the State of Siege led to the USA abstaining on an IDB loan to Chile. In June 1985, after the USA threatened similar action on a World Bank loan, the Chilean government lifted the State of Siege. The motive for such sanctions was to push the Chilean government in the right direction—that is, implementation of its constitutional promises—and not to destabilize it. Such tactics only made sense when the opposition was united enough to offer a plausible alternative, which it did with the church-inspired National Accord of August

1985. The replacement of the conservative Ambassador James Theberge with the career diplomat Harry Barnes was another sign that policy would in future favour the opposition.[13] In 1986 USA took the unprecedented step of sponsoring a resolution in the United Nations Commission on Human Rights denouncing Chile, and even applied limited economic sanctions.

The USA was, nevertheless, much more concerned than European governments with the threat from the left, and did not want the Marxist left to gain political influence. The USA liked Chile's economic model and did not want to damage the capacity of the economy to repay its international debt. Neither did the USA want to lose the emergency landing facility for polar shuttle orbits installed on Easter Island. The USA wanted Pinochet to step down because it felt that this was the best way to ensure economic and political stability in the long run, and it was worried that a prolongation of personalist rule would favour the Marxist left.

By the late 1980s the USA was confident that the democratic opposition could form a stable government, a confidence that was partly established by assiduous opposition lobbying in the USA. The support given by the US government to the opposition was important in reassuring local business sectors that the free-enterprise model would be safe in the hands of the government if the opposition came to power. As if to stress its confidence in the overall stability of the Chilean political system, the US government supported an IDB loan of US$35 million to Chile immediately after the plebiscite.

4. International Support for the Opposition: 1973–1989

One of the first manifestations of support for the Chilean opposition, apart from the reception of exiles, was the support given to exile organizations which were established and funded in countries as diverse as Sweden and Mexico. The outlawed Trade Union Confederation (CUT) established branches in a number of countries and was active both in tapping international trade-union solidarity for Chile and in denouncing the regime's policy towards labour. Academic institutes, such as the Institute for the New Chile in Amsterdam, played an important role as meeting-places for the opposition to analyse developments in Chile, in producing criticisms of the regime, in lobbying for support from foreign governments and agencies and for exile groups, as well as for agencies inside Chile that were trying to provide protection against the harsh economic and political measures of the government. One of the most public activities of the opposition was the publication of *Chile-América* in Rome. This magazine, which ran for ten years after 1974, was founded by two members of the Popular Unity alliance and two members of the PDC in exile. Its very existence was a sign that hostility between these two political forces could be overcome, and its systematic and intelligent analyses of Chile were a strong encouragement to Chileans in exile and to international opponents of the regime. At its height it had about 1,000 subscriptions from all over the world, and was read and debated by many more.

Another early manifestation of support from the international community was that given to the Catholic and other churches in Chile. Their initial activities in providing communal kitchens and in helping victims of repression were eventually supplemented by a policy of support for representative bodies such as trade unions and shanty-town organizations. The Chilean trade-union movement was largely kept alive after 1973 through the efforts of the Church and its Vicaría del Pastoral Obrero. Brian Smith estimates that between 1975 when the Vicaría de la Solidaridad was established, and 1979, some 700,000 Chileans received legal, health, nutritional, and occupational services.

Since 1973 papal, Vatican and international episcopal statements all provided strong legitimation for involvement in the promotion of human rights by national churches. Moral and political support has been given by these international Church groups to the Chilean Church's particular efforts in this area. At the regional level of Latin America itself the Latin American Episcopal Conference has focused attention on the dangers of the national security state and has emphasised the Church's responsibility to oppose it. What has been even more important has been the significant increase of financial assistance since the coup from international ecclesiastical and secular sources in support of its various programmes for the defence of human rights. Without such massive outside help none of these new commitments would have been possible.[14]

A great deal of support in various forms also came from the World Council of Churches, due to the efforts of Third World church organizations to influence the World Council in favour of support for Chile. Nevertheless, the Church in Chile faced one major obstacle in its attempts to influence the government, and that was the almost total absence of links between it and the government. The government would only accept unconditional support, and was constantly irritated by criticisms from the Church.

International support was given to a variety of research and

promotional institutes, and they were to assume crucial importance
not only in sustaining academic criticism of the regime, but later
in the political organization of the opposition itself, especially in the
plebiscite campaign. The Church was quick to respond to the attack on higher education by the government. The Church founded
the Academia de Humanismo Cristiano in 1975 to help the 1,000
academics expelled from the universities, and to express its dis-
pleasure with the continuing military intervention in the universities. Apart from the value of its own research and publications,
and efforts at social organization, the Academia also lent vital
Church protection to other independent research agencies, or to
specific groups like the Grupo de los 24, a group of opposition lawyers who sustained a continuous criticism of the government's constitutional proposals and provided a forum to draw up alternatives.[15]

Research institutes like the Academia and a host of others
were of major political importance to the opposition parties. In some
cases they were, effectively, the headquarters of the party in academic disguise. Where else could a party leadership meet, formulate alternative plans, obtain employment for key persons, engage
in sustained critiques of the government, and show to the outside
world that there was opposition in Chile, even if such opposition
had to be couched in careful academic language? Indeed precisely
because such institutions were subject to government scrutiny their
work had to be academically respectable, and some of the finest
social science research in Latin America came to be associated
with the Chilean informal academic sector. No one doubted the
overall identification of these institutes with the opposition, nor
even in some cases with specific political parties, but there was no
doubt either that they were serious academic enterprises—much
more so than many of the departments in the Chilean universities.

Such institutes could not have survived without funding from
abroad, and they were probably the main conduit for international
funds to reach the political opposition. Intellectuals have always
played a prominent role in Chilean political parties. The new
context increased their importance and diminished the role of the
old party-machine politicians, at least until open party activity
resumed.[16]

Figures are difficult to obtain, but in the late 1980s there were
about seventy research institutes, of which about ten were major.
At a rough guess 95 per cent of their budgets came from abroad,
and at an even rougher guess their funding amounted to about $1
million annually. The Ford Foundation, for example, made eighty-
five grants to Chile of a value of US$7.57 million between 1980 and

1988. Not all of these grants went to research institutes in the informal sector, but twenty-four of them went to the various research institutes of the Academia de Humanismo Cristiano, and twenty human rights projects were funded as well as eighteen concerned with women's issues. Such institutes were the only way that the opposition could enter into, albeit in a very limited way, debate with the government, for the government did respond to technical criticisms in a way that it did not to overt political criticism.[17] Justifying the role of institutions like the Ford Foundation, one of their officials wrote that,

Because of their stature and independence, foreign assistance institutions are often uniquely able to influence local authorities by protesting restrictive policies, probing the limits of acceptable behaviour, and protecting threatened groups. These critical, exploratory and protective powers may be especially important within repressive regimes, where significant segments of the society may have no other source of support. Those foreign assistance institutions that choose to withdraw may contribute indirectly to a deepening of the impact of totalitarian policies. The arguments in favour of staying and attempting to mitigate the effects of restrictive policies are therefore strong and compelling. Activities of this type may constitute the only contact that moderate elements have with the outside world.[18]

The research institutes played a vital role in the opposition's plebiscite campaign. Three major institutes—CED, ILET, and SUR—formed an overall political campaign group, the CIS, which organized a regular series of meetings to brief, if not instruct, politicians on the policies necessary for the campaign. The CIS played a considerable role in bringing together the parties to form the coalition for a 'no' vote, and masterminded the brilliant television campaign on behalf of the opposition. In the plebiscite campaign organization, an important role was played by the technical committees composed of researchers from these and from other institutes.

International support was also given to the opposition press and radio. The only opposition media tolerated in Chile for many years were two radio stations, Cooperativa and the church station Chilena. Although Cooperativa is now so successful that it can probably support itself from advertising, that was not the case in the early days. Similarly when the mild liberalization of the mid-1980s allowed some opposition press to flourish, notably the dailies *La Epoca* and *Fortín Diario*, such publications would not have been possible without support from a variety of sources (in the case of *Fortín*, notably from Italian NGOs and the Italian trade-union movement).

The trade-union movement, to take another example, was largely funded from abroad. Union salaries were paid by international funds. Training programmes were paid from abroad, and international aid allowed trade-union leaders to travel abroad to present their point of view in international assemblies. The trade-union movement in Chile was not only weakened by the economic and labour policies of the Pinochet government, it was also internally divided, and both sides of the ideological division were financed from abroad.

Finally, the political parties were dependent upon foreign funding, though as so much was indirect, not to say secretive, any estimates are likely to be very misleading. But it is hardly a secret that the moderate socialists received very considerable support from like-minded parties in Europe, or that the small Radical Party had considerable influence in the Socialist International, or that the PDC relied heavily on support from West German sources. This was inevitable when it was not possible to collect party dues, when parties had none of the perks of government even at the local level, and when the business community was very unlikely to annoy Pinochet by funding the opposition.

Who Gave Money and Why?

How much money went to Chile to support the opposition? An accurate answer would mean examining the accounts of the several hundred NGOs abroad that gave support to the 300 or so Chilean equivalents. The best informed estimate is probably that of the Taller de Cooperación al Desarrollo, which calculates that after 1985 about US$55 million per annum went to Chile.[19] Of course, this was not all specifically for the political opposition, but drawing the line between the aid programmes in terms of political and non-political does not always make a great deal of sense in the real world. The British Government spent £11 million over a ten-year period giving grants to some 900 Chilean exile students and academics.[20] Can this just be regarded as technical assistance?

Support to Chile went from a wide variety of countries, through the mechanism of NGOs, but often funded by their governments, as with the four major Dutch agencies that were very active in Chile. In per capita terms amongst the most generous of the aid donors was the Netherlands. Cuba played a role in training members of parties of the left in clandestine operations. Italian parties and unions provided considerable assistance. Germany was an important contributor to the parties via its foundations: Pinto-Duschinsky estimates that the four major German foundations gave DM39.4 million to Chile (about US$26 million) in the period 1983–8. That was substantially more than went to Brazil for example, and even more than went to Spain. It was much more than the American contribution via the NED, the AID, and the American Institute for Free Labour Development. Two-thirds of the German total was sent by the Adenauer Foundation, and it is safe to assume that much of it directly or indirectly benefited the Chilean PDC.[21] The European countries, apart from their individual efforts, also worked inside the EC to condemn the repressive measures of the government and to provide help to the opposition. In 1986 the European Parliament made a special allocation of ECU 2 million for the work of NGOs in Chile.[22] The European Parliament was consistently hostile to the Pinochet government, and warmly welcomed the formation of the opposition alliance to oppose Pinochet in the plebiscite.

Both the Socialist International and the Christian Democrat International were deeply affected by the events in Chile and mounted special programmes to aid groups with which they sympathized. Much of the finance of the internationals comes from the German foundations, so the support given by the internationals was not primarily financial. But it was of importance in helping the parties to organize, both in Chile and abroad, and lent a useful international legitimacy to the opposition's claims to represent the majority of the Chilean population.[23] At one special meeting of the Socialist International in 1977, representatives from the Chilean CP became the first Communists to attend a meeting of the SI since 1922. The Chilean Radical Party, a long-time member of the SI, and with a decidedly more leftist orientation than in the past, became influential in the organization of the SI's Latin American activities. The growing importance of the Spanish and Portuguese Socialist parties also helps to explain the concern of the SI with Chile.[24] Mexico was an important political base for the opposition and the Mexican PRI gave support, particularly to the Radical Party. Venezuela gave substantial support to the moderate left and to the Christian Democratic Party.

Official US help was centred on the plebiscite of 1988. Although private US foundations had given generous help to the opposition well before the date of the plebiscite, the US government had been far less active than European governments in funding opposition activities. There were no direct party links of the kind that existed between European and Chilean parties, and there was still considerable suspicion towards the US government on the part of many

Chilean politicians. It is not difficult to understand why there was support for the opposition in the dramatic and well-publicized plebiscite, but this was late in the day.

What had inspired fifteen years of international support for Chile? Was there some ulterior motive? No doubt motives were very mixed. Overtly political groups wanted to aid their counterparts in Chile, and no doubt to influence the political outcome. Giving aid was a way for the Left in Italy, Spain, and Germany to demonstrate idealistic attachment to international solidarity with the repressed peoples of the Third World, to show that whatever the changes in its domestic orientation, the socialist parties of Europe remained on the left. But what would explain Dutch support for Chile? Trade is hardly an important consideration, and political events in Chile are most unlikely to have much influence on the Netherlands. In the Netherlands, as in many other countries, Chile became symbolically linked to internal political debate; giving aid to the Chilean opposition was a way of publicly supporting the cause of democracy in the Third World. For a country like the Netherlands, support for the Chilean opposition was a way of projecting an image of tolerance and progressive views—and perhaps revived memories of Dutch resistance to Nazi rule.

European governments and parties felt a special affinity with Chile. The Chilean opposition had a concept of democracy that was clearly similar to that of most European political movements, based upon a combination of fair elections, social justice, and the observance of basic human rights. Support for the Chilean opposition was a way of affirming belief in the basic tenets of democracy. Moreover, without denying for a moment the genuine feelings of solidarity for Chile, and genuine dislike of a brutal dictatorship, support for the opposition was not likely to incur any penalties. Chile's economy is not as vital to the international economy as those of the larger Latin American republics, so that trade sanctions against Chile were not likely to damage domestic economies. And the strategic significance of the country is not enormous. Chile, then, became a symbol, and exiled politicians were only too ready to use the enormous wave of international sympathy in order to organize opposition to the government.[25]

International Support for the Opposition in the Plebiscite

President Pinochet announced his candidature officially when he was nominated by the military junta on 30 August 1988. But he had been campaigning for many months, and the opposition campaign effectively started in February of the same year, when sixteen parties (not including the Communist Party) formed the Comando por el NO.

International support for the Chilean opposition in the plebiscite campaign was not only financial. One incident two nights before the 5 October plebiscite is worth recounting. The US State Department issued a statement that it had received information that plans existed to interfere with the result of the plebiscite if the vote was going against the government, and that it viewed such reports with the gravest alarm and could not but consider what measures to take if such interference took place. It is difficult to conceive that this statement would have been issued without some prompting from the opposition in Chile. The government was furious. Yet it is a fairly commonly held belief that at least certain sectors of the army were prepared to take action on the night of the plebiscite to annul the result. The American statement was undoubtedly an important expression of support for the opposition, but did it also act as a deterrent to such action inside the regime? It would not have been enough by itself had there been complete agreement inside the armed forces on a plan to annul the result, but in the absence of that level of agreement, the US declaration may well have had a positive effect in strengthening those inside the government who opposed any illegal action. However, it is difficult to evaluate the effect of the statement, and it was also argued that the public way in which the statement was made meant that it was intended as much for domestic consumption in the USA as to have an effect in Chile. There were similar, if less dramatic, declarations by the presidents of a number of democratic countries in Latin America, and by the EC.

There were also about 1,000 observers present at the plebiscite, half from various parliaments, and half from a variety of other associations. The presence of these observers was not welcomed by the government, but was certainly appreciated by the opposition. The opposition argued that the presence of observers would make fraud more difficult, and would lend encouragement to local groups. International press coverage of the event was intense, and there is no doubt that the government saw both foreign press and TV as hostile to them and favourable to the opposition. (In one ugly incident shortly after the result, some twenty reporters were beaten by the local police.) Even if every reporter was strictly neutral, the opposition was convinced that the presence of so many journalists would make fraud on a large scale impossible.

In its anxiety to counter the possibility of electoral fraud by the government, the opposition attempted to minimize the threat by setting up three parallel computer systems linked to an intricate network of fax machines. This was based upon the premiss that months of active campaigning had removed the fear of voting. The major concern of the opposition was that voters would not believe that the vote was secret, and that they would be unable to resist the various kinds of pressure employed by the government, especially at the local level, to ensure a vote favourable for the government.

Support came from the USA for the registration of voters, and for computer counting systems on the day of the poll. The AID made a grant of $1.2 million to the Centre for Free Elections (CAPEL) in Costa Rica in December 1987 (one motive being to keep the US Congress happy that something was being done about Chile). In turn CAPEL made the grant over to Civitas, a church-linked group in Chile which created a campaign called the Cruzada Cívica to encourage voters to register. At the same time the US Congress approved a $1 million grant to the National Endowment for Democracy to support the activities of the opposition. Most of this money went to the National Democratic Institute for International Affairs. Even before the special grant in 1987, the National Endowment had been making grants to the opposition in Chile. Grants had gone to research institutes for polling purposes, to publishing houses and to the press ($50,000 to *La Epoca* in 1988), to community organizations and trade unions ($856,000 to the anti-Communist trade-union confederation, the CDT, from 1984 to 1988), and to a variety of seminars, meetings, discussions, and training programmes. According to an internal National Endowment document dated September 1988, the total spent by it in Chile (with a small contribution from the AID) was $3,824,000 from 1985 onwards.[26] However, to put this in perspective, one should note that the rather larger sum of $9 million was approved by Congress for use in the Nicaraguan elections in 1990, and that similar amounts had been spent in recent elections in Honduras and Haiti: all three being countries with substantially smaller electorates than Chile. In the Chilean elections of 1989, the AID made a grant of $470,000 to CAPEL to help the church-sponsored Participa organization do what the Cruzada Cívica had done in the plebiscite.

The National Endowment is an agency created by the Reagan Administration, associated with the research centre Freedom House, and then headed by Carl Gershman, a former adviser to Jeanne Kirkpatrick. According to an interview with Mr Gershman in *El Mercurio* in January 1988, the purpose of the Endowment was 'to promote democratic values throughout the world, and to actively engage the North American people and private sector in this task, in a manner consistent with UN proclamations, international law and North American ideals'. The total budget was about $16 million in 1988, of which about 45 per cent went to Latin America and of that proportion, about 15 per cent to Chile. The only other special appropriation made was to Solidarity in 1987. Asked by the interviewer if this sort of activity was tantamount to interfering in Chilean politics, Mr Gershman replied,

Look, one has to distinguish between supporting democratic forces and intervening in electoral processes. In those cases where a free and democratic process exists and where diverse groups can compete freely, it is illegitimate for the NED to intervene in the results. But efforts to promote free and democratic processes are a form of solidarity, and not intervention.

If one adds the million dollars which was received by Civitas for the Cruzada Cívica and other funds from agencies like the Ford Foundation, then something like at least $5 million went into Chile from the USA in the last couple of years before the plebiscite to assist in the organization of the opposition. Sweden is also reported to have made considerable donations to the opposition. No doubt some funds also went to the political right in Chile to fund the government's campaign but there are no details of this support.

On the day of the plebiscite, there was neither fraud nor military intervention to annul the result. Over 90 per cent of the total potential electorate was registered to vote, and over 90 per cent of those actually voted, 55 per cent supporting the 'no' option and 43 per cent the 'si'. It was a remarkable event that few would have predicted two years before it took place. It was also remarkable for the extent to which it was played out under close international scrutiny. The government enjoyed so many advantages—years of political propaganda, control over TV, state resources—that at first the opposition's task looked almost impossible. International support was surely crucial in overcoming those disadvantages. But it was a special event at a special moment. The elections of 1989 were more clearly a Chilean internal political contest in which international influence was much less marked. But had the plebiscite not produced the result it did, there would have been no elections.

5. Conclusions: The Effects of International Support for the Opposition

The real basis of opposition to a dictatorship must come from internal developments. The waves of protest that started in May

1983 were not directed from abroad, nor even influenced from abroad. Chilean opposition politicians needed help, but the strongest force for the opposition came from the immense desire of most Chileans to return to a democratic system. Yet international support for the Chilean transition to democracy was arguably more important than support for the transition in other Latin American countries. This was partly a consequence of exile, partly a consequence of a political structure similar in many ways to Western democracies, partly because of sympathy for the overall objectives of the Allende government, partly because of reaction to the brutality of the coup, and partly because all these factors combined to make Chile a symbol of democracy versus dictatorship.

The Inter-American Dialogue, in a report issued in 1984, stated that, 'We doubt that any government (perhaps least of all that of the most powerful country in the Hemisphere) can contribute much in a very direct way to building democratic institutions in other countries.' There are good reasons for sharing this scepticism. It is easier to provide humanitarian help for the victims of human rights abuses and to denounce such practices in international organizations than it is to mould political developments in a predictable and satisfactory way. Help to church-based organizations is not very controversial, and is generally praised as bringing practical benefits without the danger of direct political interference. But direct assistance to political parties is of a rather different and more controversial nature. Manuel Antonio Garretón has sounded a warning note in this area.

International influence must avoid two types of action. Firstly, linking the question of the fight against the military regime and the re-establishment of democracy with the East–West conflict, and this refers principally to the USA. And secondly, complementary with the first, dividing the opposition into 'democratic' and 'non democratic' in a way that has effects not only in the political sphere but also upon social organizations especially the trade unions.[27]

There is evidence that international support has helped some opposition forces more than others. The Radical Party was badly divided at the time of the coup and its overall vote was insignificant. Yet its privileged position within the Socialist International gave it a leverage that owed more to its international linkage than to its internal significance. The moderate socialists received a great deal of support from European sources, and this might have worked to their advantage compared with the Almeyda socialists (though this group received aid from East Germany). No doubt the Christian

Democrats have maintained their reputation as the best organized party in Chile in no small part due to international help.

But what is the alternative? Should opposition parties refuse to accept aid from abroad on the grounds that it might distort the internal balance of forces? Some aid may carry unacceptable strings, but there is little evidence that much aid to Chile was of that variety. The most serious distortion would seem to be, as Garretón points out, in introducing the Cold War into the allocation of resources. It is difficult to explain the large amounts of money going, for example, to the anti-Communist union confederation, the CDT, on other grounds. But even this may not bring more than initial advantage. Once normal political, electoral, and union activity is resumed, domestic considerations will play a greater part, and unionists will vote for the union leaders who most closely represent their demands. And distortions do not go only one way: Communists as well as anti-Communists received support. The difference is that we know a lot more about support for the latter than for the former. On balance I would argue that external support for Chilean democracy has been both important and positive, that it has not represented the simple imposition of the aims of the donor countries on Chilean recipients, and that a hard-pressed opposition had little alternative but to look for support from democratic forces abroad in order to help the process of democracy internally. Sympathy for the cause of Chilean democracy should, however, be tempered with respect for the autonomy of local political groups.

International interest in Chile has diminished since the inauguration of the Aylwin government in March 1990. On international comparisons, Chile is not regarded as a poor country, and as the spotlight of attention moves away, the country can expect a reduction of international interest. Indeed, as the economy is in much better condition than that of most other Latin American countries, the need for aid has lessened as international investment has reached record heights.

Nevertheless, the Aylwin government continues to seek international support in the process of consolidating the democratic system in Chile. The USA has already helped by removing conditions imposed on Chile for human rights violations. This allows a resumption of economic and development assistance, and paves the way for the restoration of trade benefits under the Generalized System of Preferences, and the Overseas Private Investment Corporation.[28] The government of President Aylwin has created a Fondo de Solidaridad e Inversión Social (FOSIS) in order to channel resources, both domestic and foreign, to projects to help the poor.

The political importance of this is obvious, for such help, if it were given on a sufficient scale, would reinforce the commitment of the most disadvantaged sectors of Chilean society to their newly re-established democratic system. The eventual aim of FOSIS is to spend 4–5 per cent of GDP on programmes to help those 30–40 per cent of Chilean families estimated to be living in poverty. FOSIS intends to channel international funds for these pro-grammes.[29]

The strong links that exist between Chilean parties and their counterparts in Europe and elsewhere are hardly likely to disap-pear with the return to democracy, and Chilean politics will continue to have a strong international dimension. One interesting develop-ment since the elections is the creation of a number of right-wing research institutes, such as Libertad, directed by the defeated pres-idential candidate, Hernan Buchi, and Libertad y Desarrollo, under the control of the right-wing party Renovación Nacional. These, and other earlier institutes of the right, are concerned to defend and modernize the ideas that informed the political economy of the Pinochet regime, and, like the research institutes of the former opposition, they too are seeking foreign funding, though now from foundations like the right-wing American Heritage Foundation and the German Seidel Foundation.[30] Chilean ideologists continue to seek international legitimation.

Notes

1. E. Kaufman, *Crisis in Allende's Chile: New Perspectives* (New York: Praeger 1988), 140–5 estimates that about half of the aid went to the Christian Democratic party.
2. J. Arrate, *Exilio: Textos de denuncia y esperanza* (Santiago: Ediciones del Ornitorrinco, 1987).
3. All figures in this paragraph are quoted in *El Mercurio* (Santiago), 12 June 1986, p. 6; and *Hoy* (Santiago), no. 467, 30 June 1986, p. 25. This issue of *Hoy* contains an interview with the priest in charge of the Pastoral del Exilio. The Church has played the principal role in defending the basic human rights of Chileans, including the right to live in Chile. This section on exile draws on published work by the author and Susan Carstairs.
4. All figures in this paragraph are drawn from ICEM, *Provisional Report on Movements Effected by the Intergovernmental Committee for Euro-pean Migration under the Special Programme for Resettlement from Latin American Countries* (June 1979); and CIDE, *Inserción Laboral*

para el Retorno: El caso de los exiliados Chilenos (Santiago: Centro de Investigación y Desarrollo de la Educación, 1984).

5. From the interview in *Qué Pasa?* (Santiago), 27 March 1986, 26.

6. C. Furci, *The Crisis of the Chilean Socialist Party in 1979*, working paper no. 11 (Institute of Latin American Studies, University of London, 1984). This is an invaluable source on the 1979 split. See also the exile publication *Chile-América* (Rome), dossier no. 54–5 (1979).

7. Aniceto Rodríguez, a former secretary-general of the party, exiled in Venezuela, complained bitterly that in six years of exile (1973–9) there were only two apparently representative assemblies—in Cuba and Algiers. But both, in his opinion, were used by manipulative minorities trying to prolong their power: see *Chile-América*, dossier no. 54–5, 112.

8. Interview in *Qué Pasa?*, 27 March 1986, 27.

9. B. Smith, *The Church and Politics in Chile* (Princeton, NJ: Princeton University Press, 1982), 325.

10. H. Muñóz, *Las Relaciones Exteriores del Gobierno Militar Chileno* (Santiago: Ediciones del Ornitorrinco, 1986), 19.

11. Relations between the two countries are well treated in H. Muñóz and C. Portales, *Una Amistad Esquiva: Las relaciones de Estados Unidos y Chile* (Santiago: Ediciones Pehuen, 1987).

12. From M. Falcoff, A. Valenzuela, and S. Kaufman Purcell, *Chile: Prospects for Democracy* (New York: Council on Foreign Relations, 1988), 59.

13. The personality and ability of an ambassador can also help. There is little doubt that Ambassador Barnes played an active role in obtaining financial support for the opposition's electoral efforts, in persuading the State Department to issue its famous warning to the Chilean government on the eve of the plebiscite, and even in persuading the opposition that the best way to defeat the Pinochet regime was to participate in the plebiscite rather than to boycott it.

14. Smith, *Church and Politics*, 323.

15. This is based upon an unpublished paper by Maria Teresa Lladser of the Academia. I am grateful to the author for her help.

16. Nevertheless, the sheer availability of foreign funds may well have kept alive splinter groups or smaller parties that in a more austere climate might have merged or disappeared and thereby reduced the divisions of the opposition.

17. The best-known example was the continuous criticism of the government economic model by the economists of CIEPLAN.

18. J. Puryear, *Higher Education, Development Assistance, and Repressive Regimes* (New York: Ford Foundation, 1983), 15.

19. See their publication *La Cooperación Internacional frente a los Cambios Politicos en Chile* (Santiago, 1988), 11. According to Sergio Bitar, in Chile in 1985 there were 35 NGOs in the health sector, twenty on human rights, 61 on popular education, 80 linked to the social action

programmes of the Church, 50 linked to the academic research centres, and another 60 or so engaged in diverse tasks. 'Chile: Cooperación económica international para la democracia', in H. Muñóz (ed.), *Chile: Política exterior para la democracia* (Santiago: Ediciones Pehuen, 1989).

20. See the World University Service report, *A Study in Exile* (London: World University Service, 1986).

21. M. Pinto-Duschinsky, 'Foreign Political Aid: The German Political Foundations and their US Counterparts', *International Affairs*, 67/1 (1991).

22. G. Ashoff, *La Cooperación para el desarrollo entre la Comunidad Europea y América Latina*, Documento de Trabajo no. 16 (Madrid: IRELA, 1989), 46.

23. See Chapter 8 below.

24. F. Williams, *La Internacional Socialista y América Latina* (Mexico: Universidad Autonoma Metropolitana Azcapotzalco, 1984).

25. Seeing so many opposition politicians at a reception in the US Embassy two nights before the plebiscite, I asked one of them what on earth they were all doing there. His reply was, 'Where do you think the opposition has been meeting all these years?' He was referring not just to the United States Embassy, but rather the embassies of all those countries critical of the government of Pinochet. Given the difficulties that opposition politicians faced in organizing even their own parties, holding meetings in embassies was one way of avoiding government restrictions.

26. I am very grateful to Carol Graham for obtaining information from the National Endowment. An interesting article on the subject is J. Muravchik, 'US Political Parties Abroad', *Washington Quarterly* (summer 1989).

27. M. A. Garretón, *Transición hacia la Democracia en Chile e Influencia Externa*, Documento de Trabajo no. 282 (Santiago: FLACSO, 1986), 27.

28. On 20 March 1990 Senator Edward Kennedy introduced on the floor of the Senate the 'Support for Democracy in Chile Act of 1990'. This requests a modest US$50m. for expenditures on housing, health, and education, but also includes funds for technical assistance to help the Chilean congress to function more effectively: J. Heine, 'Support Latin Democracies: Give Chile a Hand', *Miami Herald*, 6 May 1990.

29. For an acute analysis of the possible path of Chilean–European relations, see J. Heine, 'Chile y el Desafío Europeo', *Cono Sur* (Santiago), 9/2 (1990). He points out that the European Parliament has budgeted ECU 5m. for Chilean NGOs, and is proposing to double that amount; that the German Parliament has allocated DM30m. for help in the financial area and another DM31m. for technical co-operation; and that the German, Italian, and Spanish governments have all expressed their intention to establish co-operative projects.

30. See the report in *Hoy*, 23 April 1990.

International Support for Democracy in Contemporary Latin America: The Role of the Party Internationals

WOLF GRABENDORFF

According to Andreas Khol, Executive Secretary of the European Democrat Union, the primary function of international party associations consists of providing its members with democratic legitimacy.[1] The act of admitting a candidate to the association of democratic parties entails sanction of the former, that is the Internationals' support for world-wide democracy is reduced to the very act of granting access to the 'democratic club'. This clinical, very passive view of the Internationals' function in evolving democratic regimes contrasts sharply with the scandals that surface from time to time, such as West German political party foundations being accused of meddling in some Latin American countries' internal affairs.

The truth about the Internationals' support for democracy, however, does not lie somewhere in between. Rather, it is characterized by poles of extremity and the different forms that transnational party contacts can take. It is extremely difficult to develop a systematic approach to the subject in question, precisely because of the diffuse network of relations in which individual actors, forms, and channels of influence are superimposed over each other. Moreover, mere lack of information, such as the size of financial flows in transnational party relations, often impedes a proper evaluation. Therefore, this chapter will limit itself to developing a set of criteria that might shed light on some of the links in the network mentioned above.

However, even in the absence of an exhaustive examination of the topic, a general overview would suggest that the influence of the Internationals on processes of (re)democratization and consolidation

of nascent democracies in Latin America is, at best, limited. Two
basic observations point to this thesis:

- *Geographical scope.* The two Internationals with the longest
  presence in Latin America—the Socialist International (SI)
  and the Christian Democrat International (CDI)—are primarily based in those countries possessing both a European-type
  party spectrum and a democratic tradition, in some cases more
  consistent than in many European countries. In contrast, the
  dominance of a non-European origin party spectrum—namely
  the populist tradition in countries such as Argentina and
  Brazil—has a priori prevented the Internationals from exerting considerable influence on the processes of democratization
  that these countries experienced during the 1980s.
- *Type of influence.* Party Internationals have, by definition, a
  very limited policy-making capacity. An International issues
  declarations and resolutions and sends fact-finding missions
  in support of democracy or attacking governments' alleged
  violation of democratic rights. Yet apart from (limited) financial
  assistance, Internationals lack the necessary instruments to
  implement policy as expressed in declarations. That is, on the
  one hand, policy-making has to be surrendered to governments.
  On the other hand, the very fact that the Internationals' weight
  depends largely on the member parties in government tends
  to make them susceptible to government influence. Therefore,
  the influence which Internationals—as non-governmental
  organizations—can exert hinges very much upon governmental support.

1. The Internationals within European–Latin American Relations

Bi-regional relations between Western Europe and Latin America
are relatively recent in nature.[2] It was not until the end of the
1970s that the European Community sought a systematic approach
to and regular contacts with Latin America on a regional or sub-
regional basis. EC indifference to political developments on, and
economic relations with, the continent was not an isolated phenomenon. Latin America is a latecomer on the international stage;
the United States' traditionally preponderant role in Latin American foreign policy had long impeded serious attempts to diversity
external contacts on the part of the continent itself. Moreover, the

international community perceived Latin America as a US protection zone in which meddling would cause nothing but friction in the Western hemisphere.

For reasons emerging from the post-war international order, Western Europe has long been particularly attentive in its respect for US international interests. Western Europe's specific security interests committed it to the transatlantic system as much as Latin American (economic) dependence on the United States tied it to the inter-American system. Both Western Europe and Latin America, although for different reasons, shared the experience of vulnerability *vis-à-vis* the United States. Similarly both, though again to a different degree, did not enjoy a widening of their respective room for manœuvre until US hegemony over the Western world began to be eroded at the beginning of the 1970s.

Western Europe and Latin America share a further experience. On both sides of the Atlantic, the 1960s brought about an almost simultaneous process of integration. The creation of the European Economic Community in 1957 was followed in Latin America by the setting up, in 1960, of both the Latin American Free Trade Association (LAFTA) and the Central American Common Market, and, in 1969, of the Andean Pact. Although these efforts were never greeted with the same success as in Europe, Latin American integration schemes were often modelled on the European example.

Although Latin America was one of the first regions of the Third World to boast integration institutions, early attempts to set up group-to-group contact with the EC lacked success. West European foreign policy continued to be dominated first by an East–West approach to world affairs, and secondly by a Euro-centric concern with prosperous economic and political integration. Accordingly, external relations obeyed rules imposed by the East–West division of the world and/or were governed by interests geared to reinforcing the Community's evolving role as an important political and economic actor in the international system. EC–Latin American relations fit into this picture. Inactive in the face of Latin America's economic problems, the EC did not pay attention to its political conflicts either, at least until the Central American crisis offered the opportunity to raise Europe's voice in a conflict which would attract international attention for some time.

The response to Latin American demands for closer contact with Europe came from the Internationals first, and from the SI in particular. The 'dialogue of the deaf' in bi-regional governmental relations contrasted with mutual understanding at the transnational level of inter-party relations. Acting under fewer constraints than those imposed upon official foreign policy strategies and goals, the Internationals were supportive of the specific, particularly economic, problems of Latin America.

Much has been said about the Internationals operating as representatives of governments and specific European economic interests.[3] However, such a view ignores the fact that all the Internationals have recently been concentrating their activities on Central America, a region in which no European economic interests are at stake. The history and record of European party contacts with Latin America suggests that they follow different rules. An important factor has undoubtedly been the existence of a counterpart as receiver and transmitter of international party policies.[4] In this sense, it is not accidental that Latin America became the Internationals' preferential field for contact. A common cultural legacy, and in some cases a similar tradition with respect to political systems, had encouraged a party spectrum greatly resembling the European example in many Latin American countries.

However, the very factor which tends to facilitate transnational party contacts—a common political culture tradition—also puts limits on international influence. In terms of international support for democracy, the very many political parties in Latin America boasting a long political tradition of their own have often proved inappropriate subjects for patronizing lectures by their European counterparts. There is no better illustration of this point than the Internationals' contribution to the search for conflict solutions in Central America. The Contadora as well as the Esquipulas peace plans were designed by Latin Americans alone.[5] The Internationals' support for peace and democratization in the region was largely limited to congressional resolutions and to pressing their 'allies' into various forms of domestic dialogue. Their actual influence on the process depended mainly on the number of affiliates in government among the countries of Central America and the Contadora group.[6]

2. The Concept of Democracy

Although most recent among the ideologies represented by the Internationals,[7] the Christian Democrats alone have created a genuine Latin American school of thought. The Chilean Eduardo Frei and the Venezuelan Rafael Caldera were the protagonists of a Latin American Christian Democrat ideology which achieved the development of a political profile largely independent of European influence. Thus, the Organización Demócrata Cristiana de América

(ODCA), founded at a meeting of the Argentine, Brazilian, Chilean, and Uruguayan Christian Democratic Parties on 23 April 1947 in Montevideo, never adhered to the strong anti-Communism that so characterized their European counterparts in the Cold War period. Neither was the Latin American Christian Democrat movement confessional as such. 'Christianism' was a moral rather than a religious category, indicating commitment to the defence of individual rights and collective welfare.[8] In terms of economic policy, the CEPAL project of autonomous industrialization through import-substitution played an important role in the formulation of Christian Democrat economic strategy at the time.

The 1960s were the Christian Democrat heyday. In 1963 Belaúnde Terry won the elections in Peru, followed by the 1964 electoral victory of Eduardo Frei in Chile and, in 1966, of Caldera in Venezuela. However, the beginning of the 1970s witnessed an economic reorientation in Latin America as a result of the global economic crisis. The import-substitution model proved increasingly unable to cope with Latin America's economic problems.[9] Consequent social unrest threatened structures that had been built according to the model of economic and political modernization. The new trend ousted Christian Democrats from power, bringing in leftist or social democratic governments, as in the case of Chile and Venezuela, or the military, as in Peru. At the international level, Kennedy's concept of Communist containment in the aftermath of the Cuban Revolution (the Alliance for Progress), which had prompted good contacts with Latin American Christian Democratic parties, was replaced by a strategy of 'roll-back' when the United States assisted the toppling of the Allende government in Chile.

Indeed, the 1973 *coup d'état* in Chile was a bench-mark in the Internationals' involvement in Latin America. For the Latin Americans, the coup fuelled doubts as to the viability of reforms without international support and a deep suspicion of the United States. The Europeans, and particularly the SI, regarded the rise of what was perceived in Latin America as new US imperialism as an appropriate opportunity to strengthen European influence.[10] Furthermore, the 1970s brought about peaceful transition from authoritarian to democratic rule in three European countries. The successful democratization processes in Spain, Portugal, and Greece became a symbol of Europe's credibility as a valuable broker on the continent. It was not by accident that all Internationals—except for the IDU—attempted to increase influence in Latin America by establishing or strengthening links with their respective Iberian counterparts, placing the latter's representatives in leading positions within the organizations.[11]

It was the SI that most quickly and coherently reacted to the demand for political and economic alternatives in Latin America. The replacement of clear-cut socialism by the more flexible concept of social democracy paved the way for the SI to broaden its base in Latin America. International socialism coincided in Latin America with three basic trends:

- Political oppression in some countries, and the limited opening of military regimes in others, gave rise to opposition groups which the SI was quick to recognize and to support.
- Against the background of a widening North–South economic divide, the SI supported the Latin American demand for a new international economic order.
- Inherent contradictions in US President Carter's more liberal approach to US Latin American policy left the SI enough room to broaden its influence in the region and to claim the role of truly advocating human rights.[12]

The Liberal International (LI) is a latecomer on the Latin American scene. It was not until the early 1980s that Liberals established contacts with sister parties in Central America. The LI faced the problem of adapting its concept of democracy to Third World needs. The basic liberal principle regarding the indivisibility of freedom, democracy, and human rights lacked the prerequisite social component with which to recruit counterparts in Latin America. Beyond the industrialized world, liberalism has long been seen as the ideology of the rich, advocating economic *laissez-faire*, and giving freedom priority over social justice when the choice had to be made. Thus, the opening of the predominantly European— until the end of the 1970s—LI to developing countries required ideological tolerance in showing respect for different forms of liberalism. Specifically, natural liberal reservations about state intervention in the economy and encouragement of private initiative 'should not be regarded as a holy writ'.[13]

In April 1984, against a background of crisis in Central America, the Presidents of the SI, CDI, and LI issued the first common declarations on Latin America. The 'Common Appeal on Latin America',[14] though referring to a broad range of economic and political problems on the continent, revealed the overriding attention now paid to the Central American conflict. Interestingly enough, the common standpoint expressed in the declaration very much echoes the basic principles of EC dialogue with Central America set up the same year:

- the perception of Latin America's political problems as a result of long-standing economic and social injustice;
- the danger of identifying social and economic strife in Latin America with East–West confrontation;
- the special responsibility of the United States for peace, democracy, and prosperity on the continent; and
- the support for the Contadora initiative.

As in the case of EC involvement in Central America, the Internationals' attempts to mediate in the conflict came to be the litmus test of European self-assertion *vis-à-vis* the United States.[15] However, the shift of Central American policy in Western Europe towards more conservative positions and the tightening of the US grip on Nicaragua prompted serious constraints on the Internationals' room for manœuvre. Thus, the double pressure from the US administration and from some Western European governments eventually led ODCA to abandon positions—such as the principle of self-determination for the Central American nations and a general sympathetic understanding of the causes of armed opposition—to closer alignment with the United States.[16]

The SI, on the other hand, faced an even more difficult situation in Central America. Rhetorical commitment to the revolutionary change in El Salvador and Nicaragua drove the SI into a position which left no room for mediation either within the region or between Central American parties and the United States. Thus, at the beginning of 1981, several attempts to mediate in the Salvadorean conflict failed because, among other things, full-fledged support for the Salvadorean guerrillas made SI policies appear more directed towards participation in the conflict than mediation.[17] In Nicaragua the SI failed to express its disagreement with the direction of the Sandinista regime openly, for it feared being accused of backing the United States in its policy of confrontation. Through its tacit endorsement of developments in Nicaragua, the SI tried to moderate Sandinista positions, but in doing so lost some opportunities to influence US policy. Instead, the Reagan Administration turned increasingly to the Christian Democratic parties as its interlocutor in the region.

SI influence in the region suffered a further setback as the Contadora group and its peace initiative lost momentum. With affiliates in government in Costa Rica and Venezuela, as well as good relations with Mexico's PRI, the SI had been granted some say in the Contadora process. However, the US administration's decision to boycott the Contadora peace proposal, and the presentation of a plan of its own in April 1985, split the parties involved. In addition, long-standing disenchantment with the Sandinistas within the SI eventually surfaced. The harsh criticism of the Sandinistas on the part of two regional member parties, Costa Rica's PLN and Venezuela's AD, as well as their efforts to distance themselves from the Contadora peace plan, contributed decisively to diminishing SI support for the Sandinistas.[18]

3. The Institutional Structure

Each of the large Internationals has a counterpart organization in Latin America. The CDI branch—ODCA—has twenty-one members and is itself a member of the International.[19] The Federación de Partidos Liberales de Centroamérica y del Caribe (FELICA), the counterpart organization of the LI, is composed of seven member parties from Central America and the Caribbean.[20] As in the case of ODCA, FELICA is an autonomous organization which holds observer status before the LI.

Latin American socialist parties are organized in different fora with—in some cases—overlapping membership. The Socialist International Committee for Latin America and the Caribbean (SICLAC) is comprised of twenty regional member parties.[21] In addition, in 1979 Mexico's PRI created the Conferencia Permanente de Partidos Políticos de América Latina (COPPPAL) as a platform for anti-imperialist and democratic forces throughout Latin America.[22] The first meeting was attended by twenty-three parties from the continent, most of which were members of the SI or observers at its congresses.

A third organization was set up at Uruguayan initiative in 1986 in the wake of the First Political Conference of Latin American Socialism that took place in Montevideo in April of the same year. The Coordinación Socialista Latinoamericana (CSL) is composed of sixteen South American socialist parties, most of them small splinter groups which do not play a significant role in their respective party spectrums.[23] As opposed to a large coincidence in membership between SICLAC and COPPPAL, CSL parties do not generally[24] form part of either organization.

Given their long-standing presence in Latin America, the CDI and SI are—in quantitative terms—the most important of the transnational party organizations. Both count on a solid base in Central America and, to a lesser extent, on very similar representation in South America. It is interesting to note that the main pillars of both Internationals not only are the same, but that they happen to be some of the countries of longest democratic tradition: Costa Rica in Central America and Venezuela on the southern part of the continent. Moreover, both CDI and SI have a member party in Chile, but neither has any influence of importance on the Southern Cone parties heading the transition from military to democratic rule in Argentina, Brazil, and Uruguay.

However, there are important qualitative differences between CDI and SI representation in Latin America. ODCA was established in 1947, that is, simultaneously with its European mother organization. As stated above, this was an important factor in allowing ODCA to develop a genuinely autonomous political profile. ODCA's weight within CDI has been repeatedly indicated by two factors. First, ODCA representatives have long formed part of the top management of the International and, in 1989, for the second time a Venezuelan was elected president of the CDI.

Secondly, ODCA and its single most important member and financier, Venezuela's COPEI, have been decisive in shaping Christian Democrat Central American policy. Thus, the 1982 electoral victory of Napoleon Duarte, whose political orientation was largely influenced by the Venezuelan Christian Democrats during his seven years of exile in that country, can be partially put down to concerted Christian Democrat action, headed and managed by the Venezuelan lobby.[25] Moreover, under its Venezuelan Secretary General Aristides Calvani, ODCA actively promoted the creation of new Christian Democratic parties thus ensuring its control over their political orientation. Therefore, under the leadership of COPEI, ODCA was transformed into a political organization of considerable homogeneity,[26] a factor which for some time provided it with a clear-cut political profile in its Central American policy.

However, ODCA's political coherence has in recent years been challenged by attempts to strengthen ties between Christian Democrats and conservatives in Latin America. In the absence of a solid basis in Central America, IDU—with the support of the West German Christian Democrat Union (CDU) as a dominant member of both the CDI and the IDU—has been increasingly eager to challenge ODCA in favour of a more conservative policy in Central America. Tensions have already been manifest when ODCA parties have wanted to join IDU, as demonstrated in the case of the Nicaraguan Partido Social Cristiano. Keen to preserve its political character and role in Latin America, ODCA has so far rejected applications for dual membership in transnationals.[27]

As opposed to Latin American Christian Democrats, SI policy to integrate a broad spectrum of progressive forces created, in the specific case of the Central American conflict, a political entanglement which prevented the SI from taking full advantage of its influence in the region. In order to allow for broad recruitment in Latin America at a very early stage the SI created different statuses ranging from full membership to consultative members and congress-observers. The membership of the Salvadorean MNR and the admission of the Sandinista Front as an observer before the SI led to strong tensions within the International as the Central American conflict sharpened. Thus, even prior to general SI disenchantment with some of its partners in Central America, Costa Rica's PLN and Venezuela's AD lobbied openly for national reconciliation in El Salvador instead of unilateral support of the Frente Democrático Revolucionario, and harshly criticized the Sandinistas for failing to democratize its regime. SI disagreement on Central America culminated in 1982 when the AD's refusal to allow Sandinista participation in an SI conference prompted the suspension of the meeting.[28]

It can be argued that beyond the actual differences in position over which strategy to follow in Central America, European socialist protagonism in Central America prompted resentment among Latin American powers with considerable influence in the region. This is certainly true for Mexico. Like Venezuela, Mexico was a member of the Contadora group. However, unlike Venezuela, Mexico's understanding of the origin and the character of the Central American crisis as a process of revolutionary transition from traditional regimes to a new political and social order drew it very close to the SI perception of the conflict. Yet it was precisely this situation that laid the ground not just for SI–Mexican co-operation, but also for a certain competition for influence in Central America. Mexico's creation of COPPPAL was partly intended to restrain SI influence in Central America. However, the often-stated fraternal relationship between both party organizations did not hide the fact that both organizations competed for influence over the same terrain. This became even more obvious when the creation of COPPPAL allowed the Latin American SI members to press for regional representation within the SI. The creation of SICLAC in 1980, shortly after the foundation of COPPPAL, has to be seen in this context.[29]

The experience of the Liberal International was quite different. FELICA was set up in 1986. As opposed to the other Internationals, the LI counterpart is a rather small, regionally concentrated organization covering only Central America and the Caribbean. However, precisely since it is an essentially sub-regional organization in character, FELICA has, as compared with the other Latin American party organizations, achieved unique protagonism in Central America. The Honduran Liberal Party has been in office since the restoration of democracy in 1981, apart from a single term in opposition (1990–3); in Nicaragua after the 1990 electoral defeat of the Sandinistas the leader of the Independent Liberals became Vice-President, before breaking with President Chamorro; and similarly in Panama in the early 1990s the National Liberal Movement held the Vice-Presidency. During this period, therefore, the Liberal International had important counterparts, and at least nominal weight, in Central American party politics.

4. Channels of Influence

Parties in Government and Opposition

Between the mid-1970s, when the Internationals became active in Latin America on a larger scale, and the present, Social Democrats, Liberals, and Christian Democrats–conservatives have headed or participated in West European governments. The broad range of countries, each with their respective interests in Latin America as well as the different role of each of the parties within the respective Internationals, makes it difficult to draw general conclusions about transnational party influence on government and opposition policies and vice versa. However, by considering the political parties of countries that in the main have shaped West European official policy and—within the Internationals—transnational relations with Latin America, some basic assumptions can be made.

- From the viewpoint of the Latin American counterpart, an International is the more attractive, the more European members it has in government. Alignment with the strong is tempting, because congress declarations and resolutions reflect to a certain degree government standpoints, that is statements of intent are more likely to reach the stage of implemented policy.
- However, official foreign policy has underlying constraints that tend to run counter to transnational party influence on government policy. Apart from specific national interests, EC–EU foreign policy co-ordination and transatlantic relations within the Atlantic Alliance context are factors constituting the primary framework of foreign policy design for most West European countries.

- Transnational party associations may be a useful tool in allowing opposition forces to exert international influence and in demonstrating international solidarity in the context of domestic
intra- and inter-party debate.

In this context, the Latin American policy of three West European
EU and NATO member countries may be illustrative, though not
exhaustive.

Spain.   Prior to taking office in 1982, the Spanish socialist party
PSOE had already become prominent on the Latin American
scene.[30] The SI greatly helped PSOE in establishing international
contacts while still in opposition. In terms of socialist links with
Latin America, the interests of the SI and the PSOE were complementary. While the Spanish socialist party asked the SI for support in renewing their contacts with Latin America, the PSOE, as
a party directly involved in the successful transition from authoritarian to democratic rule in Spain, came to be the centre-piece of
the SI project for democracy in Latin America.

The inauguration of the Socialist term in government coincided
with the negotiations on Spanish EC membership and the redefinition of the terms under which the country had joined the Atlantic
Alliance. Such constraints on its external room for manœuvre
brought about a shift in PSOE's Latin American policy, towards a
position that adjusted to the overall European and Atlantic framework, and gradually moved away from SI positions. Thus once in
power, the government under Felipe González has been increasingly careful about any open involvement in Central American
issues. As an opposition party, in 1980, the PSOE agreed to head
the Socialist International's Committee for the Defence of the
Nicaraguan Revolution. Once in government, González avoided an
overly assertive posture that would have jeopardized the EC consensus on Central America, even though more than once he has
used indirect channels to circumvent constraints set by the US
influence on EC policy in the region. His personal role in supporting the democratization process in some Latin American countries
can hardly be overestimated.

France.   French foreign policy operates, in general, independently
of transnational party associations. The point of reference in con-
ducting foreign policy is—however vaguely defined—that of national
interest ultimately prevailing over France's European or Atlantic
commitments. In spite of increasing economic ties, French Latin

American policy has traditionally been characterized by the predominance of political rhetoric and symbolic gestures.[31] The French socialist government in particular developed a style in which periodic resort to the tradition of the French Revolution is combined with France's sensibilities *vis-à-vis* the 'oppressed' Third World. Thus, the French–Mexican declaration which recognized the Salvadorean FMLN as a 'representative political force' has to be seen in this context rather as a political message with a calculated short-term effect than as the pursuance of a specific long-term policy goal in Central America. However, the ideological discourse often ends where hard national interests come into play. The support given by the Mitterrand government to the United Kingdom during the Falkland Islands–Malvinas conflict, and the socialist refusal to endorse the SI calls for Puerto Rican independence, illustrate a French tendency to conservative nationalism whenever foreign policy touches upon its status as a former colonial power with territories in Latin America.

West Germany. In the case of the large West German political parties, the question is not so much about reciprocal influence, but about the overlapping identity of party and International. The SPD as well as the CDU dominate their respective transnational party organizations to such an extent that abroad the latter has often been identified with either one or the other West German party or their respective political foundations. However, as opposed to the CDU, West German social democrats have often been divided over SI policy towards Latin America.[32] SI positions are, indeed, most represented by the 'Euro-internationalist' wing of the SPD, which was headed by Willy Brandt until his death in October 1992. Moreover, as the initiator and single most important figure of the International's North–South campaign, Brandt came to be more strongly identified for his SI function rather than with the party he headed as honourable president. Having extended the SI into Latin America he became probably the most influential European politician in the region, without even being in government.

The 'realist' wing, headed by former chancellor Helmut Schmidt, rejected any revolutionary rhetoric and advocated political and developmental assistance to the Third World, often—as in the case of Central America—as a means of immunizing it against East–West rivalry. With its pragmatic and non-ideological approach, the Schmidt government did not hesitate to sign a nuclear power-plant contract with military-ruled Brazil, which provided it with the necessary know-how to develop a nuclear military capability if so desired. While this contract raised world-wide concern over the potential threat it implied to regional stability, the West German government primarily felt uneasy about the deal's negative impact on relations with Washington.

The alterations to West Germany's Central American policy after the change in government in 1982 served to highlight the FRG's foreign policy commitment to the Alliance and EC framework. Thus, the shift in West German policy towards more conservative positions largely followed the general trend in Western Europe; this was itself partially a result of the change in US policy *vis-à-vis* the region. In this sense, it is noteworthy that the EC embarked on a large-scale involvement in Central America at the initiative of the Liberal junior partner in the West German conservative government coalition and in co-operation with socialist-ruled France. Like no other joint action abroad, the EC dialogue with the countries of Central America raised US suspicion and anger about foreign meddling in its sphere of influence.[33]

However, government policy contrasted considerably with CDU activity within the Internationals. The FDP under Hans-Dietrich Genscher promoted an EC approach to Central America that was designed to demonstrate its distance from US policy, while in transnational party activity the CDU toed the US line. Thus, while supporting at governmental level EC efforts to steer the regional conflict clear of superpower rivalry, within ODCA Helmut Kohl echoed the US thesis of Soviet expansionism in Central America.[34]

The European Parliament

All the Internationals are represented in the European Parliament (EP) by political groups whose respective composition largely reflect that of membership in the particular International. Thus, the Socialist Group (SG) of the EP—with 198 seats in 1994, once again the largest group—is an associated organization of the SI. In the case of the CDI, the European People's Party (EPP)—once again the second largest faction—is a full member of the International. The IDU (from 1978 to 1983 purely European in make-up) is interesting chiefly for the minor EP role it performs for one of its largest and most influential members, the West German CDU, and has, at the European level, joined the Christian Democratic EPP.

Unlike the functions of a national parliament, the EP is not the legislative body of the Union. Its powers, though considerably broadened by the provisions of the Single European Act (SEA) of 1987, and the Maastricht Treaty of 1992, are limited to supervising the work of the Commission and Council, participation in the legislative process of the EC through consultation, as well as the approval of the budget. In terms of relations with third countries, the EP's consent is only required for the admission of a new member state and for association agreements. In the case of important commercial and co-operation treaties the EP has to be consulted (mandatory consultation) before the document is signed.

However, the Parliament's participation in shaping the Community's foreign policy can hardly be defined in terms of legal provisions. Instead, leverage is exerted through co-ordination with the Commission—wherever it comes into play—in order to jointly influence the Council's final decision, and by the increasing weight conferred upon the Parliament's opinion by third parties.[35] In both cases, consensus among the European deputies certainly plays an important role. Issues like the European Agricultural Policy have often prompted debates with divisions along national political lines, thus duplicating clashes which take place in the Council of Ministers. However, considerably more consensus can be found among members of the European Parliament on a broad range of foreign policy issues than in comparable national situations. Moreover, the very interdependence between consensus-building and the degree of influence on the Council's foreign policy decisions is in itself undoubtedly an important incentive for the EP to set aside national preferences and political differences.

The EC's co-operation agreement with Central America, which was signed in November 1985 and came into force in July 1987, is a case in point for policy co-ordination between the EP and the Commission. At all stages of its preparation the EP endorsed the Commission's proposal for a far-reaching co-operation agreement with the countries of the isthmus.[36] The Council of Ministers did not fully adhere to the position of Commission and Parliament. Yet one of the basic features of the EC–Central American dialogue and in particular the co-operation agreement—economic aid as a prerequisite for the promotion of peace and democracy in Central America—came in response to the basic ideas of a parliamentary resolution that had been approved in 1982.

As opposed to participation in the Community's legislative process, where the EP's activity is only of reactive character, i.e. it can state an opinion only on the basis of a Commission proposal, the EP possesses a set of instruments which it can use on its own initiative. This primarily involves resolutions, fact-finding missions, and inter-parliamentary contacts. Admittedly, these activities have produced no more than a limited impact on specific issues of the Council's foreign policy agenda.

However, the many resolutions through which the EP expresses its particular point of view as well as its various inter-parliamentary contacts have contributed to the shaping of a specifically EP foreign policy profile. In particular, the defence of human rights and continous efforts to remind the Union of its responsibility in assisting nascent democratic regimes have transformed the Parliament into the moral body of the EU and an important interlocutor for third parties' concerns. Two examples may illustrate this point.

The EP came to play a key role in the EC's support for the establishment of the Central American Parliament. MEPs threw their full support behind this initiative; in the wake of the Esquipulas II agreement they led the advocation of EC financial assistance for the setting-up of the regional body.[37] Moreover, more than once MEPs were prepared to promote and participate in an exchange of opinions and experience with Central American representatives involved in the creation of the regional Parliament.[38] In the case of the Chilean plebiscite held in October 1988, the EP even went so far as to explicitly welcome the Concertación de los Partidos Politicos por el No and to 'jointly express ... their rejection of Pinochet', provoking the harshest of protests from officials of the former regime.[39] Its outspoken rejection of the Pinochet dictatorship and unconditional support for Chile's democratic forces has transformed the EP into an important interlocutor for the new regime. Thus, the EP played a decisive role in both the creation of a special credit-line for the support of democracy in Chile and Central America, as well as in the Commission's proposal in 1989 for negotiations for a co-operation agreement with this country.[40]

The Political Foundations

Characterizing political foundations as a channel for the Internationals' party relations may be misleading in a double sense. First, foundations are national organizations; that is they represent the non-governmental policy of a certain country rather than that of a transnational party organization. Secondly, at least in the West

German case, the foundations (*Stiftungen*) are not political in character. Since all West German foundations are almost exclusively financed by public money, they are not allowed to conduct political activity, be it at home or abroad. That is, legally, there is no formal relationship between the political parties and the foundations.

Reality, however, is different. Not only are the West German foundations genuinely linked to political parties, but they can also be considered as the 'executive organs' of their political mother organization, allowing the party to participate to a certain extent in the domestic politics of another country at a non-governmental level without violating the rule of non-interference in inter-governmental relations.

Given their overwhelming protagonism in Latin America, it seems appropriate to concentrate on the German political foundations.[41] The activities of the FES (Friedrich Ebert Stiftung) and KAS (Konrad Adenauer Stiftung) are particularly impressive. In size alone the international department of the FES has the dimensions of a small foreign ministry. The Foundation's international work has traditionally concentrated on Africa and Latin America, the latter being allotted 31 per cent of the budget devoted to foreign activities in 1989.[42] Within the KAS's budget for international co-operation, Latin America is assigned over 50 per cent of the funds.[43] Broadly speaking, their operations in the Third World are devoted to the promotion of political pluralism and democratic development. Thus, among other activities, the foundations have helped to fund political, economic, and social development projects,[44] the building up or improvement of local media infrastructures,[45] education programmes, and research.[46]

Owing to their supposedly non-political character, foundations are required to co-operate with independent institutions abroad. However, these institutions or particular projects often serve or have been set up to provide the local partner with a proper medium to develop organizational structures and to transmit its political ideology. Indeed, the training of personnel and the stress on professionalism in party-building is usually of much greater importance than actual financing of party activities.

Concern in Latin America as well as in Bonn has at various times been raised over specific activities of the foundations. An example which may serve to illustrate the point was the 1987 allegation that the HSS (Hanns Seidel Stiftung) and KAS had interferred in Ecuador's internal affairs by financing Ecuador's main opposition party.[47] Other allegations with regard to KAS activities range from a substantial contribution to Duarte's electoral campaign in El Salvador to the supply of economic aid to the Nicaraguan resistance.[48] Similar concerns have been voiced with regard to the FES's financial support for the Instituto del Sandinismo in Managua.[49]

Many of these cases have been brought to trial; few of them, however, have been sufficiently clarified. The lack of public control tends occasionally to shed negative light on their activities abroad. However, perceptions which establish a direct link between the foundations' influence on political actors and the size of budget allotted to them falls short of reality. Experience in Latin America has demonstrated the competence and high motivation of the foundations' personnel working abroad. More than money, it is the possibility of contacting partners within their political, economic, and social environment that transforms the foundations into a very efficient tool of transnational party relations.

The Policy of Good Intentions

Obviously, the Internationals' support for democracy in Latin America is not limited to the simple test of admitting parties to the club of democratic associations. Size alone assigns the main Internationals the role of important allies, whose support of a specific party might contribute decisively to the political direction of a country in a process of profound political and social changes. This applied as much to SI support for the Sandinistas as to systematic Christian Democrat promotion of the Duarte option in El Salvador.

Yet there is an inherent contradiction in transnational party influence. Party Internationals are not free from constraints imposed by the international system. However, they are sometimes granted much broader room for manœuvre than governments, allowing them to experiment with new policies at a sub-governmental level. Undoubtedly, the North–South campaign of the SI set a trend which European governments successively integrated into their foreign policy.

However, it is precisely this room for manœuvre at a non-governmental level that tends to prompt political statements characterized by rhetorical over-commitment. This may not be a problem as long as member-parties are not in office and are not required to implement the policy they have been endorsing within the Internationals. However, once in government the emergence of national or international—rather than purely party–ideological—priorities usually encourages parties to adopt more pragmatic stances and to become less active in their respective party associations. The latter tends to create a further paradox: while member-parties holding government office increase the International's weight in principle, they do not necessarily strengthen influence. A case in point is the Latin American policy of the Spanish socialists, which has clearly moved away from the SI to be determined by the framework of the EPC.

An International can become even more constrained by the presence of some of its members in national governments. The Internationals' support for democracy in Central America—the endorsement of the Contadora initiative and, subsequently, the Esquipulas peace process—relied at any given moment on the member-parties involved in conflict settlement. Thus, for example, CDI and ODCA threw their full support behind the Christian Democrat government of Luis Herrera Campins in Venezuela at the onset of the Contadora process. But later on, the SI had to withdraw support simultaneous to the abandoning of the Contadora approach by its Venezuelan partner Carl Andrés Pérez. This factor, along with the conservative tide of West European governments' Central American policy and a parallel hardening of the US position on regional events, determined that the Internationals could not live up to their intention of influencing crucial stages of democratization in Latin America.

It is notable that inasmuch as the formerly purely European party associations have been opened up to Latin America, other regions play hardly any role in any of the four Internationals. However, the necessity of supporting parties allied with the regime even when their policies are not entirely congruent with the Internationals, and the need for inter- and intra-party consensus as well as foreign policy constraints imposed on European parties in power, are factors which make long-term policies for the Internationals in Latin America extremely difficult. Furthermore, the conflicts which had to be resolved within the respective organizations led to a much more limited influence on the outcome of democratization processes in Latin America than is often either suspected by their enemies or assumed by their friends. Once parties of the same International are in power in both regions, their respective policies become radically different and co-operation is reduced to good intentions.

Appendix: Latin American Parties' International Affiliations

TABLE 8.A1. *Party affiliations in Central America*

Country/Party	IS: SICLAC	LI: FELICA	CDI: ODCA	IDU
Guatemala				
DCG			full	
MAS				full
PSD	full			
UCN		full		
El Salvador				
AD		full		
MNR	full			
PDC			full	
Honduras				
PDCH			full	
PL		full		
PNH				full
Nicaragua				
PLI		full		
PNC				assoc.
PSC			full	
Costa Rica				
PLN	full			
PUSC			full	
Panama				
PDC			full	
PL		full	full	

Note: membership status—full or assoc(iated).

TABLE 8.A2. *Party affiliations in South America*

Country/Party	IS: SICLAC	LI: FELICA	CDI: ODCA	IDU
Argentina				
PDC			full	
Bolivia				
PDC			full	
MIR	cons.			
Brazil				
PDT	full			
PFL		obs.		
Chile				
PDC			full	
PR	full			
Colombia				
PDC			full	
PSC				full
Ecuador				
DP-UDC			full	
ID	full			
Paraguay				
PDC			full	
PLRA		full		
PRF	full			
Peru				
APRA	cons.			
PDC			full	
Surinam				
PPP			full	
Uruguay				
PDC			full	
Venezuela				
AD	full			
COPEI			full	

Note: membership status—cons(ultative), full, or obs(erver).

TABLE 8.A3. *Party affiliations in the Caribbean*

Country/Party	IS: SICLAC	LI: FELICA	CDI: ODCA	IDU
Aruba				
AVP			full	
MEP	cons.			
Barbados				
Labour P.	full			
Belize				
UDP				full
Cuba				
MDC			full	
Curaçao				
MAN	full			
PNU			full	
Dominica				
Freedom Party				full
Dominican Republic				
PL		full		
PRD	full			
PRSC			full	
Grenada				
NDC		obs.		
NNP				full
Guyana				
WPA	cons.			
Haiti				
PANPRA	cons.			
RVDP			full	
Jamaica				
JLP				full
PNP	full			
St Lucia				
PLP	cons.			
St Kitts and Nevis				
PAM				full
St Vincent and the Grenadines				
NDP				full
SVGLP	cons.			

Note: membership status—cons(ultative), full, or obs(erver).

Notes

1. A. Khol, 'Die Internationale Demokratische Union in Lateinamerika', *Zeitschrift für Lateinamerika Wien*, 33 (1987), 77–84 at 83.
2. For an overview see my article 'European Community Relations with Latin America: Policy without Illusions', *Journal of Interamerican Studies and World Affairs*, 19/4 (winter 1987–8), 69–87. For this particular context see also 'Las relaciones entre América Latina y Europa Occidental: Actores nacionales y transnacionales, objetivos y expectativas', *Foro Internacional*, 33/1 (1982), 39–57.
3. See for example T. Evers, 'Die westdeutsche Sozialdemokratie in Lateinamerika', in Forschungs- und Dokumentationszentrum Chile-Lateinamerika, *Sozial-demokratie und Lateinamerika* (Berlin: FDCL, 1982), 15–92; 23–30.
4. Cf Ch. 9, below, on the Christian Democrats, A. F. Williams, *La Internacional Socialista y América Latina: Una visión crítica* (Mexico City: UAM-Azcapotzalco, 1984); and L. Whitehead, 'International Aspects of Democratization', in G. O'Donnell, P. Schmitter, and L. Whitehead (eds.), *Transitions from Authoritarian Rule*, iii: 2–31.
5. U. Schoettli, 'Der internationale Liberalismus und Lateinamerika: Ein Beitrag zur demokratischen Solidarität', *Liberal*, 28/1 (Feb.), 19–29.
6. See Sections 2 and 3 below.
7. C. Jackisch, 'Las corrientes ideológicas europeas y su impacto sobre América Latina', *Contribuciones* (Buenos Aires, 1987), 27–47.
8. Ibid. 44–5.
9. T. A. Vasconi, 'La socialdemocracia en América Latina', mimeo, Socialist International.
10. A. F. Williams, 'El sur de América Latina y las Internacionales políticas europeas: La International Socialista y la International Demócrata Cristiana', in A. Borón and J. Faúndez (eds.), *Malvinas hoy: herencia de un conflicto* (Buenos Aires: Puntosur, 1989), 365–89 at 374.
11. Felipe González (of PSOE) has been vice-president of the SI since 1978 and Adolfo Suárez, leader of the Spanish Centro Democrático y Social (CDS), was elected president of the LI at the 1989 LI congress in Paris, only a year after the CDS had joined the International: S. Johnson, 'LI Congress Bears Witness to Today's Revolutions', *Liberal International Newsletter*, 52 (December 1989), 2–4.
12. U. Kopsch, 'Grenzen und Möglichkeiten transnationaler Parteienkooperation am Beispiel der Sozialistischen Internationale in Lateinamerika', *Zeitschrift für Lateinamerika Wien*, 33 (1987), 51–64; 53–4.
13. U. Schoettli, 'New Challenges for the LI in Latin America', *Liberal International Newsletter*, 49 (May 1989), 12–14.
14. 'Declaración conjunta de los presidentes de la International Demócrata Cristiana, International Liberal e Internacional Socialista sobre América Latina', *Desarrollo y Cooperación* (Bonn), 3 (1984), 3.
15. See, for example, the Final Resolution of the November 1980 Socialist Congress, *Socialist Affairs* (January–February 1981), 22.

16. J. C. Santucho, 'L'Internazionale Democratico Cristiana in America Latina', in Instituto per le relazioni tra l'Italia e i paesi dell'Africa, America Latina e Medio Oriente (IPALMO) (ed.), *America Latina, Europa, Italia: Un rapporto da rinnovare* (Rome: IPALMO, n.d.), 1–36 at 25–9. See also 'La DC se define contra Contadora', *El Día* (Mexico), 12 April 1986.

17. E. Mujal-León, 'European Socialism and the Crisis in Central America', *Orbis* (Philadelphia, Pa.; spring 1984), 53–81 at 68–9.

18. See the critical statement by Jürgen Wischnewski, member of an SI delegation that visited Central America in February 1986, in *Frankfurter Allgemeine Zeitung*, 15 February 1986.

19. See R. Combellas, 'ODCA, América Latina y Europa', *Contribuciones* (Buenos Aires, 1989), 35–7.

20. 'FELICA: El liberalismo se organiza en Centroamérica', *Perfiles Liberales* (Bogotá), 1 (April–June 1989), 12–13.

21. In addition, SICLAC includes two parties from the United States and one Canadian socialist party.

22. See the information about COPPPAL provided in *Nueva Sociedad*, 89 (May–June 1987), 82–6.

23. See the information about the CSL in *Nueva Sociedad*, 92 (November–December 1987), 95–100.

24. Six socialist parties from Argentina, Brazil, Chile, and Venezuela are members of COPPPAL and CSL. Out of these, only the Brazilian PDT is also a member of the SI.

25. W. Grabendorff, 'The Central American Crisis and Western Europe: Perceptions and Reactions' (Bonn: Research Institute of the Friedrich Ebert Stiftung, 1982), 52; 'The Party Internationals and Democracy in Central America', in L. W. Goodman, W. M. Leogrande, and J. Mendelson Forman (eds.), *Political Parties and Democracy in Central America* (Boulder, Colo.: Westview, 1992), 355–68.

26. Williams, 'El sur de América Latina', 380.

27. R. M. Goldman, 'Transnational Parties', 12.

28. P. Schori, *El desafío europeo en Centroamérica* (San José: EDUCA, 1982), 256.

29. See A. F. Williams, *La International Socialista y américa Latina: Una versión crítica* (Mexico: Universidad Autónoma Metropolitana, 1984), 267–73.

30. For an overview see E. Mujal-León, 'European Socialism', 56–8.

31. D. Moïsi, 'Mitterrand's Foreign Policy: The Limits of Continuity', *Foreign Affairs* (New York: winter 1981–2), 347–57 at 354–5.

32. See E. Mujal-León, 'The West German Social Democratic Party and the Politics of Internationalism in Central America', *Journal of Inter-American Studies and World Affairs*, 29/4 (winter 1987–8), 89–123 at 95–7.

33. For the German role in setting up the EC–Central American dialogue see K. Bodemer, *Europa occidental–América Latina: Experiencias y desafíos* (Barcelona: Alfa, 1987), 93–5. With regard to the effects

on the Atlantic Alliance see my article 'Central America: A Dilemma for European–US Relations?, *Harvard International Review*, 9/1 (November–December 1986), 37–9.

34. J. C. Santucho, 'L'Internazionale', 23.
35. D. Buchan, 'A Mandate which Goes Beyond 1992', *Financial Times*, 30 June 1989.
36. See G. Ashoff, *La Cooperación para el Desarrollo entre la Comunidad Europea y América Latina: Experiencias y desafíos*, Documento de Trabajo no. 16 (Madrid: IRELA, 1989), 26–9.
37. See the Resolution on Central America of 11 February 1988, repr. in Institute for European–Latin American Relations (IRELA), *The Central American Parliament: Alternatives for its Establishment and Elections*, dossier no. 24 (Madrid: IRELA, 1990), 33.
38. Instituto de Relaciones Europeo-Latinoamericanas (IRELA), *El futuro del Parlamento Centroamericano*, Informe de Conferencia CR-88/3 (Madrid: IRELA). See also W. Grabendorff, 'El Parlamento Europeo y el Parlamento Centroamericano', in J. Roy (ed.), *La Reconstrucción de Centroamérica: El Papel de la Comunidad Europea* (Miami: North–South Center, University of Miami, 1992).
39. European Parliament, 'Resolución sobre la situación en Chile', *Acta de Sesión* (Doc. A2–336/87/A) (Luxembourg: European Parliament Publications Office), 3–8. 'Firme rechazo a decisión de organismo europeo sobre Chile', *El Mercurio* (Santiago de Chile), 6 July 1988.
40. *Agence Europe* (Luxembourg–Brussels), 16–17 October 1989.
41. At present there are four foundations, each of which belongs to the same ideological camp as one of the four major parties of West Germany: the Friedrich Ebert Stiftung (FES), associated with the SPD; the Konrad Adenauer Stiftung (KAS), associated with the CDU; the Friedrich Naumann Stiftung (FNS), associated with the FDP; and the Hans Seidel Stiftung, associated with the Christian Social Union (CSU).
42. Friedrich-Ebert-Stiftung (FES), *Jahresbericht 1989* (Bonn: Presse- und Informationsstelle der FES, 1990), 58.
43. See, for example, Konrad-Adenauer-Stiftung, *Jahresbericht '86* (Bonn, n.d.), 91.
44. In Ecuador the FES started a project aimed at advising the government in its designing of the fiscal reform. For several years the KAS has been supporting the Guatemalan association of coffee-producers in their attempts to improve the marketing concept.
45. In 1987 the FES, for example, sent an expert to the Caribbean to advise members of the 'Caribbean Broadcasting Union' on building up a regional news network: FES, *Jahresbericht 1989*, 50.
46. This is, among other things, the function of the FES-founded Instituto Latinoamericano de Investigaciones Sociales (ILDIS) with branches in Ecuador, Venezuela, and Brazil, or the Centro Interdisciplinario de Estudios sobre el Desarrollo Latinamericano (CIEDLA) set up by the KAS in Buenos Aires, Argentina.

47. 'Parteienfinanzierung statt Entwicklungshilfe betrieben?', *Frankfurter Rundschau*, 16 May 1987.
48. S. Knauer, 'Die schwarzen Geschäfte', *Stern*, 4 (1987), 11. G. Selser, 'Las fundaciones alemanas, la democracia cristiana en América Latina y sus negocios en Ecuador y Nicaragua', *El Día* (Mexico), 15 February 1987.
49. Mujal-León, 'European Socialism', 94.

International Political Finance: The Konrad Adenauer Foundation and Latin America

MICHAEL PINTO-DUSCHINSKY

1. Introduction

The primary objective of this chapter is to start the process of mapping foreign sources of political funding in Latin America, focusing on the activities in Latin America of one donor organization, the Konrad Adenauer Foundation, based near Bonn. Although it is only one of a number of international bodies with a strong interest in Latin American politics, it can be used as a case-study to illustrate the way the foundations operate.

The subject of international political funding raises important questions for policy-makers. Is it legitimate for governments, companies, trade unions, private organizations, and individuals to give money (and other forms of assistance) to politicians in a foreign country?[1] Should such activities be characterized positively as 'promoting democracy', 'political education', or 'political aid'? Or is it more appropriate to use unflattering terms like 'interference', 'neo-colonialism', or even 'subversion'? Besides such moral questions, how can the effects of such foreign payments be evaluated? Do

I gratefully acknowledge financial support received from the British Foreign and Commonwealth Office (Policy Planning Staff and Overseas Development Administration), guest scholarships from the Woodrow Wilson International Center for Scholars, Washington DC, and facilities as a guest researcher provided by the Konrad Adenauer Foundation at its headquarters in 1989 and 1990. I also wish to thank present and past officials of the Foundation for providing documents and information in interviews. Most of the statistics in this chapter are based on these sources. I alone am responsible for any errors of fact and for the opinions expressed.

foreign donors frequently succeed in fulfilling their objectives or is intervention from abroad likely to prove ineffective or even counter-productive? Though these are vital matters, it is not possible to discuss them effectively without first obtaining information about the flows of money that are involved.

Apart from problems of evaluation, the task of obtaining information about international political funding presents obvious difficulties. In the past, foreign sources of money have often been secret (the problem of secrecy often applies to domestic funding as well). If research is restricted to donor and repicient countries and funding bodies from whom accurate information is most readily forthcoming, the results will inevitably be skewed.

A related problem is that of complexity. It is all too easy to oversimplify situations and judgements. Even within a single donor country or a single ministry within that country, political aid projects may be undertaken by a considerable number of different units and by separate (sometimes competing and unco-ordinated) organizations. Political bodies receiving foreign funding may also receive help from a large number of organizations from different countries. For example, in one small African country, a number of trade-union organizations from a variety of foreign countries recently found it necessary to meet with each other to ensure that they were not duplicating their assistance to a particular local trade-union federation.

An additional source of uncertainty arises from varying definitions of what constitutes political money. Here, too, the same question applies to internal as well as international sources. The study of political financing has traditionally concentrated on the funding of election campaigns (as in the United States) and on the financing of political parties (as in Germany). However, money may be given through other channels and yet be clearly intended to influence the political process. For instance, funds may be given to a political pressure-group or to an individual politician (rather than to his or her party organization).

Legal definitions of what constitutes 'political' as opposed to non-political funds vary from country to country. Moreover, a country's tax and other laws relating to political donations may not necessarily reflect the realities of political life. In practice, it may not be possible to determine whether a project is political without looking closely at its operation and without being privy to the intentions of recipients and donors. For example, in many countries there exist research centres which are legally independent from political parties but which, in practice, have links with a party. In some instances, the connection between research institute and party is so intimate that a donation to the institute is, in practice, like a payment to the parent party. Whether or not such payments are to be interpreted as political depends upon the facts of each case.[2]

Flows of political money across frontiers do not always involve single donor countries. Organizations providing political aid may pool their efforts. Therefore, a full picture would need to give an account of such co-ordinated ventures as well as of the work of international party and trade-union organizations. For purposes of simplicity, this chapter will use the term 'international funding' to refer to all money from abroad regardless of whether it comes from a private organization or an individual, from a single government, or from a body involving a number of countries.

2. The Main Actors

Before proceeding to a description of the particular foreign political grants that are the central subject of this chapter—those of the German Christian Democrats—it will be useful to mention four of the main foreign actors involved in funding Latin American politics.

The Superpowers

Struggles between the major world powers have for a long time led to their involvement in the internal politics of Latin American countries. Both world wars saw intense political warfare within the Americas inspired by the main combatants. The Cold War then led to competition between Soviet-backed and US-backed movements.

Our knowledge of Cold War operations in Latin America is distorted by limited access to information about Soviet activities compared to US involvement. Unlike its Soviet counterpart, the US press has frequently investigated its government's secret political undertakings. The fact that the United States has so many universities and such a large corps of political scientists means that the volume of research and of writing about anything American far exceeds publications about other nations. Moreover, former officials of the Central Intelligence Agency have been far more open and more inclined to publish than their counterparts in other secret services. Finally, US laws about the declassification of secret documents are somewhat more liberal than those of most other countries.

An assessment of various US involvements is complicated by the fact that the CIA has sometimes used other government departments, trade-union organizations, and private foundations as fronts for its activities. However, this does not mean that all or most of these bodies have been used in this way or that they are now being used in this way.

Latin American Countries

It would be wrong to assume that foreign sources of political money have always originated from outside Latin American or that Latin American countries have invariably acted as tools of extra-continental interests. Significant cross-frontier aid has moved from one Latin American country to another, but these activities have not always been productive. Argentina's attempt in the 1950s to create a continent-wide trade-union organization, CUSLA, proved abortive. But Latin American countries have sometimes been successfully involved in their neighbours' political affairs. In particular, Venezuelan politicians and organizations appear to have been especially active on the wider Latin American scene. For example, considerable funding for Napoleon Duarte's victorious campaign for the presidency of El Salvador in 1984 appears to have come from Venezuelan sources.

Church Organizations

Adherents of the Catholic Church vary not only in their political leanings but in the degree and nature of their political involvements. Any generalization about the political activities of the Catholic Church is particularly hazardous. Nevertheless, some Church-linked organizations with European connections have clearly played a major role in Latin American politics.

A significant development during recent decades is the allocation by several governments in Northern Europe of public funds to domestic-based church organizations for use in relief and other programmes abroad. It is reasonable to surmise that organizations which benefit from such grants have become more powerful in the world of Catholic politics, especially in view of the Vatican's reported financial problems.[3]

European Nations

Apart from the United States and the Soviet bloc, a variety of other countries have from time to time sponsored political projects in the Americas. A comprehensive picture would need to include Canadian activities (especially in the trade-union and human rights fields)[4] and, according to the US Department of State, the Libyan involvement. The most important foreign-funded political projects in Latin America, apart from those of the superpowers, seem to be those of some West European countries. These projects have often involved the Church-related European organizations mentioned above. Italian, Belgian, Dutch, and—above all—German bodies have been important participants.

3. Latin America and German Political Foundations

There have long existed communities of Germans in Latin America. At various times, they have had an impact on the internal politics of Latin America. Therefore it is not surprising that, when the West German government set up its development ministry, Bundesministerium für wirtschaftliche Zusammenarbeit (BMZ), in 1961, it gave considerable attention to Latin America. A feature of West German development aid was its use of German non-governmental organizations as channels for foreign aid. The BMZ started to give increasingly generous grants both to relief organizations linked with the main German churches and to foundations connected with the political parties represented in the Bundestag.[5] These German bodies subsequently used the money for foreign projects, some in Latin America.

The work of German church organizations such as the Catholic Bishops' Fund, Misereor, will not be considered in this chapter. Although, formally, the activities of Misereor are not political, they have sometimes plainly been of political importance in aiding anti-Communist bodies in Latin American countries. For example one can note the role of Misereor in Chile in the years preceding Eduardo Frei's election as president in 1964.

The oldest of the German political foundations (*Stiftungen*) is the Friedrich Ebert Foundation. It was set up in 1925 as an educational body linked with the German Social Democratic Party. It was banned in 1933 and re-established in 1947. By 1957 the Ebert Foundation was using money from the West German foreign ministry for its work with the organization of anti-Communist trade unions in Latin America, ORIT. As part of the German Social Democratic Party network, the Ebert Foundation had close connections with the West German trade-union federation, DGB. This federation had been set up after the Second World War with the assistance of the American union federations (the AFL and the CIO) and the US Central Intelligence Agency. By the 1950s the US and German union federations were both active in the world organization of anti-Communist unions, the International Confederation of Free Trade Unions (ICFTU), ORIT being the Latin American branch of this confederation.

The Ebert Foundation's earliest activities in the international field consisted mainly of courses and scholarships in Germany for foreign unionists and politicians. In the early 1960s its international projects were rapidly extended. Foundations linked with the other political parties represented in the Bundestag started similar activities. They too received almost all the funds used for these overseas projects from governmental sources.

In the early 1960s the use of political foundations as channels for the West German government's assistance to foreign political organizations developed for a number of reasons. In the late 1950s the USA had been pressing Adenauer's Christian Democratic government to give more money towards the costs of stationing American troops in West Germany. As an alternative to this US demand, the West German government agreed to contribute to the Western anti-Communist effort by building up its programme of development aid.[6]

From 1962 the BMZ gave regular grants to the political foundation linked with each major political party: the Friedrich Ebert Foundation (Social Democrat), the Konrad Adenauer Foundation (Christian Democratic Union), and the Friedrich Naumann Foundation (Free Democrats). It was not until the mid-1970s that the Bavarian Christian Social Union's political foundation, the Hans Seidel Foundation, started to receive grants from the BMZ for overseas projects. Each foundation, although legally independent from its parent party, is, in practice, closely linked with it by interlocking directorates. The funds allocated by the BMZ had the twin objectives of promoting 'socio-political education' and of supporting 'social structures' the Third World. The Konrad Adenauer Foundation's official statement of its aims and objectives was 'for furthering and promoting democratic and political education on a Christian basis'.[7]

In addition to these formal aims, the *Stiftungen* seem to have had some additional functions. In accordance with the Hallstein doctrine (which linked West German diplomatic relations with foreign countries' refusal to recognize East Germany), West Germany felt compelled in the 1960s to counteract Communist influence in the Third World. At a time when memories of the Nazi era were still fresh, and when many West German ambassadors in Latin America had started their careers under Hitler, aid for democracy-building was thought to be more acceptable abroad if it came in the name of political parties rather than from the German government. Above all, the use of German party foundations arguably permitted the Federal Republic to become a force in world politics without creating alarm.[8]

The regular deployment of German political foundations as intermediaries for the German government's international political payments began at a time of heightened tension in Latin America. Following the rise of the Castro regime in Cuba, and the American failure in 1961 to overthrow the regime by the guerrilla action at the Bay of Pigs, President John Kennedy's administration in Washington feared the spread of Castroism and of Soviet influence in Latin America. Chile and Venezuela appeared to present vulnerable and tempting targets for the Communists. As part of their anti-Communist effort, the US authorities sought help from various European allies. The European Social Democrats and the International Confederation of Free Trade Unions could help the anti-Communist left in Latin America, particularly in urban areas.

Another task was to counteract Communist influence in rural areas and in slums where inhabitants had no regular places of work. Here, the population was likely to heed a Christian Democrat message. The formation of rural co-operative movements and Church-linked political organizations had been tried out by the Catholic Church in Italy as part of the anti-Communist strategy in that country. By the early 1960s, Christian Democracy was also beginning to enjoy growing popularity in parts of Latin America. Though the rhetoric and policies of many Christian Democrats were frequently anti-American and radical, it was usually anti-Communist too.

European Christian Democrats thus became active, with tacit US approval,[9] in aiding their Latin American counterparts. In particular, they had a role in helping Eduardo Frei, the Christian Democrat candidate, in his fight for the Chilean presidency in 1954. This election's importance stemmed from the threat from Salvador Allende. Some of the techniques of political organization that had been tested by the Christian Democrats in Europe were now exported to Latin America. Institutes linked with Chancellor Adenauer's Christian Democrat Union (the Institute for International Solidarity and the Political Academy Eichholz) became and remained the most active of the German political foundations on that continent.

TABLE 9.1. *Foreign expenditure of the German party foundations from BMZ funds, by continent (DM m.)*

	Konrad Adenauer Stiftung		Friedrich Ebert Stiftung		Friedrich Naumann Stiftung		Hans Seidel Stiftung		All	
	1963–72	1983–8	1963–72	1983–8	1963–72	1983–8	1963–72	1983–8	1963–72	1983–8
Africa	9	73	54	101	13	37	—	95	76	306
Asia	16	83	36	119	6	60	—	87	57	349
Latin America	76	241	15	127	8	73	—	35	99	477
Europe and North America	—	26	—	45	—	32	—	16	—	120
SUB-TOTAL	101	425	105	392	27	202	—	233	—	1,252
Supra-regional	7	24	26	67	4	6	—	4	37	101
TOTAL	108	449	131	459	31	208	—	237	270	1,353

Note: Supra-regional includes headquarters costs for 1963–72 but not for 1983–8.
Source: Ministry for Economic Co-operation documents.

As shown in Tables 9.1 and 9.2, in the early years the Adenauer Foundation's activities concentrated on Latin America, whereas the other German political foundations focused on different areas of the world. In 1963–72, three-quarters of the Adenauer's expenditure was for Latin America, compared with under one-third of Naumann's (Free Democrat) spending and under 15 per cent of Ebert's (Social Democrat) spending. Gradually, the territorial divisions between the different German *Stiftungen* became less marked, though Latin America has remained the continent where the Adenauer Foundation has concentrated its activities.[10] In 1983–8 the percentages devoted to Latin America by each *Stiftung* were as follows: Adenauer—57, Ebert—32, Naumann—36, Seidel—15.[11]

In the first ten years after the system of regular grants to the political foundations was introduced by the BMZ (1963–72), DM99 million—DM10 million per annum—was channelled by the ministry through the foundations to Latin America. By 1983–8 the *Stiftungen* were spending DM80 million per annum in Latin America. Between 1962 and 1990, the German *Stiftungen* spent DM1.3–1.4 billion (approximately US$750 million) in Latin America.[12]

The totals spent by each *Stiftung* in every country in Latin America and the Caribbean between 1983 and 1988 are shown in Table 9.3. Though the statistics give a good impression of the scale of activities and of the areas where they are concentrated, they need to be treated with care. The foundations—particularly Ebert—sometimes administer projects on a regional basis. Thus, the absence of a listing of expenditure by Ebert in Nicaragua does not mean that it was inactive in that country. Further statistics for Adenauer Foundation projects in 1989 are given in Table 9.4.

From the beginning, the Adenauer Foundation's programme in Latin America was intended to support a network of Christian Democrat parties and of ancilliary political organizations. In July 1961 the significance of Latin America for international Christian Democrat politics was symbolized by the fact that the Christian Democrats of Chile acted as host to the congress that established the World Union of Christian Democrats (later to be called the Christian Democrat International). The three main blocs that combined to form the new World Union were: first, a series of European Christian Democrat parties which had formed an organization in 1947 called Nouvelles Équipes Internationales (NEI); second, a rather dubious group of exiled politicians organized into the Christian Democratic Union of Central Europe (CDUCE); and third, an organization of Latin American Christian Democrat affiliates named

TABLE 9.2. *Foreign expenditure of the German party foundations from BMZ funds, by continent, as a percentage of total expenditure*

	Konrad Adenauer Stiftung		Friedrich Ebert Stiftung		Friedrich Naumann Stiftung		Hans Seidel Stiftung		All	
	1963–72	1983–8	1963–72	1983–8	1963–72	1983–8	1963–72	1983–8	1963–72	1983–8
Africa	9	17	51	26	48	18	—	41	33	28
Asia	16	20	34	30	22	30	—	37	24	28
Latin America	75	57	14	32	30	36	—	15	42	38
Europe and North America	—	6	—	13	—	16	—	7	—	10
TOTAL	100	100	100	100	100	100	100	100	100	100

Note: Excludes supra-regional expenditures.
Source: Ministry for Economic Co-operation documents.

TABLE 9.3. *Expenditure of the German party foundations in Latin America and the Caribbean, 1983–1988 (DM m. of BMZ funds)*

	Konrad Adenauer Stiftung	Friedrich Ebert Stiftung	Friedrich Naumann Stiftung	Hans Seidel Stiftung	All
Argentina	22.0	8.9	4.8	3.4	39.1
Barbados	0.03	—	—	—	0.03
Belize	0.1	—	—	—	0.1
Bolivia	6.4	5.8	—	2.5	14.7
Brazil	14.4	5.6	10.6	1.7	32.2
Chile	24.8	9.8	2.2	2.6	39.4
Colombia	16.8	6.7	6.0	—	29.5
Costa Rica	9.8	26.6	1.5	3.8	33.4
Curaçao	2.2	—	—	—	2.2
Dominica	1.1	—	—	—	1.1
Dominican Rep.	5.9	3.8	1.6	1.5	12.9
Ecuador	15.5	12.6	1.5	3.8	33.4
El Salvador	16.9	—	—	0.8	17.9
Grenada	0.4	—	—	—	0.4
Guatemala	20.3	2.3	4.9	1.6	28.7
Haiti	0.9	—	0.03	—	0.9
Honduras	3.0	3.8	2.8	—	9.6
Jamaica	5.1	4.2	—	—	9.3
Mexico	3.0	7.1	6.7	—	16.8
Nicaragua	9.2	—	0.5	—	9.7
Panama	2.4	—	2.5	—	4.9
Paraguay	4.0	—	2.0	4.5	10.4
Peru	22.4	8.1	9.0	—	39.4
Uruguay	2.3	2.7	3.1	4.3	12.4
Venezuela	32.7	7.3	1.1	4.2	45.3
Regional TOTAL	—	12.0	5.2	0.2	17.1

Note: The totals for some countries, such as Venezuela and Costa Rica, are enlarged by the fact that they serve as a base for regional projects. The figures include the costs of the foundations' field representatives.
Source: Ministry for Economic Co-operation documents.

ODCA (Organización Demócrata Cristiana de América). Until the early 1960s, ODCA had been poorly organized, but it expanded its activities with European assistance.[13]

The two most active members of ODCA were the Chilean and Venezuelan Christian Democratic parties, between which there was rivalry for the leadership of ODCA. The Adenauer Foundation soon began to give grants to organizations linked to both parties

TABLE 9.4. *Konrad Adenauer Foundation expenditure in Latin America, by country, 1989*

	Expenditure (DM m.)	Number of German field-workers	Number of projects
Argentina	4.8	4	7
Bolivia	1.5	2	5
Brazil	2.6	4	7
Chile	4.3	3	11
Colombia	2.35	3	8
Costa Rica	1.4	1	3
Curaçao	0.5	—	1
Dominica	0.3	—	3
Dominican Republic	1.0	1	3
Ecuador	2.4	1	7
El Salvador	2.9	2	8
Grenada	0.04	—	1
Guatemala	3.9	2	6
Haiti	0.3	1	1
Honduras	0.15	—	1
Jamaica	0.6	1	1
Mexico	0.6	1	2
Nicaragua	2.0	1	7
Panama	0.6	1	1
Paraguay	0.8	1	3
Peru	3.65	4	10
St Lucia	0.2	—	1
Uruguay	0.8	1	2
Venezuela	4.4	2	4
TOTAL	42.3	36	103

Note: Column 1 includes costs of German field representatives; column 2 excludes locally employed staffs.
Source: Konrad Adenauer Foundation report.

as well as to ODCA. In the early 1960s ODCA headquarters was in Santiago de Chile and it later moved to Caracas. As described below, the organization of Christian trade unionists (CLASC) was also to move from Santiago to Caracas. The Adenauer Foundation stationed its first field representatives in Chile and in Caracas.

From 1963 the Adenauer Foundation financed an institute of political education for ODCA, called IFEDEC (Instituto de Formación Demócrata Cristiana). Based in Caracas, it was intended to stimulate the organization of Christian Democrat parties throughout the continent, to aid the Venezuelan Christian Democratic party

(COPEI), and to provide services to the headquarters of ODCA. In addition, the *Stiftung* subsidized a series of similar institutes which were designed to train Christian Democrat cadres in different parts of the continent.[14] Between 1969 and 1974 the Adenauer Foundation spent DM15.4 million from BMZ funds on these projects.

The Adenauer Foundation also invested heavily in the Latin American movement of Christian trade unions. These unions were organized into a continental organization, CLASC, which was part of a world-wide Christian union movement, the International Federation of Christian Trade Unions (IFCTU, not to be confused with its Social Democrat counterpart, the ICFTU). In order to widen its appeal the 'Christian' label was later removed from both titles, the IFCTU becoming the World Confederation of Labour and, in 1971, the Latin American branch being renamed CLAT (Central Latinoamericano de Trabajadores).[15]

As with its strategy regarding party-building, the Adenauer Foundation's approach to fostering Christian trade unions was to support a series of training institutes. In the early 1960s the main Adenauer-sponsored institute, responsible for the entire continent, was called IIES (Instituto Internacional de Estudios Sociales) and was jointly based in Chile and Venezuela. It was then recast as the Venezuela-based ILATES. In 1974 ILATES was combined with two other projects to form the ambitious UTAL (Universidad de los Trabajadores de América Latina). This was quartered in a set of residential buildings at San Antonio de los Altos near Caracas, formerly operated by the Salesian Order. By 1975 UTAL's pay-roll of teachers, researchers, administrators, and domestic helpers had risen to 56. Members, officials, and likely recruits of Christian trade unions were brought from all over Latin America to attend seminars and courses. These included strategy seminars for officials, courses and meetings designed for unions representing particular industries, and courses designed to teach skills such as press relations and propaganda.

Besides UTAL, in the 1960s the Konrad Adenauer Foundation started to finance other institutes responsible for Christian trade unions in groups of countries or in individual countries. Between 1969 and 1974 the Foundation spent DM25.9 million on eleven union projects.[16]

Apart from minor variations in the partner institutes, the *Stiftung*'s funding of Christian Democratic and Christian trade-union institutes has remained remarkably stable since the 1960s. The totals contributed have grown considerably. In 1986 the Adenauer Foundation spent DM8.4 million on its projects linked with

TABLE 9.5. *Konrad Adenauer Foundation: Grants to Christian Democratic organizations and to institutes connected with Christian Democratic parties in Latin America, 1986*

Region/ Country	Organization receiving grant	Size of grant (DM '000s)	Party connected to organization receiving grant
Latin America	ODCA (Organisación Demócrata Cristiana de América)	762	Latin American member parties
	IFEDEC (Instituto de Formación Demócrata Cristiana)	1,404	ODCA (the Latin American regional organization of the Christian Democrat International)
Belize	BEWESO (Belize Welfare Society)	70	Christian Democratic Party
Bolivia	INADEC (Instituto de Aprendizaje Demócrata Cristiana)	120	Christian Democratic Party of Bolivia
Chile	ICHEH (Instituto Chileno de Estudios Humanísticos)	1,090	Christian Democratic Party
Costa Rica	INDEP (Instituto de Estudios Políticos)	338	Partido Union Social Cristiano
Dominican Republic	IFP (Instituto de Formación Política)	320	Partido Revolucionario Social Cristiano
Ecuador	FESO (Fundación Ecuatoriana de Estudios Sociales)	700	Democracia Popular
El Salvador	ISEP (Instituto Salvadoreno de Estudios Políticos)	640	Christian Democratic Party
Guatemala	INCEP (Instituto Centroamericano de Estudios Políticos)	501	(This organization was for Guatemala and Honduras in 1986)
	IGESP (Instituto Guatemalteco de Estudios Políticos)	124	Christian Democratic Party
Nicaragua	INCESP (Instituto Nicaraguense de Estudios Sociales y Políticos)	65	Social Christian Party

Panama	ECAM (Escuela Campesina)	440	Christian Democratic Party
Uruguay	IFIPED (Democracia Popular)	80	Christian Democratic Party
Venezuela	C 21 (Conciencia 21)	470	COPEI (Christian Democratic Party

Notes: Totals include salaries and costs of German field representatives (normally about 20 per cent of the project).
The statistics are of the budgeted sums.
Source: Konrad Adenauer Foundation document.

Latin American Christian Democratic parties and DM7.1 million on projects involving the CLAT unions. These totals include the expenses of German field-workers responsible for the projects. Since the early 1960s the Foundation's regular payments have made it a mainstay both of ODCA and of the CLAT trade unions. The *Stiftung*'s projects in 1989 relating to Christian Democratic parties and to CLAT unions are shown in Tables 9.5 and 9.6.

Although projects involving parties and unions are arguably the most central of the Adenauer Foundation's undertakings in Latin America, there are several other types of project, for instance with employers' associations, political research institutes, the media, and co-operatives. These other types of project are especially useful in some countries where military dictators and juntas make it hard to sustain activity that is openly seen as involving political parties. They are useful in countries where Christian Democratic parties and Christian unions are weak and where the Foundation must look for other partners. The Adenauer Foundation's projects in a country typically include several different but complementary categories. The multi-layered approach is illustrated by the examples of the Foundation's work in Nicaragua and El Salvador given in Table 9.7.

According to the rules of the BMZ, projects of the German political foundations may not consist of general-purpose financial aid to unions, parties, or election campaign funds. The regulations specify that the aid must be tied to specific party or union activities such as research or training. The main focus of the German political foundations is, therefore, on the middle-term and long-term building of political institutions.

Nevertheless, German aid has in some past cases been of direct, short-term assistance to specific election campaigns. First, the *Stiftung*-funded party institutes have frequently trained some of the main campaign organizers of partner parties. Secondly, in the

TABLE 9.6. *Konrad Adenauer Foundation: Grants to institutes connected with Christian trade unions*

Region / Country	Organization receiving grant	Size of grant (DM '000s)	Trade union connected to organization receiving grant
Latin America (based in Venezuela)	UTAL (Universidad de los Trabajadores de América Latina)	2,150	CLAT (Central Latinoamericano de Trabajadores) (Latin American branch of the World Confederation of Labour)
Caribbean (based in Curaçao)	INFOSCAR (Instituto de Formación Social del Caribe)	625	The Caribbean branch of UTAL
Central America (based in Costa Rica)	ICAES (Instituto Centroamericano de Estudios Sociales)	1,220	The Central American branch of UTAL
Andean region (based in Peru)	INANDES (Instituto Andino de Estudios Sociales)	150	Works mainly in Peru
Southern Cone (based in Buenos Aires)	INCASUR (Instituto de Capacitación del Sur)	1,370	Branch of UTAL for the Southern Cone
Colombia	INES (Instituto Nacional de Estudios Sociales)	450	Confederación General del Trabajo
Dominican Republic	INFAS (Instituto de Formación Agraria Sindical)	500	Confederación Autónoma Sindical Clasista
Ecuador	INEFOS (Instituto Nacional Ecuatoriano de Formación Social)	700	Central Ecuatoriana de Organizaciones Clasistas

Source: Konrad Adenauer Foundation document.

TABLE 9.7. *Konrad Adenauer Foundation: Projects in El Salvador and Nicaragua, 1989, by type of project*

	Nicaragua	El Salvador
Political education (i.e. aid to Christian Democratic parties)	INCESP[a]	ISEP[a]
Policy advice		ISAM
		CENITEC
Trade unions	CTN[b]	INEFOS[b]
Employers' and professional associations	INIESEP	
	CONAPRO	AMPES
Co-operative organizations		FUNDE
Media	Radio Católica	Radio Cadena Libertad
Churches	Community work	
Human rights	CPDH	
Universities		UNIPAZ
Cultural		ICAL

Notes: [a] See Table 9.5.
    [b] See Table 9.6.
    ISAM—Instituto Salvadoreño de Administración Municipal.
    CENITEC—Centro de Investigaciones Tecnológicas y Cientificos.
    INIESEP—Instituto de Investigación Económica y Sociales de la Empresa Privada.
    CONAPRO—Confederación Nicaraguense de Asociaciones Profesionales.
    AMPES—Asociación de Medianos y Pequeños Empresarios Salvadoreños.
    FUNDE—Fundación Nicaraguense de Desarrollo.
    CPDH—Permanent Human Rights Commission.
    UNIPAZ—Universidad de La Paz.
    ICAL—Instituto de Cultura y Arte Latinoamericano (under the aegis of the political education institute INCESP).
Source: Konrad Adenauer Foundation document.

past, German electoral experts have been sent on short-term secondments as campaign advisers. Thirdly, there are unconfirmed reports that, at least in some exceptional cases in the 1960s, the work of the *Stiftungen* in Latin America was supplemented by grants to favoured candidates from secret and separate German sources.[17] But it should be stressed that such additional payments, if indeed they existed, would have been separate from the foundations' projects and probably unknown to the foundations' field representatives.

Apart from its money from the BMZ (and further grants for use in industrialized and socialist countries from the German Foreign Ministry), the Konrad Adenauer Foundation has raised independent funds, apparently on a relatively small scale, as 'solidarity' payment, typically to exiled Christian Democratic leaders. Their aid to exiled politicians has been a significant part of the work of several of the German *Stiftungen*.

As shown in the tables, a notable feature of the Konrad Adenauer Foundation's Latin American operations is their scope. In 1989 the *Stiftung*'s permanent field representatives were present in nineteen Latin American and Caribbean countries. Its most costly operations (totalling at least DM3.5 million in each country in 1989) were based in Argentina, Venezuela, Chile, Guatemala, and Peru. The Foundation spent at least DM2 million in each of the following: El Salvador, Brazil, Ecuador, Colombia, and Nicaragua. Relative to their populations, the Foundation's activities in 1989 were most heavily concentrated in El Salvador, Nicaragua, Costa Rica, the Dominican Republic, and Guatemala, followed by Chile, Bolivia, Ecuador, and Venezuela.

Chile

In its earliest days, the Adenauer Foundation was involved in helping the Christian Democrats in the lead-up to the presidential election of 1964, although the Foundation's overseas organization was still in its infancy at the time and probably was not the only West German organization involved. During the quarter-century between Eduardo Frei's victory in that year and Patricio Aylwin's successful campaign as Christian Democrat candidate for the presidency in 1989, the Adenauer Foundation has been a constant force behind the Chilean Christian Democrats. Its efforts have sometimes caused controversy within the Foundation itself and have had uneven effects.

In the years following Frei's election in 1964, there were complaints at the Foundation's headquarters that some of the projects in Santiago had been unduly side-tracked by disruptive, left-wing elements within the Chilean Christian Democratic movement. The attempt to aid Frei in building a centrist political organization was therefore regarded as a failure, especially after the Christian Democrat defeat by Salvador Allende in the 1970 presidential election. When Allende was ousted in 1973, there seems to have been renewed controversy within the Foundation about what attitude it should adopt towards the Pinochet regime. In general, field representatives (both in Chile and, on other occasions, elsewhere) appear to have favoured more radical stances than the *Stiftung* leadership.

During most of the period of military rule under Pinochet, the *Stiftung* aimed to sustain Christian Democrat politicians in readiness for the time when competitive party politics could resume. The Foundation's approach was to back a series of research institutes, co-operatives, and self-help organizations whose activities were permitted because, formally, they were independent of party connections. According to an internal Adenauer Foundation report of 1985, it was a monthly meeting of the Chilean Christian Democratic party which co-ordinated eight projects, funded by the Foundation, ranging from an agrarian institute (Instituto de Promoción Agraria) and a self-help project for slum-dwellers (Acción Vecinal y Comunitaria), to three academic institutes (Instituto Chileno de Estudios Humanísticos, Corporación de Promoción Universitaria, and Fundación Eduardo Frei).[18]

The sustained aid given to such Christian Democrat-linked bodies in the final years of the Pinochet regime contrasts with the shorter-term, more limited political aid supplied by the United States. It is no coincidence that it was the Adenauer Foundation that organized Aylwin's high-level diplomatic tour of Europe during the final stages of the 1989 presidential election campaign, which he subsequently won.

Venezuela

As in Chile, the Adenauer connection with the country's Christian Democratic party, COPEI, dates back to the early 1960s. Although political parties in Venezuela have been able to rely on more generous domestic contributions than their counterparts in most other Latin American countries, German support has nevertheless been significant. A highlight of the Konrad Adenauer Foundation's work was its backing for the 1968 presidential campaign of Rafael Caldera of COPEI, who became president of Venezuela in 1969. The Foundation's staff organized extensive training courses before the campaign, designed to build up Christian Democrat cadres. Prominent West German political scientists from Cologne University (schooled in the survey research methods taught at the University of Michigan) provided advice on polling and strategy.

Assistance for survey research was still a feature of the Adenauer Foundation's Venezuelan programme in the late 1980s. Since 1974 it had supported a research organization named Conciencia 21 (a component of the Fundación Humanismo Integral). One of Conciencia 21's functions was to carry out studies of voting and mass media for the benefit of COPEI.

The Adenauer Foundation's most important links with COPEI are based in common support for the previously mentioned Latin American Christian Democrat organizations, headquartered in Venezuela. The three principal Adenauer projects in Venezuela have involved support for the umbrella organization of Latin American Christian Democrats (ODCA) and for its training institute (IFEDEC), and the financing of the Latin American organization of Christian trade unionists—CLAT.[19]

Guatemala

The election of the Christian Democrat Vicinio Cerezo as president led to a rapid expansion of the Adenauer Foundation's activities in Guatemala in the late 1980s.[20] Cerezo's personal connections with the Foundation dated back to his student days. There was a strong—but not universal—feeling at the *Stiftung* headquarters that a heavy commitment of money could ensure that the new president received the expert advice needed to enable him to exercise power in the face of the forces of the military.

One of the main vehicles used by the Adenauer Foundation was the Asociación de Investigación y Estudios Sociales (ASIES, part of the Fundación Centroamericano do Desarrollo). ASIES aimed to provide advice on legislation, economic expertise, and advice to ministers. The *Stiftung* funded several additional projects. The Instituto Guatemalteco de Estudios Socio-Políticos (IGESP) was a training institute for Guatemalan Christian Democrat cadres. This institute was part of a Guatemala-based organization with responsibility for Christian Democrat political education in several Central American countries (Instituto Centroamericano de Estudios Políticos—INCEP). A programme at the Catholic University Rafael Landívar was intended to promote curricula and expertise in the West German 'social market' approach. In the trade-union field, the Adenauer Foundation backed the Instituto Guatemalteco de Estudios y Formación Social (IGEFOS), linked with the Guatemalan member of CLAT, the Central General de Trabajadores de Guatemala. From 1986 the Foundation supported another organization which represented fifty-seven coffee-growers' co-operatives.

These projects failed to solve a central problem of Guatemalan politics: how to control the military and its death squads, although the Foundation did organize meetings about the question. The *Stiftung* found itself in the awkward position of backing a president who had become subject to strong, public criticism from the United

States government for the abuses of human rights which continued under his regime.

4. The Effectiveness of German Political Aid to Latin America

In a recent work on *Exporting Democracy: The United States and Latin America*, Abraham Lowenthal has suggested that

recurrent efforts by the government of the United States to promote democracy in Latin America have rarely been successful . . . From the turn of the century until the 1980s, the overall impact of U.S. policy on Latin America's ability to achieve democratic politics was usually negligible, often counterproductive and only occasionally positive.[21]

Do Lowenthal's negative conclusions also apply to parallel German efforts and, in particular, to those of the Konrad Adenauer Foundation? It will not be possible to give a firm answer to this question until a series of detailed case-studies has been carried out. Even then, there are likely to be varying judgements on different projects and on the role of foreign political aid in different Latin American countries. After making these caveats I turn to an analysis of the impact of the German interventions.

First, although Christian Democratic parties have won elections or have entered coalition governments in several Latin American countries, the hopes of the 1960s for the spread of Christian Democracy have largely been disappointed. The Adenauer Foundation has been obliged to recognize this by abandoning its earlier policy of financing only Christian Democrats. By 1989 the Foundation had non-Christian Democrat partners in Argentina, Brazil, Colombia, Dominica, Grenada, and Jamaica.[22] The Foundation was by now a member of the Conservative International and the International Democrat Union, as well as of the Christian Democrat International. In Nicaragua, the *Stiftung* backed Violeta Chamorro's presidential campaign, even though she was not the official candidate of the local Christian Democrat party.

Secondly, the Adenauer Foundation's long-standing (one might even say long-suffering) support for CLAT has not resulted in any obvious advance of its affiliated Christian trade unions. These remain marginal and fragmentary in most countries. In 1990 the CLAT unions represented at the Congress of the World Confederation of Labour could claim a combined membership of only 277,000. Apart from Venezuela, the total membership in the rest of Latin

America and the Caribbean was only 143,000. These statistics are unreliable and possibly incomplete, but they appear to represent a considerable fall in membership since the early 1970s.

Apart from their small memberships, the CLAT unions appear to remain dependent upon foreign money. In the 1950s the budget of CLASC (CLAT's predecessor) was minuscule. It rose rapidly in the early 1960s following the establishment in 1958 of an 'International Solidarity Fund' by the world organization of Christian trade unions, based in Europe (as mentioned earlier, it was then titled the IFCTU and was later renamed the WCL). The increase in this European source of funding may have been a response to the challenge of Castroism. With help from the IFCTU, CLASC's budget rose from under $30,000 in 1960 to $450,000 by 1964. By 1966 IFCTU's total solidarity fund contribution to the CLASC was $618,402. The IFCTU reportedly raised its solidarity funds from its European member unions, but the ultimate source of the money is uncertain.[23]

With the exception of operating grants to CLASC from the IFCTU, CLASC's training institutes, which were developed in the 1960s, were almost entirely funded by the Adenauer Foundation, with occasional supplements from Dutch, Belgian, Irish, and Canadian sources. Almost none of the funds came from membership subscriptions or from Latin American sources. Between 1967 and 1969, 85 per cent of the costs of the CLAT's central training institute came from Adenauer grants (which, in turn, came from the BMZ). Despite repeated efforts to develop independent sources of funding, in 1987 the UTAL—CLAT's Latin American workers' university— was still dependent upon the Adenauer Foundation for 60 per cent of its income and on other foreign sources for a further 22 per cent.[24]

In view of these facts, the CLAT could—at first sight—be caricatured as an insignificant set of organizations propped up by overseas money, mainly from Catholic or Catholic-related sources. Whether this is a fair characterization is a matter of judgement. It could be claimed that Christian unions have a political significance and an influence among poor workers that is out of proportion to simple organizational statistics. A close examination would be needed to illustrate this.

Several further points can be made to support the argument that the Adenauer Foundation has not been very successful in Latin America.

1. Even in countries where Christian Democrat friends of the *Stiftung* have been elected to office, the help from Germany has

sometimes failed to help them to build a solid base once they have entered government. As mentioned above, after Frei's election to the Chilean presidency in 1964, a series of Konrad Adenauer projects failed to assist in consolidating the Christian Democrat Party or to avoid the doctrinal splits that paved the way for Salvador Allende's victory in the presidential election of 1970. Similarly, in Guatemala, Vicinio Cerezo's presidency appears to have been a failure despite the heavy funding of Adenauer projects designed to provide him with policy advice.

2. Occasionally, the management of projects has led to charges of misuse of funds. For example, in 1987 the German magazine *Stern* accused Konrad Adenauer field-workers in Costa Rica of black marketeering with Foundation money.[25]

3. In Ecuador, the activities of the Adenauer and Seidel Foundations themselves became controversial issues and a source of friction between the Ecuadorian and West German governments.[26]

4. On some occasions, organizations receiving *Stiftung* grants have proved awkwardly independent-minded. In particular, US officials linked with the AFL–CIO and with AIFLD (American Institute for Free Labour Development) frequently grumbled, especially in the 1960s, that support for Christian unions had the negative effect of splitting the anti-Communist unions of Latin America. They argued that some of the Christian union leaders who were being funded from Western Europe were little better than Marxists. In 1965 the Argentinian CLASC leader Emilio Maspero seemed to provide proof of his anti-American radicalism when he smuggled himself into the Dominican Republic to organize the local CLASC trade-union federation, CASC, in opposition to the US military action.[27]

Another, more favourable, interpretation of the Adenauer Foundation's record in Latin America is possible. While three decades of activity over such a large continent have obviously been accompanied by failures and very occasional scandals, there have also been notable successes. In general, it may be claimed that the Adenauer Foundation has given its backing to political moderates opposed both to military dictatorship and to left-wing revolution. The Foundation contributed to the consolidation of democracy in Venezuela in the 1960s and aided several democratic transitions—for example in Nicaragua and in Chile in the late 1980s.

An evaluation of the success of the German *Stiftungen* needs to consider the system of the four foundations as a group. For in countries where the Konrad Adenauer's favoured candidate or party has lost, one of the other *Stiftungen* may have backed the winner.

This system of channelling German government money to different political tendencies within the same country may be viewed as a cynical ploy of backing all the horses in the electoral race so that Germany gains a friend whichever of them wins. Alternatively, it may be interpreted as a useful and legitimate support for democratic pluralism. A US expert has expressed the point as follows:

when the West German Social Democrats were in power under Chancellor Helmut Schmidt, this party's Friedrich Ebert Foundation had close ties with Venezuela's Acción Democrática party. When the Venezuelan elections were won by the Christian Democratic party [COPEI] official West German diplomatic relations were not seriously frayed. A major reason was that the governing COPEI party had its own connections with the West German Christian Democratic Konrad Adenauer Foundation. COPEI also understood that the overall West German aid program was aimed at strengthening Venezuelan democracy in general, not at getting a particular party into power at a particular time.[28]

An ambassador stationed in a Latin American country reportedly expressed the envious view when he returned to his home base that the *Stiftungen* constituted Germany's most powerful diplomatic asset in that country. There are several reasons for this apparent influence. The sheer extent of the financial commitment by the German political foundations makes them significant. Since 1962 the *Stiftungen* have spent over DM1.3 billion—about US$750 million at current exchange rates—in Latin America. Current spending by the four foundations is probably nearly DM100 million a year (about US$50 million). In 1989 the Adenauer Foundation's total expenditure in Latin America and the Caribbean was DM42.3 million (over US$23 million at current exchange rates). The multiplicity of US political aid programmes makes a direct comparison difficult. However, the size of German political aid compares favourably with that of counterpart US bodies. The Adenauer Foundation's spending in Latin America in 1989 was larger than the combined expenditure in the continent by the US National Endowment for Democracy and its grantees and by the American Institute for Free Labor Development.[29]

The system of German field representatives sometimes enables the *Stiftungen* to forge personal links with important élites and leading opposition as well as government leaders. Eduardo Frei, Rafael Caldera, Napoleon Duarte, Violeta Chamorro, Patricio Aylwin, Vargas Llosa, Luis Herrera Campins, Aristides Calvani, Vicinio Cerezo, and Osvaldo Hurtado are among the Latin American leaders who have reportedly been close to the Adenauer Foundation.

A further diplomatic advantage of German activism in Latin

America is that, historically, the United States has normally welcomed the work of the Adenauer Foundation, since the Foundation has been in a position to approach some anti-Communist political leaders who would be more reluctant to receive aid from the USA. At the same time, Germany has been able to develop an independent policy, independent contacts, and considerable prestige. From the viewpoint of Latin American countries, political aid from Europe has had the advantage of being removed—or appearing to be removed—from the conflict between the superpowers.

Notes

1. For a legal discussion, see L. Fisler Damrosch, 'Politics across Frontiers: Nonintervention and Nonforcible Influence over Domestic Affairs', *American Journal of International Law*, 85 (1989).
2. Another form of payment that may be counted as political is payment intended to improve the electoral process rather than to aid a particular party or faction. For example, some governments and organizations have specialized in giving advice and assistance on the security of ballot boxes, on methods of drawing up accurate electoral rolls, and on other matters of electoral administration.
3. I am grateful to Margaret E. Crahan, Ralph Della Cava, and Jose-Maria Ghio for their ideas in discussion and for their chapters on religion and politics in Latin America in D. A. Chalmers, M. d. C. Campello de Souza, and A. Boron (eds.), *The Right and Democracy in Latin America* (New York: Praeger, 1992).
4. See G. Cote-Harper and J. Courtney, *International Cooperation for the Development of Human Rights and Democratic Institutions: Report to the Rt. Hon. Joe Clark and the Hon. Monique Landry*, Mimeo, Canadian Ministry for External Affairs, Ottawa.
5. Funding given by the BMZ for projects in developing countries has grown as follows: grants to German church organizations rose from DM34m. in 1962 to DM256m. in 1988. The total granted between 1962 and 1988 to the German church agencies was DM3.2bn. Grants to the German political foundations from the development ministry rose from DM130,000 in 1962 to DM265m. in 1988 and totalled 2.9bn. between 1962 and 1988. See *Development Cooperation between Non-Governmental Organisations and the Federal Ministry for Economic Cooperation in 1988* (Bonn: Federal Ministry for Economic Cooperation, 1989).
6. This historical summary has been based mainly on interviews with participants and on archival sources. See also H. von Vierrege, *Parteistiftungen: Zur Rolle der Konrad Adenauer-, Friedrich-Ebert-, Friedrich-Naumann-, und Hanns-Seidel-Stiftung im politischen System der Bundesrepublik Deutschland* (Baden-Baden: Nomos Verlag,

1977). For additional English-language material on the foundations' international activities, see V. Forrester, 'The German Political Foundations', in C. Stevens and J. Verloren van Themat (eds.), *EEC and the Third World: Survey*, v. *Pressure Groups, Politics and Development* (London: Hodder and Stoughton, 1985); M. Pinto-Duschinsky, 'Foreign Political Aid: The German Political Foundations and their US Counterparts', *International Affairs*, 67 (1991). For the foundations' domestic activities, see M. Pinto-Duschinsky, 'The Party Foundations and Political Finance in Germany', in F. L. Seidle (ed.), *Comparative Issues in Party and Election Finance* (Toronto: Dundurn Press, 1991).

7. G. Deussen, *Konrad-Adenauer-Stiftung* (Dusseldorf: Droste Verlag, 1979), 90.

8. Pinto-Duschinsky, 'Foreign Political Aid', 34.

9. It is beyond the scope of this chapter to explore the complex course of US–West German relations concerning political aid to Latin America, or the extent to which there has been consultation between donor bodies in the two countries or between the US and German governments. It is worth noting that the Adenauer Foundation's original overseas grantee—the Venezuela-based training institute for Christian Democratic parties in Latin America, IFEDEC—also received backing from the United States.

10. Some of the Friedrich Ebert Foundation's activities in Latin America are analysed in E. Mujal-León, *European Socialism and the Conflict in Central America* (New York: Praeger, 1989).

11. See Pinto-Duschinsky, 'Foreign Political Aid', 37 and Table 1.

12. The total excludes the administrative costs of the political foundations and also omits the costs of projects involving visits to West Germany by Latin American political leaders, trade unionists, journalists, etc.

13. H. Portelli and T. Jansen (eds.), *La Democratie Chrétienne: Force Internationale* (Paris: Institut de Politique Internationale et Européenne, 1986).

14. In 1974 the Adenauer Foundation funded CENADEC (Centro Andino de Estudios y Capacitación), which served Peru, Ecuador, and Bolivia; IDEP (Instituto de Estudios Políticos), which served the Chilean Partido Demócrata Cristiano; IDEC (Instituto de Estudios Comunitarios), based in Argentina and intended to train Christian Democrat activists in Argentina, Uruguay, and Paraguay; and INCEP (Instituto Centroamericano de Estudios Socio-Politicos), based in Guatemala, with a remit for Guatemala, El Salvador, Honduras, Nicaragua, Costa Rica, and Panama. In the Andean region, Adenauer also gave smaller grants to CEFEDEC in Bolivia and to FESO in Ecuador, as well as grants to two subsidiary institutes in the Southern Cone (a PDC institute in Paraguay and CENADEC in Uruguay). Between 1963 and 1972, Adenauer's expenditure on these projects from the funds of the BMZ was as follows: IFEDEC—DM7.9m., CENADEC—DM2.5m., IDEP—DM2.3m., IDEC—DM3.2m., and INCEP—DM1.5m. (includes

grants from 1969–72 only). In the early 1970s, the annual cost to the *Stiftung* of its nine projects designed to aid Latin American Christian Democratic parties was about DM3m. a year.

15. Studies of CLASC/CLAT include J. J. Palisi, 'The Latin American Confederation of Christian Trade Unions (CLASC), 1954–1967', Ph.D. thesis (American University, Washington DC, 1968); R. D. Bright, 'The Influence of North American Organized Labor in Latin America', Ph.D. thesis (Howard University, Washington DC, 1969). A recent study, based on access to CLAT archives and concentrating on ideological debates, is G. Wahlers, 'CLAT: Geschichte einer lateinamerikanischer Gewerkschaftsinternationale', Doctoral Diss. (Westfalischen Wilhelms-Universität, Munster, 1989). Unless otherwise stated, the statistics on CLAT and UTAL given in this chapter are based on Adenauer Foundation or BMZ documents.

16. INES (Chile), INEFOS (Ecuador), CEDOC (Ecuador), INES (Colombia), INPES (Peru), INCASUR (Argentina), ICAES (Costa Rica), ILATES–ILACDE (renamed UTAL from 1974) (Venezuela), ILATES (Caribbean), INFAS (Dominican Republic).

17. Konrad Adenauer's chancellorship saw the revival of the Bismarckian 'Reptile Fund'. This was a secret, discretionary fund used by the Chancellor for political purposes within Germany or abroad.

18. In 1986–8 the Foundation's expenditure (in thousands of DM) on its Chilean projects was as follows (statistics include costs of German field representatives but not of overhead costs in Bonn): (1) 'research institutes': CPU—1,466, ICHEH—2,960, FEF—726, Instituto Latinoamericano de Doctrina y Estudios Sociales (ILDES)—1,234; (2) trade-union education and promotion: Fundación para el Desarrollo y la Cultura Popular (DECUP), mainly for the National Workers' Command —1,350; (3) aid to small businessmen—650; (4) aid to self-help groups and slum-dwellers' leaders: AVEC—1,210; (5) rural, Church-related institute: INPROA—1,342; (6) co-operative organizations: Instituto Chileno de Educación Cooperativa (ICECOOP)—503, Confederación Nacional de Cooperativas Campesinas (CAMPECOOP)—1,995.

19. Venezuela-based projects (1986–8): (1) aid to Venezuelan Christian Democratic party: Conciencia 21—490; (2) continental Christian Democratic parties: ODCA—3,316, IFEDEC—5,657; (3) continental trade-union organization: UTAL—5,233.

20. Guatemala-based projects (1986–8): (1) political projects: ASIES—1,972, INCEP–IGESP—7,498, Universidad Rafael Landívar—4,317; (2) trade-union education: IGEFOS—600; (3) co-operatives: Federación de Cooperativas Agricolas de Productores de Café de Guatemala (FEDCOCAGUA)—5,054; (4) media: Instituto Guatemalteco de Escuelas Radiofonicas—396 (education by radio for K'etchi-speaking Indians).

21. Ed. A. F. Lowenthal (Baltimore: Johns Hopkins University Press, 1991), 383.

22. According to an internal report of 1989, the Foundation's work with parties not belonging to ODCA was as follows: Argentina: party or

party group—Reform Peronists (institute connected with party and supported by the Adenauer Foundation—FUDEPA); also, with multi-party connections, FUNDECO; Brazil: PMDB (São Paulo) (IBEAC); Colombia: Conservative Party (FSB); Peru: Partido Popular Cristiana (APD); Jamaica: Jamaica Labour Party (JIPE); Grenada: New National Party (GIDE); Dominica: Dominica Freedom Party. In Grenada and Dominica, aid was given through a regional body for the East Caribbean (ECID).

23. Palisi, *Latin American Confederation*, 369–70.

24. Even the statistic of 18 per cent of self-financing may give a wrong impression. A considerable source of such independent income came from letting out facilities at the UTAL complex that had been supplied with foreign funds. It should be noted that the percentages of UTAL income derived from self-financing have varied from year to year. Between 1975 and 1987, they ranged between a maximum of 39 per cent and a minimum of 4 per cent. A development since the 1960s is that the Adenauer Foundation appears to have had some limited success in finding other foreign donors to share some of the costs of the UTAL project.

25. How serious are problems of accountability and is there a problem of corruption relating to the Adenauer Foundation's Latin American projects? The BMZ in Bonn imposes strict guidelines on the political foundations for their accounting and documentation procedures. Receipts and counterfoils are examined annually by the Ministry's accounting control department. In addition, the Bundesrechnungshof (federal audit office) may (and sometimes does) conduct its own investigation into accounts of the *Stiftungen*. The Bundesrechnungshof's confidential reports are submitted to the BMZ. If the ministry is unable to answer its criticisms of aspects of the *Stiftungen*'s accounts, the Bundesrechnungshof may then submit its findings to the federal legislature (the Bundestag). Despite these checks, some of the procedures of the foundations were criticized by the Constitutional Court in a 1986 judgment of a case brought by the Greens. Further criticism was reportedly included in a subsequent report by the Bundesrechnungshof. Interviews with *Stiftung* officials produce widely differing opinions as to the extent to which recipients of German grants have managed in the past to use the money for corrupt purposes. The 1987 exposé in *Stern* magazine (15 January 1987) concerned two former field representatives of the Adenauer Foundation in Central America who were reported to have given forged receipts for the currency exchange of project grants to the value of DM1.96m. While claiming to have exchanged the money at the official rate, evidence was produced that they had actually exchanged grant cheques at the black-market rate. The matter was later the subject of an official reply to a written question in the Bundestag. (Deutscher Bundestag, *Antwort der Bundesregierung auf die Kleine Anfrage des Abgeordneten Volmer und der Fraktion DIE GRÜNEN*—Drucksache 11/20: Missbruch öffentliche Zuwendungen durch die Konrad-Adenauer-

Stiftung. *Drucksache* 11/233, 6 May 1987.) Some opposition politicians alleged that the profits from the currency transactions had been used to aid the Contras who were fighting the Sandinista regime in Nicaragua. According to the Adenauer Foundation, the former field-workers (against whom it was later involved in legal proceedings) had used the additional money for the benefit of its Costa Rica-based regional trade-union institute, ICAES. For an official Adenauer Foundation response to the story, see Professor Dr Bruno Heck's letter to *Stern*, 29 April 1987. The politically charged context in which this matter arose will be evident. The underlying accusation was not so much of sloppy accounting or corruption as of implied collusion with American intelligence (an allegation for which solid evidence does not appear to have been given). The Adenauer Foundation subsequently tightened its rules for money transfer. Money for grantees is now transferred directly to foreign banks and the proceeds are made available to field representatives in local currencies.

26. Examples of press reports are *Frankfurter Rundschau*, 16 May 1987, *Die Tageszeitung*, 29 May and 10 June 1987. See also Deutscher Bundestag, *Antwort der Bundesregierung auf die Kleine Anfrage des Abgeordneten Volmer und der Fraktion DIE GRÜNEN*—Drucksache 11/379: Tätigkeit der Hanns-Seidel-Stiftung und der Konrad-Adenauer-Stiftung in Ecuador, *Drucksache* 11/509, 10 July 1987.

27. *Re* AFL–CIO opposition to CLASC and its constituent union federations, see Bright, *Influence*, 198 ff., Palisi, *Latin American Confederation*, 195 ff., and S. Romualdi, *Presidents and Peons: Recollections of a Labor Ambassador in Latin America* (New York: Funk & Wagnalls, 1967). Maspero's radical rhetoric emerges from the interview included in D. Parcero, *La CGT y el Sindicalismo Latinoamericano: Historia crítica de sus relaciones, Desde el ATLAS a la CIOSL* (Buenos Aires, 1987). The opposition to Maspero within some AFL–CIO circles was not shared by all agencies of the US government. An alternative view was that, for all its anti-American, pro-Castro rhetoric, Christian trade unionism was preferable to Communist unionism. Several CLAT unions were to receive supplementary funding from US government sources. See, for example, R. J. Alexander and H. S. Hammond, *Report on United States Government Labor Programs in Latin America* (Washington DC: Agency for International Development, 1975), 84–5 (Confidential report, declassified 31 December 1981).

28. W. A. Douglas, in R. A. Goldman and W. A. Douglas (eds.), *Promoting Democracy: Issues and Opportunities* (New York: Praeger, 1988), 250.

29. For a detailed comparison between West German and US political aid to Chile during 1984–8, see Pinto-Duschinsky, 'Foreign Political Aid', 40. Total US expenditure in Chile by the National Endowment for Democracy and its grantees, and by the Agency for International Development (including grants to the American Institute for Free Labor Development and to other bodies) totalled an estimated $6.8m. During the same period, the expenditure in Chile of the four *Stiftungen* amounted to the equivalent of approximately $26m.

PART III

Europe

The European Union does not impose democracy on neighbouring states. It is a treaty-bound association of democratic states, which has grown from six founder members in 1957 to fifteen in 1995, with the likelihood that by the beginning of the twenty-first century it may contain more than twenty member states. Some of the latter additions were long-standing democracies, but this was not true of Greece, Portugal, and Spain, nor of the German Democratic Republic (incorporated through Reunification in 1990), nor will it be true of Cyprus and Malta (which were still British colonies in the 1950s), nor of post-Communist applicants from East-Central Europe. Undemocratic regimes in such countries were under no direct threat from the Community (indeed some critics have accused core EU states of being altogether too accommodating to such regimes) but so long as they remained undemocratic they could not join the club. Brussels had no military or even political capacity to coerce them into democratizing; nor any intention of doing so. But as the Community grew and prospered it created an ever stronger pole of attraction. Those in undemocratic countries who wished to join the Community were made to understand that the price of admission would have to include not just economic but also political convergence towards the liberal standards set by the established membership. The Community imposed no deadline for democratization but, as Chapters 11 and 12 below record, it did respond positively when first Greece and then the Iberian countries relinquished authoritarian rule. Thus 'democracy by convergence' emerged as an important path to democratization, at least in those countries eligible for Community membership. Considering the consultative processes by which such convergence had to be negotiated, and the associated requirements of popular or parliamentary ratification, this can be regarded as a 'democratic' and sovereignty-affirming path to democratization, in contrast to the cases of imposition considered earlier.

As the term implies, 'imposition' characteristically involves rather
clearly defined and powerful external forces acting upon relatively
weak and dependent domestic actors. The contrast between internal and external causes is therefore likely to be rather sharply
drawn. In the case of democracy-by-convergence, on the other hand,
internal actors will seem relatively unconstrained by external
compulsion. However, powerful long-term external influences and
incentives may shape their perceptions and guide their strategic
choices. Equally, although it may seem as if the European Union
is free to take its own decisions on enlargement uncontrolled by
the internal politics of aspiring members, in reality when, say, the
Greek political élite or the East German populace embarked upon
a democratic transition, by that decision they mobilized powerful
forces that would almost inevitably alter the course of Union development. The logic of democratization-by-convergence is that it
tends to lock in commitments from both external and internal
actors at the same time. Indeed, at least in the southern European
cases under consideration in these chapters, it mobilized shared
political symbols and values in a manner which partially redefined
the identities of all participants in the convergence process.

There are two key aspects of such identity politics where the
contrasts between the alternative international paths to democratization are of greatest significance: they concern national sovereignty, and the authenticity of domestic democratizing forces. In
the extreme case of democracy by incorporation, of course, the counterpart of democratization within a larger polity is the extinction
of a separate state and the dissolution of its autonomous political
identity. This is not to say that all political distinctiveness will
necessarily be lost (it turns out that the East German electorate
has quite a distinct profile and set of perceptions from that of West
Germany, and the same would doubtless be true of Puerto Rican
voters if they obtained statehood). But such democratization entails the abandonment of one potential national identity, and the
acceptance of a different and broader allegiance. In consequence
domestic political parties and actors become latecomers and secondary participants in a much larger political system to which
they are forced to adapt. Whatever separate authenticity they may
have attained prior to incorporation must now be subordinated to
the requirements of acceptability and integration within the larger
polity.

As we saw in Chapter 3, above, democracy by imposition raises
different issues of identity politics. The undemocratic, or imposed,
route through which democratization was achieved tends to impair

the sovereignty of the post-transition state. Yet democratization does end with the preservation of a separate national polity, however precarious and tension-ridden its status may be. Therefore, political parties and actors competing for support from within this bounded political system will face the problem of how to project and establish their authenticity. On the one hand the facts of imposition and continuing dependence may require them to defer to externally defined power realities, thus to some extent mirroring the experiences of domestic political actors in democratizations through incorporation. On the other hand, however, they cannot rely on permanent and institutionalized ties of subordination structured from without, since the privileges and responsibilities of incorporation are not in fact being offered to them, and since in formal terms they are only answerable to the separate national electorate of their own country. (Whether the voters of Panama really feel democratically empowered by their right to select their own president is another question. They might achieve more influence over their political destinies with an extremely diluted participation in US presidential contests.) In other words, democracy by imposition leaves a legacy of impaired sovereignty and inauthentic representation that impedes the formation of clear and strong political identities; and that may therefore give rise to artificial and exaggerated displays of authenticity (as when President Endara of Panama publicly denounced a visiting emissary from President Clinton as a 'pro-consul', or when his successor in office, President Peréz Balladares, declared the fifth anniversary of the invasion a 'day of mourning'). On the surface this can give the appearance of a sharp division between internal and external forces (even a clash of nationalisms), although behind the scenes there can be a culture of collusion with, and subordination to, external power centres.

Democracy-by-convergence also raises issues of identity politics that may be difficult to categorize in terms of a strong separation between domestic and international factors. In this case democratization is likely to be accompanied by strong affirmations of national sovereignty (which is why the question of US bases proved such a delicate issue in the Mediterranean transition processes). As Chapters 11 and 12 below illustrate, such key actors as King Juan Carlos and President Karamanlis may have depended at crucial junctures on support from outside, but they also (and perhaps more vitally) derived their leverage from the possession of long-standing domestic assets and resources. Similarly, both the PSOE and PASOK secured major symbolic and even material resources from abroad, giving them major advantages over their domestic party rivals, yet their successes depended above all on the cultivation of domestic support bases and traditions. At times they showed no hesitation in mobilizing domestic sentiments against external insensitivities, and indeed such campaigns were integral to their party-building activities, and served to guarantee their national authenticity. But these sovereign democracies governed by these authentic parties were in no way façades for covert collusion with external controllers. Moreover, for all their assertions of sovereignty and national authenticity, these new democratic regimes voluntarily selected policies of integration and strategies of convergence that corresponded surprisingly closely with the hopes and preferences of their European Community partners. Thus, even in the absence of the overt forms of control that characterize democracy by incorporation and by imposition, the southern European new democracies have largely been steered in the directions required by international co-ordination. The fact is that a particular form of identity politics has played a crucial role in these democratic consolidations as well. (The wish for full acceptance and equality of status within the European Union has played a decisive role in regime and policy choices over the longer run.) Once again, therefore, it would be somewhat misleading to segregate domestic from international components of the processes at work. Both components are closely entangled in the affirmation of a new democratic identity. Thus, in contemporary democratizations the boundaries between these two elements are characteristically fuzzy.

10

Democracy by Convergence: Southern Europe

LAURENCE WHITEHEAD

Philippe C. Schmitter wrote in the introduction to the southern European part of *Transitions from Authoritarian Rule* that 'one of the firmest conclusions' was that such transitions 'were largely to be explained in terms of national forces and calculations'. 'External actors tended to play an indirect and usually marginal role, with the obvious exception of those instances in which a foreign occupying power was present.'[1] Since that pioneering study more detailed work on the southern European transitions (including Chapters 11 and 12 in this volume) have made it clear that a significant shift of international orientation (perhaps even of perceptions of national identity) is likely to accompany any major regime change from authoritarian rule to liberal democracy. The European Community has acted as a powerful catalyst both of democratization and of national redefinition in contemporary southern Europe. It has achieved this influence not through military occupations, but by offering an elaborate structure of economic and social incentives for changes in group and national behaviour. Thus, although the key actors involved in regime change and democratization may have been overwhelmingly internal, their strategies and calculations have often been strongly shaped by the pressure of externally designed rules and structures. An actor-focused interpretation certainly sheds considerable light on the logic of the transition process, but more impersonal and durable structural relationships must be invoked to account for the permanent entrenchment of democratic institutions ('consolidation') in southern Europe, and for the convergence of these new regimes towards the common model of liberal democracy exemplified by the European Union.

1. The Various Routes to Democratization

Alfred Stepan laid out eight 'paths to redemocratization', and his typology is certainly applicable to southern Europe, especially since Italy in the 1940s and Greece, Portugal, and Spain in the 1970s were all cases of redemocratization—i.e. the return to competitive party systems and forms of constitutional government which could claim substantial antecedents in the political history of each nation.[2] Stepan's analysis also has the merit of embracing both the recent southern European cases and the European redemocratizations of the 1940s, in the wake of the Second World War. However, his eight paths do not encompass all the possibilities, in part because he considers only redemocratization, in part because he considers only post-war Western Europe and Latin America. Moreover, they are all paths to democratic transition rather than to the consolidation of democracy. Lastly, more refinements to the classification could be introduced on the question of critical importance to this chapter, namely the precise balance between the external and the internal forces that are involved.

Stepan proposes three mainly external paths to redemocratization (in each case precipitated by conquest from abroad), and five essentially domestic paths (precipitated either by elements from the authoritarian coalition, or by some initiative from the opposition). The first three paths are ones in which warfare and conquest play an integral part in the redemocratization process. The great majority of historical examples of successful redemocratization, most of them European, in fact fall into these first three categories. The balance between prior democratic strength, the political unity and disunity of the conquered country, and the role of external powers can be sufficiently different to warrant the identification of three distinct categories: (1) internal restoration after external conquest; (2) internal reformulation; and (3) externally monitored installation.'[3] As examples of the first alternative Stepan cites the Netherlands, Belgium, Norway, and Denmark in 1945. The second route (in which, although external force is predominant, there are also internal resistance movements unconnected with previous democratic leadership) is best exemplified by post-Liberation France and Greece. Archetypal instances of the third alternative are provided by West Germany and Japan, with Italy falling somewhere between the second and third routes. (Although Stepan does not explicitly stress the point, the third route refers to defeated countries whereas the first two refer to liberated countries, which is why the statuses of Italy and Austria are open to debate.) Although these three paths need to be distinguished, they share some highly restrictive common features: notably all the European examples occurred at the end of the Second World War[4] and the driving force in all cases was 'democratization-through-defeat'.

The idea of democratization-through-defeat seems on the face of it quite paradoxical. For any country to defeat another in war, and to occupy its territory, requires a sacrifice of men and resources that can only be justified by reference to some very vital national interest. A distinctly implausible degree of altruism would be required to induce any country to carry out such an act solely for the purpose of transmitting democratic institutions to other nations. (Thus none of the Allies were willing to incur casualties by invading Franco's Spain after 1945; and what apparently drove President Bush to invade Panama was not so much the electoral fraud of May 1989 as the threat Noriega was thought to pose to the US interest in the Canal and in the matter of drug-trafficking; as for the September 1994 American troop deployment in Haiti, it only took place after a succession of postponements motivated by the wish to avert resistance and so avoid casualties.) Therefore democracy is most likely to be imposed as a by-product of conquest, rather than as its motive force. Any conquering force will have to give priority to other objectives (for example, pacifying and normalizing the territory in order to reduce the costs of occupation; minimizing the risk of subsequent revanchism; denying great-power rivals—or even allies—political or strategic influence).

These high-priority objectives may all fit neatly together, and they may all be readily served by the second-order procedure of establishing (or restoring) a democratic form of government. But, as Sandino demonstrated to the USA in Nicaragua in the 1920s, and as ELAS taught the British in post-war Greece, not all 'democratizing invasions' go as smoothly as the operations in Grenada and Panama. What the occupying forces want from a newly installed democratic regime may, or may not, harmonize well with what local political forces (perhaps even the most single-mindedly democratic local forces) have in mind. This was certainly a problem for Woodrow Wilson when he attempted to teach 'good government' to the Mexicans, and, of course, it is one that British troops stationed in Northern Ireland since 1969 have found it difficult to overcome. If the first-order objectives of the external power are not adequately served by the installation of a democratic regime then, of course, there are other well-tried methods through which an occupying force may hope to achieve the pacification of a territory they control.

A second paradox of democratization-through-defeat is that for a democratic regime to become entrenched (or consolidated), it must secure the allegiances of a wide array of domestic political forces. Both winners and losers must come to view the system as reasonably fair or open to revisions, and must learn to view their rivals as authentic expressions of local opinion, not puppets of some foreign interest. These requirements would seem prima facie in conflict with the inherent logic of conquest (that is military defeat of the pre-existing regime) and the occupying power's need for security. This suggests that the requirements for effective democratization via this route are indeed highly restrictive. Not just external military defeat is required, but the total discredit of the defeated regime. Stepan's three paths all refer to 1945, when six of the European countries in his typology were being liberated from oppressive armies of occupation, and the Axis regimes were comprehensively destroyed in the eyes of their own people. Furthermore, the democratization must occur securely within the sphere of influence of the occupying power (and not, as in Greece in 1944, in a zone of geopolitical conflict). The military victors must, to a considerable extent, have won the hearts and minds of the population they are overrunning (or liberating) before their military success is completed.

A third qualification can be added to the notion of democratization-through-defeat, namely that the element of conquest may not always be necessary or even helpful. Some authoritarian regimes have been forced by military defeat to recognize their lack of internal support, and to accept the need to stand aside for democratically elected successors, without succumbing to foreign occupation. The Greek Colonels provoked a Turkish invasion of Cyprus; and the Argentine Generals provoked the establishment of a British military exclusion zone around the disputed territory of the Falklands–Malvinas; but in neither case was there a direct conquest of the internationally recognized national territory. Indeed, if either the Turks or the British had overstepped that limit they might well have breathed new life into the military regimes whose provocations they were resisting. One reason why Franco escaped defeat after 1945 was that he had resisted Axis pressure to become involved in military operations outside his territory, as he had also resisted the stationing of German forces on Spanish soil. In like manner the invasion of Cuba might well not create favourable conditions for the implementation of democracy on that island; whereas the defeat of Cuban troops abroad could perhaps destroy the Castro regime, particularly if they were deployed in some unpopular cause.

The notion of democratization-through-defeat therefore requires careful examination because to varying degrees this may help to illuminate the cases of Italy, Greece, and Portugal. But this is by no means the only possible path to democracy in which international processes would be dominant. Other possibilities, not discussed by Stepan, include democratization-through-decolonization, democratization-through-incorporation, and democratization-through-convergence. There is no space here to discuss the possibility of democratization-through-decolonization, although there are Mediterranean cases worthy of consideration (Cyprus and Malta). It might, however, be interesting to consider whether there has not been an element of decolonization in the process by which democratic Greece, in particular, has asserted itself against an 'informal American empire' which, for good reasons or bad, had come to be identified with the Colonels' dictatorship. Verney quotes Papandreou as saying he founded PASOK not as a political party, but as a national liberation movement struggling to free Greece from imperialist control.[5]

Democratization-through-incorporation requires a brief discussion. By the conventional definitions, both Puerto Rico and Hawaii have well-established democratic political regimes. These were achieved (possibly at an unacceptable price in terms of national sovereignty) by full, or virtual, incorporation into the United States (the Puerto Rican case is analysed in Chapter 5). Similarly, Guadeloupe, Martinique, and Réunion are fully incorporated overseas departments of France, and as such share most of the essential features of French political democracy. Late Victorian Britain tried to incorporate the whole of Ireland in a similar manner, but contemporary Britain is shrugging off its responsibility for democracy in Hong Kong. It is worth noting that the Azores, the Canaries, and the Balearics achieved democracy at the same time as Portugal and Spain, and in the same way; whereas Angola, Guinea, Mozambique, Cape Verde, East Timor, and the Spanish Sahara did not. Thus some territories achieve (or fail to achieve) democratization not primarily because of the balance of local political forces but more as a side-effect of their incorporation (or non-incorporation) into a larger national entity. Geographical location helps to determine which territories are included or excluded, but, as the southern European evidence demonstrates, the boundaries of new democracies are not always beyond dispute (consider Trieste, Cyprus, and Ceuta and Melilla).

In the case of democratization-through-incorporation it is very clear why the territory being incorporated must first achieve a high standard of democratic practice. If not, the quality of the democracy achieved in the incorporating state might be jeopardized or undermined. Incorporation has to be viewed as a one-way process—that is to say, it is virtually unthinkable that a new state joining the American Union could so irredeemably fail to meet the standards required by the US Constitution that it would subsequently be expelled. Thus, when Honolulu became the 50th state capital in 1959, the USA effectively pledged the entire solidity of its political institutions as a guarantor that, whatever it might take, Hawaian politics could be brought into line with US practice.

Finally, and of central concern in this context, there is a less binding, but still forceful international route to democratization via the enlargement of a pre-existing democratic community of sovereign states (democratization-through-convergence). Whereas incorporation within an existing democracy leaves virtually no margin of discretion to local political forces, the enlargement of a democratic community of states allows each applicant for admission to negotiate over conditions of entry and to set its own timetable. This is, of course, the route taken by Spain, Portugal, and Greece, and also the route envisaged by Turkey when it applied for admission to the European Community in April 1987. It raises in starker form than any of the other routes discussed so far the problem of how to disentangle and attach separate weights to the internal and international components respectively of the democratization process.

In the case of democratization-through-convergence within a community of democratic states, the question arises once again of the quality and the irreversibility of the new democracy. The situation is similar to democratization-through-incorporation, although of course a lesser degree of intervention is permissible by the enlarging community in the political affairs of the new member (since the sovereignty of each state must be protected); and the ultimate guarantee against expulsion or withdrawal is necessarily less absolute (for the same reason). Perhaps this implies that a democratic community of states has to demand a higher standard of democratic performance before admission than is necessary for incorporating democracy, since the latter has more freedom than the former to take remedial action after the event.

2. EC Membership and Democratization

In the case of southern Europe, as I have described elsewhere,[6] the European Community, following the Birkelbach Report in 1962, adopted clear and binding political conditions for admission which precluded acceptance of Franco's Spain or Salazar's Portugal, and which resulted in a freeze on relations with Greece during the rule of the Colonels. Once democracy was established in those three countries, negotiations for admission could begin. But these negotiations were long drawn out, and in practice it was not until the evidence of consolidation in all three democratic regimes had accumulated that enlargement eventually occurred. This is not to imply that the negotiations involved any explicit test of democratic purity. Obviously they were mainly concerned with economic questions, but it was understood by all concerned that solid democratic institutions were a pre-condition for entry.

In 1976, for example, the Commission explicitly linked a favourable response to the Greek application for full membership with the consolidation of the new democratic regime.[7] From seven to ten years separated the start of transition from the entry into the European Community (Greece joined in 1981, Portugal and Spain in 1986). Since 1986 further opportunities have arisen to observe what the EC's and later EU's minimum requirements for political democracy really are, and to assess how long an applicant may have to wait before the Community/Union is satisfied that those conditions have been met.

In April 1987 Turkey submitted an uninvited application for full membership of the EC, pointing out that twenty-three years had elapsed since the Ankara Association Agreement was signed. Although EC foreign ministers undertook to deal with the case in a non-discriminatory manner, and strictly in accordance with the Treaty of Rome, the Greek government promptly announced its intention to veto Turkish accession, citing various considerations, not least of which was its continuing disputes with Turkey both over Cyprus and over territorial sovereignty in the Aegean.

Whereas in 1987 Turkey unsuccessfully sought membership, Malta and Cyprus are currently preparing for accession after the 1996 intergovernmental conference. In 1995 the twelve (including an enlarged Germany following Reunification in October 1990) became fifteen (with the accession of Austria, Finland, and Sweden) so Turkey's place in the queue for membership has kept slipping back. If Athens gets its way and Cyprus becomes the seventeenth member of the Union, it seems probable that only the democratic and Greek-Cypriot-controlled part of the island will initially be admitted. The Turkish-controlled part will automatically be added at the time of Reunification (following the German precedent). As if this were not galling enough, mainland Turkey has also found itself subjected to unwelcome criticism from the West, some of which has been interpreted as reflecting European prejudices against Muslims.

The worst conflict has been with the European Parliament, which, in June 1987, passed a resolution opposing Turkish accession to the EC, until such time as there would be public acknowledgement of Ottoman genocide against Armenians in 1915. The resolution also listed other 'insurmountable obstacles to consideration of the possibility of Turkey's accession', including 'the maintenance of Turkish occupation forces in Cyprus' and 'denial of the existence of the Kurdish question'. It will be recalled that since 1987 the admission of new members requires the approval of the European Parliament by an absolute majority. It should also be noted that Turkish political parties lack close ties with Western European counterparts such as can be found in southern Europe, or, indeed, in parts of Eastern Europe. Thus, the lobbyists on Turkish issues most likely to influence the votes of Members of the European Parliament (MEPs) are Turkish migrants, exiles, and refugees living in Western Europe, whose accounts of the quality of political life within Turkey often contrast rather sharply with the official line propagated from Ankara.

Following Maastricht the European Parliament gained greater access to information about the conduct of the EU's external relations, and became more assertive in exercising its power of assent to international treaties and customs unions (including accession agreements), but in these matters it can still only grant or withhold ratification, on a single 'take-it-or-leave-it' basis.

The Commission considered itself under no obligation to produce a speedy response to the unsolicited Turkish application, and thirty-two months elapsed before a formal, two-part 'opinion' was issued, which appeared on 19 December 1989. The first part of this opinion dealt with the Turkish economy and recognized the rapid progress achieved in the 1980s. However, Turkish purchasing power remained only one-third of the EC average, and overall the economic analysis pointed to the need for an indefinitely long delay before Turkey would be ready for full membership. Given all these 'objective' difficulties, it is easy to understand why, on the political side, the Commission was much more tight-lipped. Nevertheless, in the brief second part, while conceding that Turkey now had a parliamentary democracy 'closer to Community models' and had made progress in the fields of human rights and the respect for minorities, 'these had not yet reached the levels required in a democracy'. Moreover, the dispute over Cyprus continued to raise additional difficulties. In conclusion, then, the opinion recommended that the EC should continue its Association Agreement with Turkey.

But the Commission advised member states against beginning early negotiations with the Turkish government on an eventual Turkish accession. In practice the Turkish application has been indefinitely deferred, but Brussels has offered a stronger co-operation agreement in compensation. The Commission has gone to considerable length to avoid an outright rebuff, or directly to link its negative opinion with any adverse judgement about the country's internal political affairs. Indeed the December 1989 *avis* was so muted that for some it raised the question 'why the defects of democracy are allocated just a few words in a nine page commission opinion' and 'why during contacts with Turkish government officials EC officials refrained from giving the impression that democratization was one of the defects of the Turkish political system barring it from EC membership'.

Turkey's geopolitical location and its strategic value to the West is stressed in an analysis by Huri Tursan.[8] In her view this international security dimension has been on balance unhelpful to democratic consolidation in Turkey. Although she attributes more negative influence to the US than to Western Europe, she considers that the European Community's relatively unimpressive record on the defence of political freedoms in Turkey reflects the same security reasoning that characterizes Washington's approach. Similarly, Ali Karaosmanoglu also stresses Turkey's geopolitical location, but in contrast to Tursan he takes a much more favourable view of US influence, and of the quality of current democratic practices in Turkey.[9] He therefore views the European role as unduly and inappropriately meddlesome, particularly when the defence of human rights led some Europeans to condone what he calls 'terrorist' threats to Turkish democracy, notably from the Workers Party of Kurdistan (PKK) and from other leftist movements. He also refers to the existence of historical prejudices which he thinks have limited co-operation between Turkish democrats and the potential transnational allies in Europe to further the cause of democracy. However, he does consider that, despite the various factors that have undermined European credibility, pressures from Western Europe must have exerted an accelerating influence on the process of democratization.

Whichever of these two viewpoints one adopts, it is too soon to be sure of the eventual impact of the European Community on Turkish democratization. The December 1989 Commission opinion did not finally resolve the issue, but merely postponed it to an indefinite future. However, following the Maastricht Treaty, Turkey's membership aspirations received a second rebuff from the Commission. In November 1992 Brussels sought to repair some of the damage by reactivating the long-dormant EC–Turkey Association Agreement, and using it to promote both a political dialogue and a customs union with this strategic neighbour. However, even this temporizing strategy has run into a series of major obstacles. First, the Turkish economy has slipped into a severe crisis, raising grave doubts about whether it will be feasible to constitute a full EU–Turkish customs union by the target date of 1 January 1996. Second, although Greece is unable to veto the customs union proposal (which is not subject to ratification by national governments, only by the European Parliament) it has been able to continue blocking the Community financial assistance needed to alleviate the crisis and prepare the way for the customs union. Third, Greece succeeded in using its presidency of the European Union (in the first half of 1994) to extract a promise that the next applicants in line for admission after the Scandinavians would be Malta and Cyprus (an island currently partly under Turkish military occupation). Fourth, just when Turkey was being internationally outmanœuvred in this way, the Turkish parliament chose to lift parliamentary immunity from MPs representing the Kurdish region, thereby exposing them to long prison sentences for expressing the aspirations of their constituents. No doubt both Brussels and Ankara have powerful incentives to find a path through this obstacle course, and it would be a mistake to overstress the significance of what may prove temporary impediments to convergence, but the recent history of EU–Turkish relations indicates the potential for vicious circles of estrangement (which could weaken processes of democratization) as well as for virtuous circles of political and economic integration.

Nevertheless, taking a much longer view, Karaosmanoglu argues that throughout the twentieth century Turkish modernizers have sought to transform their nation along Western lines, and have generally understood that this requires the strengthening of political pluralism as well as economic modernization. Reportedly, the emergence over the past generation of a larger, more prosperous, and more cohesive European Community has reinforced that intention, at least among some very influential groups in society:

Turkey's leading industrialists share with most of the intelligentsia the belief that membership of the European Community could provide almost a deus ex machina solution to guarantee the victory of liberal, westernising tendencies in their country over Islamicising and oriental ones. Even the government has recently begun, *sotto voce*, to argue that for Turkey—as for Greece and Spain—membership of the European Community is a legitimate way of guaranteeing a fragile parliamentary democracy against possible further military takeovers.[10]

This is a particular illustration of the more general argument that membership of the European Community has offered critical external guarantees to the business and propertied classes of southern Europe. Whatever parties the newly empowered electorates of Greece, Portugal, and Spain might favour, the EU would insist on prompt and adequate compensation for all private property acquired by the state. It would create a very strong momentum for tax and welfare harmonization with the rest of (capitalist) Western Europe, and it would ensure relatively free movement of capital. With all these provisions assured, democracy would lose much of its sting for the rich. (There would conceivably have been far less need for them to support Franco against the Spanish Republic if such external guarantees had been available in the 1930s.) However, the EC was bound to withhold these highly prized guarantees from all openly undemocratic regimes, whether of the Left or of the Right.

Between the mid-1950s and the mid-1970s this situation set up most powerful, immutable, and long-run incentives for democratic transition and consolidation in southern Europe. Particular importance may be attached to the non-discretionary character of these incentives, and to the permanence of their effects. These two features may have limited the flexibility with which the EC could respond to the uncertainties of the democratic transition phase, but they greatly added to the Community's effectiveness as a long-term external guarantor of democratic consolidation. Although this chapter only concerns southern Europe, it is notable that the same logic is likely to apply to the new democracies of Eastern Europe in the 1990s, and that these potential members will present a more serious test of Union commitment than the easy accessions of the 1980s.

3. *The Fuzzy Boundary between Domestic and External Factors*

When democratization comes about in the course of invasion or decolonization, the separation between the domestic and the external factors at work is thrown into sharp relief. But if the operative process is the incorporation of an incipient democracy within a larger and securer democratic polity, the boundary between the two categories will by definition be dissolved. And in the case of most relevance to southern Europe, democratization-by-convergence, these processes of mutual political adjustment will tend to soften—though not to obliterate—the distinction between external and internal causes. In effect, as a democratic community of states comes into being, national boundaries become more porous, and political co-ordination across frontiers becomes more open and flexible. Moreover, although during the transition phase in may be reasonable to concentrate on the parts played by various political actors, the most important of whom will typically be domestic, during the consolidation phase more long-term structural constraints become more determinant; these will often embody some combination of domestic and international elements. The incentives for consolidation provided by the prospect or reality of EC membership have represented a durable and compelling set of inducements to remould the political regimes of southern Europe (a powerful 'confining condition' of the democratization process). It is unhelpful to classify such inducements as either external or internal, since they operate at various levels, and they reshape the calculations and conduct of numerous political actors both at home and abroad.

However, it is a matter for careful comparative study to determine for each country the importance of the European Union issue, as compared with other more internal causes of democratization. As Geoffrey Pridham indicates, we should not overstress the importance of external variables.[11] The southern European experiences seem to confirm that the unfolding of what appear as primarily domestic political processes largely accounts for the establishment of new democratic regimes, and also for their consolidation. The main apparently domestic processes have been analysed and classified in detail in the *Transition* study (especially pt. 4, *Tentative Conclusions*), and so can be summarized very briefly here.[12]

Where an authoritarian regime reaches the point of termination, some form of disintegration of the authoritarian coalition is almost certainly involved, together with some strengthening and realigning of the forces of democratic opposition. Internal processes likely to trigger a disintegration of the authoritarian coalition typically include: a succession crisis; the defection of sections of the business community and/or the professional classes; and institutional shifts within the armed forces involving a return to barracks in order to protect institutional integrity. A variety of domestic mediating or bridging institutions may play a critical role in facilitating the transition: the monarchy in Spain; the Church in parts of Latin America; Karamanlis and his party-in-exile in Greece. Where such bridging institutions are weak or absent (Portugal in 1974, Argentina in 1982), the transition may take the form of a drastic and destabilizing 'democratic rupture'. In some cases the various components of the civilian opposition may facilitate a negotiated or 'pacted' transition by agreeing in advance on a framework for the new regime that defines the scope and limits of the sectoral changes accompanying democratization. In other cases, the role of the opposition may be more confrontational: mobilizing a mass following, campaigning in a plebiscite, or even undertaking acts of violence, to force the outgoing regime to speed its exit.

Clearly these are all very general alternatives, and each specific situation presents some complex combination of the various features just outlined. Although these alternatives appear at first sight to represent overwhelmingly domestic routes to democratization, closer examination of the southern European experiences indicates that there is often a significant international input, and that the internal–external boundary can be highly permeable. This can be illustrated by a brief consideration of the international factors affecting the three main categories just discussed: the authoritarian regime, the bridging institutions or actors, and the democratic opposition. The point can be further elaborated by returning to the structural influence exerted by the European Community.

Authoritarian regimes will naturally seek to prolong their existence by bolstering their cohesion and by wrong-footing their challengers. The international posture of a regime often plays an important part in this process, as the southern European cases demonstrate. During periods of international isolation (such as in Franco's Spain after 1945) the posture may be to turn away from a hostile, outside world, and to seek cohesion through autarchy and invocations of nationalism. But this is seldom an optimal strategy, certainly not in southern Europe during the Cold War. In those conditions it made more sense to adopt an opposite tactic, and to seek the security of a protective international alliance which might serve to shelter the authoritarian regime from both internal and external disintegrating forces. Such alliances have normally stressed strategic considerations, such as the offer of military basses or loyalty in a common ideological front. But economic ties or incentives may also be offered. Thus Salazar relied on the Azores (and the 'Anglo-Portuguese Alliance' of 1386), and after 1949 membership of NATO. Franco could not gain admission to NATO, but in 1953 secured a bilateral treaty with the USA that helped stabilize the Spanish dictatorship. The Greek authoritarians could invoke the Truman Doctrine, and their victory in the civil war (although in truth that legacy was more ambiguous than they wished to acknowledge). The Turkish military also invoked their security function within NATO as one justification for the periodic exercise of their political veto power. These protective alliances were not just imposed from without, but actively promoted and cultivated from within, where the driving motivation was as much the wish to stabilize the authoritarian regime as commitment to some world-wide political or ideological allegiance.

Bridging institutions or actors (like the Church or the monarchy), generally need a considerable degree of international support and protection if they are to carry out a stabilizing role in the cause of a democratization. At one extreme there are cases where the external support is virtually the sole source of backing for such an intermediary (e.g. Governor-General Sir Paul Scoon of Grenada). On the other hand, one can sometimes find virtually moribund domestic institutions, lacking all international legitimacy, which nevertheless come to life as a transitory vehicle for regime transition (Pasquino has described the case of the Fascist Grand Council in Italy in 1943,[13] and the Spanish Cortes may be viewed in this light in the mid-1970s). The more normal case lies somewhere in between. The more substantial and more complex role played by the Portuguese armed forces apparently involved little direct external instigation; and the Turkish military have also been described by some as relatively autonomous and as bridges to democratization. The clearest southern European case where external support substantially reinforced the authority and bargaining power of a bridging actor, and therefore helped to stabilize a potentially disruptive democratization, is provided by Greece. There, President Karamanlis, returning from exile in France, played a decisive role in reconciling elements of the outgoing regime to the need for a thorough regime change.[14] He was, of course, a well-established figure in domestic Greek politics, but his role in the transition was also substantially enhanced by the backing he received from Western Europe, and by the priority he attached to securing Greek entry into the European Community.[15]

In the absence of adequate internal bridging institutions or actors, there are international agencies—such as the UN, the OAS, the European Union, and the Contadora group—which could act as a functional equivalent for the missing domestic agency. With the backing of US troops the OAS played such a role in the Dominican Republic in 1965 (although whether or not this served the cause of democracy may be disputed); and the US government assumed this role more directly in the same country in 1978 (this time genuinely assisting democratization, and without sending troops). There are several other Latin American examples, although, like the US invasion of Panama in 1989, they tend to be somewhat embarrassingly neo-colonial in form.

So far this type of international substitution for weak or absent bridging institutions has hardly arisen as a factor shaping the recent democratizations of southern Europe, perhaps because the domestic bridging institutions were themselves relatively effective, or perhaps because too overt an external intervention would have been counter-productive, or at least unacceptable, to some of the parties. The US military occupation decisively shaped the course of Italian democratization in the later 1940s,[16] but it was not acting as a bridging institution in this case, since the defeat of Fascism had created a *tabula rasa*. Cyprus provides the regional exception, where international forces may play a bridging role, but it is not easy to summarize. Among the bridging institutions that have at various times since independence in 1960 attempted to mediate the twin problems of decolonization and democratization in Cyprus, one would have to consider NATO, the UN, the USA, the British government, and perhaps even the Greek Orthodox Church, not to mention the governments in Athens and Ankara. In the 1990s it is only through Graeco-Turkish co-operation that Cyprus may be reunited and redemocratized. So far, however, all these bridging institutions, whether acting alone or in concert, have proved inadequate to the task of promoting reconciliation between the two communities in Cyprus. It remains to be seen whether the eventual prospect of entry into the European Community might achieve the hitherto unattainable. But to date all Cypriot bridges have proved fatally weak in the middle.

The democratic opposition is another apparently domestic category that may in practice be closely linked to international politics. When opposition parties undertake realignments or negotiate pacts, there is usually a substantial international infrastructure of support (often but not always from such non-governmental organizations as the Socialist International and the World Council of Christian Democracy—see Chapters 8 and 9, above). It is hardly necessary to emphasize the international backing received by the various anti-Pinochet parties in Chile (see Chapter 7 above), or the rival contenders for power in El Salvador. There is a wide range of Latin American examples of this kind, indicating that various forms of international support—ranging from 'good offices' to funding and even direction of local parties—need to be considered when assessing the nature and success of democratizing pacts. (Of course, such international support can be obstructive or can distort the process of pact-making, as well as assist it.)

Among other things, many key opposition politicians may have had to operate from exile, as Mario Soares worked from London, Constantine Karamanlis from Paris, and the PSOE from Toulouse. Even Bulent Ecevit sought support from the Socialist International in the 1970s, although Karaosmanoglu stresses the relatively weak links between Turkish democratic parties and the party internationals.[17]

The evidence from southern Europe is mixed, but in general it seems that the various parties were relatively autonomous and chose their strategies mostly for domestic reasons. Apparently, neither the Spanish parties nor their Greek counterparts were guided much in their negotiations by their external backers or their co-religionaries. In some cases there was latent friction between the national organization and its international sympathizers, and more generally there was simply no advantage to be gained from playing up foreign alignments. In Turkey it was a positive handicap to be too aligned with international currents, and PASOK in Greece evidently chose to differentiate itself from West European social democracy. Even the Italian parties seem to have acted with a considerable degree of local initiative, despite their dependence on powerful external sponsors.

The case of Portugal appears less clear-cut. The Socialist Party received substantial funding and advice from such sources as the German SPD, and the CP allegedly received massive assistance from Moscow. One observer even claims that the support democratic forces received from Western parties was critical to the defeat of the Communist Party.[18] It could also be argued that Portuguese influence affected the subsequent process of transition in Spain, if only by indicating the pitfalls to be avoided.

The contrast between Spain and Portugal was in part a contrast between a 'pacted' democratization and one achieved through a process of 'rupture' and open confrontation. In a pacted transition the democratic forces usually keep their distance from external backers, whose involvement might taint the authenticity of a national agreement (although there are exceptions when foreign sponsors try to promote a pact that may be unattainable in the absence of international pressure).[19] In the more unusual case of a successful 'democratic rupture', the opposition's capacity to bring down an authoritarian regime will usually depend in part upon enlisting some international support. To create the necessary democratization within the regime, and to establish the requisite level of confidence in the opposition, it is likely to matter greatly how much international sympathy the challengers can appear to command. It was a fatal defect of the Dominican uprising of 1965 that the insurgents lacked international solidarity in their struggle against a military dictatorship; and the 1991 attempt to democratize Haiti under the freely elected presidency of Jean Bertrand Aristide also alienated some major sources of international support (evidently including the CIA), thus opening the way for a return of the military, who ousted the constitutional President and for three years sustained a military dictatorship, despite international protests.

It could be instructive to reconsider both the Greek and the Portuguese transitions from this standpoint. Soares and Karamanlis were well known internationally, and their credentials were reassuring to external backers. Indeed, like Betancourt in Venezuela and Aquino in the Philippines, these were democratic leaders who could be trusted by their Western backers to resist undue radicalization of the transition process. Moreover, the outgoing authoritarian regimes had deprived their foreign backers of any justification for coming to their assistance. Salazar and Caetano had persisted with their unwinnable and indefensible colonial war until the patience of the Portuguese military was exhausted; and the Greek Colonels had put NATO solidarity at risk. It was these blunders by the authoritarian regimes, rather than the strength of external support for their democratic challengers, that contributed most to international acceptance of the respective democratizations despite the attendant risks. (For the similarities and differences between these two transitions see Fishman.[20])

Thus, on closer inspection of the southern European experiences it appears that the main domestic actors and forces in contention (the authoritarian coalition, the bridging actors, and the democratic challengers) often derived part of their strength and cohesion and some of their objectives from external sources. In fact the external–internal distinction seems quite blurred and unhelpful when pressed too far. Despite these difficulties, the distinction can just about be sustained so long as attention is focused on actor-led interpretations of the democratization process, but it becomes considerably harder to justify when the level of analysis shifts to structural considerations, such as the 'confining condition' created by the prospect of EU membership. Actor-led interpretations seem most relevant to the transition phase of a democratization, whereas more impersonal and involuntary factors acquire greater prominence during the consolidation phase.

Viewed from a long-term comparative perspective, recent democratizations in southern Europe appear to represent the culmination of processes extending over several generations, if not centuries. Over the long haul the underlying issue was not simply democracy versus dictatorship, but rather the definition of a modern national identity and the creation of a consensus about where these nations belonged in the international system. Membership of the European Union seems to stabilize and render irreversible the democratization process because it also resolves these much larger and more profoundly unsettling issues. From this panoramic viewpoint, democratization is inextricably linked to the question of a nation's international orientation. If so it would be doubly misleading to overstress artificial distinctions between external and internal factors contributing to democratization.

Each of the authoritarian regimes of southern Europe offered its own distinctive solution to the problem of national identity and its own account of the country's place in the world. The breakdown of each regime signified the failure of its proposed solution and therefore raised the need to agree on an alternative approach. Indeed, in almost every country under consideration, a crisis over its international alignment played a critical part in the demise of the *ancien regime*. Most obviously, the collapse of Fascism was brought about as a consequence of Italy's alignment with the defeated Axis powers; the new identity established after 1945 was democratic, liberal, and European. After his victory in the Spanish Civil War Franco proposed a reactionary clerical centralist identity for Spain; he trod warily in his choice of international alignment, since both Communism and Western liberalism were viewed as enemies. However, by the time his regime terminated with his death, most of these initial positions had crumbled. In Fishman's terminology there was a crisis of 'historical obsolescence' in Spain, rather than of failure.[21] Even so this left the new Spanish democracy with a major task of national redefinition, including such contentious issues as whether to join NATO and whether to join the EC. The eventual choices were similar to those of Italy.

For Greece and Turkey the long processes of nation-building involved both economic and political Westernization, and for both countries the outcome of the Second World War was to confront them with the most painful choices of international alignment. The Greek Colonels and the Turkish Generals each regarded their respective countries as NATO's most indispensable ally in the Eastern Mediterranean, and consequently in 1974 the two allies blundered into war over technically neutral Cyprus. The ensuing crisis of identity was more profound for the losing Greeks than for the victorious Turks, which may help to explain why Athens democratized more thoroughly than Ankara. In any case, as Verney describes in depth, the redemocratization of Greece was accompanied by a far-reaching debate over international issues, and the consolidation of Greek democracy was not completed until a consensus emerged over the country's European and liberal vocation.[22] That issue remains unresolved in Turkey, as does the status of Turkish democracy.

Finally, the Salazar regime adopted the most inflexible and anachronistic stance over Portugal's national identity and vocation. Long after the other European colonial powers had bowed to the inevitability of decolonization, Lisbon still defended the myth of a multi-national Christian empire. The revolution of April 1974 was precipitated by the collapse of that myth, and the turmoil accompanying Portugal's democratization was deepened by profound uncertainty over what alternative international orientation might emerge.

Thus, in all these cases democratization involved the reopening of debates that had long been closed by repression, debate that simultaneously concerned the redefinition of domestic freedoms and of international alignments. The question linking the two parts of the debate was: 'so what kind of a nation shall we become?' In such a context it becomes artificial to disaggregate internal and external factors.

4. What Kind of Democracy? How much Variation?

In conclusion, then, some comments are called for on what kinds of nations the southern Europeans are establishing. What are their new international orientations and what will the resulting new democracies be like? Or, to put the same question another way: how far will the (sometimes utopian) hopes and aspirations aroused by the struggle for democracy have to be modified or abandoned when the eventual results crystallize?

Considering the three new southern European democracies as they now appear, one can make two observations that would have seemed quite surprising to most observers ten, or perhaps even five, years ago. First, they all seem remarkably well established, secure, and even quite flourishing democratic regimes. They all seem to be consolidated, socially entrenched, and organizationally institutionalized. (Even in the case of Greece, where this claim is perhaps most open to question, Tsingos makes the argument in forceful terms, in Chapter 12.[23]) There is, of course, no such thing as an 'impregnable' democracy, and it would be foolhardy to exclude the possibility that at some point in the future one or other of these regimes might become 'deconsolidated', but in this respect the new democracies of southern Europe are not much different from most old democracies. They are even surprisingly similar as regards the socio-economic content of their policies, for these are all rather conventional bourgeois liberal versions of democracy, with a largely private enterprise economic orientation. They also have a more or less shared set of priorities concerning welfare provision (the Social Chapter of the Maastricht Treaty), regional and agricultural policies (the structural fund and the Common Agricultural Policy), and on a widening range of other issues. As for their international alignments, they are all members of NATO (previously sensitive issues concerning American bases etc. have been resolved), they have all accepted the 1994 northward enlargement of the Union, and they are preparing to negotiate eastern and southern enlargements as well. Certainly there are conflicts of perception and priorities (not least in relation to ex-Yugoslavia and Turkey, where Greek national interests diverge from the rest[24]), but such tensions are expressed and managed politically within a collective framework of debate and decision-making. They are thus deeply immersed in the (often unseemly) routines of democratic-politics-as-usual.

These are not outcomes that were considered in any way inevitable at the outset. As recently as 1981 there were many in Spain who thought a resurgence of Francoism was possible, or who at least feared the disruptive consequences of a PSOE government. The Armed Forces Movement of Portugal retained some undemocratic 'reserve powers' until the Constitution was modified in the early 1980s. The first years of the Papandreou government in Greece could be viewed as potentially destabilizing, particularly in so far as the Western security system was concerned; and the closing years were unedifying in other ways. In the political rhetoric of these societies one can find relatively recent (and eminent) references to the dangers of 'Albanization' in Portugal, or 'Balkanization' in Spain, and of the conversion of Greece into something resembling Mintoff's Malta. From the other side of the political spectrum, not only the Communist Parties of these three countries but a wider community of leftist organizations expected to go beyond bourgeois democracy, and to establish a somehow more advanced, more progressive, more fully democratized form of society.

A simple explanation for why these regimes became so fully consolidated, and why they took such a conventional form, would be that that was what most of the population wanted or expected. Within a democratic framework, political activists or visionaries who moved too far away from this implicit social consensus (either too far towards radicalism, or too far towards reaction) would simply find their support disappearing. No doubt this is too simple and sweeping an explanation, but it evidently contains an important part of the truth. It still remains to be explained why popular political aspirations were so centrist, so conventional, and so well-established in these three historically and geographically dissimilar southern European societies.[25]

This chapter suggests one explanation. It could be that the European Union has played a major role in promoting and generalizing this pattern of political values.[26] One way this has occurred has simply been the 'demonstration effect' of security, prosperity, and moderation rightly or wrongly associated with European integration. Greece, Portugal, and Spain have long aspired to be fully recognized and equal states within the West European system. Since the 1960s that system has been more stable, more homogeneous, and more politically and economically successful than for several generations. (It may also have been less exciting, but that is a complaint for intellectuals only.) So any general European demonstration effect would act uniformly on all these southern European societies, to produce analogous expectations.

In addition to this rather abstract and intangible form of influence, the European Community also exerted some rather more direct and observable pressures on various strategic groups. Its influence on politicians, channelled through the Socialist International and the Christian Democrat International, has already been noted in Chapters 8 and 9. Its influence on businessmen, through the liberalization of trade and capital movements and the harmonization of tax and regulatory systems, deserves equal consideration.

Its influence on lawyers, journalists, academics, and similar opinion-formers probably merits special study. There was a two-fold influence on the working-class—partly via emigration and the experience of working conditions in France and West Germany, and partly via the consequent draining off of unemployment at home, so that those who remained had greater bargaining power. The influence on the military is harder to assess, but it may also have been integrative.

If this goes far to explain the homogeneity and stability of the new democracies of southern Europe, what does it suggest about the prospects for a wider extension of West European-type democratic regimes? Can Turkish politics and society be transformed in the same way? And if so, why do the societies of Sicily, Corsica, Ulster, and Cyprus seem to hold out so stubbornly against these democratizing and homogenizing influences? Democratization-through-convergence may well have been powerful throughout post-war Europe, but there are also substantial counter-currents, and southern Europe's history is far from over.

Notes

1. P. C. Schmitter, 'An Introduction to Southern European Transitions from Authoritarian Rule: Italy, Greece, Portugal, Spain and Turkey', in G. O'Donnell, P. C. Schmitter, and L. Whitehead (eds.), *Transitions from Authoritarian Rule*, pt. 1, *Prospects for Democracy* (Baltimore: Johns Hopkins University Press, 1986), 5.
2. A. Stepan, 'Paths Toward Redemocratization: Theoretical and Comparative Considerations', in O'Donnell, Schmitter, and Whitehead (eds.), *Transitions*, pt. 3.
3. Ibid. 65.
4. Ibid. 72.
5. S. Verney, 'Political Parties and Democratic Consolidation in Greece: To be or not to be within the European Community', in G. Pridham (ed.), *Securing Democracy: Political Parties and Democratic Consolidation in Southern Europe* (London: Routledge, 1990).
6. L. Whitehead, 'International Aspects of Democratization', in O'Donnell, Schmitter, and Whitehead (eds.), *Transitions*.
7. Verney, 'Political Parties'.
8. H. Tursan, 'The Impact of International Factors on Democratization in Turkey', paper presented to the Joint Sessions of the European Consortium for Political Research, Bochum, German Federal Republic, April 1990, 17–18. See also I. B. Neumann and J. M. Welsh, 'The Other in European Self-Definition', *Review of International Studies*, 17/4 (1991), 346.

9. A. L. Karaosmanoglu, 'The International Context of Democratic Transition in Turkey', in G. Pridham (ed.), *Encouraging Democracy: The International Context and Regime Transition in Southern Europe* (Leicester: Leicester University Press, 1991).
10. *Financial Times*, 16 September 1986.
11. G. Pridham, 'International Influences and Democratic Transition', in Pridham (ed.), *Encouraging Democracy*.
12. J. Linz, 'Transitions to Democracy', *Washington Quarterly* (summer 1990).
13. G. Pasquino, 'The Demise of the First Fascist Regimes and Italy's Transition to Democracy', in O'Donnell, Schmitter, and Whitehead (eds.), *Transitions*, pt. 1.
14. N. Diamandouros, 'Regime Transition and the Prospects for Democracy in Greece: 1974–83', in O'Donnell, Schmitter, and Whitehead (eds.), *Transitions*, pt. 1.
15. Verney, 'Political Parties', and ead. and T. Coloumbis, 'State-International Systems Interaction and the Greek Transition', in Pridham (ed.), *Encouraging Democracy*.
16. R. Leonardi, 'The International Context of Democratic Transition in Postwar Italy', in Pridham (ed.), *Encouraging Democracy*.
17. Karaosmanoglu, 'International Context'.
18. W. C. Opello jun., 'Portugal: A Case Study of International Determinants of Regime Transition', in Pridham (ed.), *Encouraging Democracy*.
19. L. Whitehead, 'The Consolidation of Fragile Democracies', in R. Pastor (ed.), *Democracy in the Americas: Stopping the Pendulum* (New York: Holmes and Meier, 1989).
20. R. M. Fishman, 'Rethinking State and Regime: Southern Europe's Transition to Democracy', *World Politics*, 42/3 (1990), 440.
21. Ibid.
22. Verney, 'Political Parties'.
23. Compare P. C. Iokamidis: 'Nearly 20 years after the establishment of the democratic system and 13 years after Greece's accession to the European Community, political institutions and processes appear to be more stable and consolidated than ever before in modern Greek history. It seems that Greece has . . . succeeded at long last in building up a workable political system which . . . is firmly entrenched in the social and cultural structure of the country.' 'The EC and the Greek Political System: An Overview', in P. Kazakos and P. C. Iokamides (eds.), *Greece and EC Membership Evaluated* (London: Pinter, 1994), 144.
24. Even so, Ioakimidis judges that 'Community membership and, even more than that, deeper integration appear now to be based, as policy options, on firm political consensus . . . Reaching political consensus . . . has far-reaching political repercussions for the political system and process. Consensus on EC membership practically means broader consensus on the whole range of foreign policy objectives. This is an important evolution for the stability of the political system because

it eliminates a pernicious source of dissension . . . Broad consensus on the EC seems likely to continue to underpin the dynamics of Greek politics and at the same time feed a growing political current calling for structural modernisation of the Greek economy.' (Ibid. 146.) Such modernization will be vital in the long run, given that despite EU transfer equivalent to about 5 per cent of Greek GDP per year, Greece remains the poorest country in the Union and the gap is widening.

25. Fishman, 'Rethinking State and Regime', 440.
26. 'Recent surveys show that membership of the Community has had a beneficial impact in gradually erasing the attitudes of uncertainty/ mistrust, replacing them with a sense of security as to the future of the country as a member of the Community.' Ioakimidis, 'EC and Greek Political System', 145–6, on Greece. This confirms a prediction by Arendt Lijphart, Thomas Bruneau, Nikiforos Diamandouros, and Richard Gunther, referring to all the southern European democracies. In 1988 they noted 'a trend of decreasing partisan differences. Especially the foreign policy and regime support issues are likely to become less salient as these democracies mature and as the major parties gain governing experience. Of course this trend will also make the southern European democracies less different from the other democracies.' 'A Mediterranean Model of Democracy?', *West European Politics*, 2/1 (Jan. 1988), 22.

International Aspects of Democratization: The Case of Spain

CHARLES POWELL

Introduction

Given the abundance of literature on Spain's transition to democracy, it is remarkable how little attention has been paid to the
international dimension of this process.[1] By and large, authors
writing on Spain appear to have accepted Schmitter's view that
'transitions from authoritarian rule and immediate prospects for
political democracy [are] largely to be explained by national forces
and calculations', and that 'external actors [tend] to play an indirect and usually marginal role, with the obvious exception of those
instances in which a foreign occupying power was present'. While
accepting the first half of this statement, this chapter will explore
the relationships linking domestic and external actors in Spain
during the period of pre-transition (1969–75) and transition proper
(1975–8), which have hitherto received scant attention. Additionally, it will attempt to provide answers derived from the Spanish
experience to some of the questions raised by Whitehead in his
International Aspects of Democratization concerning matters such
as the 'promotion of democracy' as a foreign policy objective, the
nature of the instruments available to those pursuing such a goal,
and the ability of domestic actors to benefit from it.[2]

As had already happened during Spain's first transition from dictatorship to democracy in the early 1930s, in the mid-1970s rapid
political change took place at a time of international economic crisis.
After benefiting from over a decade of sustained European growth,
the Spanish economy, always heavily dependent on imported oil
for its energy, was severely hit by the sudden increase in prices
in 1973–4, and entered a period of stagflation. Some authors have

argued that this crisis contributed to democratization by undermining confidence in a regime which had staked much of its prestige
on the socio-economic achievements of the previous decade. Contemporary opinion polls, however, suggest that the Spanish public
did not attribute this severe economic crisis to the government,
but rather to factors beyond its control. Nevertheless, the widespread labour unrest which accompanied the crisis may have contributed to underlining the regime's inability to provide answers
to the nation's most pressing problems.[3]

Be this as it may, successive transition governments postponed
economic adjustment to the oil shock and the ensuing crisis until
the Moncloa Pacts of 1977, largely out of fear of upsetting an already
delicate balance. Although this delay was to prove extremely damaging in economic terms, leaving Spain unprepared for the second
oil crisis of 1979, in the short term it undoubtedly eased the transition process. According to one author, it was Spain's high level of
reserves and general credit-worthiness, and indeed the attitude of
the international finance community as a whole, which allowed it
to overcome circumstances not unlike those which had contributed
to the collapse of the Second Republic in the 1930s.[4]

The international political climate of the mid-1970s was undoubtedly more favourable to democratization than it had been in
the 1930s. Above all, by 1975 Spain's major neighbours and partners were democratically governed, and regarded its authoritarian
regime as an anachronistic relic of the inter-war years. Additionally, the early stages of the transition coincided with a thaw in the
Cold War still being waged by the superpowers, a phase marked by
the Ford–Brezhnev summit meeting at Vladivostock in late 1974,
and the signing of the Helsinki Final Act in the summer of 1975.

The Cold War

Spain had effectively taken sides in the Cold War in 1953, when
it signed its crucial bilateral agreement with the United States,
whereby the latter provided military and economic aid in return
for the use of military bases. This agreement, which effectively integrated Spain in to the Western defence system, was subsequently
renewed in 1963, 1970, and 1976. The United States had favoured
Spanish membership of NATO ever since its creation, but had
invariably stumbled on Scandinavian, Dutch, and British opposition to Franco's authoritarian regime, notwithstanding the fact
that the similarly dictatorial Salazar had been a founding member
of the Alliance.

In the early 1970s, developments in Spain's vicinity contributed to augmenting her already considerable geo-strategic importance to the West. Above all, the world economic crisis triggered by the 1973–4 oil shock increased the strategic value of the Straits of Gibraltar, since most Middle East oil reached Western Europe and the USA via the Mediterranean. In October 1973 the Yom Kippur war underlined the importance of the Spanish bases, even though the Franco government, anxious not to antagonize its Arab allies, forced US aircraft in transit to Israel to refuel in the air. Shortly afterwards, the collapse of the Portuguese dictatorship following the military coup of 25 April 1974 seriously threatened to undermine NATO's southern flank, prompting the United States to press for Spanish membership with renewed vigour. Several months later, at the other end of the Mediterranean, the Cypriot crisis resulted in the departure of the Greek Colonels, who were succeeded by a government which saw in NATO a symbol of US support for the military junta. What was more, the conflict over Cyprus led the USA to impose an arms embargo on the Turks, who in turn threatened to seek Soviet support. Finally, throughout this period, the French and Italian Communist parties steadily improved their electoral performance, to the extent that many in the West expected them to participate in future coalition governments.

The most important of these events, in terms of its impact on the domestic political situation in Spain, was undoubtedly the Portuguese Revolution.[5] One unexpected by-product of the revolution was the creation in Spain of the Unión Militar Democrática (UMD), a clandestine organization consisting of several hundred young officers dedicated to the establishment of a democratic system of government and the political independence of the armed forces. The UMD did not aim to emulate the Portuguese MFA (which provided them with considerable support), but rather to prevent the more reactionary sectors of the Spanish military from intervening against a civilian uprising against the regime. The UMD grew rapidly in 1974–5, but collapsed when its leaders were court-martialled and expelled from the armed forces in 1976. In spite of their failure, the discovery that not even the military were immune to contagion from the democratic virus provided reformists within the regime with fresh evidence of the need to find a new institutional role for the armed forces, something which could best be achieved in the context of a constitutional democracy.

The Left opposition naturally read Caetano's failure to perpetuate the Salazar dictatorship beyond his retirement as evidence that something similar could be expected in Spain after Franco's death.

More specifically, the Communist Party (PCE) initially believed that events in Portugal vindicated its own efforts to attain a broad-based, cross-class 'pact for freedom', but the Portuguese Communist Party's subsequent attempt to seize power by non-democratic means (which the Spanish Party hastened to condemn) undermined its case somewhat. In marked contrast, the far smaller, recently renovated Socialist Party (PSOE) concluded that decades of clandestine struggle against a dictatorship did not guarantee electoral success, and that, with sufficient external support, a relatively new party could soon challenge better-established rivals.[6]

Reformists within the regime who had become increasingly outspoken in demand of constitutional reforms which might pave the way for more substantial changes after Franco's death also felt vindicated by events in Portugal. These sectors had repeatedly warned that Prime Minister Carrero Blanco's refusal to contemplate such measures could only lead to a violent outburst from below, and they consequently stepped up the pressure on his successor, Carlos Arias Navarro, though to little avail. Most importantly, the Portuguese Revolution taught the reformists that, after decades of right-wing authoritarianism, political parties capable of representing the more moderate, even conservative, sectors of society could not be improvised overnight.[7]

Finally, the events in Portugal appear to have had a significant impact on Juan Carlos, who had been waiting in the wings since his appointment as Franco's successor in 1969. The Prince had spent part of his childhood in exile near Lisbon, and, unusually for a Spaniard, spoke Portuguese and knew the country well. Juan Carlos was personally involved in assisting prominent Portuguese financiers and industrialists who fled the country in the aftermath of the coup, an experience which appears to have strengthened his resolve to carry out the necessary reforms to prevent something similar occurring in Spain.[8]

Events in Portugal were also important in that they influenced the major external actors' perceptions of Spain's immediate prospects. The threat of a Communist take-over in Portugal initially led the US administration, and particularly Henry Kissinger, Secretary of State in 1973–6, to view further political change in the Iberian Peninsula with deep apprehension. Paradoxically, by late 1975 the Portuguese experience had discouraged the USSR from becoming entangled in Spain. Most importantly of all, the success of the German-led intervention in Portugal, aimed at defeating Communist efforts to take power while strengthening Soares's PSP, proved that even a situation which seemed lost could be turned around to the West's advantage.[9]

Kissinger has claimed that 'America's contribution to Spain's evolution during the 1970s has been one of the major achievements of our foreign policy.' However, Wells Stabler, US Ambassador in Madrid from 1975 to 1978, is of the opinion that 'one might have spposed that . . . the United States would have developed some form of policy toward the future of Spain, already having some idea of what the dynamics were . . . but the fact is that the United States really didn't do a great deal'. On the whole, US governments adopted a largely passive attitude, while endorsing the democratizing process in as far as it proved compatible with the existing balance of power in southern Europe, and in particular, with their continued access to Spanish military bases.[10]

Given its excellent relations with the Franco regime, we should first ask ourselves whether the US had any substantive interest in a change of regime. On the one hand, it was reasonable to expect future democratic governments to become increasingly demanding when it came to renewing the crucial bases treaty, as indeed was to be the case. A democratic Spain, however, would finally be free to join NATO, thereby strengthening the southern flank which so obsessed Kissinger. Equally, a democratic Spain would also be able to join the European Community, something the US had advocated even against its own economic self-interest, on the grounds that it would anchor the country permanently in the Western camp. As one senior US diplomat serving in Spain in 1974–8 observed, in theory 'the security relationship itself [would] be more soundly based for the long term if founded on a democratic consensus than if derived from the will of one man'.[11]

In Kissinger's view, during the final years of the Franco regime, the US administration had been faced with the choice of having to 'ostracize and oppose the existing regime or, while working with it, to extend our contacts and therefore our influence for the post-Franco period'; it opted for the latter course of action. President Nixon undoubtedly showed some concern for the Spanish situation during his mandate, particularly after his visit to Madrid in late 1970, at a time when, in Kissinger's words, 'the post-Franco transition was a subject too delicate for even the most oblique allusion'. Nixon concluded that he should support Prince Juan Carlos, and invited him to Washington in early 1971. Shortly afterwards, he sent the deputy head of the CIA, Vernon Walters, on a secret fact-finding mission to Spain, which included an interview with Franco.

In spite of the latter's efforts to reassure Walters that existing arrangements would guarantee a peaceful transition to a somewhat more democratic monarchy after his death, the US administration remained uneasy about the future.[12]

The Secretary of State's high opinion of the US's ability to cultivate 'moderate elements in Spanish government and society' was largely unjustified, however. Indeed Washington was barely in touch with even the most moderate sectors of the democratic opposition until shortly before Franco's death. In May 1970, for example, the US Embassy in Madrid acted in collusion with the Spanish government in preventing a delegation of moderate opposition leaders from presenting Secretary of State William Rogers with a document opposing the renewal of the bases treaty. In 1974 a deputy assistant secretary travelled to Madrid to meet a handful of moderate opposition leaders, prompting a furious response from the authorities. A year later the newly appointed US Ambassador, Stabler, arranged a meeting between moderate opposition leaders and President Gerald Ford, but later cancelled it at the request of the Spanish government. In spite of this, Stabler gradually established contact with leaders of the non-Communist opposition—including the socialist leader Felipe González—in the course of 1975–6. Even though the Communist Party was the largest and most well-organized opposition group, the US administration refused to have any dealings with it, as a delegation from the Communist-led Junta Democrática platform discovered on visiting Washington in mid-1975.[13]

As both Kissinger and Stabler have acknowledged, on the eve of Franco's death the top priority for the US administration was not democratization, but rather the renewal of the bases agreement, which was due to expire in 1975. This determination to secure a military presence in Spain at any price caused concern and dismay in some West European capitals. In May 1975 German chancellor Helmut Schmidt reminded President Ford that the Franco era was obviously coming to an end, in view of which 'we should be encouraging those we hope will govern after Franco; that means we must deal not only with those who are in power now'. Ford objected that the renewal of the bases agreement was of vital interest to the West, to which Schmidt replied that 'so that you can be sure of your bases and your special strategic ties with Spain beyond today, you should talk about it with tomorrow's rulers as well'. Ford ignored this advice, however, and in October 1975, at the height of a major international campaign against the regime triggered by the execution of five anti-Franco activists, the US signed a pre-agreement for the renewal of the lease on the bases.[14]

Kissinger initially behaved as though Franco's death in November 1975 and Juan Carlos's proclamation as King of Spain had no direct bearing on US–Spanish relations, but the new authorities in Madrid thought otherwise. Although Juan Carlos inherited a prime minister, Arias Navarro, who was lukewarm about undertaking substantial reforms, his new foreign minister, José María de Areilza, was firmly committed to the establishment of a Western-style parliamentary monarchy. The latter immediately insisted on elevating the US–Spanish agreement to the status of a treaty, which required the approval of the US Senate, a body traditionally hostile to the Franco regime. Areilza thereby hoped to underline US recognition of the fact that it was no longer dealing with an authoritarian regime, but with a future democracy. The new Treaty was duly signed in January 1976, paving the way for Juan Carlos's visit to Washington in June, in the course of which he openly committed himself to a Western-style democracy in a speech to the US Congress.[15]

In spite of this explicit support for the young monarch, Kissinger remained highly sceptical as to the short-term prospects for democracy in Spain, and resented West European pressure in favour of democratization. In particular, as Areilza soon realized, the Secretary of State was unenthusiastic about the legalization of the Communist Party, an issue which would soon dominate the domestic political debate. Responding to claims that the US had vetoed Communist participation, in June 1976 the State Department declared that, while this was a purely internal affair, 'in our judgement it would be absurd to make legalization of a party dedicated to authoritarian principles a litmus test as to whether or not democratization is taking place'. This statement failed to convince many observers, notably the Communists themselves, who hastened to declare that they would not object to a democratically elected government applying for NATO membership.[16]

The Carter Administration, which took office in late 1976, appears to have adopted a somewhat more pragmatic stance towards Communism in Western Europe generally, an attitude which may have tempered earlier opposition to the legalization of the PCE. In early 1977 Secretary of State Cyrus Vance defended legalization on the grounds that 'icebergs are more dangerous when they are submerged', though he was still in favour of excluding the Communists from the first elections. Adolfo Suárez nevertheless legalized the PCE in April 1977, on the eve of his first visit to the US, during which he was treated somewhat coldly by the Carter Administration. Ambassador Stabler would later reflect that 'if we took the view that we supported Spanish democracy, then we ought to have followed through so that people involved believed we supported them'.[17]

The Soviet Union played a far less prominent role in the Spanish process than the United States. The USSR had come to accept Spanish membership of the Western bloc, and although the Franco regime had refused to establish diplomatic relations with Moscow, the early 1970s witnessed a marked improvement in commerical relations. In Portugal the Soviets had lent substantial support to the Communists in the hope that domestic turmoil would lead to the independence of the African colonies and a significant shift in the regional balance of power at the expense of the West. Spain offered no comparable possibilities, since the USA and France had already indicated their support for Moroccan ambitions in the former Spanish Sahara. Additionally, Soviet involvement in Portugal had briefly threatened to jeopardize *détente*, and the USSR was unwilling to risk irritating the West further with renewed incursions in the Iberian Peninsula.

Contrary to what decades of anti-Francoist rhetoric might suggest, the existence of an authoritarian regime in Spain had suited the Soviets well, in spite of the bases agreement with the USA. Precisely so as to compensate for the latter, in the 1960s Spanish foreign-policy-makers had displayed a strong independent streak, notably in relation to Latin America (including Castro's Cuba) and the Arab world, thereby irritating the West. Democratization was expected to pave the way for Spanish integration into the EC and NATO, which Moscow paradoxically equated with an increase in US influence in Western Europe. Seen in this light, the USSR had little to gain from a successful transition to democracy in Spain, except the establishment of full diplomatic relations, and hence the improvement of commercial ones.

In marked contrast with the Portuguese case, Soviet involvement in Spain was also limited by the absence of a powerful domestic ally. The PCE had become increasingly critical of the USSR since the invasion of Czechoslovakia in 1968, and was anxious to distance itself from Soviet foreign policy. In 1974 the PCE strongly opposed the Portuguese Communists' attempt to take power by non-democratic means, and read Moscow's support for Cunhal as evidence of Soviet determination to undermine Spanish efforts to build a broad, democratic anti-Franco alliance. Relations deteriorated further after the conference of European Communist parties held in East Berlin in mid-1976, at which Secretary General Santiago Carrillo announced he would never take part in another such gathering. Given this increasingly independent stance, and Carrillo's efforts to influence other Communist parties in a similar direction, the Soviets may have come to contemplate the PCE's legalization and possible electoral success with some trepidation. Significantly, Moscow established full diplomatic relations with Spain in February 1977, at a time when there was still uncertainty as to the PCE's legalization.[18]

Even if relations had been more cordial, the Soviets had reason to doubt whether the PCE would be an efficient obstacle to US influence in Spain. Already in 1974 the party's Eurocommunist policies had led it to acknowledge the impossibility of dismantling US bases in Spain as long as the USSR kept a presence in Central and Eastern Europe. Although the PCE remained hostile to Spanish membership of NATO, as we saw above, by mid-1976 it was willing to accept a democratically adopted decision to join. Furthermore, since the late 1960s, the PCE had been firmly committed to the cause of European integration.[19]

The European Community

On the eve of Franco's death, the consensus amongst leading West European powers concerning Spain's immediate future was qualitatively different to that predominant in the United States. Broadly speaking, while for the latter Spain's future was primarily a defence and security issue, for the former it was essentially a political one. This discrepancy reflects fundamentally different attitudes towards the promotion of democracy generally, which Whitehead has attributed to their contrasting histories, their distinctive geopolitical roles, and their differences of political structure.[20] In practice, it resulted in a much more assertive role being played by leading West European governments, notably that of the Federal Republic of Germany. Unlike Kissinger, Chancellor Schmidt and his leading West European partners thought that 'the chances were particularly good for a shift to democracy in Spain', and tended to act accordingly.[21]

It should nevertheless be remembered that, in spite of their post-war hostility to the Franco regime, the leading West European nations had gradually established a reasonable working relationship with Spain. The opening-up of Spain's economy in the late 1950s took place with the full acquiesence of all OECD countries, not just the United States, and the economic miracle of 1960–73 would not have occurred if Western Europe had not supplied direct capital investment, tourists, and jobs for Spanish emigrants in abundance. France and Germany in particular appear to have encouraged Spain's economic development—and closer ties with Europe—in the hope that this would eventually create conditions conducive to the restoration of democracy, an attitude which was of course fully compatible with their own economic self-interest.

It could also be argued that thanks to the US–Spanish bases agreement of 1953, the European democracies had benefited from Franco's indirect contribution to Western defence without having to offer anything in return. One possible exception to this was France, which obtained its own limited military agreement on 1970, with a Spanish government determined to show the USA that it had allies elsewhere.

In spite of these growing links, Franco's Spain failed to overcome its pariah status. This situation was somewhat alleviated by Juan Carlos's appointment as Franco's successor in 1969, which allowed West European governments to cultivate him, thereby appearing to bolster the Franco regime. The prince made his first official visit to France in 1970, and to Germany in 1973. Other European states, notably the Scandinavians, did not invite him until after the restoration of democracy.

The leading West European governments also expressed their commitment to democratic change by becoming increasingly outspoken in their support for the domestic opposition. The latter's contacts abroad gradually raised the cost of repression for the regime, thereby providing them with a degree of protection, if not immunity. Indeed the semi-toleration of the moderate opposition so characteristic of the early 1970s was partly the consequence of the proliferation of external links. The contrast between US and European attitudes is particularly striking in this respect. The same Spanish government which prevented Secretary of State Rogers from meeting a group of opposition leaders in May 1970 had acceded to German foreign minister Walter Scheel's request for a similar interview in April. This type of discrepancy did not go unnoticed by the domestic opposition.[22]

Governmental willingness to intervene in support of opposition groups depended largely—though not entirely—on the degree of ideological affinity. Schmidt has claimed that 'we supported *all* democratic parties and labour unions to the best of our ability', but there is in fact no evidence of German government intervention on behalf of the PCE or the Communist-controlled Workers' Commissions. Nevertheless, the German SPD–FPD coalition governments of 1969–82 proved considerably more interventionist than

Pompidou's government of 1970–4, or Heath's Conservative government of the same period.

The German government's efforts proved particularly effective in this respect. In 1971 the German Embassy secured the release of a group of prominent socialist leaders, amongst them González, accused of membership of an illegal organization. In 1975, at the Helsinki summit, Schmidt successfully requested Arias Navarro to restore González's passport. Months later, with the help of Prince Juan Carlos, a different German ambassador obtained the release of another prominent socialist, responsible for his party's external relations, who had been arrested for criticizing the government during a visit to Sweden.[23]

Diplomatic pressure from West European governments did not always succeed, however. In early 1974, for example, a young anarchist was garrotted by the authorities in spite of pleas for clemency from abroad. In September 1975 five activists belonging to the terrorist organizations ETA and FRAP were also executed by the regime in defiance of international public opinion, in response to which every major European government recalled its ambassador from Madrid. It is no doubt significant that in both cases the victims lacked substantial support from abroad, not least because European public opinion was divided over the question of the use of violence against a non-democratic regime.[24]

In November 1975, the major European governments reaffirmed their condemnation of the regime by abstaining from sending high-level representatives to Franco's funeral. This was in marked contrast to the presence of President Giscard d'Estaing, President Scheel, and the Duke of Edinburgh at Juan Carlos's proclamation ceremony held shortly afterwards. The French president, who had been recruited to the young monarch's cause by the latter's father, Don Juan, became a staunch advocate of Spanish democratization. Even Prime Minister Harold Wilson, hardly a friend of the Franco regime, became quietly supportive when he learnt of the king's intentions from Lord Mountbatten.[25]

In the wake of Franco's death, leading European governments pursued two separate though complementary strategies with regard to Spain. One the one hand, they did their best to urge the king and his successive governments to move slowly but surely along the road to full democratization. At the same time, they supported the moderate opposition—and, in the Italian case, the Communists as well—in their efforts to conquer official recognition and win the right to participate in free elections to a constituent assembly.

The German government, which had intervened so decisively in events in Portugal, was particularly anxious to ensure that the PCE did not establish itself as the hegemonic party of the Left, and strongly supported the PSOE in its transition from clandestinity to legality. Thus, in late 1975 the German ambassador complained to foreign minister Areilza that Chancellor Schmidt came under pressure from his party, the SPD, every time the Spanish police acted against the PSOE. On other occasions, it was the PSOE's initiatives—such as the decision to join the PCE in a broad opposition alliance in March 1976—which prompted Areilza to seek German government support in requesting the SPD to apply pressure on their Spanish allies.[26]

The ability of West European governments to deal with both government and opposition in this manner is best understood against the background of Spain's relations with the European Community, and, to a lesser extent, the Council of Europe. Both these institutions had consistently refused to accept Spain as a full member on account of the non-democratic nature of its regime, effectively imposing a long-standing veto which served both to undermine its credibility and to encourage those committed to democratic change.[27]

Spain's application for associate membership of the EEC in 1962 had prompted an immediate response from European socialists in the form of the European Parliament's Birkelbach report, which stated that 'only states which guarantee in their territories truly democratic practices and respect for fundamental rights and freedoms' should be eligible. The leaders of both the internal and the exiled anti-Franco opposition subsequently met at Munich under the auspices of the European Movement, formally requesting that Spain be excluded from the major European institutions until democracy was restored. Despite the changes which subsequently took place within the opposition camp, this aspect of their programme was to remain unaltered during the ensuing fifteen years.

The European Parliament's recommendation did not prevent the EC Commission from exploring closer links with Spain, a process which eventually led to the signing of a preferential trade agreement in 1970. Although this was extremely favourable to Spanish economic interests, Britain's accession in 1973 threatened to disrupt it, forcing Madrid to seek fresh talks with Brussels, a process still under way at the time of Franco's death.[28]

In the Spanish case, the EC represented a complex system of medium- and long-term incentives and guarantees tending to favour democratization. On the one hand, by depriving Spain of the real (and imagined) benefits of full integration in a rapidly developing community, the EC's veto contributed to undermining the ruling authoritarian coalition, elements of which began to regard the regime's continued existence as a hindrance to their present and future prosperity. Economic élites became particularly anxious after the 1973 enlargement, due to the importance of the British market for Spanish goods. The literature produced by the regime's reformists in the 1969–75 period, particularly in the wake of Prime Minister Carrero Blanco's assassination in 1973, provides ample evidence of this growing dissatisfaction.[29]

Additionally, the veto enforced by the EC (and to a lesser extent, that of the Council of Europe), together with the growing prosperity and stability of Western Europe in the 1960s, contributed to enhancing the appeal of parliamentary democracy as practised in EC member states in the eyes of Spanish élites and public opinion at large. More specifically, regardless of its shortcomings, the EC came to be seen as the embodiment of European values, notably liberal democracy, and an antidote to the regime's authoritarianism. It was thus widely accepted that the democratizing process would be incomplete until it had been formally sanctioned by Brussels, while Spain's continued exclusion from the EC would represent an insult to national pride as well as a negation of democratic credibility.[30]

Finally, both before and during the transition to democracy, the prospect of EC membership provided guarantees and reassurances to those who faced a post-authoritarian future with apprehension. As Whitehead has observed, membership could be expected to guarantee the free movement of capital, the freedom to travel and seek employment abroad, and legal protection against arbitrary confiscation of property, all of which were highly valued by Spain's wealthy classes. The same author has argued that if such external guarantees had existed for these classes in the 1930s, they would have been far less inclined to take up arms against the Second Republic.[31]

The mere fact that by the early 1970s even the Communists were enthusiastic advocates of EC membership for a democratic Spain represented a significant guarantee. The Communists were evidently aware of this, and never missed an opportunity to publicize their commitment to European democratic values. Thus when they finally succeeded in forming their own opposition platform, the Junta Democrática, in 1974, they hastened to present their political programme to the EC authorities in Brussels. The socialist-inspired Plataforma de Convergencia Democrática, formed in 1975, proved equally anxious to have its European—and hence democratic—credentials endorsed by the EC.

In his enthronement speech of November 1975, King Juan Carlos proclaimed Spain's renewed commitment to full integration in Europe's major institutions, a goal subsequently reaffirmed by his first government. By so doing, those in power effectively invited the EC (and the Council of Europe) to monitor developments in Spain and pass judgement as to when and how the political requisites for membership should be met. This simultaneously enabled the democratic opposition to open an external, European front in their ongoing struggle with those in power.

Both the European Parliament (EP) and the Parliamentary Assembly of the Council of Europe had already begun to perform this task in the wake of Carrero Blanco's assassination in late 1973, largely, though by no means exclusively, at the instigation of their socialist members. The March 1974 execution of the young anarchist, combined with government threats of expulsion against the Bishop of Bilbao for his defence of Basque minority rights, prompted the EP to warn Madrid that this behaviour was unacceptable from a candidate for EC membership. In October 1975, after appealing to the Spanish authorities for clemency, the EP responded to the execution of the five anti-Franco activists with a resolution demanding the suspension of the talks then taking place between the EC and Spain for the updating of the 1970 agreement, which the Commission and the Council promptly endorsed. As we saw above, with the exception of Ireland, the governments of all EC members states recalled their ambassadors from Madrid. Much to the irritation of many MEPs, however, the Council agreed to resume talks in early 1976, before the new Spanish government had proved its democratizing intentions.

The EP held a major debate on Spain in February 1976, in the course of which Socialist and Communist MEPs dismissed Arias Navarro's programme as a half-hearted liberalization of the existing political system. Earlier, a debate in the Council of Europe's Assembly had produced similar conclusions, and a resolution reminding the Spanish authorities that admission to the major European institutions required the legalization of all political parties and the election of a parliament by universal suffrage. Significantly, the resolution also called on all political parties represented in the Assembly to assist their Spanish counterparts by every means available.

Areilza's subsequent tour of the nine EC capitals failed to convince Brussels of his government's willingness or ability to carry out far-reaching reforms. Relations reached their lowest point in April 1976, following the arrest of opposition leaders who had met to announce the creation of a single opposition platform, thereby foiling government efforts to exclude Communists from the democratizing process. This prompted a formal protest from EC heads of government which greatly embarrassed both the king and his foreign minister.[32]

In May 1976 the EP adopted a text by its rapporteur on Spain, Maurice Faure, which explicitly linked Spanish membership of the EC to progress on the road to democracy. Faure specifically condemned Arias Navarro's plans for a bicameral Cortes, in which a democratically elected Congress would share power with a 'corporatist' Senate, on the grounds that such a Parliament 'would not measure up to the democratic standards we in the countries of Western Europe set for ourselves'. Significantly, he also objected to government attempts to exclude the PCE from the first elections, arguing that 'the legal existence of communist parties is a characteristic common to our Western democracies' and consequently a requisite for Spanish accession to the EC. As we have seen, this was in marked contrast to the US State Department's stance on the issue.

The king's decision to replace Arias Navarro with Suárez in July 1976 paved the way for a rapid improvement in Spain's political relations with the European institutions. After discussing Suárez's programme with government and opposition representatives in Madrid, the EP and Assembly rapporteurs agreed to give him the benefit of the doubt. In December, Faure returned to express EP satisfaction at the success of the referendum on the decisive Political Reform Law, and advised the government to bring the PSOE into the political process as soon as possible so as to avoid a return to the popular frontism of the 1930s. Interestingly, he also recommended that Spain adopt a system of proportional representation like the German system, on the grounds that majoritarian systems were better suited to well-established democracies. In the event, the government adopted an electoral system not unlike that proposed by Faure.[33]

In April 1977 the EP responded to the legalization of the Communist Party with a resolution which amounted to an enthusiastic endorsement of Suárez's performance to date. Three months later, in the wake of Spain's first democratic elections in over thirty years, the EP expressed the 'political will to see Spain occupy its place in the European Community as soon as possible', in view of which the newly elected government immediately submitted its application. The Assembly also hastened to recognize the new democratic Cortes, and invited its representatives to attend its meetings as observers, which paved the way for full membership of the Council of Europe in November 1977. That autumn, Suárez embarked on a tour of the nine EC capitals, in the course of which it became apparent that, in spite of having met the political requisites laid down by Brussels, Spain's road to full membership would be a difficult one. Nevertheless, this exernal, largely symbolic endorsement of Spanish democratization was extremely important in the eyes of domestic actors.

The ability to monitor and influence developments in Spain from abroad in this manner—even during Franco's lifetime—may largely be attributed to the existence of effective transnational party networks.[34] Thus, the presidents of the EP's Socialist, Christian Democratic, and Liberal groups were in constant communication with their Spanish allies, who kept them fully informed of the latest developments. At the same time, these links enabled the Spanish opposition to have a direct say in the formulation of motions and questions debated by the EP and the Assembly.

As well as enabling the European institutions to influence events in Spain, these transnational links proved highly beneficial to the democratic opposition. After forty years of authoritarian rule, only highly committed anti-Francoists were fully satisfied as to the opposition's right to speak on behalf of Spanish democrats. Access to European institutions which were widely associated with democratic values thus played a crucial role in the domestic opposition's efforts to establish their credibility in the eyes of potential voters.

The Socialist International

The most effective transnational party organization active in Spain was undoubtedly the Socialist International (SI). Partly due to the prominent place occupied by the Civil War in the collective memory of the European Left, the SI had been consistently hostile to the Franco regime since its relaunching in 1951, and one of its first acts was to protest against the United States' *rapprochement* with the Franco regime, on the grounds that 'democracy cannot be defended by measures which would reinforce the position of dictatorship in the world'. It was thus by no means coincidental that Birkelbach, the author of the report which largely stymied Spain's 1962 EC application, should have been the president of the EP's socialist group.

Although the PSOE had been a founding member of the SI, in the 1960s its lack of social support within Spain and the shortcomings of its exiled leadership led some European parties to cultivate the increasingly attractive and independent PCE as well as other socialist groups. Professor Tierno Galván's Partido Socialista del Interior, formed in 1968, was particulary successful in attracting support from the German SPD. Indeed, for much of this period, the PSOE relied very heavily on the financial assistance of its sister union, the UGT, which was in turn largely provided by West European and North American labour organizations. In 1972, however, the younger, more dynamic sectors of the party, both in Spain and abroad, successfully challenged the exiled faction led by Llopis, whose desperate attempt to remain in control by calling his own congress merely formalized the split within the party. After failing to arbitrate a friendly reconciliation, the SI temporarily suspended the PSOE's membership until it could determine which faction was entitled to speak on behalf of Spanish socialists, finally settling for the larger group, active within Spain, in early 1974.

In many ways, the defeated historic faction led by Llopis was more in tune with the major parties of the SI—particularly those of northern Europe—than the renovated PSOE. Llopis was moderate, pro-Western, and deeply anti-Communist, while his rivals cultivated a radical left-wing rhetoric, were highly critical of the US presence in Spain, and understood the need to collaborate with the PCE, which was after all by far the largest opposition party. In spite of this, the SI opted for the latter because it believed it to have a much more active presence in Spain. The renovated PSOE lobbied hard in several countries to win external support, but it was the visits to Spain by Italian socialists and by Michael Foot during 1973 which proved decisive.[35]

Paradoxically, once they awoke to its potential, it was the more moderate, northern European members of the SI—notably the German, Swedish, and Austrian parties—which proved most supportive of the renovated PSOE. Mitterrand was initially very sceptical as to the PSOE's possibilities, and showed far greater interest in the PCE. This was of course fully in keeping with his own electoral strategy, which envisaged an alliance with the PCF capable of taking him to the presidency. Largely due to his rivalry with the Stalinist PCP, at first Soares also courted Carrillo, who was the guest of honour at his party conference in late 1974, much to the PSOE's chagrin. Although relations with the PSF improved considerably after Franco's death, the PSOE systematically opposed Mitterrand's efforts to forge a Mediterranean socialist identity, which were clearly aimed at reducing the SPD's influence in the SI.[36]

The SI's immediate goal in Spain was the establishment of a Western-style parliamentary democracy. Member parties applied pressure on the Spanish authorities both directly, through the national governments in which they held or shared power, and indirectly, through their representatives in the major European institutions. At the same time, SI parties offered the PSOE substantial financial, political, and diplomatic support, thereby contributing to the process whereby the small, ill-organized faction which emerged in 1972–4 was able to develop into the major opposition party by 1977.[37]

The SI owed much of its clout to its ability to influence Spain's relations with both the EC and NATO, notably the former. On the eve of Franco's death, parties belonging to the SI held office— alone or in coalition—in six of the nine EC members states. In mid-1975 the SI formally reminded member parties that 'as long as there is not a democratic government in place, Spain should not be associated with NATO or with the European Community', urging them to 'ensure that the present status of Spain *vis-à-vis* NATO and the EEC is not modified'. In October the SI played a major role in the international campaign unleashed against the regime in protest at the executions mentioned above, with Swedish Prime Minister Olof Palme taking the lead. Only days before Franco's death, the SI urged parties currently in office in Western Europe to apply pressure on the United States and France 'not to establish any new military or political relations with the new regime and to avoid giving Juan Carlos new prestige', while encouraging the latter to 'establish a full democracy in Spain and to end the structure and institutions of the Franco regime'.[38]

Not surprisingly, in his tour of EC capitals in early 1976, Areilza soon discovered that ministers were anxious to discuss—and if possible influence—his government's attitude towards the PSOE and other socialist parties. In Britain, Denmark, and Germany (where he visited the headquarters of the SPD), it was made clear to him that the prompt legalization of the PSOE would significantly improve Spain's standing with EC members. In Luxembourg Areilza was even advised to establish diplomatic relations with Israel, given the Israeli Labour party's ability to influence SI attitudes to Spanish membership of the EC.[39]

As well as encouraging democratization, the SI hoped to contribute to the emergence of a well-organized, broad-based democratic socialist party capable of attaining power in the not too distant future. In 1974 the SI duly created a special Spain Committee, consisting of representatives from the major member parties, which was given the task of channelling financial and political support to the PSOE. Indeed, when the PSOE established its headquarters in Madrid in 1975, it largely relied on funds raised abroad to do so. Member parties also played a prominent role in promoting González, who only stepped into the limelight after his election as first secretary in October 1974. It was then that he met Willy Brandt, the SI's most influential figure, who formally launched him on to the European stage at the SPD party conference held at Mannheim in late 1975.[40] In January 1976 the SI sent a high-level delegation to Spain, providing the PSOE with its first opportunity to publicize its status as the only internationally recognized Spanish socialist party. SI support for the party reached its climax at the PSOE's XXVIIth Congress, held in Madrid in December 1976, which was addressed by Brandt, Palme (both in Spanish), Mitterrand, Nenni, and Foot, amongst others. In June 1977 prominent SI leaders returned to Spain to play a leading role in the PSOE's first highly successful election campaign.

This highly visible external support for the PSOE proved crucial in a number of ways. First, by recognizing and publicly endorsing the renovated PSOE, the SI largely decided the outcome of the ongoing struggle between rival socialist groupings, which had hitherto competed for international support. The PSOE's external recognition even led Tierno Galvan's group—which had failed to obtain observer status from the SI in March 1974—to change its name from Partido Socialista del Interior to Partido Socialista Popular (PSP). Deprived of the support of the major European parties, the PSP was forced to seek material assistance from Third World socialist parties such as those of Libya and Iraq, which partly accounts for its increasingly radical, anti-imperialist image. This no doubt undermined its appeal in the eyes of a predominantly moderate would-be electorate.[41]

More importantly, perhaps, the SI's endorsement enabled the PSOE to adopt an increasingly independent stance *vis-à-vis* its major rival on the Left, namely the PCE. Without such explicit external support the PSOE leadership would have been less successful in resisting Communist efforts to include them in their Junta Democrática in 1974, thereby jeopardizing their ability to pursue their own, significantly more pragmatic, strategy. (Similarly, it was partly the support of European and North American labour organizations which enabled the socialist trade union UGT to resist the hegemonic ambitions of the Communist-controlled Workers' Commissions.) When the PSOE finally agreed to join the PCE in a new Coordinación Democrática in March 1976, it was able to do so on its own terms. In the event, it was the PSOE rather than the PCE which benefited most from the *reforma pactada* process, with the latter obtaining a mere 9 per cent of the vote in the first elections. Finally, association with the leading figures of the European socialist movement—many of whom were in office in their respective countries—enabled the PSOE to project a democratic, responsible image at home, at a time when the would-be electorate remained apprehensive about the outcome of the transition.

It is difficult to gauge the exent to which SI support—and in particular that of its most influential member, the SPD—influenced the PSOE's strategy during democratization. According to Suárez, when Brandt visited Madrid in December 1976 to attend the PSOE conference, he advised its leaders to take part in the first elections regardless of whether the PCE was also allowed to do so. In spite of public statements to the contrary, however, it would appear that González had already reached this conclusion of his own accord.[42] The SI's external pressure complemented the PSOE's strategy most effectively, but this was essentially an indigenous product.

It is equally problematic to ascertain the SI's ideological impact. As we have seen, the young men who took over the PSOE in 1972–4 were initially characterized by their radical political discourse, which is probably best understood in terms of the party's rivalry with the far better established PCE. The 1976 conference, so well attended by SI leaders, ironically produced the most radical programme ever adopted by the PSOE, though not much of it found its way into the 1977 election manifesto. Frequent contact with more moderate—particularly north European—socialist leaders may have influenced González's outlook, and critics both within the party and outside it have often attributed his alleged rightward shift to external pressures. This evolution, however, is probably best explained in terms of domestic demands and possibilities.[43]

Other Transnational Influences

The PSOE was not the only party to benefit from the existence of transnational party links. In 1972 the major Christian Democratic parties active in Spain had joined forces as the Equipo Demócrata Cristiano del Estado Español (EDCEE), precisely so as to take fuller advantage of the support available from the European Union of Christian Democrats (EUCD).[44] The latter was generally less active than the SI during this period, and less able to apply pressure on major European governments, but its members played a major role in EP and Council of Europe initiatives relating to Spain.

The EUCD's support was essentially political. Its representatives attended the EDCEE's second and third conferences in 1975 and 1976, and came out in force for the 'Encounter with Europe' staged by the Spaniards in January 1977. The absence of Germany's CDU at this gathering did not augur well for the EDCEE, however. The Germans were fully aware of the latter's leadership problems and overall lack of social support, which they largely attributed to a left-wing programme which was out of tune with their potential electorate. The CDU therefore opted for the more moderate sectors of the Christian Democratic family, which had gradually accepted the need to join forces with the reformists then in power. This did not prevent the rest of the EUCD parties from actively supporting the Federación Demócrata Cristiana, which finally fought the 1977 elections, in which they failed to win a single seat. Indeed it could be argued that in this case the external support enjoyed by the EDCEE proved counter-productive, in that it encouraged them to stand alone rather than ally with the reformists. With the exception of several regional parties, the only Christian Democrats to win seats in the new Congress were those who joined Suárez's loose electoral alliance, Unión de Centro Democrático (UCD), who received limited material support from the CDU and the Venezuelan COPEI.[45]

The Suárez government also sought to benefit from the transnational Christian Democratic network. Given his initial lack of democratic credentials, when he formed his first cabinet in July 1976, Suárez was careful to include a large contingent of Christian Democratic reformists in the hope that this would make his government more acceptable to European democratic opinion. Similarly, in January 1977, he made much of his meetings with leading ECDU leaders, notably the Belgian prime minister Leo Tindemann. Deputy Prime Minister Alfonso Osorio also took advantage of their presence in Madrid to seek their support for a future broad-based, government-led Christian Democratic party, though without success.[46]

Inevitably, the effectiveness of transnational party networks depended not only on their own willingness and ability to intervene in Spain, but most importantly on the social support and organizational skills available to domestic counterparts. This was particularly evident in the case of the Liberal International (LI), the least active of three major transnational organizations, whose ability to influence events in Spain was severely limited by the absence of substantial domestic interlocutors.[47]

In spite of this, the transnational liberal network operated in a very similar manner to its Socialist and Christian Democratic counterparts, in relation to both national governments and European institutions. Aware of the precedent established by the other two political families, in March 1977 the Spanish Liberal parties hosted a major gathering, which was attended by the LI's leading figures. In the Liberal case, the German FDP proved more successful than the CDU, and convinced its Spanish friends to join Suárez's nascent coalition. Suárez—who once again publicized his meeting with Europe's only liberal prime minister, Gaston Thorn of Luxembourg—has admitted that he invited these tiny liberal parties into his coalition largely on account of their standing with the LI.[48]

In spite of the absence of an institutionalized transnational organization which could come to its assistance, external support also played a significant role in the case of the PCE. Given that the existing transnational Communist network was dominated by the CPSU and its allies, Carrillo was forced to look elsewhere for external support.[49] The PCE initially sought a *rapprochement* with the SI, but the SPD's hostility to Communism and the PSOE's reluctance to collaborate with the PCE frustrated its efforts. Carrillo therefore turned to the more independent and unorthodox Communist parties, partly with a view to enhancing the PCE's democratic credibility in the eyes of potential Spanish voters.[50] The PCI was a particularly attractive partner, because of both its Eurocommunist strategy and its electoral success. Italian Communists proved particularly effective in the EP when it came to defending the PCE's legalization, and it is significant that the latter should have chosen Rome as the venue for the public presentation of its Central Committee in July 1976. Berlinguer and Marchais undoubtedly contributed to the PCE's legalization by attending Carrillo's Eurocommunist summit in Madrid in March 1977, which the Suárez government was forced to allow in order to avoid an international scandal.

The prominence of German political parties within the transnational networks discussed above is partly attributable to the role played by their political foundations, which established themselves in Spain in 1976–7.[51] The most active of these was undoubtedly the Friedrich Ebert Foundation, linked to the SPD, which opened an office in Madrid in 1976, at a time when the PSOE had not yet been legally recognized.[52] The Konrad Adenauer Foundation, associated with the CDU, was generally less active in Europe at this stage, but nevertheless provided the EDCEE parties with a degree of support.[53] In view of their lack of success in the 1977 elections, it subsequently backed the Christian Democratic parties which joined the UCD. Similarly, the FDP's Friedrich Naumann Foundation associated itself with the liberal groups which entered Suárez's coalition. Finally, the Hanns Seidel Foundation, linked to the CSU, whose leader, Strauss, had cultivated several of Franco's ministers in the 1960s, lent its support to Fraga's Alianza Popular after 1976.

The above discussion would appear to validate Whitehead's view that the democratic opposition is an apparently domestic category which may in practice be closely linked to international politics, and that 'when opposition parties undertake realignments or negotiate pacts, there is usually a substantial international infrastructure of support'. Another domestic institution whose role in the Spanish democratizing process was greatly conditioned by its external links, in this case with the Vatican, was the Catholic Church.

The Spanish Catholic Church was initially one of the mainstays of the Franco regime, a relationship formally acknowledged by the Concordat of 1953. In the 1960s, however, social changes taking place within Spain and the new attitudes aired at the Second Vatican Council led the Spanish Church to adopt an increasingly independent, even critical stance. This was greatly resented by the regime (notably by Franco himself), which clung to its anachronistic privileges in a desperate attempt to retain control over Spanish Catholics. In 1973, however, the Episcopal Conference, the collective voice of the Spanish hierarchy, publicly advocated disengagement from the regime and the formal separation of Church and state. Relations reached their lowest point in early 1974, when the government ordered the Bishop of Bilbao out of the country, only to discover that he could not be removed without the Pope's permission, which was not forthcoming. This scandal had a major impact on Catholic reformists within the regime, for it revealed the extent to which the latter had become incompatible with their long-term goal of upholding the Church's influence in Spanish society.[54]

By the early 1970s, the Vatican had very specific reasons for wanting a change of regime. In 1941 Franco had reluctantly been granted the right of presentation to bishoprics, which granted him a considerable degree of influence over the appointment of bishops. This was incompatible with the Second Vatican Council's insistence on the Church's autonomy relative to all political systems, and in 1968 Pope Paul VI asked Franco to renounce the right of presentation, thereby earning the lasting hatred of regime hardliners. The Head of State refused, however, and was unmoved when the Spanish bishops themselves reiterated the Vatican's request in 1973. Over time, it became clear to bishops and Pope alike that only a change of regime could result in a separation of Church and state such as that desired by Rome and the majority of the Spanish population.

The Church's attitude towards democratization was defined by Cardinal Tarancón, archbishop of Madrid and president of the Episcopal Conference since 1971, in a homily read in Juan Carlos's presence to mark his enthronement. In it, Tarancón advocated disengagement not only from the confessional state, but from authoritarianism as well. Arias Navarro initially resisted the Vatican's efforts to renegotiate the Concordat, but his dismissal allowed Juan Carlos to impose his own views on the matter. In July 1976 he formally renounced the right of presentation he had inherited from Franco, paving the way for the negotiation of a series of agreements which effectively replaced the Concordat. When Foreign Minister Oreja subsequently met Pope Paul VI, the latter urged him to inform the king that he had nothing to fear from the Church, which supported him in his efforts to bring about democratic change. Earlier, Areilza had found him equally supportive.[55]

It could also be argued that the Vatican's policies—as interpreted by the Spanish Church—had a significant impact on the future party system. The absence of a large, broad-based Christian Democratic party in Spain after 1975 has generally been attributed to the process of rapid secularization experienced by Spanish society in the preceding decades, as well as to the lack of a well-established pre-Francoist democratic Catholic tradition. Equally importantly, however, the emergence of a Christian Democratic party in the 1970s would not have been in keeping with the spirit of the Second Vatican Council, and under Tarancón the Spanish Church never lent its support to the many political groups which sought its blessing. Indeed, some of those who struggled in vain to bring about the creation of such a party in time for the 1977 elections have partly attributed their failure to the opposition of the Vatican and the Spanish hierarchy. Be this as it may, it could of course be argued that the UCD ultimately performed a role not unlike that of the Christian Democratic parties of Western Europe in their own post-war democratic restorations.[56]

One of the defining characteristics of the Spanish transition process was undoubtedly the leading role played by the restored monarchy as a bridging institution. As we have seen, Juan Carlos's appointment as Franco's successor in 1969 enabled him to establish links abroad which allowed Western democracies to express support for the future king without antagonizing the existing regime. Thereafter, it was largely through Juan Carlos that Western governments channelled their support for a gradual, non-violent transition to democracy. From the king's point of view, access to Western leaders who had traditionally spurned Franco was also beneficial in that it enabled him to acquire badly needed democratic credentials at home.

The king occasionally turned to external actors when he wished to communicate with domestic actors who were beyond easy reach. In the spring of 1976 Juan Carlos wished to reassure Carrillo personally of his determination to legalize the PCE, while simultaneously convincing him of the impossibility of doing so in the near future. Unable to relay this message directly, he turned to the Romanian autocrat Ceaucescu, whom he had met in Iran in 1971, and who was known to be close to Carrillo. The latter duly travelled to Bucharest to receive the king's message, which, while failing to appease him, nevertheless provided him with first-hand evidence of Juan Carlos's democratizing intentions.[57]

Ceaucescu was not the only foreign dictator to whom the king appealed for help in advancing the democratizing process while simultaneously consolidating the monarchy. In June 1977, shortly after the first democratic elections, Juan Carlos wrote to the Shah of Iran, whom he had actively cultivated as a prince, requesting $10 million 'on behalf of the political party of Prime Minister Suárez', as the autocrat's 'personal contribution to the strengthening of the Spanish monarchy'. In order to justify this appeal, Juan Carlos claimed that the PSOE's excellent performance in the recent elections constituted 'a serious threat to the country's security and to the stability of the monarchy', in view of which it was essential to secure Suárez's victory at the forthcoming municipal elections (which were subsequently postponed until 1979).[58] Given the king's behaviour throughout the transition process, and the Shah's own ideological preferences, it is reasonable to assume that the letter was worded thus so as to increase the likelihood of a favourable response. Unfortunately, it is not known how the Shah reacted to this request, though it would appear that Juan Carlos had been successful in obtaining financial assistance from him in the past.[59]

Conclusion

Whitehead has observed that the methods used against Franco's Spain in 1946–8 (such as exclusion from the United Nations and from Marshall Aid, closure of the frontier, and recognition of a government-in-exile) probably represent the most drastic attempt to induce redemocratization anywhere in the post-war period, short of outright invasion. In spite of these efforts, the Franco regime survived for almost another thirty years. Given this precedent, it is perhaps not surprising that those hoping to advance the cause of democracy in Spain from abroad should have opted for a more subtle approach, based on longer-term inducements and disincentives. This chapter has argued that it was essentially the West European actors—national governments, multinational institutions, transnational party organizations, and political foundations—which proved most effective in applying pressure or channelling support. Given the extent of their involvement, it is perhaps not the least of their achievements that Spaniards only rarely perceived such activities as improper, to such an extent that once their own democracy had been consolidated, Spanish actors would seek to emulate these practices elsewhere.

Notes

1. The major exception is J. Story and B. Pollack, 'Spain's Transition: Domestic and External Linkages', in G. Pridham (ed.), *Encouraging Democracy: The International Context and Regime Transition in Southern Europe* (Leicester: Leicester University Press, 1991).
2. L. Whitehead, 'International Aspects of Democratization', in G. O'Donnell, P. C. Schmitter, and L. Whitehead, *Transitions from Authoritarian Rule: Comparative Perspectives* (Baltimore: Johns Hopkins University Press, 1986).
3. G. Gortázar, 'El último franquismo: actitudes y preocupaciones de los españoles según los sondeos del Instituto de Opinión Pública', in H. de la Torre (ed.), *Portugal y España en el cambio político* (Mérida, 1989), 130–2.
4. A. Tovias, 'The International Context of Democratic Transition', in G. Pridham (ed.), *The New Mediterranean Democracies: Regime Transition in Spain, Greece and Portugal* (London: Frank Cass, 1984), 169.
5. The impact of the Portuguese Revolution on Spanish public opinion at large should not be exaggerated. According to a major poll, in October 1974 only 48 per cent of the urban Spanish population knew the revolution had taken place, and only 20 per cent expressed any sympathy: Instituto de Opinión Pública, Study number 1,075, 1974.
6. Felipe González, statement to the Seminar on Spain's Transition to Democracy, organized by the José Ortega y Gasset Foundation (Toledo, 1984).
7. See for example the views of the Tácito group, many of whose members were in office in 1975–8, in *Tácito* (Madrid, 1975), 237–40, 385–7.
8. In 1977 Juan Carlos explained to the Shah of Iran that on acceding to the throne he had 'vowed to tread in the path of democracy, endeavour-

ing always to be one step ahead of events in order to forestall a situation like that in Portugal which might prove even more dire in this country of mine': A. Alam, *The Shah and I: The Confidential Diary of Iran's Royal Court, 1969–1977* (London, 1991), 553.

9. According to Willy Brandt, 'in the spring, late summer and early autumn it looked as though [the Communists] would take over the country completely. I urged the mobilization of a counter-force, not only out of solidarity with our Portuguese political allies but for the sake of European development as a whole. There followed a relief operation whose full story cannot yet be written. It was the product of secret collaboration between a handful of social democratic party leaders': W. Brandt, *People and Politics: The Years 1960–75* (London: Collins, 1976), 489–90.

10. H. Kissinger, *The White House Years* (New York: Center for the Study of Foreign Affairs, Foreign Service Institute, US Dept. of State, 1982), 870; W. Stabler, 'The View from the US Embassy', in H. Binnendijk (ed.), *Authoritarian Regimes in Transition* (Washington: Center for the Study of Foreign Affairs, Foreign Service Institute, US Dept. of State, 1987), 192. See also A. Tovias, 'US Policy toward Democratic Transition in Southern Europe', in Pridham (ed.), *Encouraging Democracy*.

11. S. D. Eaton, *The Forces of Freedom in Spain, 1974–79: A Personal Account* (Stanford, Calif.: Hooker Institution Press, 1983), 116–17.

12. Kissinger, *White House Years*, 870. V. A. Walters, *Silent Missions* (New York: University of Wisconsin Press, 1978), 551.

13. For the opposition's view of the Rogers visit, see J. M. de Areilza, *Crónica de Libertad* (Barcelona: University of Wisconsin Press, 1985), 150–5, and E. Tierno Galván, *Cabos Sueltos* (Barcelona: University of Wisconsin Press, 1982), 414–19. Stabler, 'View from Embassy', 192–6. S. G. Payne, *The Franco Regime, 1936–1975* (Madison and London: University of Wisconsin Press, 1987), 611.

14. H. Schmidt, *Men and Powers: A Political Retrospective* (London, 1990), 167. For a similar exchange between Kissinger and the Irish prime minister, see G. Fitzgerald, *All in a Life* (London: Macmillan, 1991), 180. Defense Secretary James Schlesinger admitted that Madrid had threatened to block the renewal of the agreement if Washington issued pleas for clemency: *Time*, 13 October 1975.

15. On the 1976 Treaty talks, see J. M. de Areilza, *Diario de un ministro de la Monarquía* (Barcelona, 1977), 14–15, 45.

16. Areilza, *Diario*, 61, 65–7, 195–6. Eaton, *Forces of Freedom*, 127–8.

17. A. Osorio, *Trayectoria política de un ministro de la Corona* (Barcelona, 1980), 280. Stabler, 'View from Embassy', 197.

18. According to the PCE's Secretary General, Brezhnev himself urged Juan Carlos—via the Venezuelan president Carlos Andrés Pérez—not to legalize the party until after the first democratic elections: S. Carrillo, *Memorias* (Barcelona, 1993), 633.

19. See R. Legvold, 'The Soviet Union and West European Communism',

and E. M. Mujal-León, 'The Domestic and International Evolution of the Spanish Communist Party', in R. L. Tokés (ed.), *Eurocommunism and Détente* (Oxford: Martin Robertson, 1979).

20. See Whitehead, *International Aspects of Democratization*, 10–16.
21. In Schmidt's view, in both Portugal and Spain, 'Bonn gambled on positive changes and tried to contribute to that end, while Washington remained sceptical.' Schmidt, *Men and Powers*, 168. 'In view of Germany's own experiences', Brandt wrote with reference to Spain, Portugal, and Greece, 'I did not think it right to sit in moral judgement, but we could not remain indifferent to the fate of these nations. We had to show solidarity wherever possible. I was never in any doubt that dictatorships hamper Western co-operation and do not belong in the European Community': Brandt, *People*, 164.
22. See Areilza, *Crónica*, 103–6, 109, and Tierno Galván, *Cabos Sueltos*, 421–2.
23. W. Brandt, *My Life in Politics* (London, 1992), 315; A. Papell, *Conversaciones con Luis Yáñez* (Madrid, 1992), 104.
24. When Garret Fitzgerald discussed this episode with Kissinger, the latter 'mumbled something about European countries taking a free ride and making mock-heroic decisions so long as they don't have to pay for them'. The secretary thought European governments had been 'hypocritical in the extreme', and could not understand why 'the execution of convicted cop killers [should] be turned into a moral issue': Fitzgerald, *All in a Life*, 180.
25. Valéry Giscard d'Estaing, *Le Pouvoir et la vie* (Paris: Compagnie 12, 1988), 283. In December 1975 Wilson told President Ford that 'I recognise, even if it cannot be put bluntly in public, that King Juan Carlos has a very hard row to hoe. So we shall encourage him privately to move as fast as possible, but try to avoid public condemnation when we can, if the pace is slower than public opinion expectation here may demand': P. Ziegler, *The Authorised Life of Lord Wilson of Rievaulx* (London: Weidenfeld and Nicolson, 1993), 464.
26. Areilza, *Diario*, 15, 122.
27. See G. Pridham, 'The Politics of the European Community: Transnational Networks and Democratic Transition in Southern Europe', in Pridham (ed.), *Encouraging Democracy*.
28. The proportion of Spain's imports from the EC rose from 25 to 49 per cent during 1960–70, and trading figures increased substantially after the 1970 agreement and the EC's enlargement in 1973.
29. See for example the articles of the Tácito group, whose members later made a major contribution to the Suárez reform, in *Tácito* (Madrid, 1975).
30. On the nature of Spanish Europeanism in this period, see F. Morán, *Una política exterior para España* (Barcelona, 1980), 289–98.
31. Whitehead, *International Aspects of Democratization*, 23.
32. Areilza, *Diario*, 125.
33. Osorio, *Trayectoria politica*, 157–8. Areilza's successor, Marcelino

Oreja, received identical advice from foreign minister Genscher in August 1976: author's interview with Oreja, 1994.

34. See P. Letamendia (ed.), *L'Intervention des organisations partisanes transnationales dans le processus de democratization espagnol* (Université de Bordeaux, I, 1982).

35. R. Gillespie, *The Spanish Socialist Party: A History of Factionalism* (Oxford: Clarendon Press, 1989), 285–7.

36. Mitterrand hosted two conferences of southern European socialist parties—in January 1976 and May 1977—which ostensibly studied specifically southern problems, such as the presence of large Communist parties, the viability of EC enlargement, etc.

37. Membership of the renovated PSOE grew from 3,400 in August 1972, to some 10,000 in December 1976, and to an estimated 200,000 by late 1977.

38. Minutes of the third meeting of the Spain Committee, 10 July 1975, Circular No. S 6/75. Minutes of the fourth meeting of the Spain Committee, 16 November 1975: Socialist International archive, Amsterdam.

39. Areilza, *Diario*, 47, 100.

40. In July 1975 the Spain Committee had advised the SI to invite PSOE delegations led by González to conduct highly publicized tours of member countries, the 'principal goal being to make the First Secretary of the PSOE better known, especially in Northern Europe'. Brandt would later write that 'I am still proud to think that under my leadership, the SPD sent more than fine words to help Spanish democracy to its feet': Brandt, *My Life*, 315. The PSOE also received aid from the French, Italian, British, Swedish, Austrian, Dutch, and Venezuelan parties.

41. The PSP's first party conference, held in June 1976, was attended by delegates from parties in Libya, Yugoslavia, and Mexico, amongst others. In the 1977 elections, the PSP obtained 4.4 per cent of the vote (and only 1.7 per cent of the seats in the Congress), as compared to the PSOE's 29 per cent (and 33 per cent of the seats). After lengthy negotiations, a debt-ridden PSP finally agreed to its absorption by the PSOE in 1979.

42. Author's interview with Suárez, 1985. González's statement to the Seminar on Spain's Transition to Democracy.

43. For a PSOE view of SPD influence on the SI see Menéndez del Valle, *El Socialista*, 23 October 1977. Already in April 1976, a prominent SI figure, Austrian Chancellor Kreisky, told the Spanish ambassador in Vienna that he found González surprisingly conservative for his age: L. López Rodó, *Claves de la transición* (Madrid, 1993), 233.

44. The EDCEE consisted of Ruiz Giménenz's Izquierda Democrática, Gil Robles's Federación Popular Democrática, the Basque Nationalist Party, and the Catalan Unió Democrática. The first two parties subsequently formed Federación Demócrata Cristiana.

45. F. Alvarez de Miranda, *Del 'contubernio' al consenso* (Barcelona, 1985), 84–5, 122.

46. Author's interview with Suárez, 1985; Osorio, *Trayectoria politica*, 297.

47. The Spanish members of the LI were Garrigues Walker's Federación de Partidos Demócratas y Liberales, Camuñas's Partido Demócrata Popular, and the Esquerra Democrática de Catalunya of Trias Fargas.

48. Author's interview with Suárez, 1985.

49. In 1975 the Mexican PRI gave the PCE-led Junta Democrática $400,000 for its activities abroad. Carrillo, *Memorias*, 604. The Mexicans had never recognized the Franco regime, and only agreed to establish diplomatic relations in 1977, once democratic elections had been called.

50. Amongst those who came to the PCE's assistance were the Communist parties of Yugoslavia, Japan, and Romania, where its clandestine radio station was based.

51. See M. Pinto-Duschinsky, 'Foreign Political Aid: The German Political Foundations and their US Counterparts', *International Affairs*, 67/1 (1991), 33–63.

52. In 1985 Dieter Koniecki, the Ebert representative in Madrid, informed a Spanish parliamentary committee that during 1976–80 his foundation had invested over DM2.7m. in Spain. Another source estimates that Ebert spent DM4m. in the Iberian Peninsula in 1977 alone. Pinto-Duschinsky, 'Foreign Political Aid', 56.

53. Alvarez de Miranda, *Del 'contuburnio'*, 89.

54. See *Tácito*, 28–9, 46, 193–5.

55. Note that these Church–state agreements were signed by the Spanish foreign minister and the Vatican Secretary of State, without the formal participation of the Spanish Church. Where the Catholic Church is concerned, therefore, conflicts with a domestic regime automatically acquire an external dimension: author's interview with Oreja, 1994; Areilza, *Diario*, 143.

56. See C. Huneeus, *La Unión de Centro Democrático y la transición a la democracia en España* (Madrid, 1985), 175–90.

57. S. Carrillo, *El año de la peluca* (Barcelona, 1987), 37–8.

58. In his letter, the king claimed that in the recent elections the PSOE had received support from 'Willy Brandt, Venezuela and the other European Socialists', while the PCE had been financed 'by the usual means'. Juan Carlos attributed the PSOE's excellent performance partly to the fact that many had voted for them 'in the belief that through Socialism Spain might receive aid from such major European countries as Germany, or alternatively from countries such as Venezuela, for the revival of the Spanish economy': Alam, *Shah and I*, 552–4.

59. In his reply, the Shah displayed much greater caution than Juan Carlos, promising to 'convey my personal thoughts by word of mouth'. In his own letter, the king had thanked him for 'providing me with a speedy response to my appeal at a difficult moment for my country': Alam, *Shah and I*, 554, 552.

Underwriting Democracy:
The European Community and Greece

BASILIOS TSINGOS

1. Introduction: Reassessing the Democratic Transition Literature in a New World Order

The role of international factors in the democratization process has become the focus of considerable scholarly attention in the wake of the events in Eastern Europe in 1989. The monumental regime changes in Eastern Europe have sparked renewed interest in the international factor because they seem to have challenged many of the assumptions and conclusions upon which much of the literature on the establishment of new democracies was grounded. Many of these assumptions and conclusions emerged from the *Transitions from Authoritarian Rule* series.[1] Drawing upon Latin American and southern European cases, the comparative and theoretical *Transitions* series helped to crystallize a scholarly consensus in the 1980s concerning the nature of the democratization process. In particular, it highlighted the domestic political forces of regime change and concluded that 'transitions from authoritarian rule and [the] immediate prospects for democracy were largely explained in terms of national forces and calculations', rather than international factors or external environments.[2]

This chapter is a condensed version of several chapters of a doctoral thesis in International Relations prepared at Oxford University. I would like to thank Nikiforos Diamandouros, Robert Fishman, Susannah Verney, and Ngaire Woods for helpful analytical guidance and feedback. Laurence Whitehead, who supervised the larger project out of which this essay arises, merits special mention. For additional editorial comments and suggestions on earlier versions of this essay, I am further indebted to Tanya Pollard. I also owe an acknowledgement to the Rhodes Scholarship Trust, whose generosity made this project financially feasible.

It is this conclusion, already the subject of some debate,[3] that Eastern Europe can be said to have called into question. The events of 1989 gave a new lease of life to new or previously marginalized interpretations that underscore the importance of international factors in democratization,[4] and lent force to others which call into question the very idea of a definable distinction between 'national forces' and 'external actors'.[5] In the search for explanations for the recent Eastern European cases, the literature on regime transitions has now cast a retrospective look at the earlier southern European and Latin American cases in order to re-evaluate the influence of the international environment.

Among the cases being reconsidered by a growing body of scholarship are those of southern Europe including that of Greece. The challenge to the conclusion reached in the *Transitions* series can broadly be said to consist of two positions. The first, that of White-head and others, is that the distinction between domestic and international factors is in reality a blurred one, with domestic and international factors assuming different degrees of importance at different stages. Cross-national structural factors, Whitehead argues, are relatively more important in the later, consolidation phase of democratization, rather than in the earlier, transition phase.[6] In the southern European cases, he concludes, the European Community has been central to democratization to the extent that it has helped to 'permanently entrench' democratic institutions by offering 'an elaborate structure of economic and social incentives for changes in group and national behaviour' that are beneficial to the prospects for democracy.[7] Other scholars go one step further in their re-evaluation of international influences on regime change, particularly the role of the European Community in the southern European cases. For instance, in an insightful and tightly argued essay on the Greek case that builds on an earlier article with Panos Tsakaloyannis,[8] Susannah Verney argues that the EC can be viewed as 'an exporter' of democracy.[9] The Community, in her view, played an important role in undermining authoritarian rule and catalysing the transition to democracy.

The past danger in the literature on transitions was to dismiss or underestimate the importance of international factors in the democratization process. The present danger, however, is to overcompensate for this deficiency by exaggerating the role of international actors or forces and downplaying those of the domestic arena. This tendency, as we shall see, is particularly present in the emerging scholarship on the EC and Greece.

This chapter considers this literature and evaluates the role that the EC and its member states can be said to have played in the breakdown and transition from authoritarian rule, and in the consolidation of the new Greek democracy. It locates ways in which the EC and its member states affected the democratization process, but concludes that they cannot be properly labelled as 'exporters' of democracy. The Community and its partners certainly played a role during the transition to and consolidation of democracy in Greece, but this role was supplementary, not central or decisive. Nevertheless, the chapter goes on to suggest that the EC has played a decisive role in influencing the prospects for democracy in Greece, but that this influence has primarily been felt after the consolidation of democracy, with the EC acting as a 'guarantor' or 'underwriter' of democracy.

2. The EC and the Greek Transition from Authoritarian Rule

A growing body of scholarship on the Greek case has advanced the argument that the EC's firm stance against the Colonels (backed by the force of the Community's economic and diplomatic weight), together with Greek perceptions of the EC, significantly helped to undermine the military junta and to catalyse the transition to democracy in Greece. In Susannah Verney's words, 'Greece's relationship with the EC . . . clearly played a role in the pre-transition period by contributing to the lack of legitimacy which caused the Junta to collapse.'[10]

On this view, the EC's role in the democratization process largely stemmed from its increasing economic and political importance for Greece, and in particular from the EC–Greek association agreement (signed in 1961; entering into force in 1962) which explicitly referred to the eventual accession by Greece to full Community membership. Greece's 'prior relationship with the EC allowed the latter to take direct action' in response to the Colonels' coup in April 1967. The EC accordingly 'froze' its association agreement with Greece following the military coup and 'began actively promoting the export of parliamentary democracy beyond its existing frontiers', having as its primary aim 'the establishment of a new role for the EC as an exporter of democracy'.[11]

The novelty and force behind recent accounts in the growing literature on this aspect of the Greek case rest not so much in their analysis of EC responses to the 1967 coup (other works have covered that[12]), as in their assertion that the EC response to the dictatorship affected the political trajectory of Greece in a direct and decisive fashion. The arguments in this body of scholarship revolve around two related, but separate, contentions—a maximum and a minimum claim. On the maximum view, the EC is said to have pushed the Colonels into a liberalization attempt which then failed, thereby provoking the hardline backlash of November 1973, leading eventually to the disastrous intervention in Cyprus. At the very least, however, the EC is seen to have helped preclude the dictatorship's consolidation. Verney, for example, argues that the EC undermined the regime's efforts to legitimize its hold on power and effectively compelled it to experiment (disastrously) with liberalization. Antagonistic EC policies, she reasons, harmed the Greek economy, helped fuel popular and élite discontent, and eventually led the Colonels into an economic and political impasse which they were increasingly hard-pressed to escape.

In the first place, Verney explains, the European Commission took the firm position that normal relations between Brussels and Athens could not be resumed until the latter re-established parliamentary democracy. This decision, she argues (in a joint article with Panos Tsakaloyannis), slowly but surely twisted the arms of the Colonels. Unlike the Council of Europe—which Greece contemptuously[13] quit in December 1969, hours before that body planned to vote on whether to expel Athens for human rights violations—'the EC had economic teeth and, therefore, could not be ignored'.[14] Indeed, by 1972, the Community provided and absorbed roughly half of all Greek imports and exports respectively.[15]

The two most direct results of the 'freeze' were the suspension of financial aid to Greece from Brussels, and the suspension of negotiations over the harmonization of Greek agriculture with the EC's Common Agricultural Policy (CAP). This precluded additional EC funding sought by Greece through the Agricultural Fund (FEOGA). Preferential trade agreements concluded by the EC with other Mediterranean countries further threatened the Greek economy.[16]

The EC's actions, Tsakaloyannis and Verney explain, were felt in Athens with particular force: 'Greece simply could not afford to allow the balance-of-trade with the EEC to worsen; in 1971 the trade deficit with the Nine exceeded the total value of the country's exports. Thus Greece was particularly vulnerable to pressure from the EC.'[17] According to their account, the Colonels

were caught in a dilemma. Either they had to reduce imports from the Community to alleviate the country's worsening balance-of-payments (which would have exacerbated public discontent); or Greece had to expand its exports to the Nine which meant coming to an accommodation with Brussels [concerning the return to Greece of democratic institutions].[18]

On this view of the Greek case, the EC's firm anti-dictatorial stance thus had the effect of frustrating attempts by the Colonels to establish a popular base of support, most notably by decreasing their ability to point to positive economic performance. Moreover, the EC's stance had the further effect of hindering the regime's ability to reach out and cultivate the support of important political élites. This inability is seen in part as the result of élite perceptions in Greece of Europe and the Community, and in part as a function of the EC's changing nature in the early 1970s. Accelerated moves towards European integration and the high-water mark of *détente* in this period were accompanied, recent scholarship notes, by a 'Europhoria' to which Greek élites were not immune. To Greek élites watching such developments in the early 1970s, Verney concludes, 'there seemed the distinct danger of Greece becoming a pariah on the margins of a rapidly uniting Western Europe'.[19]

Growing isolation from the Community was a 'mortal threat' for the Colonels, recent accounts on this aspect of the Greek case note, because it helped to isolate and emasculate them politically, driving a wedge between them, civilian élites, and popular opinion. In particular, Verney and Couloumbis explain, 'Greece's isolation by the EC seems to have been an important factor [in] splitting the anti-Communist bloc' which had supported and underlined the Greek political system in the decades following the Civil War.[20] This split is seen as a result of perceptions by both conservative and liberal Greek élites of the importance of European integration for Greece's future.

These élite perceptions, Verney explains, were conditioned by Greece's geopolitical location, her recent history, and her internal political composition. Excepting Turkey, Greece had emerged out of the ashes of the Second World War as the only non-Communist state and Western ally in the Balkans. This was the result of the Left's military defeat during the Greek Civil War, made possible or at least facilitated by British assistance and intervention,[21] and later reinforced by large amounts of American military and economic aid extended under the Truman Doctrine.[22] For the ruling political class and establishment élite which had triumphed during the Civil War, the scars of the 1940s and the Left's political resilience, Verney argues, 'made exclusion from European integration a life-and-death matter for the maintenance of a non-communist Greece . . . [since] integration was seen as a way to tie Greece more firmly into the Western strategic bloc'.[23]

It was on the basis of such political calculations, Verney explains, that 'during the Junta's latter years former civilian politicians and

economic analysts, promoted the need to reactivate relations with
the EC as an argument for democratization'.[24] By 1973 prominent
élite figure such as Xenophon Zolotas, the former Governor of the
Bank of Greece, Georgios Mavros, the leader of the liberal Center
Union party, and Constantine Karamanlis, the exiled former prime
minister and founder of the right-wing conservative ERE party,
were all 'publicly calling for the restoration of democracy on the
grounds [that] this would facilitate Greek accession to the EC'.[25] If
the political Centre and Right had been 'riven for years' by disagreements, then the 'issue of Greek accession became for them
a unifying factor, for it was something on which they could all
agree'.[26] And since the military regime jeopardized Greece's future
in Europe, these élites concluded that it had to go. The direct and
indirect economic and political pressures brought to bear on the
Colonels by the Community, Verney concludes, thus played an
important role in undermining the ability of the regime to legitimize
itself either in élite circles or with the public at large. It was
largely this lack of legitimacy 'which caused the Junta to collapse
overnight following its external defeat in Cyprus in July 1974'.[27]

But the scholarship in this area suggests that the European
Community did more than merely help preclude the legitimation
of the Colonels' regime. Tsakaloyannis and Verney argue that the
EC also played an important role in compelling the military junta
to undertake the failed liberalization experiment that led to the
hardline counter-coup of November 1973 and, ultimately, to the
desperate gamble in Cyprus. As they put it, by 1973 'the junta
[was] moving towards a form of "guided democracy" to avert exclusion from the proposed European Union'.[28] This assertion, which
I have referred to as the 'maximum' claim in the recent scholarship on the Greek case, directly challenges a conclusion that rests
at or near the heart of the *Transitions from Authoritarian Rule*
series, as we saw above. After all, O'Donnell and Schmitter concluded in the *Transitions* series that 'it seems . . . fruitless to search
for some international factor or context which can reliably compel
authoritarian rulers to experiment with liberalization'.[29]

3. The EC's Role in the Greek Regime Change of 1974 Put in Perspective

The recent assessments by Verney, Tsakaloyannis, Couloumbis, and
others of the Community's role in the junta's decline are important contributions to the literature, pointing to international factors

and internal–external linkages that were neglected or not fully explored in earlier studies of the Greek case, and were in danger of being forgotten. There can be no doubt that the Community played a role in undermining authoritarian rule in Greece for the reasons mentioned above. Nevertheless, both the maximum and minimum claims in the growing literature on Europe and the Greek regime are ultimately incomplete and misleading. The Community role in the dictatorship's breakdown and collapse is magnified and distorted when viewed out of its broader domestic and regional context. The Community and the EC link may have played a role in the regime change of 1974, but a closer inspection of the historical record does not support the view that the EC exported democracy to Greece.

In the first place, the contention that 'the EC began actively promoting the export of parliamentary democracy' to Greece following the Colonels' coup in April 1967 adopts too uncritical a view of the Community, with respect to both the intent and the consequences of its policies towards the Greek regime. As for the intent claim, a fuller consideration of the Greek case reveals that the Community's policies towards the dictatorship, when considered as a whole, were much more complex, dispassionate, and hardheaded than suggested in recent accounts, in a manner which calls into question the accuracy of the 'democracy promotion' thesis. To be sure, the Colonels' coup led to the EC's so-called 'freeze' of the association agreement with Greece. But, as Loukas Tsoukalis cogently notes, the use of the term 'freeze' is somewhat misleading and requires clarification. 'Both sides', he points out, 'continued to adhere to the [association treaty's] timetable for the elimination of tariffs.'[30] Whatever else can be said about it, Tsoukalis concludes, 'in the end the freezing was not at a particularly low temperature'.[31]

In fact, the extent and impact of the freeze on financial aid from Brussels is also frequently exaggerated or distorted. A financial protocol attached to the treaty of association envisaged $125 million in EC loans to Greece over a five-year period ending in October 1967. When the freeze was imposed in the months which followed the Colonels' coup in April 1967, Greece had already absorbed $69 million of this amount. It was the remaining $56 million that the Community withheld following the protocol's expiration in October.[32] While this was not a negligible amount, on its own it clearly was not a big enough carrot or economic stick to cause the Colonels to doubt the wisdom of their conspiratorial ways.

On the contrary, the Colonels amply demonstrated they could

secure foreign loans with or without EC assistance, and indeed
financed short-term prosperity and economic growth on the back
of long-term borrowing—much of it from West European sources.
By far the largest source of Western financial assistance to the
Colonels—including assistance from Community members—came
from within the framework of the Cold War strategic alliance and
NATO.[33] All told, the nature and magnitude of these and similar
financial dealings on both government and private levels qualified
and called into question both the economic and symbolic impact of
the suspension of the EC financial protocol. As *The Economist*
explained in 1972, the regime's overall success in securing loans
from alternative Western sources enabled it to shrug off just about
any impact that the suspension of financial assistance from Brussels might have had.[34]

Assertions that the EC vigorously and actively promoted the restoration of democracy in Greece seem further suspect when one
probes and examines the many and complex reasons underlying the
other feature of the EC's freeze: its suspension of negotiations with
Greece on the harmonization of agricultural policies. As Tsoukalis
explains, this decision was not based on 'pure idealism'. On the contrary, as far as many Community policy-makers were concerned,
'the political change in Greece provided a *deus ex machina* for the
elimination of agriculture from the agenda' of EC–Greek relations.[35]
This argument was one that regime officials also made. Indeed, it
could be argued that the Colonels' coup produced not only a complicating factor, but also an agreeable smokescreen behind which
the Community's partners could hide and which could eliminate or
postpone the troublesome question of agriculture from the agenda
of EC–Greek relations. To be sure, the decision to break off the
negotiations on agriculture was not devoid of a moral component.
Still, as Coufoudakis explains, it seems clear that the Community's
decision to freeze the association and suspend negotiations was
not motivated 'by absolute idealism—as many of the speeches at the
European Parliament would indicate'.[36] The reasons lying behind
EC decision-making in this area were rather more complex and
morally ambiguous than the interpretation that they were driven
by principled considerations of democracy promotion would imply.

Indeed, as George Yannopoulos suggests, the EC's continuing
relationship with the Greek regime, its reluctance to suspend or
void the association agreement *in toto*, and its subsequent entry
into negotiations with the regime on the question of Greek wines,
all help to illustrate 'one vital point, namely that once the degree
of market interdependence among nations reaches a critical point

it makes their relationship one that often transcends and bypasses political preferences'.[37] In fact, contracts, jobs, export strategies, and balance-of-payments crises were seen in many European capitals as important reasons not to alienate, or at least to remain on good and amiable terms with, the Colonels. As C. M. Woodhouse explains, West European governments typically displayed a greater interest in promoting their economic agendas and self-interests *vis-à-vis* the largely untapped Greek market than in denouncing human rights abuses by the regime in Athens.[38]

The assertion that the EC vigorously and actively promoted the restoration of democracy in Greece seems further suspect when one views EC policy towards Athens in the broader regional context of the time. A full and accurate assessment of the Community influence on events in Greece needs to look beyond a Brussels-centred view of the EC and its formal institutions. In fact, Community policies towards the Colonels' regime and their influence on events in Greece cannot be properly understood outside the context of the dealings of individual member governments with the Colonels, both bilaterally and within other regional organizations with partially overlapping memberships. And in the end, Community members—far from actively trying to pressure or topple the Colonels from within the EC, as much recent scholarship has suggested—generally co-operated with, supported, and even courted them (albeit reluctantly in some cases) for strategic, geopolitical, and security reasons, both in their independent, bilateral relations with Greece, and within other organizations, most notably NATO.[39]

This was evidenced in the attitude and behaviour of EC member states towards Greece, but recent scholarly accounts frequently fail to report or explore this feature of European–Greek relations during the dictatorship. As Tsoukalis rightly explains, it is 'worth pointing to the apparent contradiction between the attitude of Western European governments—at least the majority of them—as members of the Community . . . and their attitude as members of NATO or in bilateral relations with the colonels'.[40] For instance, one member of the European Parliament, perplexed by what he termed 'la politique du contrepied', pointed out how many of the EC countries which had voted to freeze the association agreement with Greece were helping to supply 'the junta with the arms by which it imposed its rule on the Greek people'.[41] If the EC and its member states were actively promoting democracy in Greece, they were doing so in a most curious fashion. The contradictory behaviour of EC member states in their various capacities *vis-à-vis* the Colonels, Tsoukalis concludes, helps to explain at least partly the different attitudes adopted subsequently within Greece itself on the subject of full [EC] membership. There were enough arguments to be found for both supporters and opponents. While one would point to the ostracism of the colonels' regime by democratic Europe and the need to consolidate democracy by becoming a member of the Community, the other would prefer to emphasise the NATO dimension of member countries and the tolerance/support of the dictatorial regime.[42]

The 1974 Cyprus crisis is often seen as the *locus classicus* of the Greek transition's 'international dimension' in accounts emphasizing the foreign influences on the regime's fall. To be sure, the Cyprus issue was, and continues to be, a long-standing point of contention between Greece and Turkey. However, this particular crisis and the form it took seems to have been an outgrowth of factors which lay more in the tottering regime in Athens than in Cyprus itself.[43] As Constantine Danopoulos explains, 'Ioannidis and his co-conspirators' were '[c]ognizant of the regime's downward slide' and accordingly 'attempted to precipitate a national crisis; they were banking on the notion that an externally emanating threat would lead the people to close ranks behind the[ir] leadership to save the nation'.[44]

Indeed, the course of events makes it difficult to see the Cyprus crisis as a crisis which confronted the regime independently. On the contrary, this was a situation of its own making, created as a possible, if dangerous, exit from its political cul-de-sac.[45] As Van Coufoudakis explains, 'the attitudes of the Greek junta toward the Cyprus dispute and the Cypriots in general support the argument that the coup in Cyprus would have occurred regardless of Makarios['s] actions'.[46] A closer inspection of the events surrounding the crisis thus leads one to concur with O'Donnell and Schmitter in their conclusion that it is more accurate to interpret the crisis created by the plot against Makarios 'as the result of an already tottering and stalemated regime launching a *fuite en avant* rather than as the cause of the regime's having reached such an impasse'.[47]

Together with Cyprus, the European Community no doubt provided one of several international backdrops or 'contexts' to the essentially domestic process detailed here by which authoritarian rule in Greece unravelled and ultimately collapsed. However, it would be stretching and distorting the importance of the EC's role in this process to say that it directed the course or timing of events, as the emerging literature in this area suggests. The Community may have provided some incentives for a move away from dictatorship, but the experience of dictatorship itself was enough of an incentive for a move to democratic rule, not only for civilian political élites and broad sectors of the population, but, increasingly, for the regime's most important and only real constituency, the armed forces themselves.

A response to this argument may well be that the most important way in which the EC affected the transition was in helping to prevent the entrenchment or consolidation of authoritarian rule in Greece. A central tenet of recent accounts in the literature is that EC actions and mass and élite perceptions within Greece of the Community helped to preclude the military junta from moving beyond its initial base of support in the armed forces, and thus helped to prevent the regime from cultivating the legitimizing support of either national political élites or a broad section of the Greek electorate. This inability to move beyond its base of support in the armed forces may well have been a mortal blow to the regime, for as Nietzsche incisively argues in *The Genealogy of Morals* (1887), that which creates a situation cannot necessarily be called upon or assumed to sustain it. But was the regime's inability to consolidate itself a product of EC actions or Greek perceptions of the Community, as recent scholarship contends?

On this score, it can be said that the inability of the military junta to legitimize itself or to cultivate support among, for instance, civilian élites was not so much a result of Greek isolation from the EC as of the coup itself and the political crisis which preceded it. The military junta had, from the early morning hours of 21 April 1967, jailed, reviled, and otherwise attacked the national political leadership, not recklessly, but because these élites were part and parcel of the 'problem' at which the coup was directed.

The junta's attacks on the discredited politicians of the pre-1967 political system (*politikandides*, in the regime's derogatory parlance) served to alienate potential political partners from the regime's inception. This, far more than the issue of possible exclusion from a hypothetical European Union in 1980, as Verney has argued, isolated the dictatorship from its most likely civilian constituency, the conservative right, over seven years of dictatorial rule.

The regime's domestic isolation was reinforced by social class differences between the ruling junta and the establishment élites of the *politiko kosmo* (political world). The élite and aristocratic status of the Greek officer corps had been progressively eroded in the decades preceding the coup as a result of the recruiting reforms in the earlier part of the century. The protagonists of the 1967 coup in particular were 'socially unknown quantities' and, as a rule, hailed from substantially humbler, inferior, and more rural backgrounds than did the nation's prominent political figures, who, on the contrary, typically hailed from a seemingly hereditary and professional political class of well-to-do, Athenian socialite families.

In short, the reasons underlying the military regime's failure to consolidate itself by gaining the legitimizing support of civilian political élites seem not to have been moulded by EC actions or Greek élite perceptions of the Community so much as they were rooted in a host of domestic factors. The EC may have played a role in the Greek transition, but it did not play the decisive role attributed to it in some recent accounts in motivating political action within either the armed forces or the élite political class. Nor does it appear to have appreciably affected the timing of events leading to the regime's breakdown and collapse.

4. The European Community and Democratic Consolidation in Greece

While the European Community and its member states played a less than central role in the process that led to the breakdown of authoritarian rule in Greece, the European or Community link can be seen to have played a more (and increasingly) prominent role in the process by which democracy in Greece was established and consolidated. Having said this, there remains the danger of over-emphasizing or distorting the Community's importance on domestic events in Greece, even in the later, transition and consolidation phases of the democratization process. Recent scholarship is right to point out that the consolidation of parliamentary rule and the entrenchment of democratic procedures in Greece cannot be thought of divorced from events which included the EC. However, the nature and timing of the EC's influence on the transition and consolidation processes are areas requiring further examination and more precise analysis.

On a view recently advanced in the literature (Chapter 10, above), the most direct and visible way in which the EC and its member states affected the incipient transition stage of the democratic consolidation process in 1974, following the dictatorship's collapse in July, was in buttressing the claim to legitimacy and the domestic bargaining power of a key bridging actor: the new civilian prime minister, Constantine Karamanlis. 'Bridging institutions or actors', Whitehead explains, 'generally need a considerable degree of international support and protection if they are to carry out a stabilizing role in the cause of a democratization'. The Greek case, in his view, provides a clear case in which 'external support substantially reinforced the authority and bargaining power of a bridging actor and therefore helped to stabilize a potentially disruptive democratization'.[48] Karamanlis's role in the transition, Whitehead goes on to explain, was 'substantially enhanced by the backing he received from Western Europe and by the priority he attached to securing Greek entry into the European Community'.[49]

Susannah Verney similarly highlights the degree to which 'Karamanlis was surrounded by the aura of West European approval'. This was especially important, she explains, because 'the prestige which the EC had acquired as a defender of democracy during the dictatorship, meant that the West Europeans' attitude towards the new government carried particular weight'.[50] French president Valéry Giscard d'Estaing lent Karamanlis his own private jet so that Karamanlis could make the triumphant flight back to Athens and be sworn in as prime minister. The president of the European Commission cabled the new prime minister a congratulatory message the next day. Within a month, the president of the European Parliament and the Dutch foreign minister had visited Karamanlis in Athens. Such 'clear external approval', Verney rightly notes, 'added to the new government's legitimacy during its difficult early weeks'.[51]

Nevertheless, there is a danger in the recent literature of exaggerating the importance of Karamanlis's 'external support'. Verney and Whitehead point to West European approval of Karamanlis without fully exploring the domestic factors which proved to be much more crucial in lending him the legitimacy and bargaining power he needed to be a successful bridging actor. Indeed, Karamanlis was unique among members of the Greek political élite and ideally suited for his role as a stabilizing actor not so much for the West European approval he received, but rather because his undoubted conservative credentials, his clash with the king and military in the 1960s, and his subsequent self-exile gave him credibility, legitimacy, and a constituency base in both the conservative Right and the liberal Centre. This was essential and more important than is often realized, given the enduring and bitter divisions in Greek politics between the Right and the Centre. As Diamandouros explains, Karamanlis, the leader of the anti-Communist Right as prime minister from 1955 to 1963, was '[a]cceptable to the military on account of his past anti-Communist record', could 'command the support and confidence of the nonroyalist Right and of large segments of the traditional Center' owing to his clashes with the king in the early 1960s, and was 'tolerated as the lesser of two evils by monarchists opposed to the military regime'.[52]

Many of the international and domestic factors that lent Karamanlis legitimacy, authority, and political capital as a bridging actor
were no doubt reinforcing and reciprocal. However, the domestic factors were indispensable. That these domestic factors were
crucial—and more important than West European approval in
providing Karamanlis with the requisite legitimacy and authority
he needed to be a successful stabilizing actor—is made evident if
we consider two things. First, one could have expected almost any
other prominent Greek political figure, and certainly King Constantine, to have received West European approval had they been
placed in a similar position to that held by Karamanlis. But the
authority and domestic bargaining power of any of these figures
would almost certainly have been compromised by the fact that
they did not enjoy the broad political or 'statesman-like' appeal of
Karamanlis, who alone, it seems, was able to straddle the political
divide separating the Centre and the Right.

Secondly, 'the aura of West European approval' which surrounded
Karamanlis upon his return from exile in Paris detracted from as
well as 'added to the new government's legitimacy during its difficult early weeks'—something the recent literature in this area does
not examine or note. This effect was a domestic political result of
the contradictory behaviour of most Community member states
vis-à-vis the dictatorship. It was demonstrably *not* the case that
West European governments, because of EC actions, had (in contrast to the United States) somehow acquired the prestige of defenders of democracy during the dictatorship and that, as a result,
their favourable attitude towards the Karamanlis government carried particular weight.

On the contrary, the NATO connections of many member
states, and their tolerance or support of the Colonels in that guise
or in their bilateral relations with the regime, meant that the
West Europeans were resented alongside, and for similar reasons
as, the Americans. 'Bitter disillusionment with American policy in
Greece', as Clogg notes, 'was compounded by frustration at the
pusillanimity of the West European reaction to the establishment
of a dictatorship' in Athens. Nor did this reaction seem difficult to
understand. For when all was said and done, Clogg explains, it
remained the case that '[n]either NATO nor the EC proved willing
to exert real pressure on the military dictatorship'.[53] As *The Economist* retrospectively concluded in 1975, the United States and other
'member states of the Nato alliance . . . merely expressed with varying degrees of conviction, sadness at the turn of events' in Greece
during the dictatorship. 'They were not prepared to jeopardise the

west's defensive structure in the eastern Mediterranean by putting the Greek regime into purdah.'[54]

The mixed emotions many Greeks felt towards the West, it is important to note, were not simply the views of disaffected Left-Communist radicals. They extended well beyond the socialist Left into the liberal Centre and encompassed the conservative Right New Democracy Party as well.[55] These feelings of ambivalence towards the West, spanning the entire political spectrum, were compounded by widespread Greek disillusionment and indignation following the conspicuous aloofness of both the United States and Western Europe during the initial Turkish invasion of Cyprus in July 1974, and the second Turkish offensive in August. As Tsoukalis puts it, in Greece 'there was strong resentment of the fact that the United States and the other Nato allies had been unwilling or unable to prevent the Turkish invasion' of Cyprus—a resentment which only grew in view of 'the continuing occupation of about 40 per cent of the island's territory'.[56]

Accordingly, Karamanlis's popular legitimacy, political capital, and bargaining power at home increased as much, if not more, for tactfully rebuking and effectively condemning the West Europeans (along with the Americans) for their support of the dictatorship and tolerance of the Turkish invasion of Cyprus as it did for receiving public support and visible approval from West European governments. This was above all done through Karamanlis's decision to withdraw Greece from NATO's military wing.[57] This action was subsequently complemented by the Karamanlis government's public demand that Joseph Luns be removed from his position as NATO Secretary-General.[58] The move against Luns was somewhat ironic, in view of his 'pre-NATO' role as the Dutch foreign minister in raising the question of the Colonels' human rights record in the Council of Europe. But the call for Luns's removal, if nothing else, served to symbolize the degree to which the limited efforts taken against the regime by European governments in bodies such as the Council of Europe or the EC were seen, even in responsible Greek eyes, to pale in comparison to the actions these same states (in this instance, the same individual) had taken in NATO or in their separate bilateral dealings with the Colonels.

In the end, then, West European approval for Karamanlis proved to be a two-edged sword that restricted as well as enhanced his domestic bargaining power and legitimacy. In the context of 1974, foreign support was something that was partly welcomed, but also something that had to be partly avoided. With Greece's Western allies distrusted and popularly resented in Greece because of their ineffectiveness against the junta and over Cyprus, Karamanlis could not hope (or afford) to have his authority or bargaining power too 'substantially enhanced' by external Western support, especially during the volatile Cyprus crisis, in the shadow of which Karamanlis operated during the transition.

Indeed, one is perhaps better served by looking towards the Cyprus crisis and the showdown with Turkey if one wishes to locate an international factor that significantly enhanced Karamanlis's ability to play the role of a stabilizing 'bridging actor' in the transition to democracy. The Cyprus crisis, as we saw above, can more appropriately be said to have dealt authoritarian rule in Greece a *coup de grâce* rather than a mortal blow. Nevertheless, the threat of war with Turkey over Cyprus and the Aegean[59] did play an important role in the process by which democracy returned to Greece—but not so much in the immediate breakdown of authoritarian rule (as is often argued) as in the months and years subsequent to the collapse of the military regime. As Diamandouros points out,

the very real threat of war which the crisis [in relations with Turkey] produced acted as a powerful counterweight, containing radicalizing forces, imposing self-restraint on mass actors, and producing a wave of national solidarity which greatly expanded the new civilian leadership's freedom of movement and effectively neutralized substantive opposition to its handling of the transition.[60]

The crisis over Cyprus and the Aegean dampened Greek political reactions in the post-dictatorship period in a number of crucial ways conducive to a stable process of democratization. Opposition leaders deferred to Karamanlis in the interests of national security 'given the near universal perception of a Turkish threat'.[61] Moreover, the crisis in relations with Turkey importantly served to reduce the threat of street violence or social disorder. Beyond the attitudinal effects of the threat of war, this minimization of social disruption was greatly facilitated by the general mobilization called by Greece in July 1974 to counter the Turkish invasion of Cyprus. The nationwide call-to-arms helped 'to remove from Athens and all other major cities the more militant civilian elements, thus weakening potential demonstrations or strikes'. Moreover, 'by putting young Greeks into uniform', the mobilization helped 'to reconcile them to the idea that the army [wa]s now not the enemy inside the tanks that had shot up the Polytechnic . . . but part of the democratic state' standing ready to defend Greece. This shared national experience helped to recast the collective consciousness and furthered the difficult process of political healing in the wake of the domestic wounds left by the dictatorial experience.[62]

The traumatic showdown with Turkey over Cyprus was crucially important in the relatively rapid and smooth Greek transition to democracy not only to the extent that it modulated and moderated national political differences, but also in so far as it helped to alter the military's guiding mission and long-standing relationship to domestic politics. The hectic summer days of 1974 constituted a rebaptism of fire for the Greek armed forces. From their Cold War mission of home defence against potential internal Communist subversion, the military was recast virtually overnight into the role of a force mainly geared to deal with an external threat to Greek security. The significance of this change can hardly be overstated.

This change in military attitude was further helped by the 'gigantic rearmament programme' which the Karamanlis government undertook in light of the deterioration in relations and the threat of war with Turkey. In the years following the dictatorship's collapse, the Greek defence budget grew enormously. Defence expenditure doubled in 1975 compared with the preceding year, and grew again by 30 per cent in 1976.[63] The acquisition of newer and better equipment, and the generous personnel provisions which the expanded military budget permitted, helped to discourage the formation of 'professional grievances' of the type which had 'constituted an important force behind the coup of 1967'.[64]

The attitudinal removal of the armed forces from politics was further matched by a literal and physical removal of the military from Athens itself, also a result of the Cyprus and Aegean disputes and the threat of hostilities with Turkey. The powerful military organization which had been installed by the regime in the Greater Athens area was dissolved 'since many troops had to be moved to the north' in anticipation of a possible Turkish offensive in Thrace.[65] Crucially, the tanks and armoured divisions which the conspiracy of officers had used to assume power so effortlessly in 1967, and which had helped to maintain their control over the capital city, were also sent out of Athens.[66] The threat of war with Turkey provided the 'perfect excuse' for all these movements, many of them aimed as much at asserting civilian control over the military as anything else.[67]

Of course, to say that the showdown with Turkey affected mass and military politics in ways that substantially enhanced the prospects for democracy in Greece is not to say that the Community and its member states had no effect on the consolidation process. On the contrary, recent scholarship has attempted to demonstrate that democratic consolidation in Greece during the course of the 1970s was facilitated by Greek perceptions of the democratic advantages of EC membership, as well as by the EC's 'elaborate structure of economic and social incentives for changes in group and national behaviour' conducive to the prospects for democracy.[68] Prominent members of the élite in Greece (none more prominent than Karamanlis) and the ruling conservative New Democracy Party, it is explained, advocated Greek accession to the Community on the grounds that EC membership would 'inevitably strengthen the political fabric of the country, eradicate the negative elements that weakness and poverty breed, and permit a greater sense of security towards adverse influences from within and without'.[69] Whitehead and Verney (among others) have accordingly argued along lines that the Community helped to consolidate democracy in Greece to the extent that it convinced ruling political élites and, more broadly, the majority of the Greek electorate of the plausibility and desirability of the following process: democracy → EC membership → EC aid → modernization and development → prosperity → political and democratic stability. It is primarily through this consensus-building mechanism of desire, aspiration, and expectation, Whitehead notes, that convergence with the democratic political and social models offered by EC member states came about, thereby helping to further and facilitate the consolidation of democracy in Greece.[70]

There is much of relevance in these arguments. However, there is also a sense in which they provide only a selective vignette of EC influence on domestic politics in post-junta Greece over the course of the 1970s. It is analytically important to note both how the process of democratic consolidation in Greece was facilitated by factors largely independent of the question of Greek accession, and also how, for a time, and in several important ways, it proceeded in spite of it. This point is something that recent scholarship, which in many respects usefully draws attention to factors that had previously been ignored or left unexamined, has unfortunately not acknowledged or examined more closely. European Community or no, the experience of the dictatorship itself (reinforced by the threat of war with Turkey) was enough to discredit the idea of a return to authoritarian rule among New Democracy's conservatives and free-market liberals, PASOK's populists and social democrats, and, perhaps most importantly, the military itself. The dictatorship's bitter legacy and (less centrally, though still importantly) the threat from Turkey, not the promise or possibility of EC membership, were sufficient to create the broad democratic consensus and national unity necessary to facilitate and make possible the entrenchment of democratic institutions and procedures.

In fact, Greek attitudes towards the Nine and the West in general poignantly suggest that the question of Greek entry into the Community helped to hinder democratic consolidation in significant ways, at the same time as aiding it, in other respects, over a crucial span of years in the late 1970s. As had been the case in the United Kingdom, Norway, and elsewhere, the question of accession to the EC was controversial in Greece and occupied a particularly prominent position in national politics, especially from 1977.[71] In this sense, the EC in the late 1970s was as much a point of domestic political conflict as it was a model or aspiration. Indeed, the aggravation and magnification of political differences occasioned by the debate on Europe eroded the sense of national consensus which observers noted had emerged after the dictatorship's fall in 1974.[72] The national debate over EC membership helped to polarize the political spectrum and to undermine the development of a minimum level of national consensus on the internal–external political identity of Greece, the latter arguably being a necessary pre-condition for democratic consolidation.

Accordingly, a contention of this chapter is that it was no mere coincidence that the conclusion of the process by which democracy was consolidated in Greece largely came hand in hand with, and on the heels of, Greek entry into the European Community in 1981. The debate and controversy surrounding accession precluded, and by its very nature postponed, the formation of a consensus concerning the political identity of post-dictatorship Greece, and thereby precluded the full consolidation of the new political system. So long as Community membership was a subject of debate, the most fundamental questions concerning the future domestic and international identity of the republic were, by definition, open to confrontational challenge in the political arena.

The degree to which the far-ranging and bitter debate over EC membership stalled the process of democratic consolidation is perhaps most evident if one considers the Greek parliamentary debate (25–8 June 1979) on the issue of ratifying the treaty of accession to the Community. Opposition parties expressed their hostility to Greek entry by boycotting the four-day debate. The principle of EC membership was finally approved by a parliamentary vote of 193–0 (with three abstentions), while the actual accession treaty itself was ratified 191–2 (again with three abstentions). However, 104 of the parliament's 300 members were absent for these votes, the absentees being members of Papandreou's PASOK and the Greek Communist Party (KKE).[73] The refusal of opposition parties to participate in the parliamentary debate—and most especially their refusal to participate in the vote—illustrates the extent to which hostility to Greek membership undermined, or, at the very least, interrupted and complicated the process of, democratic consolidation. The opposition's convictions concerning EC membership were such that the democratic procedures and institutions which were giving effect to accession were seen as less than legitimate—so much so that the opposition displayed an unwillingness to work within these procedures and institutions (for instance, by voting against the treaty). On the contrary, the anti-Europe opposition cast aspersions on the legitimacy of the parliament's decision and its competence in general, maintaining that only a national referendum could decide a matter of such historical importance for the nation.

Although this challenge in retrospect can be seen not to have caused irreparable damage to the consolidation of democracy, in the context of a new democratic regime seeking to legitimize its governmental structures and executive decisions, it amounted to a most serious challenge to the system. Importantly, it raised the spectre of destabilizing future conflicts over the regime should the opposition not come to power and get a chance to articulate and legislate its political platform. The incipient formation of a 'sore loser' mentality called into question whether a prerequisite for consolidated democracy and the avoidance of praetorian politics—regime acceptance and a willingness to work within agreed and accepted democratic procedures—would come to pass or, in repetition of past Greek history, recede beyond the reach of the new republic.[74]

It can perhaps be said that PASOK's opposition to EC membership (though certainly not the KKE's) was by this time tactical, not strategic, and had as its motivation a desire to win votes and public support, rather than deeply rooted ideological convictions. This may very well be true. What is important from the point of view of democratic theory and the present study, however, is the way in which PASOK and the KKE chose to register their dissent on the subject of full membership. Their willingness to resort to extra-parliamentary tactics demonstrated a readiness to bypass or work outside recognized democratic procedures. As Juan Linz's seminal work on democratic deconsolidation suggests, the incipient development in the late 1970s of 'semi-loyal' opposition patterns (as opposed to those of a loyal opposition), as well as the disintegration of the traditional Centre and polarization of the political spectrum, for a time (short, yet in many ways crucial) marked an inauspicious turn in the young republic's history.[75]

Having said this, however, it is important to note a distinction between the effects of the debate on Greek entry into the Community, on the one hand, and actual entry, on the other. Indeed, while the debate over Greek entry may have in many ways disrupted and, for a time, complicated the consolidation process, the ratification of the accession treaty, and particularly EC membership, promoted and helped to bring the process of democratic consolidation to a close. Most importantly, this was because of the real or perceived irreversibility of the 1979 ratification of the accession treaty, and especially because of entry into the Community in 1981. This sense of irreversibility seemed to proceed from and illustrate a point of central importance to liberal interdependence theory, namely that 'once the degree of market interdependence among nations reaches a critical point it makes their relationship one that often transcends and bypasses political preferences'.[76]

This chapter adopts the position that the process of democratic consolidation in Greece was largely completed by 1981. The question of when, or even whether, democracy in Greece has been consolidated since 1974 is a point of some contention in the literature and as such warrants further consideration. The notion of 'democratic consolidation', like many social science concepts, clearly presents something of a problem.[77] There is no single indicator to which one can point to discern whether a given democratic system is consolidated or not. Following Whitehead, I take consolidation to mean the 'entrenchment of democratic institutions'.[78] To what evidence can one point in order to say that a democracy is consolidated rather than fragile? Regular non-fraudulent elections, the alternation of parties, civilian control of the military, and signs that governing and principal opposition groups more or less see their future as tied to working within the polity's procedural and constitutional rules, all add up, I would argue, to a reasonable level of consolidated democracy (this being an extensive but not an exhaustive list). Verney and Pridham have argued with respect to Greece that the 'quality' of a democracy affects its 'credibility'.[79] However, consolidated democracies need not be perfect, or even particularly attractive.[80] They might happen to be strong, weak, corrupt, or dominated by political parties (partitocracy). Nor need they be impregnable. Consolidated democracies can succumb later on and be victims of processes of deconsolidation.[81]

The process of democratic consolidation in Greece can be said to have been well advanced by 1977, the year in which Andreas Papandreou's Centre-Left PASOK party emerged as the major opposition party, and can almost certainly be said to have been nearing completion by 1981, when Papandreou and PASOK assumed power.

Following its emergence as the major opposition party in the 1977 general elections, one can detect a gradual change in PASOK's previously radical stance and attitude as it began to smell power.[82] For instance, while Papandreou went to the polls in 1977 campaigning vociferously for complete Greek withdrawal from NATO, after the election he qualified his party's position, 'intimating that the timing and the manner of the Greek withdrawal would have to obey realistic considerations of Greece's defence requirements'.[83]

The change in PASOK's stance and attitude effectively marked the first stage of a reconciliation between the fledgling Hellenic Republic, on the one hand, and Papandreou and the Greek Centre-Left, on the other, which had been conspicuously excluded from the 'national unity' government of 1974. The transformation (or so-called 'maturation') of PASOK, beginning in 1977, from a radical anti-system movement into a loyal opposition party and its effective acceptance of both the national and international rules of the game—and the ramifications of this for the prospects of political, social, and economic stability in Greece—greatly furthered the process of consolidating the new Greek democracy. The aftermath of the 1977 general elections can thus be seen as having marked the beginning of the end of a phase in which democratic institutions had been created, put into operation in a satisfactory way, and accepted as more or less legitimate by the major actors on the national political stage. The 1981 elections, the elevation to power of Papandreou, and the relatively smooth transfer of power and alternation of parties helped to complete this process.[84]

Once in power after 1981, PASOK, a party which in opposition had tenaciously opposed Greek entry into the EC, even at the risk of placing one foot outside normal democratic procedures and questioning the legitimacy of governmental decisions and structures, gradually reconciled itself to the reality of EC membership. Papandreou and PASOK essentially accepted it as a *fait accompli*. Given the flow of EC money from Brussels which membership brought with it, Papandreou immediately came to recognize (even if he only came to say so later) that 'withdrawal from the EC would have harmful effects on the economy'.[85]

The apparently irreversible nature of EC membership, as Whitehead has suggested, provided a sense of closure, preventing the perpetual re-examination of the issue of Greece's domestic and international political identity, something which could quite conceivably have permanently destabilized the Greek polity.[86] Thus, while the effect of the debate on EC membership may have been deleterious to the consolidation process, the resolution of that debate and Greece's subsequent entry into the Community (and all that seemed to imply for Greece's external and internal political identity and her material and institutional interdependence with 'Europe') helped to bring that process to a close. The 'finality' of the new economic and institutional relationship with the EC, and particularly the flow of EC money to Greece, encouraged the major anti-establishment political groups to accept and work within the established procedures of the new republic and the international political order, rather than persisting in challenging them.

5. *The European Community and the Consolidated Greek Democracy*

Greek integration into the Community framework may have helped to restructure group and national political behaviour in Greece, as well as Greece's pattern of foreign relations, in ways conducive to the prospects for democracy, much as Whitehead, Verney, and others have argued in recent literature on the EC and Greek democracy, but the bulk of this integration effect was felt in the 1980s — that is, after Greek entry to the Community and after the effective completion of the consolidation process. Accordingly, the present chapter argues that the EC can more appropriately be seen as underwriting democracy in Greece following its consolidation, rather than exporting it there in the first place.

Much of the recent Greek case literature holds or suggests that EC membership helped to export democracy to Greece because it views the consolidation of democracy in Greece, and southern Europe more generally, as a lengthy process that was ongoing during the 1980s. This chapter has already argued that the consolidation of democracy in Greece was largely completed by 1981. It accordingly views membership in the Community not so much—note the qualification—a cause as a result of democratic consolidation. As Whitehead notes, democracy in Greece (as in Spain and Portugal) was 'pretty well consolidated' by the time accession or enlargement occurred, it being 'understood by all concerned that solid democratic institutions were a pre-condition for entry'.[87] The relationship between democratic consolidation and accession was not, of course, simply a one-way street. On the contrary, it was reciprocal and reinforcing in a number of important ways, as we saw in the preceding section. However, the great bulk of the EC's influence on domestic politics in Greece must be seen as having followed Greece's accession to the Community as a democratic state.

As I conceive this term, the EC helped to *underwrite* democracy in Greece in the 1980s by reinforcing and broadening its attractiveness and stability, and thus helping to guarantee its domestic and international credibility. The process of underwriting democracy in part involved the extension of material resources as tangible incentives and reasons for maintaining democracy, above and beyond normative commitments to democratic values. These incentives can be conceived of as external supports (or reasons for staying democratic), which could, if need be, bear some of the burden of proof for the desirability of maintaining a democratic polity. In this sense, underwriting democracy meant helping to instil the belief and holding forth the prospect that democracy was closely interrelated with prosperity in a mutually supporting and interdependent manner, thereby helping to preclude the situation in which the attractiveness of democracy might be questioned or constrained by perceptions that its maintenance involves a trade-off with material well-being or economic welfare. The provision of resources contingent on the presence of democracy—backed by strong, legally binding material commitments based on international treaties and European law, as embodied in a framework of authoritative institutions—helped to convince domestic groups and actors representing large sections of society that threats to democratic values and procedures were tantamount to threats to material interest, thus raising the costs of repression in a manner significantly conducive to the Greek republic's stability, endurance, and political resilience.

The EC and its framework of economic and institutional interdependence helped to underwrite democracy, in this sense, by helping to move the reasons for democracy beyond the realm of political preferences and normative commitments and tying them, both implicitly and explicitly, to the sphere of material interests. Furthermore, EC membership helped to underwrite Greek democracy in the 1980s to the degree that it facilitated its stability by reducing the scope, or need, for praetorianism (i.e. the actual or threatened use of force by military officers) as a mechanism for asserting authority or establishing political order—and furthermore, by restructuring the pattern of foreign influences on domestic politics in a manner propitious to the character and nature of internal democracy. Viewing the EC as an underwriter instead of an exporter of democracy in the above ways more accurately conveys the nature and timing of the EC's influence on the prospects for democracy in Greece, by drawing a distinction between the strength and salience of EC incentives to stay democratic, as opposed to the lesser salience in the earlier transition and consolidation periods of possible EC incentives to *become* democratic, as seen above.

Moreover, viewing the EC as an underwriter of democracy in Greece during the 1980s helps to convey the nature of the EC's vested interests in Greek democracy more accurately than viewing the EC as a democratic exporter, or less simply, as a factor or actor affecting (a prolonged) democratic consolidation. The concept of exporting democracy to Greece casts the EC in the light of an international actor or force essentially driving or inducing a domestic political development externally. Viewing the EC as an underwriter of democracy more accurately conveys the degree to which the EC's own resources and credibility became wrapped up with the stability of Greek democracy than either this picture or that of the EC as a consolidating influence on Greek democracy, i.e. one among many. If the Community helped to lend democracy in Greece some domestic and international credibility by helping to reinforce and guarantee the attractiveness and stability of democratic institutions in both intended and unintentional ways, then at the same time, the EC's own credibility as an international actor in part came to depend on the success and maintenance of Greek democracy and would have been adversely affected in the event of the failure of democracy in Greece. In other words, characterizing the EC as an underwriter of democracy better helps to convey the shared risk-taking and partnership involved in the committal of Community resources with one eye on making democracy work in Greece. This point is partly illustrated by the EC's arguably diminished credibility and sense of future uncertainty in the wake of the ERM's collapse in 1993, despite policy commitments on the part of Community partners to make it work.

At the same time, underwriting democracy is at least as different from the concept of supporting democracy as that of exporting it. Supporting democracy does not imply the same legally and institutionally backed set of guarantees and therefore does not necessarily have anything like the same durability, credibility, or democratic outcome in terms of regime stability. Support for democracy—be it financial or political—can be withdrawn in a manner unlike the more permanent, treaty-based, and legally defined commitment to underwrite. Underwriting democracy thus signifies a form of international democracy promotion characteristic of EC membership more powerful and sustained than mere support, but less intrusive and controlling than is implied by the language of exporting.

EC membership helped to underwrite democracy in Greece during the 1980s in a number of different ways which we can only briefly consider here. Accession first of all helped to restructure Greece's relationship to external powers in a way propitious to the character and nature of internal democracy. Moreover, membership and integration into the Community's institutional framework facilitated the full incorporation of rural population into the political life of the new republic. Finally, membership enhanced the transformation of the Greek political system from one largely characterized by institutionally weak parties of notables to one characterized by more robust organized mass parties.

First, as Verney convincingly argues, the European Community allowed Greece, which had been caught between the superpowers ever since the 1940s, to move away from US tutelage without provoking an American reaction.[88] Given the post-war history of Greece this was a critical contribution to the prospects for internal democracy. Membership in the Community allowed Greece to restructure its international relations in a way conducive to the prospects for internal democracy. As Verney explains, the type of foreign influence exerted on Athens by the European Community 'cannot be compared with the old bilateral relationship with a single superpower'.[89] The nature of the differences between the two types of influence were felt most strongly upon accession. 'EC membership', as Verney continues, 'has subjected Greece to a more diffuse network of foreign influence—and crucially, one in which Greece itself has an institutionalised voice in decision-making'.[90] Most importantly, as far as the prospects for democracy are concerned, Greece's EC membership, unlike her previous relationship with the United States, 'clearly depends on the existence of internal democracy', given the Community's implicit adoption of democratic criteria for membership in the Treaty of Rome,[91] and more particularly its explicit adoption of such criteria in the Birkelbach (1962) and Luxembourg (1970) Reports, and the Copenhagen Declaration (1978).[92]

Second, EC membership also affected the post-consolidation prospects for the new democracy in the 1980s to the extent that it helped to alter the traditional political landscape of Greece. Indeed, membership in the Community helped to revolutionize the political relationship of the rural countryside to Athens, and in particular facilitated the full social and political incorporation of the previously marginalized rural population into the new democracy. As Constantine Tsoucalas, Keith Legg, and others have shown, remote rural areas were 'negatively' incorporated into the 'guided' political system of the post-war decades. Formal and informal mechanisms of intimidation and limits on the free expression and dissemination of political ideas mediated the rural population's participation in politics.[93] The major extension of local government to the countryside came only after 1974. Prior to this, as Robert Fox notes, remote rural areas were essentially under the thumb of centrally appointed governors, and villages were under the eye of gendarmes.[94]

As a result, the Greek countryside was traditionally susceptible to authoritarian politics, particularly if accompanied by promises of the forgiveness of farm debts, electrification, and other improvements in living standards (all promises made by the Colonels in their attempt to win rural support). The susceptibility of rural areas to authoritarian bribes offered to secure support or political apathy was a direct result of the fact that the practical difference between so-called democratic rule and authoritarian rule, as far as most rural dwellers were concerned, was often more apparent than real.

However, Community membership and the dollops of EC aid that came with it helped to change this state of affairs. Community membership first, and most directly, helped to cushion the shock to the new democracy of the proliferation of previously constrained rural demands, helping to absorb and underwrite some of the costs of democracy. In this way, it helped to minimize the scope of social and political disruption in the wake of the post-1974 dismantling of the *ancien regime* of rural surveillance, intimidation, and thought-leading.

Furthermore, EC money, mainly funds earmarked by the Community for regional development and the agricultural sector, positively enhanced the prospects for democracy to the extent that they helped to establish a clear, causal connection between democracy, EC membership, and prosperity for the now heavily subsidized countryside. This connection amounted to nothing less than a recognition that personal and national prosperity were inextricably linked to Greece's new identity as a liberal democracy and EC member state. This proved to be one of the most direct and powerful ways in which EC membership provided, to use Whitehead's words, an 'elaborate structure of economic and social incentives for changes in group and national behaviour' conducive to the prospects for political democracy.[95]

The manner in which EC membership helped to alter the political predilections of the rural countryside, and facilitated the full and managed incorporation of the countryside's rural population into the new democratic regime, was in important ways related to another political development also enhanced by Greek entry to the Community. This was the growth in Greece, particularly in the 1980s, of organized mass parties, and the concomitant redefinition of traditional clientelist politics.

In the democratic system which had preceded military rule, political parties had been decentralized, personal coalitions of notables, lacking any mass membership or internal organization.[96] This state of affairs did not change appreciably in the years immediately following the dictatorship's collapse. As Roy Macridis explains, 'the hastily reorganized parties remained "personal parties"'. That is to say, they remained 'loose federations and alliances of political leaders and local notables rather than centralized and disciplined entities'.[97] Indeed, despite some lip-service paid to the development of a party organization, the ruling conservative New Democracy Party in the 1977 elections 'was far less significant as a mass organization than as a group of leaders and professional politicians'.[98]

A notable exception to this state of affairs was Andreas Papandreou's socialist PASOK party. By the time PASOK was swept into office in 1981, it was clear to all, as Richard Clogg explains, that

it had created the most effective and widespread . . . grassroots organization ever achieved by a political party in Greece outside the [Communist] far left. Scarcely a village was without an office sporting the somewhat mystifying PASOK symbol of the Green Sun. PASOK was firmly entrenched in the trade unions, student unions and professional organisations, and was highly visible in the peace and women's movements.[99]

However, PASOK's biggest steps towards its self-establishment as an organized mass party came after its assumption of power in 1981, when membership figures literally mushroomed and locally based party organizations (*topikes organoseis*) proliferated accordingly, as seen in the following table.

TABLE 12.1. *The growth of PASOK's party membership and local organizations, 1980–1984*

		1980	1981	1982	1983	1984
Members		75,000	110,000	140,000	200,000	220,000
Local clubs	(*topikes*)	460	1,000	n/a	n/a	3,285

Source: compiled data presented in D. Sotiropoulos, 'State and Party: The Greek State Bureaucracy and the Panhellenic Socialist Movement (PASOK), 1981–1989', Ph.D. thesis (Yale, 1991), 111.

The rise of the PASOK party machinery was highly significant due to PASOK's identity as the first organized mass party in Greece outside the Communist Left. Its efficient organizational breadth and depth at the grass-roots and village level, as established in the 1970s and expanded in the 1980s, was unprecedented—and quickly copied by the conservative New Democracy Party in the opposition, thus recasting the face of Greek politics.[100]

Importantly, the extension and entrenchment of PASOK's party machine can be said to have been financed to a great extent on the back of EC transfer payments in the 1980s. While this was not an intended consequence of EC money, it was made possible by four related factors: the interpenetration in Greece of state and governing party, the relatively high degree of control by the latter of the former ('partitocracy'), the extent to which the EC relies on member states for the administration of its initiatives, and the Commission's apparent early tolerance of poor or politically motivated Greek management of EC initiatives in the interests of easing the shock of membership and avoiding 'disharmony and crisis within the Community'.[101]

To be sure, the lion's share of EC aid to Greece over the course of the 1980s, amounting to some $14 billion,[102] was intended as investment subsidies to aid the development of Greece's rural regions and agricultural sector. In reality, as Napoleon Maraveyas explains, 'most of the time this assistance [wa]s given without the existence of a modernization project, and therefore it is very likely that it [wa]s used as an income rather than an investment subsidy'.[103] For example, a full 60 per cent of the 1981–5 EC contribution to the structural improvement of the Greek agricultural sector (19 billion drachmas) was used to finance 'compensatory payments to marginal agricultural enterprises . . . found in the disadvantaged (mainly mountainous) regions'.[104] It is not difficult to see how party machines built around the dispensation of spoils and favours could be financed on the back of EC monies distributed in such a manner. In practice, the determination of assistance and the dispersal of EC funds could be, and became, as much a political as an economic question, and was in fact often made primarily on the basis of proven, confessed, or perceived loyalty to the party in power.[105]

Moreover, the political and economic effects of Community spending indeed extended well beyond the areas for which EC funds were nominally earmarked. The fungibility of money meant that EC resources eased public finance burdens on the Greek state, freeing up money the government would have otherwise spent on certain projects or goals for uses in other areas. Given this displacement of government spending, EC funds can thus be said to have partly, if indirectly, financed a whole array of Greek government programmes and policies in the 1980s, and in particular the huge expansion of the public sector, where an estimated 400,000 employees, mostly PASOK members or supporters, were hired over the decade. In this context, of course, it bears remembering, as C.

Lyrintzis puts it, that in Greece the 'organized expansion of existing posts and departments in the public sector and the addition
of new ones [serves as a means] . . . to secure power and maintain
a party's electoral base'.[106] Besides the direct distribution of EC
monies as income subsidies, then, there is a second, perhaps more
important, sense in which a party machine, built around the dispensation of jobs, patronage, and spoils, could be said to have been
financed on the back of EC resources.

In fact, as Pridham and Verney incisively note, whereas political
clientelism in Greece had traditionally 'revolved around personal
relationships, with the local MP as the usual clientelistic "gate-
keeper"', over the course of the 1980s 'the party card became a job
ticket'.[107] The most notable, and notorious, illustration of the change
in the political landscape and in clientelistic practice was the rise
of the *kladiki*, the quasi-corporatist, occupation-related PASOK
office or professional club where 'membership . . . became the guarantee for a job offer and/or of job security' in the highly desirable
public sector.[108]

To be sure, the expansion, redefinition, and entrenchment of
clientelist practices in the 1980s, as made possible in part by Community transfers and borrowed money, may not have been particularly savoury. However, the spread of party structures at the
grass-roots and village level, and the development of mass mobilization techniques, fostered a stronger party system over the
course of the decade. This result must be seen as a significant and,
in important ways, positive development for the long-term prospects
of political democracy in Greece. This is something which is often
overlooked in contemporary discussions of Greek politics. Admittedly, the ways in which EC membership affected democracy in
Greece during the 1980s were not all salutary. For instance, the
nearly institutionalized corruption that was in large part unwit-
tingly (or, initially perhaps, patiently) financed by the EC in the
1980s has been corrosive of democratic political culture. More
specifically, it has generated some popular resentment towards
the relatively closed Greek political class, and may be said to pose
a potential threat to the social and political bargain on which the
young Greek republic rests.[109]

Still, the effect of EC membership on democratic politics in Greece
seems to have been, on balance, largely positive. It would be hy-
perbole to suggest that popular disgust at high-level corruption
has undermined the widespread Greek democratic consensus or
significantly increased popular receptivity of the idea of an authoritarian interlude to cleanse the Augean stables of national pol-

itics. As Pasquino explains with reference to the southern European cases,

> The matter of the quality of democracy might indeed provoke feelings of *desencanto*, but seldom has this *desencanto* resuscitated desires of returning to the authoritarian past. In any case, the commitment of almost the totality of party élites to democratic politics as well as their own behaviour and the ideas they diffuse among the population at large seem to guarantee that no breakdown of democracy is likely in the near future of southern Europe.[110]

In Greece, feelings of disenchantment peaked in the late 1980s and early 1990s, when a number of financial scandals were publicized, contributing to the fall of the PASOK government and the indictment of high-level PASOK officials, including Andreas Papandreou, on charges of fraud, embezzlement, bribery, abuse of power, and other wrong-doings. Still, cross-national opinion surveys found that people in Greece were 'generally satisfied with the way democracy work[ed] in their country' at a comparable or higher rate than people in such West European countries as Belgium, France, the Netherlands, or the United Kingdom.[111]

Whether this balance would change over the course of the 1990s and beyond, to the detriment of the prospects for democracy, was an important and timely question raised in the aftermath of the Cold War. The early 1990s indeed witnessed powerful changes of the parameters within which democracy in Greece operates, not the least of those being the instability and conflagration in the former Yugoslav republics and the arguably diminished credibility and uncertain future development of the enlarged European Union. The concept of democratic consolidation, as suggested earlier, does not presuppose immutability or impregnability. In the event, what this chapter shows is the powerful ways in which the EC underwrote the already largely consolidated Greek democracy in the decade following accession in 1981.

6. Lessons from the Greek Case for Democratization Theory

The new and growing body of scholarship on the Greek and other cases has no doubt enriched our knowledge in pointing out the international and in particular the European aspects of the democratization process in Greece that were previously overlooked or under-studied in the literature, and stood the danger of being forgotten. However, it would also seem to be the case that in contributing to our understanding of regime change and consolidation in some ways, the growing literature on Greece and the EC has obfuscated our understanding in others. This paradox highlights a shortcoming in current ways of viewing the relationship between international and national forces in the democratization process, as well as an opportunity for a better conceptualization of the relationship between the two.

No doubt the preceding analysis of the Greek case has shown that both international and national forces played important roles in shaping Greek politics over the course of the 1970s and 1980s. To the extent that recent works in the literature underscore this point, one not properly explored in earlier scholarship, they perform a great service. The new literature, in this area in particular, usefully points out the fault with a long-standing academic orthodoxy, namely the dualist tendency to view the realms of national politics and international relations as separate and mutually exclusive subjects of study and fields of scholarship.

However, the present analysis does not find evidence for a 'monist' view of politics, and parts company with recent works where they suggest that 'the distinction between "national forces" and "external actors" is somewhat artificial and incomplete',[112] and that what is now 'necessary [is] to take account of the linkages between them'.[113] The boundaries between international and domestic politics may be blurred, but the Greek case warns us against doubting the usefulness of such boundaries. The present investigation suggests that the challenge facing the student of regime change is not that of discarding the dichotomous analytical categories of the old orthodoxy, as some scholars interested in 'linkage politics' theory have suggested. This analysis of the Greek case suggests that the way to meet this challenge is not by trying to stress the reality of linkages and artificiality of distinctions, but rather by trying to discern the differing importance of external vs. internal forces and actors over time, at different points, and during successive stages of the democratization process. Accordingly, this chapter suggests that the European Community played a minor role in the erosion and breakdown of authoritarian rule in Greece, that it played a smaller role as an international factor than the threat of war with Turkey in the early stages of the democratic transition, that it nevertheless went on to play an increasingly important role in the subsequent process by which democracy was consolidated, and finally, that it came to play a central role in underwriting and furthering the prospects for democracy in the 1980s.

In conclusion, this chapter suggests that domestic and international factors assume different degrees of importance at different stages of the democratization process, with transnational structural factors being relatively more important in later stages than in the earlier breakdown and transition phases. These findings support and further develop some of Whitehead's recent work, which has proposed such an argument in relation to southern Europe.[114] The thrust of these empirical and analytical conclusions, and the reasons underlying them in the Greek case, it is suggested, are perhaps best conveyed by the concept of 'underwriting' democracy, which this chapter introduced to highlight a distinctive, if delayed, form of international democracy promotion characteristic of EC membership, which is more durable, sustained, and powerful than mere international support, but less intrusive and controlling than is implied by the language or concept of exporting democracy.

Notes

1. G. O'Donnell, P. C. Schmitter, and L. Whitehead (eds.), *Transitions from Authoritarian Rule: Prospects for Democracy*, 4 vols. (Baltimore: Johns Hopkins University Press, 1986).
2. Schmitter, introductory essay in *Transitions from Authoritarian Rule* Tentative Conclusions about Uncertain Democracies, 3.
3. See, for example, the discussions by G. Pridham, 'Comparative Perspectives on the New Mediterranean Democracies: A Model of Regime Transition?', and A. Tovias, 'The International Context of Democratic Transitions', both in *West European Politics*, 7 (April 1984).
4. See, for instance, G. Pridham (ed.), *Encouraging Democracy: The International Context of Regime Transition in Southern Europe* (Leicester: Leicester University Press, 1991). For the Greek case, see the contribution by S. Verney and T. Couloumbis, 'State–International Systems Interaction and the Greek Transition to Democracy in the Mid-1970s', ibid. 103–24. Also consider P. Tsakaloyannis and S. Verney, 'Linkage Politics: The Role of the European Community in Greek Politics in 1973', *Byzantine and Modern Greek Studies*, 10 (1986), 179–94.
5. For example, see Laurence Whitehead, 'Democracy by Convergence and Southern Europe: A Comparative Politics Perspective', in Pridham (ed.), *Encouraging Democracy*, 45–61. A revised version appears as Chapter 10 above.
6. Ibid. 45.
7. Ibid. 45–6.
8. Tsakaloyannis and Verney, 'Linkage Politics: The Role of the European Community in Greek Politics in 1973', *Byzantine and Modern Greek Studies*, 10 (1986), 179–94.

9. Verney, 'The European Community as Exporter of Democracy: Lessons from the Greek Case', paper presented at the European Community Studies Association Conference, George Mason University, 22–4 May 1991.

10. Ibid. 9–10.

11. Ibid. 6.

12. See, for instance, L. Tsoukalis, *The European Community and its Mediterranean Enlargement* (London: George Allen & Unwin, 1981), 28–49, and G. Yannopoulos, *Greece and the European Communities: The First Decade of a Troubled Association* (Beverly Hills, Calif.: Sage, 1975).

13. Leading figures of the military junta at the time petulantly asserted that the Council of Europe was little more than a coffee-house and was to the regime as a mosquito to a bull. See *To Vima*, 6–13 December 1969, and C. M. Woodhouse, *The Rise and Fall of the Greek Colonels* (London: Granada, 1985), 56–7, 67–72.

14. Tsakaloyannis and Verney, 'Role of the European Community', 184.

15. Verney, 'European Community as Exporter of Democracy', 7.

16. Tsakaloyannis and Verney, 'Role of the European Community', 183.

17. Ibid.

18. Ibid. 183.

19. Verney, 'European Community as Exporter of Democracy', 7–8.

20. Verney and Couloumbis, 'State–International Systems', 111.

21. Cf. H. Richter, *British Intervention in Greece: From Varkiza to Civil War: February 1945 to August 1946* (London: Merlin Press, 1986), and G. Alexander, *The Prelude to the Truman Doctrine: British Policy in Greece, 1944–47* (Oxford: Clarendon Press, 1982).

22. Greece received $3,285m. from the USA between 1946 and 1963; 45 per cent of this aid was military, 55 per cent economic in nature: cf. Y. A. Kourvetaris and B. A. Dobratz, *A Profile of Modern Greece: In Search of Identity* (Oxford: Clarendon Press, 1987), 55.

23. Verney, 'European Community as Exporter of Democracy', 8.

24. Ibid. 9.

25. Tsakaloyannis and Verney, 'Role of the European Community', 189.

26. Ibid. 189.

27. Verney, 'European Community as Exporter of Democracy', 10.

28. Tsakaloyannis and Verney, 'Role of the European Community', 189. On this point, the article by Tsakaloyannis and Verney does not appear to be consistent, for this assertion follows the earlier statement: 'Papadopoulos' declaration on June 1st 1973 that Greece was to become a "presidential parliamentary republic" with elections to be held in 1974 under the supervision of a civilian government, was undoubtedly largely due to internal developments' (180).

29. O'Donnell and Schmitter, *Transitions*, iv. *Conclusions*, 18.

30. Tsoukalis, *European Community*, 31. See also V. Coufoudakis, 'The European Economic Community and the "Freezing" of the Greek Association', *Journal of Common Market Studies*, 16 (1977–8), 127.

31. Tsoukalis, *European Community*, 31.
32. S. Stathatos, 'From Association to Full Membership', in L. Tsoukalis (ed.), *Greece and the European Community* (Westmead, Hampshire: Saxon House, 1979), 5. See also, F. Nicholson and R. East, *From the Six to the Twelve: The Enlargement of the European Communities* (Essex: Longman, 1987), 187.
33. For a contemporary critique of Western funding policies *vis-à-vis* the regime, see 'Nato's Little Torture-Chamber', *New Statesman*, 6 December 1968.
34. 'EEC and Greece: Mansholting', *The Economist*, 20 May 1972.
35. Cf. Tsoukalis, *European Community*, 31.
36. Coufoudakis, 'European Economic Community', 121.
37. Yannopoulos, *Greece and the European Communities*, 31.
38. Woodhouse, *Rise and Fall*, 52.
39. For insights on this point, see C. Barkman, *Ambassador in Athens* (London: Merlin Press, 1989), 16, 25, 50, 60, 76, 99, 180, 207. Barkman, who served as the Dutch ambassador in Athens from 1969 to 1975, paints a candid and hitherto unavailable inside account of the moral and strategic dilemmas facing Western policy-makers, and the trade-offs they were forced to consider, in formulating their Greek policy during the dictatorship.
40. Tsoukalis, *European Community*, 32.
41. Ibid. 32.
42. Ibid. 33.
43. For a theoretical and comparative discussion of the internally driven process which often leads regimes to risk foreign adventures and war in order 'to accommodate . . . domestic constituencies . . . threaten[ing the] regime's survival at home', see B. Bueno de Mesquita, R. M. Siverson, and G. Woller, 'War and the Fate of Regimes: A Comparative Analysis', *American Political Science Review*, 86/3 (1992), 638–46.
44. C. P. Danopoulos, 'Beating a Hasty Retreat: The Greek Military Withdraws from Power', in C. P. Danopoulos (ed.), *The Decline of Military Regimes: The Civilian Influence* (Boulder, Colo.: Westview Press, 1988), 235.
45. For more on the events surrounding the crisis, see L. Stern, 'Bitter Lessons: How We Failed in Cyprus', *Foreign Policy*, 19 (1975), 35–78, and G. A. Leontaritis, 'Prasino Fos gia tin Tourkia: To Praxikopima Enantion tou Makariou Anoixe to Dromo stin Eisvoli tou Attila' ('The Green Light for Turkey: The Coup Against Makarios Paved the Road for the Attila Invasion'), *Kathimerini*, 15 July 1992.
46. V. Coufoudakis, review of K. C. Markides, *The Rise and Fall of the Cyprus Republic* (New Haven: Yale University Press, 1977), in *American Political Science Review*, 72 (1978), 1480.
47. O'Donnell and Schmitter, *Transitions*, iv. *Tentative Conclusions*, 18.
48. Whitehead, Ch. 10, p. 274.
49. Ibid. 274–5.
50. Verney, 'European Community', 10.

51. Ibid. 10.
52. Diamandouros, 'Regime Change', 158. For more on Karamanlis and the clash in the 1960s with the king and right-wing elements of the military, leading to his exile in Paris, see C. M. Woodhouse, *Karamanlis: The Restorer of Greek Democracy* (Oxford: Clarendon Press, 1982); Y. Ginis, *O Allos Karamanlis* ('The Other Karamanlis'; Athens: I Nastos, 1986), 107–33; G. B. Leontaritis, *Ta Paraskinia Mias Epoches* ('Behind the Scenes of an Era'; Athens: Filippoti, 1989), 17–24, 114–25; R. Clogg, 'Karamanlis's Cautious Success: The Background', *Government and Opposition*, 10 (1975), 332–53, at 334–5. For a view of the feud between Karamanlis and the monarchy from the royalist point of view see G. N. Tantzos, *Konstantinos* (Athens: Logos, 1991), 98–9, 118–19, 273–4, 284–92, 315.
53. R. Clogg, *Parties and Elections in Greece: The Search for Legitimacy* (Durham, NC: Duke University Press, 1987), 126.
54. 'The Sweet and Sour Pill', *The Economist*, 20 September 1975.
55. Tsoukalis, *European Community*, 108.
56. L. Tsoukalis, 'Greece in Europe: The Tenth Member', *World Today*, 37 (April 1981), 120.
57. Tsoukalis, *European Community*, 108. Cf. Norbert Kohlase, 'The Greco–Turkish Conflict from a European Community Perspective', *World Today*, 37 (April 1981), 127–35. Also consider, Economist Intelligence Unit, *Quarterly Economic Review of Greece* (London: *The Economist*, 1974), no. 4, p. 3, and K. Mitsotakis, 'Straddling the Horns of a Dilemma: How Greek Governments Reconciled International Imperatives and Domestic Pressures in Negotiating a Bases Agreement with Washington', BA thesis (Harvard, 1990), 33.
58. 'Greece Wants Luns Sacked', *Guardian*, 15 September 1975.
59. For a comprehensive discussion of the border disputes between Greece and Turkey in the Aegean, see A. Wilson, 'The Aegean Dispute', in J. Alford (ed.), *Greece and Turkey: Adversity in Alliance*, Adelphi Library, xii (Aldershot: Gower, for the International Institute for Strategic Studies, 1984), 90–130.
60. Diamandouros, 'Regime Change', 156. Cf. 'The Gods Smiled At Last', *The Economist*, 20 September 1975.
61. T. A. Couloumbis, 'Defining Greek Foreign Policy Objectives', in H. R. Penniman (ed.), *Greece at the Polls: The National Elections of 1974 and 1977* (Washington: American Enterprise Institute for Public Policy Research, 1981), 184.
62. The quotations are from 'The Uses of Crisis', *The Economist*, 24 August 1974.
63. 'Greece: Costs Up, Security Shaky', *The Economist*, 29 November 1975. Cf. Economist Intelligence Unit, *Quarterly Economic Review of Greece* (London: *The Economist*, 1977), no. 1, p. 4.
64. T. Veremis, 'The Military', in K. Featherstone and D. K. Katsoudas (eds.), *Political Change in Greece: Before and After the Colonels* (London: Croom Helm, 1987), 220.
65. 'The Greeks Are Not Themselves', *The Economist*, 3 August 1974.

66. *To Vima*, 30 August 1974.
67. 'The Army and Mr Averoff', *The Economist*, 20 September 1975.
68. Whitehead, Ch. 10, p. 261.
69. A. Chloros, 'A Contribution and an Agonising Reappraisal', in Tsoukalis (ed.), *Greece and the European Community*, 19.
70. Whitehead, Ch. 10.
71. M. G. Pateras, 'From Association to Accession: Changing Attitudes of Greek Political Parties Towards Greek Relations with the European Communities', Ph.D. thesis (London School of Economics and Political Science, 1984), 337.
72. R. Clogg, 'Greece: The End of Consensus Politics?', *The World Today*, 34/5 (1978), 184–91 at 190–1, and Couloumbis, 'Defining Greek Foreign Policy Objectives', 184.
73. F. Nicholson and R. East, *From the Six to the Twelve: The Enlargement of the European Communities* (Essex: Longman, 1987).
74. For more on the importance of regime acceptance for democracy in general, and the Greek regime in the late 1970s in particular, see Macridis, 'Elections', 1–2, 19–20. For a more sustained theoretical discussion, see S. P. Huntington, *Political Order in Changing Societies* (New Haven, Conn.: Yale University Press, 1968).
75. Cf. J. J. Linz, *Crisis, Breakdown, and Reequilibrium* (Baltimore: Johns Hopkins University Press, 1978).
76. Yannopoulos, *Greece and European Communities*, 31.
77. For a helpful overview of some of these problems and the theoretical ideas surrounding them, see S. Mainwaring, G. O'Donnell, and J. S. Valenzuela, *Issues in Democratic Consolidation: South American Democracies in Comparative Perspective* (Notre Dame, Ind.: Notre Dame University Press, 1992), and the section 'What is Democratic Consolidation?' in G. Pridham's article 'Southern European Democracies On the Road to Consolidation: A Comparative Assessment of the Role of Political Parties', in G. Pridham (ed.), *Securing Democracy: Political Parties and Democratic Consolidation in Southern Europe* (London: Routledge, 1990), 1–41 at 8–16.
78. Whitehead, Ch. 10, p. 261.
79. G. Pridham and S. Verney, 'The Coalition of 1989–90 in Greece', *West European Politics*, 14/4 (1991), 44.
80. For some more views on this point, see P. C. Schmitter and T. L. Karl, 'What Democracy Is . . . and Is Not', *Journal of Democracy*, 2/3 (1991), 75–88.
81. For more on the process of democratic deconsolidation, see J. J. Linz, *Crisis, Breakdown, and Reequilibrium* (Baltimore: Johns Hopkins University Press, 1978).
82. For more on PASOK, see M. Spourdalakis, *The Rise of the Greek Socialist Party* (London: Routledge, 1988); C. Lyrintzis, 'Between Socialism and Populism: The Rise of the Panhellenic Socialist Movement', Ph.D. thesis (London School of Economics and Political Science, 1983); and I. Papadopoulos, *Dynamique du discours politique et conquête du pouvoir: Le cas du PASOK (Mouvement Socialiste*

Panhellénique): 1974–1981, Ph.D. thesis (Geneva, 1987; Berne: Peter Lang, 1989).

83. Macridis, 'Greek Foreign Policy', 142.

84. The Greek financial scandals of the late 1980s (most notably, the Koskotas and so-called 'sale of the century' scandals), Papandreou's apparent impunity, Greece's formidable and seemingly mounting economic woes, her widespread bureaucratic inefficiency and corruption, her often bitter political competition and 'winner-takes-all' spoils system, the continuing campaign of violence and terror by the clandestine '17th of November' extremist organization, and the occasional outbreak of anarchist riots in Athens, have all been pointed to in the Athens press or the scholarly literature on Greece as evidence of the persistent fragility and non-consolidation of Greek democracy. Such features of contemporary Greece in the early 1990s, Pridham and Verney explain, cast doubt on the 'quality' of democracy in Greece and thus, they contend, call into question the very 'credibility' of the Hellenic Republic. Pridham and Verney, 'The Coalition of 1989–90', 43–4.

However, on closer inspection such features of Greek politics do not seem to be problems that cast doubt on the consolidated nature of democracy in Greece. Britain's problems in Northern Ireland, her poll tax revolts, Irish Republican Army terrorist bombings, or political party financing scandals, while no doubt matters about which no one can be complacent, would not seem to advance the case that Britain is not a consolidated democracy. Neither would the inner-city riots or Watergate and Iran-contragate cover-ups and scandals in the case of the United States. Threats to the quiet functioning or quality of a democratic system do not necessarily imply threats to the persistence of democracy, provided that the system is able to process and deal with them. Consolidated democracy may not be impregnable, but it can be said to be resilient.

In the Greek case, the *katharsis* ('cleansing') trials in the early 1990s of former PASOK officials for fraud, embezzlement, and abuse of power suggest that the system was able—however painfully and controversially—to address itself to these threats to democracy, in much the same manner that the Congressional hearings and litigation which surrounded the Watergate and Iran-contragate scandals in the US demonstrated a similar democratic resilience. To be sure, Papandreou, unlike others implicated in the Greek scandals, managed to dodge judicial proceedings because the scales of justice were subject to the vagaries of political agendas, but in this the course of events in Greece did not markedly differ from the Watergate or Iran-contragate cases.

The democratic resilience demonstrated in the case of Greece was underscored by the fact that the *katharsis* proceedings were themselves made possible by an unprecedented coalition government that linked the right-conservative New Democracy party with the far-left

Synaspismos, a coalition of Communist parties and splinter groups, in a move which both sides characterized as an act of national self-reconciliation (*ethniki symfiliosi*). Whatever motives each side may have had in participating in this political marriage of convenience, the coalition evidenced a commitment to the Greek democratic system that spanned the full breadth of the political spectrum and bridged feelings of political hatred and personal animosity stretching back over forty years to the traumatic Civil War of the 1940s.

85. Clogg, *Politics and Elections in Greece*, 141. Also consider, 'With A Profit Like That, Greece Can't Afford To Leave', *The Economist*, 20 March 1982.
86. Whitehead, Ch. 10, p. 279.
87. Ibid. 267.
88. Verney, 'European Community', 16–17.
89. Ibid.
90. Ibid. 17. Cf. V. Coufoudakis, 'Greek Foreign Policy, 1945–1985: Seeking Independence in an Interdependent World—Problems and Prospects', in K. Featherstone and D. Katsoudas (eds.), *Political Change in Greece: Before and After the Colonels* (London: Croom Helm, 1987), 236–7.
91. The question of whether the Treaties of Paris or Rome adopted democratic criteria for membership of the European Communities is an old chestnut which has divided legal and governmental experts, but a consensus may be that such criteria, while not explicitly adopted, are implicit in the texts of the treaties. The House of Lords Select Committee on the European Communities, for instance, had this to say on the matter in view of the proposed enlargement of the Community in 1978: 'The Treaties contain no express requirement that candidates should be states which are democratic in the sense understood in the present Member States. But the Committee think it implicit in the Rome Treaty, for example, that its Member States should be democratic. The free movement of persons, services, and capital which the Treaty [Articles 85–6] contemplates suggests this . . . The provision in Article 138 for elections to the European Parliament to be by "direct universal suffrage" is even clearer. This Article leaves little room for doubt that the Community is to be composed of democratic states.' Cf. House of Lords, Select Committee on the European Communities, *Enlargement of the Community*, 2 vols. (London: HMSO, 1978), i. 15.
92. Verney, 'European Community', 17.
93. See, for instance, Richard Legg, *Politics in Modern Greece* (Stanford, Calif.: Stanford University Press, 1969), 144.
94. R. Fox, *The Inner Sea: The Mediterranean and its Peoples* (London: Sinclair Stevenson, 1991), 212.
95. Whitehead, Ch. 10, p. 261.
96. Cf. R. C. Macridis, 'Elections and Political Modernization in Greece',

in H. R. Penniman (ed.), *Greece at the Polls: The National Elections of 1974 and 1977* (Washington: American Enterprise Institute for Public Policy Research, 1981), 2–3, 8, 10, 20. For more on the political parties of the pre-junta period, see Clogg, *Parties and Elections in Greece*, 17–54.

97. Macridis, 'Elections and Political Modernization', 10.
98. J. C. Loulis, 'New Democracy: The New Face of Conservatism', in Penniman (ed.), *Greece at the Polls*, 72.
99. Clogg, *Parties and Elections in Greece*, 122. Cf. A. Elephantis, 'PASOK and the Elections of 1977: The Rise of the Populist Movement', in Penniman (ed.), *Greece at the Polls*, 105.
100. Cf. D. Haralambis, *Pelateiakes Scheseis kai Laîkismos: I Exothesmiki Synainesi sto Elliniko Politiko Systema* ('Clientist Relations and Populism: Extra-Institutional Consensus in the Greek Political System') (Athens: Exantas, 1989), 296.
101. I. Barnes and J. Preston, *The European Community* (London: Longman, 1988), 137–41.
102. A figure given by Prime Minister Constantine Mitsotakis during the course of an address to EKEM, the Hellenic Centre for European Studies. Cf. C. Mitsotakis, 'I Evropaïki Politiki tis Elladas' ('Greece's European Policy'), in L. Tsoukalis (ed.), *I Ellada Stin Evropaiki Koinotita: I Proklisi tis Prosarmogis* ('Greece in the European Community: The Challenge of Adjustment') (Athens: Papazisis, 1993), 35.
103. N. D. Maraveyas, *I Entaxi tis Ellada stin Evropaîki Koinotita: Epiptoseis ston Agrotiko Tomea* ('The Accession of Greece to the European Community: The Effects on the Agricultural Sector') (Athens: Idryma Mesogeiakon Meleton ('Foundation for Mediterranean Studies'), 1989), 491.
104. Ibid. 491.
105. For an illustration of political favouritism in the dispensation of government funds, see 'Idyllic Arcadia, Idle without its Youth, Symbolizes Rural Europe', *International Herald Tribune*, 20 February 1992.
106. C. Lyrintzis, 'Political Parties in Post–Junta Greece: A Case of "Bureaucratic Clientelism"?', *West European Politics*, 7/2 (1984), 103–4.
107. Pridham and Verney, 'The Coalition of 1989–90 in Greece', 49.
108. For the quote and more on the *kladikes* and their importance for employment prospects under PASOK, see Spourdalakis, *Rise of the Greek Socialist Party*, 246, 249. Also consider, N. Mouzelis, 'Continuities and Discontinuities in Greek Politics: From Eleftherios Venizelos to Andreas Papandreou', in K. Featherstone and D. Katsoudas (eds.), *Political Change in Greece: Before and After the Colonels* (London: Croom Helm, 1987), 280.
109. See, for instance, S. Zoulas, 'Krisi Laikis Embistosynis kai sta Tessera Kommata' ('The Crisis of Public Confidence with All Four Parties'), *Kathimerini*, 27 October 1991.
110. Pasquino, 'Party Elites and Democratic Consolidation: Cross-National

Comparison of Southern European Experience', in G. Pridham (ed.), *Security Democracy*, 59.

111. Cf. C. P. Danopoulos, 'Democratising the Military: Lessons from Mediterranean Europe', *West European Politics*, 14/4 (1991), 33.
112. Whitehead, Ch. 10.
113. Verney and Couloumbis, 'State–International Systems', 120.
114. Whitehead, Ch. 10.

Democracy and Decolonization:
East-Central Europe

LAURENCE WHITEHEAD

1. Introduction

The comparative analysis of democratization processes was a flourishing branch of political science well before the dismantling of the
Berlin Wall, on 10 November 1989. That event, its timing, and the
transformations through East-Central Europe which it symbolized, were unforeseen not only by virtually all academic observers,
but also by world statesmen, foreign ministries, and media commentators. Certainly the available stock of democratization theory
was not capable of predicting—or even of strongly suggesting—the
course, speed, or sequencing of political developments that con-
verted all the six non-Soviet members of the Warsaw Pact from
Communist-ruled regimes into polities operating under more or
less competitive electoral systems within about a year. Fortunately
such predictive power is not an essential requirement of useful
work in comparative politics.

This chapter is based on the assumption that, with the benefit
of hindsight, it can still be helpful to re-examine the political up-
heavals of 1989 deploying the categories and hypotheses distilled
from earlier experiences of democratization. But equally, these pre-
existing analytical tools may have to be revised or refined in the
light of East-Central European experiences. Initial approaches to the
theory of democratization derived from a restrictive range of Latin
American and southern European processes which took place within
a securely bipolar world, with the result that the international
dimension was downplayed and conceived in a restrictive manner.
Even with regard to those earlier processes some reconsideration

may be called for, given the heightened prominence of international influences apparent in many subsequent cases of regime transition.

However, before the 1989 democratizations can be invoked to justify a possibly wholesale reconstruction of previous analytical work, we need to consider whether these processes do indeed belong in the same classificatory schema as the earlier processes. Participants in the events of 1989 certainly invoked the same vocabulary—of democratization, human and civic rights, the rule of law, and clean and open elections—as their Latin American and southern European predecessors; and indeed, they drew on powerful and long-standing shared traditions of enlightenment liberalism. To some extent they even made explicit cross-references to non-Communist democratizations. Nevertheless, the regimes they were dismantling (single-party-ruled command economies) were very different in structure from the conservative capitalist authoritarian regimes on which most theorizing was based. Transition to a market economy was viewed as an integral (possibly even the dominant) component of democratization. Social structures (universal welfare provision, absence of a strong autonomous civil sphere, or of market-related professional associations) and geopolitical settings were also very different.

The first question to consider, therefore, is whether such key analytical terms as 'democratization', 'consolidation', and 'transition' carry substantially different connotations when deployed in the East-Central European context. This topic is taken up in the second section of the chapter. Then the third section turns to a key feature of the international context that differentiates these from earlier experiences—the persistence for over forty years of a Soviet military veto over full democratization, and the reasons why that veto was lifted in the late 1980s. The fourth section turns to other distinctive features of the international environment, that can be grouped together under the heading 'the role of the West'. It considers the various influences flowing from 'the West', and their effects in shaping the course and content of local democratizing impulses. The fifth section reflects on the interactions that took place once the transitions got under way, and relates this to comparative debates on the prospects for democratic consolidation. The conclusion draws together these arguments about the relative weight of various types of international influence on the East-Central European democratizations, and reflects on the implications for pre-existing analysis.

2. Democratization in East-Central Europe: The Local Terminology

In the immediate aftermath of the collapse of the Soviet bloc, it is understandable that East-Central European conceptions of democracy should be viewed essentially as an expression of popular resistance to imposed Communist rule. However, such an immediatist perspective is likely to cloud the possibilities of locating the 1989–90 democratizations in a broader comparative framework. Certainly, forty years of living under a Soviet military veto against political reforms that would challenge the legal monopoly on power exercised by ruling Communist parties (together with vetoes against neutralism, privatization, and various freedoms of expression) constituted a profound political learning experience distinctive to this region and common throughout it.[1] By 1989 democracy in East-Central Europe was universally equated with the dismantling of an externally imposed system of Communist rule, based philosophically on the suppression of private property. Citizenship rights were therefore intimately identified with ownership rights. Indeed, in the prevailing local terminology the re-establishment of a market economy was viewed as a core ingredient of democratization, and was regarded as indissolubly linked with other distinctive aspects of the regime transition, such as the dismantling of Communist structures of political control, the repudiation of Soviet hegemony, and the reversal of international alliances. This is a radically different agenda from that associated with the earlier democratizations of conservative authoritarian regimes. Indeed, it is almost exactly the opposite to what democratization was initially thought to involve in the first of the southern European transitions (i.e. in Portugal in 1974).

Nevertheless, despite some extremely divergent local connotations of the terminology, some major comparisons between, say, East-Central and southern Europe, remain intact. Such comparisons suggest, for example, that even when such political rigidity is imposed for more than forty years (forty-six in the case of Salazar's Portugal, for example), pre-existing democratic memories and traditions may well persist and retain the power to affect the course and content of an eventual redemocratization. Moreover, such comparisons also suggest that such a very long period of authoritarian imposition will typically include a variety of different stages, interrupted experiments, lost opportunities, and so forth, which are also likely to contribute to the specific form and social meaning of democratization in each country. Furthermore, of course, the comparative literature reminds us that typically not all the forces which emerge in the course of dislodging an entrenched anti-democratic regime are themselves inherently democratic (there is also scope for considerable diversity of view over the nature of any democratizing project); and that not all the power-holders in existing regimes typically remain united in defence of a foundering status quo.

It is important to recall that the countries of East-Central Europe had a rich and diverse political history which long antedates the arrival of the Red Army in 1944–5. European liberal values were as well established in eighteenth-century Poland as in many parts of the West; and after 1848 Austrian and German liberalism achieved wide if uneven diffusion in other parts of the region. As liberalism spread eastwards it stirred up subordinated nationalisms, and these two processes did much to undermine the Habsburg and Tsarist empires. However, the international political forces that most powerfully shaped regional democratic potentialities before the imposition of Soviet control were, of course, the two world wars. Six of the present states came into existence as a result of the Treaty of Versailles, that is under the supervision of the victors of the First World War, and initially all were to some extent influenced by their international sponsors to adopt liberal constitutional forms of government. Such international actors also backed plebiscites to define the new borders and sometimes promoted minority rights through treaty provisions. Czechoslovakia and Estonia both established conventional democratic regimes which lasted for twenty years, until cut down by foreign aggression. Both the initiation and the destruction of these fragile inter-war experiments in democratization were substantially influenced by geopolitical forces beyond their domestic control. This set an enduring pattern, whereby local democratic actors would naturally formulate their strategies having strong regard to their likely international repercussions; and whereby external powers would be watchfully assessed and rated not only according to their stated sympathies, but more importantly according to their real capacities and inclinations to supply help (or to create difficulties) in times of trouble.

In the immediate aftermath of the Second World War there were some indications that post-Versailles regional experiments in democratization might be given something of a second chance. The Yalta Agreement did, after all, provide for the holding of free elections in all the countries liberated from Nazi occupation, as well as for the negotiating of spheres of influence and the redrawing of national boundaries. Such elections were in fact held, and at least in certain cases (most clearly in Czechoslovakia in May 1946) they were indeed reasonably free. Even where the reality of Soviet control was made more explicit, it would be a mistake to overlook the long-term significance of the three-year period (between early 1945 and the Prague coup in February 1948) during which varying degrees of limited pluralism and non-Stalinist experimentation were tolerated, in deference to Moscow's residual commitments to the wartime alliance. For example, in January 1947 the then Secretary-General of the Polish Communist Party (Władysław Gomułka) could still write that 'we have completely rejected the collectivisation of agriculture . . . our democracy is not similar to Soviet democracy just as our society's structure is not the same as the Soviet structure'.[2] Eight months later the Cominform was launched in Poland with 'the consolidation of democracy' given as one of its stated aims. (It is curious to find such an early use of this term of art, bracketed with 'the eradication of the remnants of fascism', and 'the undermining of imperialism'.[3])

It was, of course, no kind of pluralist regime that the Cominform was about to 'consolidate'. On the contrary, only five months later the Prague coup led to the fusion of the Socialist and Communist parties, and the adoption of a Soviet-style constitution guaranteeing a political monopoly to the new ruling party. Similar transformations in Poland, Hungary, East Germany, and so on ensured that a uniform variant of 'people's democracy' was rapidly consolidated throughout Soviet-controlled Eastern Europe, an externally underwritten system of centralized political and economic control which survived with only limited variations for the next forty years. Thus, we see that on four successive occasions in the first half of the twentieth century it was major shifts in the global balance of power (i.e. processes essentially external to East-Central Europe) which either initiated (1919, 1945) or terminated (1938, 1948) regional experiments in democratization.

Following the Prague coup, for about forty years a Soviet military veto blocked further such experiments and imposed a rather standardized form of Communist political and economic organization. Although (outside the Baltic republics) the inter-war state system was largely resuscitated, and each people's democracy acquired its own national structure of government enjoying internationally recognized sovereign status, in many respects this was a semi-imperial system of power, with essential decisions requiring if not clearance then at least the tacit approbation of Moscow. (Later in this chapter we will examine the democratizations of 1989 by comparison with earlier experiences of decolonization leading to democracy.)

Thus, in the first place, without belittling the reforms of this system achieved (in Hungary) or attempted (in Czechoslovakia in 1968, or in Poland and the USSR during the 1980s), it is important from a comparative perspective to remember that the ruling parties retained their legal monopolies on power until 1989 or 1990. Just as the political transition in Spain had to await Franco's death (even though at the social level preparations for such change had long been under way), so the Communist rulers of this region had to acknowledge that their system was not immortal before negotiations over the construction of an alternative regime could begin. Until such negotiations began there was no way of assessing either the real strength and intentions of the various contenders for power or the substantive bases on which a new regime might be constructed. Thus, in January 1989 the Solidarity movement was legalized in Poland, at about the same time that the Hungarian Party decided to abandon its leading role, and accept multiparty elections. Then, in the June 1989 elections Solidarity scored an overwhelming victory (though power-sharing continued to reserve the most strategic ministries for the hands of the Polish Communist Party). In October the Hungarian Party changed its name to the Hungarian Socialist Party and explicitly abandoned its Leninism. Then in November 1989 the Czech and German parties respectively lost their political monopolies through mass protests. Finally, in February 1990 the CPSU abolished clause 6 of the Soviet Constitution, which had for so long formally guaranteed the party's leading role in Soviet society.

If we are to extend the terminology developed in the Latin American and southern European academic literature on democratization to these East-Central European processes, we would have to say that there could be no transition to democracy before the ruling party relinquished its legal claim to a monopoly of political representation. From this standpoint, prior to February 1990 *perestroika* and *glasnost* could only be classified as episodes of liberalization, and not of democratization in the Soviet Union. Similarly, although the Hungarian Communists may have demonstrated an exceptional capacity both for economic reform and for the protection of human rights long before 1989, they too would have to be classified as no more than liberalizing authoritarians prior to 11 January 1989.[4] Whether the Polish transition to democracy began just before, or just after, the Hungarian move is a matter of controversy between democrats in the two countries. It depends whether the bench-mark is the legalization of Solidarity in January or the Round Table talks in March. In any case, Jaruzelski's reformism did not concede the principle of popular sovereignty before the end of 1988. Similarly, although the 1968 'reform Communism' of Alexander Dubček in Czechoslovakia included the abolition of censorship, and the secret election of party officials, it did not explicitly extend to abandonment of the leading role of the party, and for this reason comparativists should hesitate to apply the term 'democratization' to it.[5]

At first glance it may seem rather pedantic to worry whether liberalization turned into a transition to democracy in 1989, or a year or two earlier. It is hardly surprising that in East European parlance, processes that an outsider might regard as mere liberalization were sometimes regarded as the beginnings of democratization. Well before the explicit surrender of Communist Party monopoly control over the state, such control was *de facto* in retreat. To those accustomed to living under a supposedly monolithic system it was striking to witness the emergence of a significant degree of constitutionalism, a strengthening of the rule of law (except in the most sensitive areas), and increased evidence of limited pluralism at the élite level. Nevertheless, from a broader comparative standpoint these would all be regarded as characteristics of the liberalization of an authoritarian regime, perhaps foreshadowing an eventual transition to democracy, but still in principle controlled and reversible, and therefore not yet a democratization.

The issue of precisely when the transition began is quite critical, bearing in mind Judy Blatt's observation[6] that a distinctive feature of the East-Central European democratizations is that they were accompanied by sweeping transitions in the direction of a market economy, and a wholesale rejection of the Soviet model of the command economy. By contrast, of course, so long as the dominant logic was only that of liberalization, and not democratization, the associated goals were to reform the command economy and to refound Soviet hegemony rather than to destroy them. In fact at the political level these democratizations were inextricably entwined with movements of national affirmation, and with a comprehensive reorientation of alignments and identities from East to West. In comparison, the authoritarian regimes of Latin America and southern Europe always regarded themselves as fully identified with Western civilization, even though they may have suffered limited estrangements from some Western governments and institutions because of their human rights violations. The essential point here is that the democratizations under study took place in the context of the longer and larger process of decolonization which has now shattered the entire Soviet empire. Old political communities reasserted their long-suppressed sovereignties, and new national identities were also asserted, in a manner more reminiscent of African and Asian independence struggles than the democratizations of southern Europe and Latin America. Some fragments of the former empire were well placed to invoke democratic values and aspirations as a guiding principle for national emancipation; other constituent elements of the former empire relied on alternative organizing principles. In any case, processes of decolonization both precede and extend the democratization episodes under study in this volume. From a comparative perspective it is important to seek precision over the starting-point of these democratic transitions, not least because they were so pivotal to the broader and more protracted process of dismantling the Soviet empire.

Although the two break-points of 1948 and 1989 both seem unusually clear, abrupt, and uniform through the East-Central European region, it by no means follows that Moscow-imposed uniformity blotted out all manifestations of democratic potential across the region and over the entire intervening forty-one years. On the contrary, Soviet policies were of course highly variable in intention and uneven in impact. In part, no doubt, this variability was due to differences in the levels of resistance (and the forms of collaboration) encountered by Moscow in the six distinct and even competitive countries under consideration. As the comparative study of authoritarian regimes has already taught us, too much emphasis on shared patterns of regime control may well conceal more than they reveal about the underlying development of democratic potentialities when considering six distinct nations (or nine including the Baltic states) over a forty-year period. As we have already shown, there are some important and distinctive common features shared by these East-Central European Communist regimes. But once these obvious and basic points have been noted, the distinctive (sometimes interacting) political trajectories of these regimes would also require attention in order fully to reconstruct the various paths to democratization taken in the late 1980s (a task beyond the scope of this chapter).

This variety of interacting trajectories was also, however, in no small measure due to differences of interpretation and even of strategy within the top levels of the Soviet leadership. In fact from the death of Stalin onwards the leaders of the CPSU were engaged in a concealed, but more or less continuous, process of debate over how to restabilize and legitimize their own political system within the USSR. The questions posed to Moscow by the restless regimes within its security perimeter—how much pluralism could be tolerated, what controls over the intelligentsia and the media were most

appropriate, how much historical veracity could be allowed, etc.—
all these merely presented in more dramatic form dilemmas that
already existed within the USSR as well. CPSU responses to satellite demands for liberalization were unsteady, in part because
leaders in Moscow were divided about how to respond to such
demands from within the USSR itself. This interconnectedness
between concessions in the semi-colonies, and the pressure for
reforms at home, set up an iterative pattern whereby experiments
in one country stimulated imitation in others. And when such
experiments ran out of control the resulting backlash also spread
from country to country. Thus, for example, the frustrated democratic rebellions of 1956 were in part triggered by Moscow's vacillating attempts to de-Stalinize within the USSR; and the backlash
against the Prague Spring of 1968 dammed up the impetus for
reform not only in Czechoslovakia, but also designedly in the Soviet
Union.

Consider the key events of 1956 which gave rise to a reform-
minded (or liberalized) variant of Communism in Poland and Hungary. Under Malenkov's protection in June 1953, Imre Nagy assumed
the Hungarian premiership, curbing the secret police, relaxing
policy towards the farmers, and promoting a 'consolidation of legality'. His policies of liberalization stimulated an intense debate
among Hungarian intellectuals about how far democracy could
progress in a Communist state, and about to what extent a people's
democracy could reach sovereignty within the Soviet bloc. But in
the spring of 1955 Khrushchev's stand against Malenkov was followed by the dismissal of Nagy from the Hungarian premiership
and an attempt to reassert Communist discipline. Nagy responded
by writing a report for the Central Committee, advocating Hungarian independence, neutrality, and active coexistence between
countries with different systems. In short, a key Hungarian Communist openly advocated policies akin to those of neighbouring
Yugoslavia (which had been expelled from the Soviet bloc for its
nationalist deviations in 1948). Although Nagy did not at this
point advocate an end to the Communist Party's monopoly of power,
his arguments went beyond the limits of what was tolerable in
Khrushchev's Russia, both on questions of bloc security, and on the
issue of political liberalization.

Although from 1953 to 1955 the strongest impulse for reform
took place in Hungary, there was also a parallel process under
way in Poland. Following the dismissal of Nagy, leadership of the
revisionist movement passed to Gomułka, whose credentials as a
reform Communist preceded the split with Yugoslavia. In June 1956

there were workers' riots in Poznań, in response to which in July the Central Committee of the Polish Party invited Gomułka to argue his case. Gomułka subsequently described two main issues under consideration as '(1) the problem of Poland's sovereignty and (2) the problem of democratisation within the framework of the socialist system'.[7] On 19 October 1956, in very tense circumstances, Khrushchev endorsed Gomułka's approach to these questions, and he was restored to the post of Secretary-General of the Polish Party. Soviet troops were then ordered back to their barracks, and the Polish Party proceeded to carry through a wide range of reforms (decollectivization of agriculture, religious toleration, an enhanced role for parliament, and many other measures of liberalization). But the quid pro quo for Soviet endorsement of these measures was that the Polish Communist Party should regain its power, and that Polish–Soviet security ties should remain undisturbed. Thus the Polish crisis of October 1956 underscored the connection between continued subordination to a Russian-dominated alliance system and Moscow's veto over democratization.

The Hungarian uprising of early November 1956 underscored the same connection in a different way. On 20 October 1956 the Hungarian press published the full text of Gomułka's statement accompanying his reappointment to lead the Polish Party. This produced a climate of intense mobilization within Hungary, under which conditions Nagy was appointed Prime Minister. In the following week of intense factional conflict and popular agitation a nationwide demand developed for complete national emancipation. Particularly in the countryside (where no Soviet forces were stationed, and where the local security apparatus had mostly disintegrated) the demand was for general and free elections to be held within two months, with the participation of multiple parties, and the return of Soviet troops, not just to their bases, but to their fatherland. On 30 October Nagy responded by announcing the restoration of a multi-party system and the formation of a four-party coalition government ('like in 1945'). The following day he called for the withdrawal of Soviet troops, and for Hungary's departure from the Warsaw Pact. But rather than acquiesce to the establishment of a neutral, democratic, and no doubt non-Communist Hungary, Moscow used all necessary force to impose a regime (under János Kádár) that would operate within the same constraints as those reluctantly accepted by Gomułka in Poland.

The crushing of the 1956 Hungarian uprising is, of course, remembered throughout East-Central Europe as a watershed event, demonstrating the limits of Soviet toleration of dissent in the post-Stalinist era. Equally significant, however, was the increased scope for reform allowed within such brutally imposed limits. Khrushchev's memoirs are revealing about the confused attitudes towards political freedom that existed in the higher reaches of the Soviet system after the dismantling of Stalin's apparatus of intimidation. According to Khrushchev, 'the rift which developed (in 1960) between the Soviet Union and Albania stemmed mainly from the Albanians' fear of democratisation'. Following Moscow's break with Albania he claimed to 'stand all the more firmly for those principles of democratic leadership which the Albanians could never accept'. Khrushchev's attempt to explain those principles was a muddle: 'A democratic leader must have a good mind and he must be able to take advice. He must realise that his position of leadership depends upon the people's will to have him as their leader, not on his own will to lead the people ... In other words he is not above the Party but is the servant of the Party, and he can keep his position only as long as he enjoys the Party's satisfaction and support.'[8]

Later, in 1968 in Czechoslovakia, and then again in 1981 in Poland, the ultimate constraints that had been evident in 1956 were demonstrated yet again, albeit in somewhat different circumstances. In short, between early 1948 and late 1986 the security and integrity of the Soviet bloc system was shown to rest ultimately on Moscow's willingness to use the Red Army (if all other instruments of control failed) both to maintain the cohesion of its alliance structure, and also in an inextricable conjunction to block any threatened dismantling of the Communist Party's practical monopoly over formal rights of political representation throughout the region. The CPSU invariably barred what we have loosely termed decolonization, and it also limited internal reforms to what we should label liberalization without democratization, because from Moscow's standpoint these were two aspects of a single integrated process—'de-Sovietization', or 'de-Communization'—rather than two separable issues.

The implied parallel with West European colonialism would naturally have been rejected for one set of reasons; and the liberal theory underlying the language of democratization would have been rejected for a second set of reasons. Although Soviet political terminology is now mainly of antiquarian interest, it is as well to note that the citizens of the post-Communist regimes of Eastern Europe frequently share an unspoken assumption, inherited from pre-*perestroika* days, that democracy entails a pro-Western geopolitical orientation, and that it necessarily involves a repudiation of state socialism. These are distinctive ideas that were incubated in Eastern Europe by forty years of bitter experience. Prior to 1948, East Europeans were perhaps just as likely as Latin Americans or southern Europeans to make an analytical distinction between liberal political democracy, on the one hand, and commitment to a market economy system, on the other. They might also (like the Czechoslovak democrat and patriot Eduard Benes in 1947) hold that political democracy could be compatible with a pro-Soviet strategic alignment. It is a historically contingent, rather than logically necessary, feature of the polities of East-Central Europe that, at least for the present generation, democratization has acquired unusually prescriptive connotations both as to economic system and as to international orientation. It is a recurring problem in comparative politics that apparently standard terminology frequently carries strong overtones in one setting that are either absent, or resonate differently, in the next. The analyst must therefore guard against twin dangers of distortion. One source of distortion can arise when local realities are interpreted through an inappropriately rigid and insensitive application of a general terminology; a second equally serious distortion would arise if, for example, the whole spectrum of democratic transitions were to be subsumed under the parochial optic of East European anti-Sovietism. There can be no absolute defence against these twin distortions. The best defence is to be explicit about the contingent and local connotations of more general categories, and to specify the shade of meaning intended at each point.

3. Why Moscow Lifted its Veto on Democratization

Using the conventional terminology of the transitions literature, we would have to say that it was not until very late in 1988 that liberalization (within the framework of a continuance of the Communist system of rule) began to give way to democratization. However, it would now appear that the most crucial shift in the international context—Moscow's decision to lift its military veto over the unfolding of indigenous political processes—may have occurred, and even been announced, as long as two years earlier. Thus, according to Alex Pravda, 'it appears that by the autumn of 1986 the Gorbachev leadership had decided to distance itself from the last-resort use of force associated with their predecessors' treatment of East European crises'.[9] In the previous section we saw how, as a result of the Soviet military actions of 1956 and 1968, the issue of democratization had become deeply entangled with the issue of what may loosely be termed decolonization within the informal Soviet empire in Eastern Europe. From a comparative perspective, therefore, we need to consider how distinctive this decolonization–democratization link may have been.

In Chapter 1 I argued that thirty of the sixty-one independent states that might conventionally be classified as 'democracies' in January 1990 established such regimes in association with processes of decolonization. In a formal sense the Communist regimes of East-Central Europe were not of course 'colonies', but rather independent sovereign nations recognized as such, for example, through their membership of the United Nations. As we have just seen, however, until November 1986 Moscow kept them under quite a strict system of informal control (stricter, for example, than the restraints on various francophone republics in West Africa, which are also recognized as members of the United Nations, although periodically reliant on French paratroopers, and more constantly reliant on economic supervision from Paris). In particular, Moscow imposed a more constraining limitation on the scope for domestic political expression than is typical of most neo-colonial regimes in the Third World.[10] In that sense, therefore, it may be permissible to analyse the political consequences of the lifting of Moscow's military veto on East-Central Europe's regime transformations by analogy with the more formal decolonizations that sometimes presaged democratization in other parts of the world.

From a comparative politics perspective it would be misleading to rely on too narrow and formalistic a conception of decolonization. As John Darwin has pointed out with reference to the British Empire, direct rule was only the most overt manifestation of a much broader structure of imperial controls, which included other kinds of legal concessions, military and demographic provisions, economic advantages, and socio-cultural arrangements. Indeed, British imperial authorities sometimes sought to avoid the costs of explicit direct rule, believing that the main benefits of colonial domination could better be achieved by other means. Likewise, therefore, the decision to grant formal independence is not necessarily to be equated with decolonization in a broader sense. Indeed, Darwin's interpretation of the decolonization of the British Empire bears some striking similarities to the subsequent collapse of the Soviet bloc, in that imperial policy-makers tended to believe they could revitalize their threatened positions of dominance by relinquishing the more objectionable instruments of control. 'For much of the time, we may suspect, those who "made" colonial policy' in London 'were guessing, hoping, gambling—and miscalculating'[11]—just like their later counterparts in Moscow.

In reality, of course, the post-war termination of British colonial rule

did not proceed as a carefully planned rolling programme . . . the actual outcome was largely unexpected and thoroughly unwelcome from a British point of view . . . The rapidity of British withdrawal arose from . . . uncertainties about their ability to check disruptive elements and restore political discipline without losing the co-operation of moderate politicians on whom they depended, were compounded by the fear that confrontation might occur in a number of colonies simultaneously.[12]

While this was going on 'British opinion was shaped by a variety of expectations, but one of the most important was the belief constantly reiterated by British leaders, that come what may, Britain would remain a great world power'.[13] In the event, however,

in South Asia, the Middle East, and then in Africa, Britain lost her special position with startling speed. It is this, far more than the formal transfer of sovereignty, which indicates the true nature of the changes implicit in the term 'decolonisation'. In each region, the British found that the effort to move to a less formal kind of superiority proved unworkable in practice.[14]

The parallels with Gorbachev's failed attempt to shift the basis of Moscow's ascendancy within its post-war sphere of influence are notable.

At one level we can view all such decolonizations as conscious strategies for the divestment of a certain type of direct power and responsibility chosen and pursued by imperial decision-makers. This level of analysis requires careful attention, even if the results are unforeseen and the underlying causes are distinct. In the Soviet case this involves analysing the motives and actions of an extremely small group of Moscow power-holders. Between 1985 and 1989 we need to consider above all the political trajectory of Mikhail Gorbachev.

It was by no means a foregone conclusion that he would become Secretary-General of the CPSU on the death of Chernenko in March 1985 (the Politburo voted 4 to 4, until Gromyko broke the tie), nor that once in office he would promote such a comprehensive break with the past. What needs to be explained is why, given the enormous concentration of power in the hands of the new Secretary-General, he subsequently came to relinquish ever more of it. In 1989 his power-base shifted from the party to a newly empowered Presidency, but the erosion of strength continued until finally, six-and-a-half years later, the entire Soviet structure of command and control had been dismantled, not only in East-Central Europe, but within the USSR as well. With hindsight it can be seen more clearly than at the time that Gorbachev's major decisions concerning his European allies were all largely predetermined by the positions he was developing on East–West disarmament, and in relation to his central concern—the reform and liberalization of Communist rule in the USSR. Those positions were not uniquely his. (Their antecedents could be traced back to Khrushchev, and to a lesser extent to Andropov; and for a considerable period they were reinforced by such prominent party figures as Shevardnadze and Yeltsin; together with such influential constituencies as the intelligentsia, parts of the media, and local bureaucracies, e.g. in Leningrad and the Baltic republics.) But his authority was essential to sustain and develop them. Given the centralized nature of the Soviet system it was extremely problematic for conservatives (i.e. those who favoured preservation of the apparatus of control) to defy an incumbent Secretary-General who was prepared to use his position to push the cause of reform. Gorbachev may have been misguided, over-confident, inconsistent, and opportunistic at various points, but he was never disposed to abandon that cause. Indeed, each time his innovations encountered resistance he identified the opposition as his conservative enemies, and therefore took further liberalizing steps in order to reinforce his campaign against them. Given that this was the underlying thrust of his leadership, it was almost certainly never open to him to practise open repression or to ally with the forces of conservatism in Eastern Europe. To do so would always have been to liquidate his platform for reform within the USSR. It is perhaps unsurprising that democrats in East-Central Europe took quite a long time to recognize this reality, and even longer to feel sufficiently confident of its permanence to act out its implications.[15]

The sequence of events in Moscow was schematically as follows. Even before Chernenko's death, in December 1984, Gorbachev had established a strong following in the Central Committee, with a bold speech advocating *glasnost*, and even using the term 'democratization'.[16] On assuming supreme leadership he immediately (April 1985) launched a programme of economic reform (*perestroika*). By June 1986, in the wake of Chernobyl, he was appealing to the intelligentsia and the media for assistance, saying that 'restructuring' was going very badly, and that 'a society cannot exist without *glasnost*' ('openness, publicity, visibility'). One of his advisers, a former speech-writer to Khrushchev, commented that 'the press will be the method of democratic control, not control by administration but control with the help of democratic institutions'.[17] (All this preceded the November 1986 meeting at which Pravda believes the CMEA governments may have been told that Moscow was forswearing the last-resort use of force to control them.) By January 1987, recalling how the party apparatus had 'broken Khrushchev's neck', Gorbachev turned explicitly to *demokratizatziya*, which initially 'applied only to the Communist Party to mobilize the rank and file members to offset the power of the party bureaucracy'.[18] By 1988 the campaign had escalated further. In June of that year Gorbachev proposed a constitutional reform, to create directly elected Soviets and a strong elected President, both seen as instruments to advance the cause of reform and overcome conservative resistance. In *perestroika* he asserted that 'everything which is not prohibited by law is allowed' and this was then reinforced by the promotion of *zakonnost* (the law-governed state).[19] In short, by the end of 1988, when the East-Central European transitions began, Gorbachev had taken huge steps towards dismantling the Communist Party's monopoly of power in the USSR.

Prior to 1989 it seems fairly certain that policy-making in Moscow was based on the assumption that a successful programme of economic and political reform could rescue some essentials of the Communist system by liberalizing it. ('Everything must change so that everything can stay the same,' as Lampedusa's Sicilian aristocrat would say.) This was expected to apply both within the USSR and to those European allied regimes which were agile enough to reform and thereby legitimize themselves. In short, the Dubček model of reform Communism was still thought to be viable, and the real threat to the survival of some variant of liberalized socialism was thought to come from the inflexibility of the conservatives. As we now know, this was all an illusion, a fact that became apparent rather rapidly as the transitions of 1989 gathered momentum. By mid-year the Polish elections had administered a crushing blow to the Polish Workers Party, while the Tienanmen Square massacre had demonstrated that repression could still be effective. On 9 October 1989 the East German government attempted a similar show of force against unarmed demonstrators in Leipzig, only to be told that Russian troops would provide no back-up and that Moscow was opposed to such actions. Once it became clear throughout Eastern Europe that Gorbachev's repudiation of force would remain intact, even *in extremis*, the last external barrier to transition (the fear of a reversal in Moscow) was removed. On 5 December the Warsaw Pact publicly apologized to the Czechoslovak people for the invasion of 1968. With hindsight all this may seem self-evident, but on the information available to them at the time all political actors in the region were bound to fear that the international conjuncture might suddenly turn against democratization, just as it had done on so many occasions in the past. After all, hindsight also tells us that on 8 December 1991, as a direct consequence of Gorbachev's leadership strategy, the Communist Party of the Soviet Union would itself be dissolved. Given that fact, and the contingent nature of many leadership decisions taken since 1985, it would be ahistorical to regard Moscow's passivity in the face of the 1989 revolutions as natural, let alone inevitable. A Soviet backlash could never be entirely discounted, particularly since Russian troops remained stationed throughout the region, and even though such an extreme change in policy would probably have come too late to salvage anything of the old order, it would most certainly have disrupted all the processes of non-violent regime transition, and might even have thwarted their democratic content. The timing, course, and texture of these democratizations would certainly have been different if Gorbachev had reverted to type at this crucial stage.

This focus on decision-making in Moscow helps to explain the speed, direction, limits, and mechanisms of the East-Central European democratization process. It also invited further comparisons with the British experience of decolonization, which, we have argued, contributed to the establishment of about half the democracies in existence on the day the Berlin Wall came down. In both the British and the Soviet cases, the aim of the dominant state at the time was not to maximize its immediate power, but to create an international environment that would in the longer run be relatively unthreatening to a former great power in decline. In international politics more broadly conceived, then, there are periods when it may be good policy for a dominant state to be permissive and decentralizing in the territories it controls, even though such a situation is hard to express in the terms of strict power politics theory. This is all the more true if we allow domestic opinion within the dominant state to affect its foreign policy. The single-minded pursuit of power politics abroad normally requires fairly unwavering support for a potentially repressive security apparatus based at home. Domestic interests may feel threatened by such an apparatus, in which case the pursuit of apparently inexplicable altruism overseas may reflect a perceived self-interest in *détente* and the reduction of tension on the internal front. (Compare British support for decolonization, or French or Portuguese responses to colonial wars. Eduard Shevardnadze's declarations point to a similar pattern in Moscow.)

Neither British nor Soviet decolonizing strategies were formulated in an international vacuum. In both cases the dominant authorities had to consider not just the pressures and demands arising within the colonial or dependent territories that they still controlled, but also (and for the purposes of this chapter more crucially) the standpoints and policies of great power rivals and of the international community more generally. In the post-war period British policies were profoundly affected by the requirements of the USA and by the United Nations' commitment to the principles of the self-determination of nations. Similarly, in the 1980s, Moscow's strategy was heavily constrained by the pressure of demands from the West—not just the USA, but also Western Europe and an array of international organizations. To these pressures we shall now turn.

4. The Role of the West

Clearly, in general, the liberal democracies of Western Europe and North America exerted a range of long-term pressures on the Soviet bloc which helped nurture democratic aspirations in East-Central Europe, and which eventually contributed to Gorbachev's decision to risk decolonization. But any systematic analysis of the role of international factors in stimulating democratization in this region must carefully specify which pressures were most significant; how, when, and where they produced their main effects; and in what historical context they were embedded and constrained. Just as the record of Soviet policy towards the region extends over a long period and contains a variety of distinct phases, with a differential impact on the various countries concerned, so also the policies (in the plural) and influences emanating from the West require disaggregation. Such a deconstruction of the record is required in order to pierce the veil of Western selective recall about the Cold War, as well as to help us situate the East-Central European democratizations in their comparative context, and to clarify the part played by international factors in such processes. Such a re-evaluation is also necessary if we are to understand certain distinguishing features of the regional democratization experience—the speed of the demonstration effects; the remarkably limited resort to violence; the association between democratization and rejoining the West.

This chapter is, of course, too brief to accomplish all these tasks. It can only survey some of the major issues and suggest some provisional interpretations. A convenient starting-point is provided by David Deudney and G. John Ikenberry, who have sketched out one influential viewpoint concerning the West's role in spurring changes within the Soviet bloc. They distinguish between the causes of the Soviet crisis, which they describe as primarily domestic, and causes of the Soviet response to its crisis (most particularly the foreign affairs response) which they say 'derive from external sources'. 'Many commentators have emphasised the role of Western state policy', they note, 'and particularly American containment policy, in inducing Soviet change.' However, they consider it important to assess the 'full set of environmental factors . . . some of which have been long in the making and some of which are not a reflection of government policy'. They distinguish no fewer than eight dimensions of international influence, ranging through various types of military and economic pressure to the strength of international organizations and a final catch-all, 'the character of global society and culture'.[20] After tracing the way all these factors may have affected Moscow's choices of response to the crisis in the Soviet system, they conclude that since the 1950s 'although the West has grown militarily and economically powerful, it has presented the Soviet Union with a more benign and attractive face'.[21] 'The central role of these deeper, long-term forces puts in perspective and shows the limits of the designs and disputes of policy-makers. The real genius of the Western system has been not its coherent and far-sighted policy, but the vitality and attractiveness of its polity.'[22]

This interpretation admittedly offers some rather large hostages to fortune (will the citizens of the new democracies of East-Central Europe continue to admire the vitality of Western polities, no matter how policy-makers behave in the post-Communist era?). And although it seems mainly directed against US conservatives who may feel that the collapse of the Soviet Union vindicates their policies of containment, nevertheless it does have the merit of emphasizing the multiplicity of channels through which Western influences were exerted, and the cumulative macro-historical impact of these influences. Despite this, it seems to me that certain key decisions by Western policy-makers can be singled out for examination. Had different decisions been taken at critical junctures, I would argue that the pattern, timing, and course of democratization in East-Central Europe might well have been different. In some cases even the outcome itself might have changed.

Most importantly, for example, the artificial post-war division of Germany created the linchpin of Cold War Europe—a German Democratic Republic surrounding a partitioned Berlin. The West never openly accepted this solution (after 1970 *Ostpolitik* involved recognition of post-war frontiers subject to their eventual endorsement by a united Germany), nor did it actively challenge this cornerstone of the Soviet security system, certainly not after the erection of the Berlin Wall, on 13 August 1961. The outcome of this tacit understanding between East and West was that a liberal capitalist democracy came to flourish in West Germany and West Berlin, which never relinquished its claim to the eventual reincorporation of an East German population denied access either to democracy or to capitalism (or indeed to the West in general) by force of Soviet arms. The moment that the people of East Germany realized that Moscow would no longer use military means to block Reunification, the linchpin of the entire regional system was removed. The dismantling of the Berlin Wall soon signified not only the Reunification of Germany on a liberal capitalist basis, but also the democratization along similar lines of most if not all of the other countries in the rearguard of the Soviet alliance.

Clearly the basic Western position on German Reunification was much more long-term and deeply entrenched than most of the policy debates that consumed the energies of governmental strategists. Moreover, the structural pressures on the Soviet bloc generated by the West's dogged and successful pursuit of 'peaceful coexistence' in Central Europe were much more profound in their effects than most consciously designed strategies of selective reward and punishment. Although such pressures can be disaggregated into their military, economic, political, and socio-cultural components, it is in practice rather artificial to split up elements that were in reality indissolubly interconnected. However, there is a need to explore how this bundle of pressures changed over time, and how they acted differentially in different parts of the East-Central European region.

Taking a long historical view, it is not so clear that the Western system always displayed great vitality and attractiveness. The Western democracies may have contributed substantially to the creation of a democratic Czechoslovakia in 1919, for example, but they also played a key role in its destruction in 1938. Although they went to war in defence of a much less democratic regime in Poland in 1939, their basic concern was to maintain the balance of power. Hence their intervention only served to maximize the wartime suffering of the Polish people. And even when the war was won, neither Polish sovereignty nor Polish democracy were counted as a vital interest of the West.

It is true, and important, that the incorporation of the Baltic democracies into the Soviet Union (agreed under a secret clause of the Nazi–Soviet Pact) was never fully accepted by the West, but of course for fifty years the issue remained largely dormant in East–West relations. It only returned to haunt officialdom in Moscow when President Gorbachev opened the archives in a misjudged attempt to stabilize the USSR through historical openness. This example confirms the vital importance of retaining a long-term historical perspective when evaluating democratization processes, since suppressed political memories are frequently so potent. It also illustrates the many complex ways in which the legacy of past actions and inactions (both domestic and international) may hang over and redirect the course of contemporary democratizations. To take one specific example, the consequence of fifty years of Baltic incorporation into the USSR was the Russification of these three republics. However, when the international community recognized the restoration of their sovereignty as democratic states in 1991, it made no stipulations as to their treatment of the by-this-time substantial Russian minority populations within their borders. A consequence of this international inaction was that the Estonian parliament enacted laws restricting citizenship rights to those families already resident in the republic prior to its forced incorporation into the USSR. (This notwithstanding the fact that many Russian nationals had voted for independence in the 1991 referendum.) Thus long historical memories, and the selective application of democratic principles by the West, can markedly alter the character of the democratization processes under way in parts of East-Central Europe.

One period is of particular interest from our perspective. This is the early to mid-1970s, the era of so-called *détente*, during which a new West German government, led by the former mayor of West Berlin, sought to reassure Moscow and its Warsaw Pact allies that growing Western prosperity and freedom would not be used aggressively to destabilize the post-war status quo in the region. Although the broad framework of European *détente* was inscribed in that phase of international history, a number of specific institutional procedures, such as the Conference on Security and Co-operation in Europe (CSCE), were established that were far from inevitable. Particular Western decisions taken at that time contributed significantly to the course and pattern of the democratizations that took place a generation later. Although the Brezhnev leadership group in Moscow remained highly adversarial, Soviet memories of European *détente* contributed to the Gorbachev team's perceptions of their strategic options (which were of course also shaped by the Reagan Administration's more belligerent line in the 1980s). Gorbachev's references to a 'common European house', and his favourable posture towards the CSCE, provide tangible evidence of the significance of this contribution.[23]

Détente was formally incorporated into NATO policy on 14 December 1967, with the adoption of the Harmel Report. This reflected a broadened conception of Western security, whereby the military containment of Communism would be supplemented by attempts to stabilize some form of political relationship with it. However, the nature of that political relationship remained controversial within the West, right until the end of the Cold War. Over that twenty-two-year period, perceptions of *détente* shifted repeatedly on both sides of the East–West dividing-line. The West German position underwent a particularly sharp shift when Willy Brandt became Chancellor in 1969 (although the ground was being prepared several years earlier). The earlier position had been that there could be no *détente* before unification. Now Brandt asserted the reverse proposition. 'The basis of his thinking was that only by accepting postwar reality and giving up unrealistic territorial claims could West Germany exert influence in Eastern Europe ... *Wandlung durch Annäherung* or "change through rapprochement" was his stated aim.'[24] He thought that by stabilizing the status quo the West could pave the way for a gradual evolution in the East. Brandt's approach was always controversial in Germany, first resisted by conservatives, who said it conferred legitimacy on the fruits of conquest, and subsequently undermined from the left by those who indeed sought only *rapprochement*, reducing the pressure for change.

But at least, according to a careful account by Richard Davy, the original approach was to a considerable degree embodied in the 1975 Helsinki Final Act, which institutionalized the CSCE, and thereby provided a negotiated international framework that helped channel and contain the decolonization and regime transitions of 1989–91. According to Davy's interpretation, although both Soviet propagandists and some Western hard-liners for different reasons chose to misinterpret the Final Act as an instrument of appeasement, this was far from being the case. 'Instead of endorsing the status quo it was a charter for change. Instead of legitimizing the Soviet sphere of influence it legitimized Western intrusion into it. Instead of making frontiers immutable it specifically affirmed the principle of peaceful change. Instead of putting contacts under official control it emphasized the role of individuals. Instead of confining itself to inter-state relations it reinforced the principle that peace also depends on how states treat their people.'[25] In short, a decade before Gorbachev, the West set out in treaty form all the essential principles he would subsequently embrace. On this view it was not just the general 'vitality and attractiveness' of the Western polity, but rather a specific coherent and disputed set of Western requirements, incentives, and reassurances embodied in an international treaty that shaped Moscow's foreign policy options in response to the Soviet Union's systemic crisis.

Admittedly the CSCE process only covers a part of the West's role in the democratization of East-Central Europe. As the European Community developed and expanded, especially in the 1970s and 1980s, its achievements in such areas as personal freedom, welfare, prosperity, and law-based integration came to contrast increasingly sharply with comparable performance in the Warsaw Pact countries. Thus West European (and eventually even southern European) demonstration effects brought mounting indirect pressure to bear on the Comecon states. More directly, the EC espoused the Helsinki process (attaching particular importance to the human rights basket), and it insisted on negotiating trade issues on a country-by-country basis, thus undermining Moscow-led institutions of regional economic integration.[26] Both the CSCE process and the activities of the EC brought maximum pressure to bear on the Soviet bloc system at its weakest point—the German Democratic Republic (whose five eastern *Länder* were offered immediate and automatic incorporation into the EC via the Treaty of Rome the moment German Reunification was agreed). It will never be known whether these positive Western incentives to transform the Soviet system would eventually have achieved their goals in the absence of intensified economic and military competition between West and East in the 1980s. 'Hawks' in the West (now supported by many anti-Communists in the East) argue that it was only by re-escalating the Cold War that the Soviet system could be brought to such a crisis that the Moscow leadership would accept full implementation of CSCE conditions. Arbitration between such rival explanations would require a more precise analysis of the causes of Soviet collapse than can be attempted here. Nevertheless it should be noted that many Western hawks continued until the very end to disbelieve President Gorbachev's protestations of good faith, and to insist that Soviet power could only be destroyed through unrelenting external assault. Some hawks regarded the possibility of a non-violent and negotiated transition as a snare and an illusion, until the very moment when it was upon them.[27]

At any event European *détente* and the CSCE process produced a range of effects, which varied between countries and social sectors. It is not only the possible impact on the Soviet leadership in Moscow that requires consideration. The effects were multiple, often indirect, and at times quite different from those intended. For example, prior to 1970 the Communist regime in Poland achieved some modicum of patriotic legitimacy because it was seen as defending the nation's post-1945 boundaries against the threat of German revanchism. An unforeseen consequence of *Ostpolitik* was to deprive the Warsaw authorities of their best claim to the right to rule, thereby contributing to the rise of the broadest and most democratic mass anti-Communist movement known within the region—Solidarnosc. Timothy Garton Ash has even argued that without *détente* there would probably have been no Solidarity. But

Bonn was not prepared for the Polish revolution any more than Washington was. Solidarity was an embarrassment to the social-liberal government . . . It reacted with palpable confusion, for here (in a process that would have delighted Hegel) a policy had produced its opposite: the policy of reducing tensions . . . had produced tensions.[28]

However, there were also major intended consequences of the policy. Václav Havel's Charter 77, for example, was formed in direct response to the Helsinki Final Act, which precipitated Czechoslovakia's signature of the UN Declaration of Human Rights. More generally, as Adam Roberts has argued,

the existence of international agreements and even of some shared values—exemplified in the 1966 human rights accords, the 1975 Helsinki Final Act, and the 1989 Vienna follow-up document of the CSCE—played a part in facilitating transition, both by stressing the importance of human rights and by helping to establish a framework of general security and confidence that made major change in Eastern Europe and the Soviet Union seem thinkable.[29]

In a similar vein, Richard Davy concludes 'it is incontrovertible that, without the Final Act and the Western interest that it aroused, opposition in Eastern Europe would have been weaker, less coherent, easier to supress and slower to foster the development of civil liberties in Eastern Europe in preparation for the transition to democracy when the opportunity finally came'.[30] Moreover 'by helping to support the development of civil societies in Eastern Europe, detente paved the way for a *smoother* transition to democracy when the old regimes crumbled because it had fostered alternative structures and authorities to take their place'.[31]

5. After the Wall Came Down

The immediate post-Communist response throughout the region recalled the democratic honeymoon of 1919, before right-wing dictatorships took over everywhere except in Czechoslovakia ('the only democracy east of the Rhine').[32] This quotation reminds us both that democratization in the region has historical antecedents stretching back before the first arrival of Soviet imperialism; but also that the consolidation of democratic regimes can be threatened from more than one direction.

As in 1919–20, the years 1990–1 were occupied with the creation of new states and the confirmation of old ones; with the establishment of internationally recognized representative regimes; and with the redefinition of international alignments throughout the region. As in the earlier period these three processes were intimately interconnected. They took place all in a rush, and according to a relatively standardized formula, because although they were obviously initiated and shaped in response to internal political realities, all took place under the vigilance, not to say virtual supervision, of the extra-regional powers. Admittedly the great powers had limited control, and were deeply divided amongst themselves. They sought to sketch out the main elements of an internationally acceptable new order for the region, to substitute for the collapse of German hegemony, in the first instance, and of Russian hegemony, in the second. The main elements of this new order had to be negotiated, and reinforced by international treaty commitments and the appropriate redeployment of economic and military assets, within a fairly short time period, before international attention shifted elsewhere. In each case some international support for representative and constitutional forms of government was expressed, but the depth and seriousness of these commitments could not be gauged in so short a period.

Whether or not international support for the consolidation of fragile democracies will prove more solid and durable in the 1990s than in the 1920s remains to be seen. Progress has been particularly notable in the northern tier (where even the return to office of reform Communist parties—in Hungary and Poland—can be taken as evidence of democratic maturity), but the dismal failure of international policies towards the former Yugoslavia casts a long shadow (see Chapter 14, below). As always much will depend upon whether the main international actors can remain united in their support for democratic consolidation in the region, whether their attention becomes distracted by crises elsewhere, and whether the objective of democracy promotion remains harmonious with other externally desired objectives (the restoration of capitalism, the control of international crime, the avoidance of warfare, etc.). In the past it has been suggested that the US style of policy-making by crisis management may produce its greatest impact during the brief and turbulent period when a democratic transition is in progress; whereas the more cumbersome and bureaucratic style of the European Community may produce its greatest effects in the long run-up to a transition (when it brings cumulative economic and political pressure to bear against the *ancien régime*) and during the subsequent protracted period of democratic consolidation (when it may hold out such incentives as the prospect of full membership of the EC once sufficiently solid reforms have been implanted). While this schema worked reasonably well for southern Europe or Central America, it requires substantial modification in relation to East-Central Europe. As we have already seen, there is a counter-argument concerning the role of military strength and the risks of European *détente* as instruments for forcing reform out of the Communist apparatus before 1989. At the crucial moment of transition neither Brussels nor Washington played a leading role—Western policy-makers in general were overtaken by events they had not foreseen and could only applaud from the sidelines. Since 1990, despite a torrent of Western rhetoric expressing support for the consolidation of the region's fragile new democracies, the actual record has been quite mixed. Both North Americans and West Europeans have shown a tendency to switch attention to their own internal problems, perhaps at the cost of weakening the long-term impact of such support.

Since 1989 the European Community has proved less reliable as an agency of democracy promotion in East-Central Europe than might have been expected, given its record in southern Europe. On the one hand, the Commission responded with alacrity to the dismantling of the Berlin Wall, extending an open welcome to East Germany, whether as a separate state or as a region within a reunified Germany. (Ever since 1957 the Treaty of Rome had beeen explicit in regarding the GDR as an integral part of Germany, a founding member.) Brussels also made a quick start in establishing PHARE programmes of technical assistance to assist the transformation of seven East European countries (Yugoslavia was initially included). However, the Community failed to maintain this momentum, in part because of its internal conflicts over Maastricht and economic and monetary union, in part because the disintegration of Yugoslavia and the USSR uncovered deep differences of priorities within

Western Europe over how to handle the collapse of the Soviet bloc. The formerly Habsburg areas of Central Europe benefited from EC support far more than the rest of the region, with the Serbs and the Muslims the most conspicuous losers. The uneven impact of EC support for democracy can be traced through the record of the Europe Agreements set up by the Community as a half-way-house response to post-Communist applications for membership. The first three agreements were signed in December 1991, with Czechoslovakia, Hungary, and Poland. The preambles expressed a commitment to 'pluralistic democracy based on the rule of law and the market economy'. Subsequently Czechoslovakia split into two, each with its own agreement (and it was in accordance with this preamble that the French and German ambassadors called on the President of Slovakia in November 1994 to express the European Union's concern over a purge of the state-controlled media carried out by the Bratislava parliament). Romania and Bulgaria also signed similar agreements in 1993, and Slovenia and the three Baltic republics are expected to follow suit in 1995. At the Essen summit of the European Union in December 1994 it was publicly acknowledged that this might imply an eventual expansion of the EU to twenty-seven member states (fifteen, plus Cyprus and Malta, plus the ten eastern countries). Poland occupies a key position at the head of the queue, and the Czech Republic and Hungary have publicly set their sights on full membership by the year 2000, and the Commission has so far refused to commit itself to any timetable whatsoever. It begins to look as though the southern European experience of democracy by convergence may be replicated in at least a few Central or East European countries, and the EU may therefore assist democratic consolidation in certain instances, although the Turkish precedent could prove equally applicable in other cases. The queue for membership is uncomfortably long, and the Union is under great internal strain.

From an international relations perspective there is one particularly crucial difference between the earlier democratizations which provided the basis for transitions theory, and those occurring since November 1989. Once the Cold War had ended, the entire international context for democratization was transformed. Western reactions to earlier democratizations were by contrast shaped and constrained by the overarching context of a bipolar world. Authoritarian regimes had been supported or undermined largely according to calculations concerning their value as allies in the conflict with Moscow. When processes of democratization received support from the West it was always accompanied by the discouragement of neutralism and efforts to strengthen the electoral appeal of centrist parties against any possible challenge by the far Left. Moscow's approach to democratization in Latin America and southern Europe was a predictable mirror image to these concerns of the West. But since the Berlin Wall came down this logic no longer applies. In the euphoria of 1990 there were even Western liberals who argued that in the post-Cold War world the West would become the only important source of external influence, and it would no longer have any motive for shoring up authoritarian allies, or for intervening in a discriminatory manner between one set of domestic power contenders and another (provided all observe democratic procedures). On a more sceptical reading, once the challenge of bipolarity is removed the West no longer has a clear *realpolitik* motive for democracy promotion. Liberal idealism is unlikely to have the same staying power. In any case, in the absence of an external threat Western allies are likely to develop a heightened sense of their conflicting interests, and are therefore likely to cultivate rival protégés within each fragile new democracy, and to favour competing client states. Whether or not this proves to be the case, the disappearance of a bipolar order destroys the binary system of classification by which external actors could identify allies and enemies in complex, turbulent, and distant political conflicts. So long as the Czechs (or Croats) could be identified as 'liberals' and the Slovaks (or Serbs) as 'Communists', international chancelleries could work out where they stood. Once such spurious systems of classification have been eroded the West is left with a much weakened rationale for sustained involvement in the internal political processes of fragile regimes. The disintegration of the Soviet Union adds to this sense of disorientation, by generating a proliferation of new arenas and untried political actors, often of indecipherable antecedents, few of whom can be regarded as trustworthy democrats, or who can be relied upon to respect the democratic aspirations of their neighbours. Sustained international support for the consolidation of democratic regimes would demand hitherto untapped sources of Western maturity and tenacity in such a context.

Even in the most favourable conditions, such as those prevailing in southern Europe in the 1970s, something like a decade must pass before a transition from authoritarian rule can progress towards the consolidation of a liberal democracy. East-Central Europe has tried to change itself far more drastically and rapidly than southern Europe, acting on more fronts simultaneously. The initial conditions (prerequisites?) for democratic stability were also much weaker. Consequently it is far too early to pass serious judgement on the prospects for democratic consolidation in the region. A comparative perspective suggests a few provisional considerations, however. If consolidation does occur, it will take time and will develop unevenly. Quite a few regimes could be suspended in an intermediate condition—neither properly consolidated nor clearly headed away from democratic forms. Developments external to the region (e.g. the success or failure of reforms in the former USSR, or shifts in outlook in Western Europe) will once again exert a strong influence on the political climate in East-Central Europe, and may therefore affect the region's democratic prospects. A final intriguing point concerns the likely character of such consolidated democracies as may emerge. In southern Europe the initial expectation was that newly empowered popular forces harbouring resentments against earlier authoritarian regimes might press for a more radical and participatory type of democracy than elsewhere. In the event, however, once memories of the transition had faded, relatively conventional and unadventurous liberal democracies took the stage. Authoritarian élites were forced to reform themselves, but were in no way disqualified from eventual return to office. Does this mean that in East-Central Europe, once the initial heat of anti-Soviet and pro-market feeling has abated, the democracies that eventually achieve consolidation there will also become reconciled to the preservation of substantial continuity linking them to their Communist past? Will the distinctive overtones of the local terminology concerning democratization fade, as consolidation progresses?

6. Conclusion

The recent democratizations in East-Central Europe have introduced some important variations on the themes present in earlier transitions literature; important variations, but not an entirely new tune. Among the most important continuities I would stress the loss of cohesion within the authoritarian coalition prior to the transition; the unforeseen or unintended consequences of its attempts to liberalize the political system without relinquishing ultimate control; the dilemmas this presented to the democratic opposition (how to negotiate a non-violent transition without being co-opted); the rapid turnover of political groupings and projects during the brief quasi-revolutionary phase of full transition; the significance of pacts, constitutional arrangements, and other bridging institutions in containing the uncertainties of this phase, and channelling the outcome towards democratic institutionalization; and the relatively conventional and standardized forms of liberal democracy that emerge rather consistently as the macro-political framework for the posttransitional settlement. The existence of such continuities should be pleasing to those who theorized about democratization prior to the collapse of the Soviet system. Those who relied on totalitarianism for theoretical guidance, or who regarded Communist political systems as incomparable with pro-Western authoritarian regimes, were by comparison handicapped in their attempts to understand the transformations of 1989 (except in the case of Romania). However, such continuities are imprecise and incomplete. A number of critical features of the East-Central European transition were distinctive to the region, and to the problems of dismantling Communist forms of autocracy.

This chapter, and this volume, have focused on one particular dimension of the democratization process and one crucial respect in which East-Central European experiences differed from those of earlier democratizations. The brute fact is that a particularly antidemocratic model of Communism was imposed by Moscow, at Stalin's behest, on all territories occupied by the Red Army, and that post-Stalinist rulers of the USSR nevertheless continued to restrain political liberalization and to veto democratization by threat of military force for almost forty years thereafter. This chapter has tried to unravel the major distinguishing features of the 1989 democratizations that flow from this raw geopolitical reality.

There was a pre-1945 tradition of attempted democratization in this region, which provided quite a promising internal basis for redemocratization in at least some of the more influential and prosperous countries of the region following the defeat of Nazism. Not all the local Communist parties of the region were always pure instruments of Stalinist imperialism. On the contrary, in Poland and Czechoslovakia, at least, more democratic traditions of socialism found brief expression even at the highest party levels. However, wherever such soft-line attitudes materialized they were subjected to the same harsh disciplines that Moscow customarily dispensed to liberal dissidents at home. In consequence, all the Communist parties of the region without exception were turned into accomplices of foreign imposition, and of the suppression of popular rights and aspirations. This is the fundamental reason why all later attempts to stabilize Communist rule through liberalizing it were doomed to failure. In other parts of the world some softliners within the authoritarian coalition could manage to survive and even flourish by steering a path to full democratizations. Those who attempted this in East-Central Europe in the late 1980s were swept aside by a tide of popular indignation the moment Moscow withdrew its protection from them. Whether Nagy, Gomułka, or Dubček could have done better in an earlier generation is an experiment the Soviet leadership was not prepared to risk. In consequence, when democracy did finally return to the region it carried very distinctive connotations, not to be confused with the meaning of the term in the abstract, or with the overtones it acquired in other regions. Democracy, private property, anti-Communism, and 'embrace of the West' were all rolled into one, and linked to the rebirth of national sovereignties.

This chapter has emphasized two basic factors that probably suffice to explain the durability of the Soviet veto on democratization, independent of the personal inclinations of individual Russian leaders. One factor is strictly international, or geopolitical; the other is a matter of internal Soviet politics. But the two seem to me so interrelated that it would be artificial to claim that the real explanation was either essentially domestic or primarily international. The first is the strategic imperative of maintaining a divided Germany. This was the core of the post-war settlement in Europe, and the linchpin of Soviet bloc security. It required the imposition of a strict form of Communism on the inhabitants of the Soviet-controlled part of Germany (preferably, no doubt, with their consent, but finally regardless of their preferences). From time to time experimentation, pluralism, and the loosening of Soviet controls in other parts of East-Central Europe might well have been more tolerable to Moscow, but for the repercussions on the GDR. This fundamental geopolitical reality underlay the Soviet veto on all attempts at democratization in the region.

Equally compelling was the second factor, which must be seen in the context of the first. All Soviet reformers had to consider the implications for their own power base within the USSR of permitting the dismantling of core Communist structures in allied countries. In theory, it might seem as though there could be two alternative routes to reform, regional or system-wide—i.e. liberalism might be allowed in some or all client states, without dictating the content of reform policies within the Soviet Union. In practice, Moscow's scope for permitting deviations within the Warsaw Pact, while blocking them at home, was always highly constrained. If the Hungarians made a success of the price mechanism, that would inevitably (through demonstration effects and the pressures of international rivalry) feed into similar debates throughout the Soviet bloc. If Solidarity's trade unions proved tolerable in Poland, workers elsewhere would certainly wish to emulate the experience. If objective historical enquiry was licensed in any part of the system, it would raise questions that had to be answered throughout the bloc. In short, only a Soviet leader steeled to promote openness at home (and to take the domestic consequences, whatever they might be) would be willing to lift the essential veto on political liberalization in the neighbouring Communist countries. Prior to 1985, reform-minded Soviet leaders always drew back from the dangers of such far-reaching domestic reform and for that reason they were bound to maintain a wary vigilance over dangerous precedents anywhere in the bloc. The essential link between the two factors just mentioned was provided by the centralizing logic of the Soviet command system. Since it was known throughout the system that all essential decisions (military, political, economic, and ideological) must be initiated from the top, it followed that whatever the Moscow leadership decided (by either action or inaction) in relation to a particular challenge in a specific policy or geographical arena would be taken to apply more generally. Thus, if Moscow had not crushed the Dubček experiment in 1968, this would have signalled the raising of a veto on reform elsewhere as well (even at home). Likewise, once Gorbachev had decided on extensive liberalization within the USSR he could never afford to suppress reform elsewhere, without capitulating to the enemies or reform at home. Somewhat similar issues arise with earlier Western experiences of imperial decolonization.

The transitions literature has sometimes been criticized for focusing too heavily on élite strategies and calculations, to the neglect of broader democratic pressures rooted in society at large. This chapter's focus on the Moscow veto might seem an extreme case of such over-emphasis. However, the claim made here is that the maintenance of that veto was a crucial distinguishing feature distorting democratization patterns and timing in this region. Within the Soviet bloc most pressures from below were heavily suppressed by the Communist system of control (to this extent the totalitarian literature made a valid point, although grossly overstating it). Another distinguishing feature of the regional experience was the role played by the West both in pressing Moscow to liberalize, and in sustaining popular aspirations for democracy in East-Central Europe. This may to some extent be regarded as a partial international substitute for the missing domestic pressures from below—but of course it followed a different rhythm and operated according to a distinctive logic, as discussed above.

There is, however, another societal dimension to this process which certainly requires far more attention than it could be given here. The pro-democratic influence of the West came not only through formal treaties and public policies—it was also transmitted through culture, consumption patterns, and a proliferation of other demonstration effects.[33] These societal influences are in the long run extremely powerful, but also quite difficult to specify and evaluate.[34] Their impact on different geographical and social sectors within the region was extremely uneven depending on the extent of media control by the regime. (In Romania in 1989, for example, not only were there no private VCR's but every individual typewriter had to be separately registered with the *Securitate*, and photocopying was also rigorously supervised.) In any case it is one thing to show that by example Western social values and practices were in general undermining Communist structures of social control and quite another to link this to specific political consequences. However, it is striking, as Adam Roberts points out, that popular demands for change should have proved so nonviolent, as well as so widespread and uncontainable. Demonstration effects across international boundaries were dramatically reinforced by the impact of television news coverage. In some cases the greatest practical impact was felt by the ruling élites, whose confidence in their own legitimacy was undermined by demonstrations of the West's superior appeal. Elsewhere the biggest effect may have been to stimulate a wish to travel abroad (particularly in the younger generation)—a wish which once frustrated by bureaucratic edict could be turned into political resistance and the demand for change.

In summary, then, even though Communism may have traditionally suppressed most forms of civil society in the region, the societal push for democracy became a major independent variable as the transition process got under way. This element in the democratization process, like the others considered in this chapter, surely contained a major international component. But whether one stresses pressures from below, or the importance of élite strategies, in any case the domestic and international components were so intermingled that it would be arbitrary and artificial to disentangle them, let alone to present the former as dominant over the latter.

Notes

1. The 'region' in question therefore extends from the former German Democratic Republic to the Baltic states, and from Poland to Bulgaria.

It excludes the former Yugoslavia and Albania, which were not under Soviet control.
2. Quoted by G. Ionescu, *The Break-up of the Soviet Empire in Eastern Europe* (Harmondsworth: Penguin, 1965), 27, which also contains a discussion (25–6) of the ambiguities of the term 'people's democracy', which still retained some pluralist connotations until late 1947.
3. The speaker was Andrei Zhdanov, as quoted in A. Bullock, *Hitler and Stalin: Parallel Lives* (London: Harper-Collins, 1991), 1023. By this point, of course, the anti-Fascist alliance was breaking up, and Zhdanov's speech is primarily remembered for enunciating the doctrine of the 'two camps'.
4. According to Adam Roberts, 'in acceptance of multi-party democracy (though not in the holding of actual elections) Hungary was significantly ahead of Poland': A. Roberts, *Civil Resistance in the East European and Soviet Revolutions*, monograph no. 4 (London: Albert Einstein Institution, 1991), 174.
5. Alex Pravda is generally cautious and precise in his use of such terminology, but to my mind he goes too far when describing Dubček's influence on Gorbachev's entourage, saying 'many of the ideas underlying the Czechoslovak reform programme coincided with and perhaps catalysed the thinking and aspirations of the Gorbachev generation to a *communist-party led democratisation* of the Soviet command system' (my emphasis): A. Pravda (ed.), *The End of the Outer Empire* (London: Sage, for the Royal Institute of International Affairs, 1992), 3. It might be safer to substitute the term 'liberalization' here.
6. J. Blatt, 'The International Dimension of Democratization in Czechoslovakia and Hungary', in G. Pridham (ed.), *Building Democracy: The International Dimension of Democratization in Eastern Europe* (Leicester: Leicester University Press, 1994).
7. Ionescu, *Break-up of Soviet Empire*, 64.
8. *Khrushchev Remembers* (London: Sphere, 1971), 438. This may seem hard to take from the man responsible for the execution of Nagy, but it is of great importance that Khrushchev could be removed by a collective decision and without bloodshed. So were all subsequent Communist rulers of Eastern Europe, other than the Albanian and Romanian dictators. So was Gorbachev.
9. Pravda, *End of Outer Empire*, 70. Indeed, he thinks it 'likely' that CMEA leaders were informed of this decision when they met in Moscow on 10–11 November 1986 (17–18).
10. Interesting attempts to compare the US sphere of influence in the Caribbean with the Soviet sphere in East-Central Europe include J. E. Triska (ed.), *Dominant Powers and Subordinate States* (Durham, NC: Duke University Press, 1986); P. Keal, *Unpoken Rules and Superpower Dominance* (London: Macmillan, 1983).
11. J. Darwin, *Britain and Decolonization: The Retreat from Empire in the Post-War World* (London: Macmillan, 1988), 20. He adds that Harold Macmillan's retrospective claim that African independence was the

long-standing object of British policy, and the triumphant culmination of Britain's mission to endow less fortunate peoples with her democratic heritage, was 'a picturesque invention worthy of Disraeli'.

12. Ibid, 334.
13. Ibid. 331. However, Darwin does not attempt to answer Max Beloff's highly pertinent question, 'Why were British governmental institutions and even the party system so little affected by the retreat from Empire when the collapse of almost all other imperial systems has entailed the most profound repercussions upon the domestic polity?': Beloff, *Imperial Sunset*, i (New York: Alfred A. Knopf, 1969), 7.
14. Darwin, *Britain and Decolonization*, 335. Britain's Caribbean possessions were something of an exception, and that is where many of the more successful recent decolonization-cum-democratizations took root (with US support).
15. Paradoxically, the first Moscow-watcher to grasp the full significance of what was happening, and to act consequentially in order to protect his position, was almost certainly Fidel Castro, who launched an implicitly anti-Moscow campaign of 'rectification' in 1986.
16. R. V. Daniels, *The End of the Communist Revolution* (London: Routledge, 1983), 12.
17. Ibid. 15–16.
18. Ibid. 19.
19. Ibid. 24.
20. D. Deudney and G. J. Ikenberry, 'The International Sources of Soviet Change', *International Security*, 16/3 (1991/2), 77.
21. Ibid. 117.
22. Ibid. 118.
23. 'One symptom of the change was the revival of the CSCE, which entered a wholly new phase of its existence at the Vienna follow-up meeting of 1986–9. The Soviet Union now wanted to be accepted as a member of the world community, and especially of Europe, so it had to be seen to accept European values. The CSCE was its ticket to admission': R. Davy (ed.), *European Detente: A Reappraisal* (London: Sage, for the Royal Institute for International Affairs, 1992), 25–6.
24. Ibid. 10–11.
25. Ibid. 19.
26. J. Pinder, 'The European Community and Democracy in Central and Eastern Europe', in G. Pridham, E. Herring, and G. Sanford (eds.), *Building Democracy: The Internal Dimension of Democratization in Eastern Europe* (London: Leicester University Press, 1994), 120–3.
27. Those wedded to the theory of a 'totalitarian' Soviet bloc had to conclude that it was only through outright defeat in war or a violent and catastrophic internal revolution that the system could change. By contrast, as early as 1980, Richard Davy was pointing out the heavy drain on Soviet military, economic, and political strength arising from the East European dependencies. 'We should not write off the possibility that the Soviet Union will gradually become more flexible, perhaps

under a new leadership. It has good economic reasons for encouraging East European trade with the West, and it is learning to live with greater unorthodoxy even, for the moment, in Poland. Peaceful evolution is still possible,' he wrote in the *The Times*, 18 December 1980.

28. T. Garton Ash, *The Polish Revolution: Solidarity* (London: Granta, 1991), 336. Not that Solidarnosc should be viewed as relentlessly destabilizing—on the contrary, prior to the declaration of martial law there were some serious efforts at 'pact-making'.

29. Roberts, *Civil Resistance*, 32.

30. Davy, *European Detente*, 251.

31. Ibid. 263 (my emphasis).

32. Daniels, *End of Communist Revolution*, 132.

33. There were an estimated 700,000 VCRs in Poland in 1987, 300,000 in Hungary, and 150,000 in Czechoslovakia: M. Sukos, 'From Propaganda to Öffentlichkeit in Eastern Europe: Four Models of the Public Sphere under State Socialism', 25, paper presented to the conference Contemporary Societies in Comparative Perspective: Eastern Europe and Latin America in the Twentieth Century', Polish Academy of Sciences, Pultusk, Poland, 29 May–1 June 1990.

34. Adam Roberts goes so far as to argue that 'television played a key role in the events of 1989–91. It made East Germany aware of the flight to the West, Czechs and Slovaks aware of what was happening in all the neighbouring countries and in their midst, and Romanians aware that Ceausescu was vulnerable: indeed, much of the Romanian revolution was conducted from the television studio in Bucharest': A. Roberts, *Civil Resistance*, 12.

PART IV

A Comparative Perspective

Democratic Regions, Ostracism, and Pariahs

LAURENCE WHITEHEAD

Democratic Regional Groupings

The construction of democratic regional communities of states, and the transmission of liberal democratic practices and institutions from state to state within a region are two powerful international processes currently shaping the course, distribution, and content of democratization experiences both in Europe and in the Americas. The importance of such international dimensions of democratization seems much clearer at this regional level than at the world-wide level of analysis. This is a shift of focus from the standpoint adopted in the immediate post-Cold War period, when for a brief period it seemed possible that a 'wave' of democratization might sweep away resistance in the world as a whole, and not just in Latin America and on the periphery of Europe.[1]

Naturally any distinction between regional and global dimensions of democratization can only be approximate, especially since both Western Europe and North America currently occupy pre-eminent positions in the post-Cold War world as a whole, and not just within their own regions. As models of market liberal freedom and prosperity both societies project a way of life which attracts adherents far beyond their immediate peripheries. Among the most obvious non-governmental channels for the transmission of such influences are the Western mass media, telecommunications, tourism, and other more specific avenues such as academic exchanges, the receipt of refugees, the dispatch of charitable, religious, and other NGO personnel, and interchange between like-minded political and civil society organizations. Jean Laponce has highlighted the long-distance significance of such influences within language communities by distinguishing between 'contagion' and 'irradiation' effects.[2] In addition, of course, each of these two regions have governments and collective institutions which are now committed, among other things, to the promotion and protection of democracy on a world scale. Thus, for example, the European Union has an active and influential policy of democracy promotion in Latin America, and the USA and Canada are similarly engaged in the ex-Communist countries of Europe. For the most part these two groupings support and reinforce each other's efforts to strengthen democracy in their respective regions.

It remains an open question whether similarly effective democratic regional communities can be established elsewhere, but so far there is scant evidence of this occurring. In Asia, for example, the resurgence of authoritarian rule in post-Tienanmen China threatens to erode some of the most promising democratic advances in the region, notably in Hong Kong and Taiwan. A community of democratic states may perhaps eventually emerge around a post-apartheid South Africa, but as yet that remains a distant prospect. Where strong regional impulses towards democratization are absent, the only international forces at work are much weaker and more diffuse global tendencies, which may contain large elements of window-dressing, particularly where (as in much of the former Third World) processes of state formation and national integration remain incomplete.[3]

This volume has mostly considered the two regions in which relatively strong democratic communities of states are already being actively promoted. Accordingly, the international dimensions of democratization emphasized here have mostly to do with regional co-operation and integration schemes. But these are by no means solely (or perhaps even primarily) concerned with democracy promotion. Such regional harmonization processes are typically driven by concerns about state security, economic advantage, and the shifting balance of international power, at least as much as by shared democratic values or ideals. Consequently, even where regional communities constructed in accordance with principles of democratic convergence seem to have made the greatest progress, democratization studies may need to pay more attention to inter-state rivalries and *realpolitik* considerations than has been apparent so far. Most of the case-studies in this volume point in that direction, as does the initial discussion of conditionality, control, and decolonization. This closing chapter extends the same approach, by examining the case of those states which find themselves marginalized or discriminated against in the course of regional construction.

In the contractarian version of regime formation there is a single moment when all participants join together within a constitutional order designed to accommodate their mutual interests. From this convenient fiction the new regime can derive a claim to legitimacy—all participants regardless of their previous conditions are presumed voluntarily to have relinquished their freedom of action in a simultaneous act of mutual commitment. But this is obviously not the way in which democratic regional communities of states are currently being constructed, either in the Americas or in Europe. On the contrary, the process of enlargement is incremental and protracted. There are founder members who design the basic rules (including the terms for subsequent admission), there are latecomers (who must queue, and adjust to pre-established norms), and there are recalcitrants and marginals whose deviance may invite ostracism, or even complete exclusion. Some members join more voluntarily than others, and some potential members find their antecedent conditions (their history, their geopolitical location, or their inherited structural characteristics) constitute a major impediment to acceptance. The internal adjustments and sacrifices required of such poorly located latecomers may be so drastic that instead of conforming to external standards they had no part in shaping, they may be driven into a stance of resistance, defiance, and isolation. In extreme cases such pariah regimes (Cuba and Serbia are the instances considered here) may not merely stand aside from processes of democracy by convergence. They may actually challenge and confront the processes that exclude them. So long as they survive, proclaiming and exemplifying principles which are rejected by their regional communities, they will offer a source of resistance which must somehow be met or countered by their democratic neighbours. Analysts need to pay as much attention to how democratic regions handle the problems generated by such recalcitrant or pariah regimes, as to how they reward and strengthen the democratizing impulses of the most eager new members. Some ways of consolidating a democratic region are more democratic (more consistent with proclaimed underlying values of pluralism and tolerance) than others.[4]

There are several good arguments for the view that international efforts at democracy promotion should be conducted by the most democratic means possible. There are arguments from democratic principles, which can be traced back at least as far as John Stuart Mill's 'Few Words on Non-Intervention'.[5] In the same vein, it can be argued that since democratic behaviour involves learned restraints which are acquired through practice, democracy is best propagated by example. Specifically, then, the most appropriate and indispensable way for a regional democratic community to transmit its values would be to observe the highest possible standards of democratic practice both within each member state taken separately, between these members as they develop their community, and in the conduct of that community towards non-members. There is a prudential reinforcement to this argument, at least in the case of the European Union, namely that while in formidable measure it possesses the capacity and means to reinforce its democratic characteristics internally, it is singularly ill-equipped (lacking a military capacity) to promote democracy elsewhere by interventionist means.[6] The OAS has proved similarly toothless, at least when acting on its own. (It was only when the UN Security Council—hardly a democratic forum—took charge that intervention became effective, both in Haiti and in Yugoslavia.) To the extent that democratic regional communities do indeed eschew intervention, and therefore rely solely on political, social, and economic instruments to encourage democracy in peripheral states, their effectiveness will depend upon their ability to appeal to shared values, assumptions, and interests. Where such appeals fail the only remaining option is ostracism—a negative form of control which only postpones the issue. In the long run the propinquity of an undemocratic regime will almost inescapably prompt any regional democratic community to re-engage with it, offering some pattern of positive incentives (conditionality) and seeking to strengthen value consensus (consent).

The Americas and Europe Compared

If a democratic regional community is to develop the capacity for democracy promotion and protection in its area it must designate that function to an appropriate organization which needs to be equipped with suitable legal authority, political legitimacy, and means of action. In the Western hemisphere the December 1994 Miami summit designated the Washington-based Organisation of American States (OAS) for this purpose. From its foundation in 1948 the OAS, like the Council of Europe in its area, has been accepted as a 'regional arrangement' pursuant to Article VIII of the UN Charter. All thirty-five independent states in the region are members (although as we have seen Cuban membership has been suspended since the early days of the revolution). An awkward consequence of this is that a number of founder governments (such as Nicaragua under the Somoza dynasty, or the Dominican Republic under Trujillo) were notorious dictatorships. In contrast to the Council of Europe during the Cold War the OAS never suspended any anti-Communist government for its repressive or dictatorial practices. Indeed, in 1974 it came close to endorsing Pinochet's overthrow of the democratically elected Allende government in Chile. When at President Johnson's behest it intervened in a civil war in the Dominican Republic in 1965 it effectively tilted the balance against the democratic insurgents. With that precedent in mind, although an OAS resolution effectively delegitimized the tottering Somoza dictatorship in 1979, a majority of its members resisted a US proposal to intervene in the Nicaraguan civil war, and throughout the 1980s the United States was unable to secure OAS approval for its covert war against the Sandinistas. When the Reagan Administration sent its 'rescue mission' to restore democracy to Grenada this was done without OAS approval. Instead the Organisation of Eastern Caribbean States (OECS) provided some regional authority for what was essentially another unilateral act. In the same way following the annulment of fraudulent elections in Panama in May 1989, the OAS was only willing to send an ineffective peace mission. When, after three months, the mission failed, the US government acted unilaterally to oust the Noriega dictatorship by force, an act which the OAS officially 'regretted' (by a vote of 24 to 1 with 6 abstentions), but did not actually condemn.

Despite this unimpressive track-record, with the end of the Cold War and the elimination of almost all overtly anti-democratic regimes in the Western hemisphere, considerable efforts have been made to reposition the OAS. In June 1991 the 'Santiago Commitment to Democracy' was promulgated at the behest of the new Chilean government. Unfortunately this was quickly followed by a coup in Haiti and a presidential decree closing Congress in Peru, both of which put the Organisation's new commitment under severe pressure. In the Haitian case, after twenty-one months of ineffective OAS mediation between the exiled democratic government and the military dictatorship, the former lost patience and in June 1993 appealed to the UN Security Council. It was under Security Council rather than just OAS auspices that an oil embargo was eventually applied, and it was in fulfilment of a Security Council resolution that the US landed troops in Port au Prince in September 1994, thereby paving the way to the restoration of the elected Aristide regime. Nor was the OAS performance on Peru particularly impressive.[7] Thus, by the time of the Miami summit in December

1994 the chosen instrument for democracy promotion in the region had no more than a mediocre record of performance. Moreover, the quality of democracy practised by many of the region's elected governments was questionable, as indicated by the January 1995 Freedom House rankings, which classified only twenty as 'free' (fourteen were 'part free' and Cuba was 'not free'). On the most outstanding regional issue—how to handle the unrepentant Castro regime—in October 1994 of all OAS members only the USA voted for a continuation of Washington's unilateral US economic sanctions against Cuba in the UN General Assembly. A large majority voted against these sanctions. But far from heeding the voice of its regional 'democratic' allies the Congress in Washington proceeded to study a bill to further reinforce these punitive measures.

In contrast to the OAS, the main European regional organization engaged in democracy promotion—the European Union—is independent of the UN system. It is also more recent (founded in 1958), and at present has fewer members—originally six, increased in stages to fifteen at the beginning of 1995. Even now it does not include all the states of its region within its membership—Norway has twice voted to stay out, and Switzerland has also declined to join. Again, in contrast to the OAS, the standards of democratic performance maintained by EU member states is consistently high. On the detailed Freedom House rankings for January 1995, all fifteen countries were rated 1 (on a scale from 1 to 7) in terms of political rights. For comparison, only nine out of the thirty-five OAS members were so rated. Leaving out Cuba, the thirty-four American 'democracies' scored a total of 82 points on political rights, compared to a possible best score of 34, and a theoretical worst score of 231. On civil liberties the EU performance was somewhat weaker (23 compared to a best score of 15) but again the contrast with the OAS democracies was striking. The latter scored a total of 91, compared to a best score of 34.[8] The principal instrument of democracy promotion available to the EU is the offer of eventual membership to a prosperous and growing regional (con)federation of market democracies, where membership carried precise and detailed benefits and obligations. To some extent the EU acts more widely than this through its co-operation programmes with non-members, but in these cases the democratic conditionality is much more contingent and secondary—similar perhaps to the loose rhetoric and gentle coaxing that characterizes most inter-American activity on this subject. In contrast to the OAS, however, the European Union has yet to suspend a member state for non-fulfilment of its treaty obligations, or to develop its own collective security strategy (in principle the West European Union (WEU) has this responsibility, but in practice its role is yet to be clearly defined and the EU still operates as a civilian institution under the shelter of NATO). Just as the OAS was virtually displaced by the UN Security Council when the Haitian crisis became acute, so the EU has largely fallen in behind the Security Council as the Yugoslav crisis has deepened. When it comes to the enforcement of economic sanctions, or the dispatch of military force, neither of these regional communities has shown much cohesion or capacity for resolute and autonomous action.

With these considerations in mind, let us briefly compare the current stance of these two regions in relation to their respective pariah regimes, and how to reincorporate them into a democratic community of states. First, we shall survey the relatively unthreatening (and certainly non-belligerent) case of Cuba, after which the much more violent, dangerous, and currently unpredictable problems of the post-Yugoslav Balkans can be considered and compared.

In the case of Cuba the policy of ostracism dates back to the early days of the revolution. There was already a regional arms embargo in effect by the time the Batista dictatorship collapsed at the end of 1958, and it was never subsequently lifted. Instead the Castro regime turned to Moscow for its military equipment, a policy which led to the Missile Crisis of 1962. Cuba was then suspended from membership of the Organisation of American States for violating the charter of the regional organization. This was, of course, at the height of the Cold War when the distinction between allying with the Soviet enemy and rejecting democratic practices at home was hardly noticed. Revolutionary Cuba was beyond the pale on both counts, and so far as Washington was concerned the second was understood as a consequence of the first. From the standpoint of most OAS members Havana's worst offence was neither of these, but rather the support of guerrilla insurgencies which threatened the fragile social order prevailing in a number of Latin American countries. In any case, Cuba was suspended from the OAS in 1962, since when the main thrust of US policy has been to quarantine the Western hemisphere from Cuban subversion, rather than directly to overthrow the Castro regime. By the end of the Cold War Havana no longer represented much of a subversive threat to any neighbouring political regimes, and in 1991 when the Soviet Union finally disintegrated so did Castro's external support. What remained was a (unilateral) US trade embargo and (multilateral) suspension from the OAS, together with suspension from the IMF, the World Bank, and the

Inter-American Development Bank for non-compliance with Fund obligations. Clearly the Castro regime had brought much of this ostracism upon itself by its early revolutionary choices. But it is worth recalling here the original meaning of that term, which derives from the voting practices of direct democracy in Ancient Greece. To 'ostracize' was to banish a dangerous or unpopular citizen for a fixed term (usually five or ten years). It did not involve permanent exclusion from the political community.

The Castro regime has been ostracized in this sense for over thirty years, but the underlying assumption has always been that Cuba's membership of the American community of states was irrevocable. The time-scale and terms on which the ostracism would be lifted are increasingly a matter of dispute, but not the principle of eventual reintegration. However, it is the time-scale and terms for admission into a democratic regional community that provide the critical incentives for democratization. In the Cuban case the United States has decisive weight in determining these conditions, and Washington has consistently been far more committed to the continuance of sanctions than the rest of its OAS partners, until the Castro regime buckles. Since, contrary to long-standing US expectations, the Cuban Communist Party's monopoly on power has remained stubbornly intact, the time-scale for ending Cuba's isolation keeps being indefinitely extended, and the population of the island is subjected to what seems like an apparently endless regimen of sanctions and punishments.

Thus, in 1992, as the Cuban economy reeled under the impact of the disappearance of the Soviet bloc, Washington redoubled the pressure for a regime transformation through the enactment of the so-called 'Cuba Democracy Act', which among other things barred maritime operators doing business with Cuba from US ports of call on their way to and from the island and banned most travel to the island and dollar remittances from US sources. Then, following the Republican Party's November 1994 success in capturing majorities in both houses of Congress, a further unilateral tightening of economic sanctions against Cuba was proposed. Under the draft terms of the so-called 'Cuban Liberty and Democratic Solidarity Act of 1995' the US Congress would enable any 'US national' (including those who were Cuban citizens at the time of the expropriations) to sue in the US for compensation from anyone (including foreign investors with no US ties) who 'traffics' in property expropriated during the Cuban Revolution. The object of this proposed measure would be to scare off the European and Latin American foreign investors who were being wooed by the Castro administration, and to tie the hands of the executive branch, by ensuring that there would be no lifting of US sanctions until after all remnants of the Castro regime had been comprehensively liquidated. (The future of this measure remains uncertain at present, given the resistance it has created within the Clinton Administration, and the fact that it drives a wedge between the USA and her democratic allies, by violating treaty commitments and by seeking to extend US jurisdiction extra-territorially.) Arguably, it is the ordinary people of Cuba who suffer most from the pariah status conferred by such measures, whereas the Havana authorities gain an excuse for continued intransigence and intensified hardships on the island. Whereas most other potentially democratizing societies are offered a mixture of rewards and encouragements progressively to conform to regional standards, together with some limited sanctions on backsliding, the Cubans face much more categorical demands to undo their past, and these are backed by implacable international pressures. Whether they would be well rewarded for compliance is much less clear. Even on the assumption that in the end US policy 'works', in that the Castro regime does indeed eventually buckle, on this scenario what takes its place may not be much of a model of pluralism and tolerance. By the time Cuba is finally reintegrated into the regional community the island's economy and society will have been crippled by the many years of sanctions, and it will rejoin on the most disadvantageous terms, as the last in the queue for NAFTA or other integration benefits. In short, then, the regional policy of indefinite ostracism will at best—even if eventually 'successful', which is not yet certain—lead to the belated reintegration of polity scarred by protracted sanctions, alienated from the regional institutions it has had no opportunity to influence, and in need of external support and assistance on a scale that may well not be made available. A Cuban transition from international pariah to equal member of a democratic regional community—if it can be accomplished at all —is unlikely to follow the pattern of the other democratic transitions in the Western hemisphere. Both the path and the outcome will be heavily conditioned by international strategies of conditionality, compellance, and control.

Clearly the conflictual relationship between the EC and Serbia is only part of a much broader and more tangled relationship between the Western democracies as a whole, and the various successor states of Yugoslavia as a group, but the comparisons of relevance to this chapter can best be made by focusing on the Brussels–Belgrade sub-relationship. The European Community's estrangement from Serbia is far more recent, not a product of the Cold War, but rather of its termination. An eventual Serbian path from pariah status to re-entry into a European Union of democratic states is obviously much more uncertain and hypothetical than that of Cuba. The consequences for the rest of Europe of failing to create such a possibility are also much more threatening. Nevertheless, even at the height of the Bosnian conflagration, it is essential to recognize that the various states generated by the disintegration of Yugoslavia are all destined by geography for inclusion in whatever European system or power structure eventually emerges (whether an inclusive democratic community of states or something less satisfactory). The Serb government can be excluded, subjected to sanctions, and indeed anathemized, as the Castro regime has been in the Americas, but eventually a time-scale and conditions will have to be set for ending regional ostracism of the Serbian people. How the European Union and its prospective Eastern European members should approach the task of eventually reintegrating Serbia, and supporting democracy in all the fragments of ex-Yugoslavia, poses the same issue as how to readmit Cuba to the American regional community, but in even starker form. These hard cases may seem so speculative that nothing definite can be said, yet they are as vital to the analysis of democratization through regional integration as all the instances of voluntary convergence and co-operation.

The essential first step towards analysing such hard cases is to provide a dispassionate account of the process of estrangement. In the case of Yugoslavia, and in contrast to Cuba, it was obviously not the existence of a successful, internally led, Communist party regime that alienated democratic partners in the region. On the contrary, Tito's Yugoslavia was viewed as a security buffer by the West and it was the Soviet-dominated Communist regimes to the east who initially felt most threatened by the possibility of Belgrade-based destabilization. It was only when the Cold War was nearing its end that anti-democratic politics within Yugoslavia began to pose a problem for the European democracies. In particular the rise of a greater Serbian nationalism (associated with the person of Slobodan Milosevic, President of the Serbian Republic since 1989) provoked resistance in the Catholic regions of northern Yugoslavia which retained historical links with Austria and Germany (i.e. among the Croats and Slovenes). These destabilizing tendencies were well advanced before the dismantling of the Berlin Wall, but they were greatly reinforced and exacerbated by the expectations, fears, and illusions accompanying the Reunification of Germany.[9] By early 1992 the Bonn government had induced its reluctant European Community allies and Washington to recognize the new states of Slovenia and Croatia (both presented as democracies throwing off Communist control), even though the boundaries of Croatia had not been agreed with the rump Yugoslav authorities in Belgrade, and the various minorities living within the new state boundaries were not given effective international assurances concerning the protection of minority rights. Thus, in the name of democracy promotion the European Community endorsed the dismantling of a multi-ethnic state, without securing the consent of all the parties concerned. This intemperate recognition of Croatia jettisoned some of the most basic canons of diplomatic prudence, and disregarded international law and practice, not to mention breaching the EC's declared policies on minority rights and the observance of democratic procedures. The fact that the Serb-dominated and repressive regime in Belgrade had unexpectedly acquiesced to Slovene independence was no justification for such recklessness over Croatia, nor does the clear evidence of a prior greater Serb military build-up provide sufficient excuse for EC disregard of such basic principles. Admittedly the Yugoslav rump regime in Belgrade had brought much international discredit upon itself by its chauvinism and its ruthless use of force against non-Serbs in the areas it controlled, but if we are to understand Serbian national estrangement from the Western democracies we must recognize both sides of the process. From the Serbian perspective it was difficult to avoid the conclusion that the Western democracies in general (and reunited Germany in particular) had sought to take advantage of the collapse of the Soviet bloc by reversing the verdict of the Second World War, in so far as the internal balance within Yugoslavia was concerned. Guided by this conviction since 1991 many Serbs have been persuaded to follow a greater Serb nationalist course which has blighted the possibilities of peaceful coexistence between Yugoslav successor states, not to mention the scope for democratization (except in geographically privileged Slovenia), and which has brought down a rain of Western economic and eventually military sanctions against them. Nevertheless, an illiberal and ostracized Serb state has yet to be shattered or transformed by all these pressures, even after four years of bitter conflict. Instead the European Union may have to contemplate the indefinite persistence of an undemocratic and militarized Serbia in its midst—not only a Cuba-like pariah within the European democratic region, but even perhaps a continuing threat to processes of democratic convergence, especially if neighbouring Balkan states such as Croatia also prove to be similarly militarized, and chauvinist.

The Geopolitical Implications of Queuing

Following these extremely brief (and incomplete) sketches of the Cuban and Serbian cases, what general conclusions can be drawn concerning the construction of regional groupings of democratic states, and the consequences for democratization of ostracizing those illiberal regimes (and unreformed societies) which stand least to gain (or most to lose) from the resulting patterns of regional integration? Five points may be proposed:

1. Regional integration processes grouping democratic states into mutually supportive communities can generate powerful international processes of democracy promotion in adjoining territories, but the effects are likely to be phased, selective, and geographically uneven. Both in Europe and in the Western hemisphere in the post-Cold War period these processes involve a significant redrawing of the political map, to the benefit of some states and regions, but to the detriment of others. They affect not only the spatial location of democratizing endeavours, but also the distribution of territorial entities and the relationships of power and authority within and between such units. They promote new centres of power (Brussels, Miami, etc.), and affect the power balance between the major regional groupings, but this also means that they generate new peripheries, and new fault-lines, as some political communities find themselves left at the margins of the emerging regional blocs. Thus, it is inadequate to focus on the democracy-promoting potential of such regional groupings without also considering their power-political implications and the hegemonic tendencies they may also serve.

2. Since it takes time to construct such regional groupings, and enlargement invariably proceeds outwards from a core of founder members, candidates for eventual inclusion will be required to form a queue. The resulting geographical and temporal sequences are highly consequential for the pace and content of democratization efforts in individual countries. For example, if it is agreed that Slovenia has a strong claim to early admission to the European Union, that may produce a powerful set of incentives reinforcing and locking in democratic procedures in that particular republic. But the analysis must not stop there. Other ex-Yugoslav republics will read the same signals in a different manner, and adjust their

domestic priorities accordingly. Once inside the European Union Slovenia will no doubt attempt to exercise its enhanced European influence to promote its interests in relation to its former sister republics. It may, perhaps, become a strong advocate for the subsequent early admission of Croatia. Or it may aim to exercise its leverage to block the admission of rival republics (just as Greece tries to tilt the EU against Turkey and Macedonia, and in favour of Greek Cyprus). Similar patterns of international hierarchy and rivalry can be expected to affect negotiations over the establishment of a Free Trade Agreement covering all the Americas.[10] The early entry of Chile into NAFTA would be consequential for Argentina, for example, and the interests of Puerto Rico and the Dominican Republic would be strongly affected if a regime change in Cuba were to reorder US priorities in the Caribbean.

3. At the opposite end of the queue from such eager candidates as Chile, Poland, and Slovenia, both regions contain undemocratic and unrepentant pariah regimes which are presently taking few steps to satisfy the conditions for admission and support laid down by their respective communities of democratic neighbours. On the contrary, Cuba and Serbia are both subject to severe sanctions for their deviance, and therefore, if anything, the time-scale before they could be reintegrated with their neighbours is becoming progressively longer. Certainly, as other countries in the two regions prepare themselves for admission the relative position of these two pariah regimes continuously deteriorates. The often grave failings of these two governments cannot be overlooked by democratic opinion, but it is also important to recognize the strong international and structural components of the predicament faced by these two peoples. Many of the difficulties presented to them by surrounding processes of regional integration would persist however they were governed. Since neither Cuba nor Yugoslavia was ever subject to semi-colonial control from Moscow, neither political system could be liberated by the USSR's collapse. On the contrary, as Gorbachev's reforms weakened the Soviet empire these relatively self-driven Communist regimes reacted by defensive disengagement and preparations to withstand a long seige. This commitment to internal continuity ensured that they would have few lines of communication with the triumphant Western liberal democracies after 1989, and little capacity to promote even their most legitimate national interests in the dominant centres of world power. Their critics and foes, on the other hand (the Croats, the Cuban American exiles, and even the Bosnian Muslims), could hope for a receptive Western hearing not only for their valid criticisms,

but also for their most partisan and revanchist assertions. In short, while no doubt these pariah regimes deserved positions at the bottom of the queue for Western consideration, the peoples they led were also correct in perceiving that the democratic West was unresponsive to their objective predicament, and was predisposed against them by the disproportionate influence of the most hostile international lobbyists.

4. In view of this history and the associated structural legacies, the countries at the bottom of the queue have little prospect of receiving material or political benefits from their democratic neighbours as rewards for incremental reform. It is only by means of a virtually unconditional surrender to their Western critics that they might hope to reverse the flow of sanctions directed against them. But, barring extreme provocation or exceptional opportunity, the Western democracies are likely to remain most reluctant to commit either the force or the resources that would be required to bring about an outright regime collapse, particularly since the immediate consequence might well be waves of refugees and other forms of instability, rather than the inauguration of a new democratic order. This caution is well-merited, especially in relation to such countries as Cuba and Serbia, with their traditions of intense nationalism and armed struggle. In any case, whereas interactions at the level of dialogue and persuasion play to the strong suit of the regional democracies, any resort to compulsion is liable to shift the conflict onto a terrain on which the pariah regime will enjoy a relative advantage.

However, viewed from within the pariah regime it is difficult to envisage the kind of sweeping repudiation of the entire local political system that the external democrats are almost bound to demand. Even if it could be brought about from within, the benefits of such an upheaval would be highly uncertain, and might easily be appropriated by outsiders. Consequently the pariah status of these countries persists, and instead of inducing liberalizing or democratizing reforms, regional pressures help perpetuate the policies that provoke ostracism. In fact, regional incentives intended to force a wholesale reversal of the internal political order tend rather to entrench it, and to strengthen institutions that will then have the strongest possible interest in resisting subsequent liberalization. (Threatening the Cuban military command with wholesale punishment for narcotics trafficking, or convicting Serbian military leaders for crimes of genocide, however justifiable on moral grounds, has the inconvenient consequence of creating an all-or-nothing dichotomy, without much assurance that the West can secure the all.) In short, whatever other purposes they may serve, regional policies of ostracism and sanctions are quite likely to produce counter-productive consequences from the standpoint of democracy promotion. Where such policies become unavoidable they would need to be conducted with great even-handedness if they are to minimize the risks of such unintended consequences.

5. It is not just the subjects of the pariah regime who stand to lose if ostracism persists indefinitely without producing the intended change of course. Just as a democratic regional community will be strengthened and reinforced by each new member it successfully incorporates, it will be correspondingly weakened and undermined by each failure to promote political convergence within its region. Any such failure will tend to distract and perhaps demoralize the leaders whose co-operation is needed to carry forward the regional democratization initiative. It may also raise doubt and reduce commitment in countries still waiting in the queue for eventual admission. It offers encouragement to opponents of democratic regionalism in both the founder and the candidate countries. It may even stir sympathy for the main victims of any unconcluded strategy of ostracism: average citizens of the pariah state, whose legitimate interests get continuously deferred in the name of a democratic ideal that never seems to come within reach. After all, any collective project carried out on behalf of the peoples of the Americas needs to take ordinary Cuban needs and aspirations into account, whatever friction with the current Cuban government there may be. The same applies to the aspirations of all ex-Yugoslavs within any inclusive European project. A democratic regional community should therefore take the utmost care to behave justly and even-handedly towards the contending forces engaged in power struggles on its periphery. This may be no easy matter, when public opinion is aroused by scenes of war crimes (as in Bosnia) or by waves of Caribbean boat people. But it is precisely in such circumstances that the regional democracies most need to abide by their own declared principles if they are to create a long-term consensus on values and eventually to overcome the bitterness of ideological or ethnic polarization. Thus, Croat and Bosnian allies should be held to the same standards of conduct as Serb antagonists, and Cuban-American exiles should be expected to observe the same democratic constraints as their Communist opponents. For regional democratic authorities need to consider not just the risk that embittered citizens of the pariah state might transmit instability beyond their borders but, perhaps more importantly, the danger that by neglecting or mistreating one of the peoples in its area of

responsibility the democratic community would be undermining its own long-term cohesion and legitimacy.

Conclusion

The evidence from our two regions is clear. The construction of a regional community of democratic states is inherently an extremely long-term project. If it takes at least a generation to consolidate a fragile new democracy, one must expect it to take more like two before such individually democratic states can learn to live together in a stable and effective regional community or union, especially one capable of winning round deviant regimes on its periphery. When viewed in such a very long-term perspective, even the EU's recent extreme failure in the former Yugoslavia should be relativized. Provided a regional democratic community is eventually constructed in the rest of Europe, and provided the Europeans adhere to democratic principles in relation to their troubled Balkan neighbours, in the face of inevitable periodic setbacks, the slow processes of convergence which have proved so ineluctable elsewhere can be expected to bear down even upon intransigent Serbs and Croats. Certainly in this particular instance reliance on processes of democratic convergence will require exceptional patience and persistence. But, in fact, even where democracy has been imposed from without (and therefore apparently established far more quickly) the major tasks of post-imposition democratic construction can easily take just as long, and require quite as much firmness of regional purpose.

This discussion of the problem of pariah regimes also underscores a central thesis of this volume: geopolitical considerations need to be reintegrated into the analysis of democratization processes in general, and of those embedded in post-Cold War regional integration efforts in particular. International support for new democracies may be a moral good in its own right; and it may also serve the best political, security, and economic interests of the citizens of the established democracies in the long run; but these hortatory arguments should not blind us to the hegemonic purposes and balance-of-power consequences that are also involved. Particularly in contexts such as contemporary Europe and the Americas, where regional convergence or integration constitutes the main bearer of international influence in support of democracy, we need to be conscious that not all regional co-operation strategies are equally democracy-friendly, and that the means used to construct a regional community will affect its subsequent quality and durability.

Notes

1. See F. Fukuyama, *The End of History and the Last Man* (New York: The Free Press, 1992) and more restrainedly S. P. Huntington, *The Third Wave: Democratization in the Late Twentieth Century* (Norman, Okla.: University of Oklahoma Press, 1991). Both authors subsequently shifted their attention to the obstacles to liberal democratic uniformity at the global level. Fukuyama came to focus on the uneven distribution of the social capital required for effective voluntary co-operation, and Huntington became concerned about what he foresaw as the 'clash of civilizations' looming in the post-Cold War world.

2. 'Les Langues comme acteurs internationaux: Phénomènes de contagion et phénomènes d'irradiation', *Les Relations Internationales à l'Épreuve de la Science Politique*, Mélanges Marcel Merle (Paris: Economica, 1993).

3. These points are developed further in L. Whitehead, 'Concerning International Support for "Democracy" in the South', in R. Luckham (ed.), *Democratization in the South: The Jagged Wave* (Manchester: Manchester University Press, 1996, forthcoming) and in 'A Comparative Perspective on Democratization: Theory and Experience in the Post-Cold War World', mimeo, FLACSO, Santiago, Chile (July 1993).

4. It is on this basis that the Euro–Latin American Forum made its case for 'open integration' in the post-Cold War world: 'It is not a question of imposing a reductive, closed, westernized ideal of democracy, but of promoting an open and universalist ideal which can promote respect for different cultures and civilizations . . . The only way in which the international system can enjoy some stability is through tolerance. Tolerance is defined here as a value. As such, while it requires meaning and limits through concrete expression, it is also infinite. Democracy is the best expression of tolerance as a way of organizing life in society; it presupposes recognition of the Other, the adherence to majority rule with respect for minority rights as well as pluralism': *Open Integration: The European Union and the Mercosur and the International System*, Third Euro–Latin American Forum (Lisbon: Instituto de Estudos Estratégicos e Internacionais, Mar. 1995), 17.

5. 'There can seldom be anything approaching to assurance that interventions, even if successful, would be for the good of the people themselves. The only test possessing any real value, of a people's having become fit for popular institutions, is that they, or a sufficient portion of them to prevail in the contest, are willing to brave labour and danger for their liberation. . . . Men become attached to that which they have long fought and made sacrifices for; they learn to appreciate

that on which their thoughts have been much engaged. . . . It can seldom, therefore—I will not go so far as to say never—be either judicious, or right, in a country which has a free government, to assist, otherwise than by the moral support of its opinions, the endeavours of another to extort the same blessing from its native rulers'; originally published in *Fraser's Magazine* (Dec. 1859); repr. in J. S. Mill, *Essays on Equality, Law, and Education*, vol. xxi of *Collected Works*, ed. J. M. Robson (Toronto: Toronto University Press, 1984), 122–3.

6. Andrew Moravcsik has recently argued the case for European exceptionalism in this regard, distinguishing between three methods of international democracy and human rights promotion, where the EU has a special advantage, at least within its zone of established membership. The three methods are sanctioning, shaming, and co-optation. However, compared to the standpoint of this volume, he underplays the significance of EU enlargement, and perhaps overstresses the legal dimension: see A. Moravcsik, 'Lessons from the European Human Rights Regime', in *Advancing Democracy and Human Rights in the Americas: What Role for the OAS?* (Washington DC: Inter-American Dialogue, 1994).

7. This judgement is controversial, of course. For a generally more favourable assessment of OAS performance see *Advancing Democracy and Human Rights in the Americas: What Role for the OAS?* (Washington DC: Inter-American Dialogue, May 1994).

8. 'Freedom in the World: 1995', *Freedom Review* (Jan.–Feb. 1995), 15–17.

9. 'The European Community eventually agreed that it would accord diplomatic recognition to those successor states which showed appropriate respect for human rights, and its study group produced a report, finding that only Slovenia and Macedonia met the EC human rights requirements. But instead of recognising these two states thereupon, the EC, under heavy pressure from Germany, extended diplomatic recognition to Slovenia *and Croatia*, holding up recognition for Macedonia': S. P. Ramet, 'The Yugoslav Crisis and the West', *East European Politics and Societies*, 8/1 (winter 1994), 201. Serbs stranded in the newly recognized state of Croatia responded to what the Europeans apparently viewed as an act of democratic affirmation by rising in arms, seizing one-third of the territory, and expelling or murdering their Croat neighbours.

10. For a fuller discussion, see L. Whitehead, 'Requisites for Admission', in P. H. Smith (ed.), *The Challenge of Integration: Europe and the Americas* (New Brunswick: Transaction Publishers, 1993).

Bibliography

Books

AN-NA'IM, A. A. (ed.), *Human Rights in Cross Cultural Perspective: A Quest for Consensus* (Philadelphia: Pennsylvania University Press, 1992).

BERGESEN, A. (ed.), *Studies in the Modern World System* (New York: Academic Press, 1980).

BERMEO, N. (ed.), *Liberalization and Democratization: Change in the Soviet Union and Eastern Europe* (Baltimore: Johns Hopkins University Press, 1991).

BETHELL, L. and ROXBOROUGH, I. (eds.), *Latin America between the Second World War and the Cold War, 1944–8* (Cambridge: Cambridge University Press, 1992).

BLACKWILL, D., and KARAGANOV, S. A. (eds.), *Damage Limitation or Crisis? Russia and the Outside World* (Washington DC: Brasseys, 1994).

BLASIER, C., *The Hovering Giant: US Response to Revolutionary Change in Latin America* (Pittsburgh: Pittsburgh University Press, 1976).

BONNER, R. *Waltzing with a Dictator: The Marcoses and the Making of American Policy* (New York: Times Books, 1987).

BONVICINI, G., *et al.*, *The Community of the Emerging European Democracies: A Joint Policy Report* (London: Royal Institute of International Affairs, 1991).

BRZEZINSKI, Z., *Power and Principle: Memoirs of the National Security Adviser, 1977–81* (New York: Farrar, Straus, Giroux, 1983).

CALDER, B., *The Impact of Intervention: The Dominican Republic During the US Occupation of 1916–24* (Austin: Texas University Press, 1984).

CAROTHERS, T., *In the Name of Democracy: US Policy toward Latin America in the Reagan Years* (Berkeley: University of California Press, 1991).

CHIROT, D. (ed.), *The Crisis of Leninism and the Decline of the Left: The Revolutions of 1989* (Seattle: University of Washington Press, 1991).

CHOMSKY, N., *Deterring Democracy* (New York: Hill and Wang, 1992).

CLARK, R. P., and Haltzel, M. H. (eds.), *Spain in the 1980s: The Democratic Transition and a New International Role* (Cambridge, Mass.: Ballinger Publishing, 1987).

CRAWFORD, B. (ed.), *Markets, States, and Democracy: The Political Economy of Post-Communist Transformation* (Boulder, Colo.: Westview Press, 1995).

DAHRENDORF, R., *Reflections on the Revolution in Europe* (London: Chatto and Windus, 1990).

414 *Bibliography*

DANIELS, R. V., *The End of the Communist Revolution* (London: Routledge, 1993).

DARWIN, J., *Britain and Decolonization: The Retreat from Empire in the Post-War World* (London: Macmillan, 1988).

DAVY, R. (ed.), *European Detente: A Reappraisal* (London: Royal Institute of International Affairs/Sage, 1992).

DIAMOND, L., LINZ, J., and LIPSET, S. M. (eds.), *Democracy and Developing Countries* (3 vols.) (Boulder, Colo.: Lynne Riener, 1989–90).

—— and PLATTNER, M. E. (eds.), *The Global Resurgence of Democracy* (Baltimore: Johns Hopkins University Press, 1993).

DRAPER, T., *A Very Thin Line: The Iran-Contra Affairs* (New York: Simon & Shuster, 1991).

EVANS, P., JACOBSON, H., and PUTNAM, R., *Double-Edged Diplomacy: International Bargaining and Domestic Politics* (Berkeley: California University Press, 1993).

FOSSEDAL, G. A., *The Democratic Imperative: Exporting the American Revolution* (New York: Basic Books, 1989).

FREEDOM HOUSE, *Freedom in the World: Political Rights and Civil Liberties* (New York: Freedom House, annual).

FUKUYAMA, F., *The End of History and the Last Man* (New York: Free Press, 1992).

GARDNER, J. A., *Legal Imperialism: American Lawyers and Foreign Aid in Latin America* (Madison: Wisconsin University Press, 1980).

GLEIJESES, P., *Shattered Hope: The Guatemalan Revolution and the United States, 1944–54* (Princeton: Princeton University Press, 1991).

—— *The Dominican Crisis: The 1965 Constitutionalist Revolt and American Intervention* (Baltimore: Johns Hopkins University Press, 1978).

HAGGARD, S., and KAUFMAN, R. R. (eds.), *The Politics of Economic Adjustment: International Constraints, Distributive Conflicts and the State* (Princeton: Princeton University Press, 1992).

HALPERIN, M. H., 'Guaranteeing Democracy', *Foreign Policy*, 91 (spring 1993).

HEINE, J. (ed.), *A Revolution Aborted: The Lessons of Grenada* (Pittsburgh: Pittsburgh University Press, 1990).

HELD, D. (ed.), *Prospects for Democracy: North, South, East, West* (Cambridge: Polity Press, 1993).

HERSH, S. M., *The Price of Power: Kissinger in the Nixon White House* (New York: Summit Books, 1983).

HOFFMAN, S., *Duties Beyond Borders: On the Limits and Possibilities of Ethical International Politics* (Syracuse, NY: Syracuse University Press, 1981).

HUNTINGTON, S. P., *The Third Wave: Democratization in the Late Twentieth Century* (Norman: Oklahoma University Press, 1991).

IONESCU, G., *The Break-up of the Soviet Empire in Eastern Europe* (Harmondsworth: Penguin, 1965).

JOWITT, K., *New World Disorder: The Leninist Extinction* (Berkeley: University of California Press, 1992).

KANT, I., *Principles of Politics, including Essay on Perpetual Peace*, ed. and trans. W. Hastie (Edinburgh: T. and T. Clark, 1891).

KAYSEN, C., PASTOR, R. A., and REED, L. W. (eds.), *Collective Responses to Regional Problems: The Case of Latin America and the Caribbean* (Cambridge, Mass.: American Academy of Arts and Sciences, 1994).

KAZAKOS, P., and IOKANUDIS, P. C. (eds.), *Greece and EC Membership Evaluated* (London: Pinter, 1994).

KEMPE, F., *Divorcing the Dictator: America's Bungled Affair with Noriega* (New York: G. P. Putnam, 1990).

KIRKPATRICK, J., *Dictatorships and Double-Standards: Rationalism and Reason in Politics* (New York: Simon & Schuster, 1982).

KISSINGER, H., *Diplomacy* (New York: Simon & Schuster, 1994).

—— et al., *Report of The President's National Bipartisan Commission on Central America* (Washington: Government Printing Office, 1984).

KLEPAK, H. P. (ed.), *Canada and Latin American Security* (Laval, Que.: Méridien, 1993).

KRATOCHWIL, F., *Rules, Norms and Decisions* (Cambridge: Cambridge University Press, 1988).

LAKE, A., *Somoza Falling: A Case Study of Washington at Work* (Amherst: University of Massachussetts Press, 1989).

LOWENTHAL, A. F., *The Dominican Intervention* (Cambridge, Mass.: Harvard University Press, 1972).

—— (ed.), *Exporting Democracy: The United States and Latin America*, 2 vols. (Baltimore: Johns Hopkins University Press, 1991).

MILL, J. S., *Essays on Equality, Law, and Education*, vol. xxi of the *Collected Works*, ed. J. M. Robson (Toronto: Toronto University Press, 1984).

MOUZELIS, N. P., *Politics in the Semi-Periphery: Early Parliamentarianism and Late Industrialisation in the Balkans and Latin America* (Basingstoke: Macmillan, 1986).

MOWER, A. G., JNR., *Human Rights and American Foreign Policy: The Carter and Reagan Experiences* (New York: Greenwood Press, 1987).

MURAVCHIK, J., *Exporting Democracy: Fulfilling America's Destiny* (Washington DC: American Enterprise Institute, 1991).

NAGEL, S. S. (ed.), *Latin American Development and Public Policy* (New York: St Martin's Press, 1994).

NELSON, J., *Encouraging Democracy: What Role for Conditional Aid?* (Washington DC: Overseas Development Council, 1992).

—— (ed.), *A Precarious Balance: Democracy and Economic Reforms*, 2 vols. (San Francisco: Institute for Contemporary Studies Press, 1994).

O'DONNELL, G., SCHMITTER, P., and WHITEHEAD, L., *Transitions from Authoritarian Rule: Prospects for Democracy*, 4 vols. (Baltimore: Johns Hopkins University Press, 1986).

PACKENHAM, R., *Liberal America and the Third World: Political Development Ideas in Foreign Aid and Social Science* (Princeton: Princeton University Press, 1973).

PASTOR, R. A. (ed.), *Democracy in the Americas: Stopping the Pendulum* (New York: Holmes and Meier, 1989).

PINDER, J., *The European Community and Eastern Europe* (London: Pinter, 1991).

PRAVDA, A., *The End of Outer Empire* (London: Sage, 1992).

PRIDHAM, G. (ed.), *Encouraging Democracy: The International Context of Regime Transition in Southern Europe* (London: Leicester University Press, 1991).

—— and VANHANEN, T. (eds.), *Democratization in Eastern Europe: Domestic and International Perspectives* (London: Routledge, 1994).

—— HERRING, E., and SANFORD, G. (eds.), *Building Democracy? The International Dimension of Democratisation in Eastern Europe* (London: Leicester University Press, 1994).

PROSTERMAN, R. L., and RIEDINGER, J. M., *Land Reform and Democratic Development* (Baltimore: Johns Hopkins University Press, 1987).

PRZEWORSKI, A., *Democracy and the Market: Political and Economic Reforms in Eastern Europe and Latin America* (Cambridge: Cambridge University Press, 1991).

RABE, S. G., *Eisenhower and Latin America: The Foreign Policy of Anti-Communism* (Chapel Hill: University of North Carolina Press, 1988).

REISS, H. (ed.), *Kant's Political Writings* (Cambridge: Cambridge University Press, 1970).

ROETT, R. (ed.), *Mexico's External Relations in the 1990s* (Boulder, Colo.: Lynne Riener, 1991).

ROSENAU, J., *Linkage Politics: Essays on the Convergence of National and International Systems* (New York: Free Press, 1969).

ROY, J. (ed.), *The Reconstruction of Central America: The Role of the European Community* (Miami: North–South Center, University of Miami, 1992).

RUESCHEMEYER, D., STEPHENS, E. H., and STEPHENS, J. D., *Capitalist Development and Democracy* (Chicago: University of Chicago Press, 1992).

RUSSETT, B., *Grasping the Democratic Peace: Principles for a Post Cold-War World* (Princeton: Princeton University Press, 1993).

SCHOULTZ, L., *Human Rights and US Policy Toward Latin America* (Princeton: Princeton University Press, 1981).

—— *National Security and US Policy Toward Latin America* (Princeton: Princeton University Press, 1987).

SCHRAEDER, P. J. (ed.), *Intervention into the 1990s: US Foreign Policy in the Third World*, 2nd edn. (New York: Sage, 1992).

SCHULTZ, G. P., *Turmoil and Triumph: My Years as Secretary of State* (New York: Charles Scribner's, 1993).

SHALOM, S. R., *The United States and the Philippines: A Study in Neocolonialism* (Philadelphia: Institute for the Study of Human Issues, 1981).

SIGMUND, P. E., *The United States and Democracy in Chile* (Baltimore: Johns Hopkins University Press, 1993).

SLATER, J., *Intervention and Negotiation: The United States and the Dominican Revolution* (New York: Harper and Row, 1970).

SMITH, G., *Morality, Reason, and Power: American Diplomacy in the Carter Years* (New York: Hill and Wang, 1986).

SMITH, P. H. (ed.), *The Challenge of Integration: Europe and the Americas* (New Brunswick, NJ: Transaction, 1993).

SMITH, T., *America's Mission: The United States and the Worldwide Struggle for Democracy in the Twentieth Century* (Princeton: Princeton University Press, 1994).

SMITH, W. C., ACUÑA, C. H., and GAMARRA, E. A. (eds.), *Latin American Political Economy in the Age of Neoliberal Reform* (New Brunswick, NJ: Transaction, 1994).

SORENSEN, G., *Democracy and Democratization: Processes and Prospects in a Changing World* (Boulder, Colo.: Westview Press, 1993).

STALLINGS, B., and KAUFMAN, R. (eds.), *Debt and Democracy in Latin America* (Boulder, Colo.: Westview Press, 1989).

STANLEY, P. W. (ed.), *Reappraising an Empire: New Perspectives on Philippine–American History* (Boston, Mass.: Harvard University Press, 1984).

TRISKA, J. F. (ed.), *Dominant Power and Subordinate States* (Durham, NC: Duke University Press, 1986).

TSOUKALIS, L., *Greece and the European Community* (Westmead: Saxon House, 1979).

—— *The New European Community: The Politics and Economics of Integration* (Oxford: Oxford University Press, 1991).

UNITED NATIONS DEVELOPMENT PROGRAMME, *Human Development Report 1994* (New York: Oxford University Press, 1994).

VANCE, C., *Hard Choices: Critical Years in America's Foreign Policy* (New York: Simon & Schuster, 1983).

WALZER, M., *Just and Unjust Wars: A Moral Argument with Historical Illustrations* (New York: Basic Books, 1977).

WESTON, B. H. (ed.), *Alternative Security: Living without Nuclear Deterrence* (Boulder, Colo.: Westview Press, 1990).

WIARDA, H. J., *The Democratic Revolution in Latin America* (New York: Holmes and Meier, 1990).

Articles

ALLISON, G. T., and BESCHEL, R. P., 'Can the United States Promote Democracy?', *Political Science Quarterly*, 107/1 (1992).

ALMOND, G., 'Review Article: The National–International Connection', *British Journal of Political Science*, 19 (1989).

BLOOMFIELD, R. J., 'Making the Western Hemisphere Safe for Democracy? The OAS Defence-of-Democracy Regime', *Washington Quarterly*, 17/2 (spring 1994).

BOSTRÖM, M., 'Political Waves in Latin America, 1940–1988', *Ibero-Americana: Nordic Journal of Latin American Studies*, 19/1.

—— 'Contagion of Democracy in Latin America: The Case of Paraguay', in S. S. Nagel (ed.), *Latin American Development and Public Policy* (New York: St Martin's Press, 1994).

BUENO DE MESQUITA, B., JACKMAN R. W., and SIVERSON, R. M. (eds.), special issue of *Journal of Conflict Resolution*, 35/2 (1991) on 'Democracy and Foreign Policy: Community and Constraint'.

—— SIVERSON, R. M., and WALLER, G., 'War and the Fate of Regimes: A Comparative Analysis', *American Political Science Review*, 86/3 (1992).

CASTAÑEDA, J. G., 'Can NAFTA Change Mexico?', *Foreign Affairs*, 72/4 (1993).

COHEN, R., 'Pacific Unions: A Reappraisal of the Theory that Democracies do not go to War with each Other', *Review of International Studies*, 20/3 (1994).

DEUDNEY, D., and IKENBERRY, J. G., 'The International Sources of Soviet Change', *International Security*, 16/3 (winter 1991/2).

DIAMOND, L., 'Promoting Democracy', *Foreign Policy*, 87 (summer 1992).

—— 'The Global Imperative: Building a Democratic World Order', *Current History*, 579 (Jan. 1994).

DIXON, W. J., 'Democracy and the Management of International Conflict', *Journal of Conflict Resolution*, 37/1 (Mar. 1993).

—— 'Democracy and the Peaceful Settlement of International Conflict', *American Political Science Review*, 88/1 (Mar. 1994).

DOYLE, M., 'Kant, Liberal Legacies, and Foreign Affairs', 2 parts, *Philosophy and Public Affairs*, 12 (summer and autumn 1983).

—— 'Liberalism and World Politics', *American Political Science Review*, 80/4 (1986).

—— 'Thucydidean Realism', *Review of International Studies*, 16 (1990).

FARER, T. J., 'Collectively Defending Democracy in a World of Sovereign States: The Western Hemisphere's Prospect', *Human Rights Quarterly*, 15/4 (Nov. 1993).

FISHMAN, R. M., 'Rethinking State and Regime: Southern Europe's Transition to Democracy', *World Politics*, 42/3 (Apr. 1990).

FRANCK, T. M., 'The Emerging Right to Democratic Governance', *American Journal of International Law*, 86/1 (Jan. 1992).

GARRETÓN, M. A., 'Human Rights in Processes of Democratisation', *Journal of Latin American Studies*, 26/1 (Feb. 1994).

GOUREVITCH, P., 'The Second Image Reversed: The International Sources of Domestic Politics', *International Organisation*, 32/4 (autumn 1978).

HAKIM, P., 'The OAS: Putting Principles into Practice', *Journal of Democracy*, 4/3 (July 1993).

HALPERIN, M. H., 'Guaranteeing Democracy', *Foreign Policy*, 91 (spring 1993).

HERMET, G., 'Environnement international et dimension historique de la transition politique en Espagne', *Pouvoirs*, 8 (1984).

HOFFMAN, S., 'The Crisis of Liberal Internationalism', *Foreign Policy*, 98 (spring 1995).

HUNTINGTON, S. P., 'Will More Countries Become Democratic?', *Political Science Quarterly*, 99/2 (summer 1984).

—— 'A Clash of Civilizations?', *Foreign Affairs*, 72/3 (summer 1993).

HURRELL, A., 'Kant and the Kantian Paradigm in International Relations', *Review of International Studies*, 16 (1990).

JENTLESON, B. W., 'The Reagan Administration and Coercive Diplomacy: Restraining more than Remaking Governments', *Political Science Quarterly*, 106/1 (1991).

JOHNSON, R. H., 'Misguided Morality: Ethics and the Reagan Doctrine', *Political Science Quarterly*, 103/2 (1988).

KOBRIN, S., 'Diffusion as an Explanation of Oil Nationalization: or The Domino Effect Rides Again', *Journal of Conflict Resolution*, 19/1 (1985).

KOHLER, B., 'Germany and the Further Enlargement of the European Community', *World Economy*, 2/2 (1979).

LAKE, D. A., 'Powerful Pacifists: Democratic States and War', *American Political Science Review*, 86/1 (Mar. 1992).

LI, R., and THOMPSON, W., 'The "Coup Contagion" Hypothesis', *Journal of Conflict Resolution*, 19/1 (1975).

MEEL, P., 'Money Talks, Morals Vex: The Netherlands and the Decolonization of Suriname, 1975–1990', *European Review of Latin America and Caribbean Studies*, 48 (June 1990).

MILL, J. S., 'A Few Words on Non-Intervention', *Fraser's Magazine*, 60 (Dec. 1859); repr. in J. S. Mill, *Essays on Equality, Law and Education* (Toronto: Toronto University Press, 1984).

MORAVCSIK, A., 'Lessons from the European Human Rights Regime', in *Advancing Democracy and Human Rights in the Americas: What Role for the OAS?* (Washington DC: Inter-American Dialogue, May 1994).

MUÑOZ, H., 'The OAS and Democratic Governance', *Journal of Democracy*, 4/3 (July 1993).

OSIEL, M., 'The Making of Human Rights Policy in Argentina: The Impact of Ideas and Interests on a Legal Conflict', *Journal of Latin American Studies*, 18/1 (May 1986).

PASTOR, R. A., 'Securing a Democratic Hemisphere', *Foreign Policy*, 73 (winter 1988–9).

PINDER, J., 'The Future of the European Community: A Strategy for Enlargement', *Government and Opposition*, 27/4 (1992).

PINTO-DUSCHINSKY, M., 'Foreign Political Aid: The German Political Foundations and their US Counterparts', *International Affairs*, 67/1 (1991).

RUSTOW, D. A., 'Transitions to Democracy: Toward a Dynamic Model', *Comparative Politics*, 2/3 (Apr. 1970).

—— 'Democracy: A Global Revolution?', *Foreign Affairs*, 69 (autumn 1990).

SCHMITTER, P., and KARL, T., 'Modes of Transition in Latin America and Southern and Eastern Europe (Democratic Transition in the East and in the South)', *International Social Science Journal*, 43/2 (May 1991).

SCHWELLER, R. L., 'Domestic Structures and Preventive War: Are Democracies More Pacific?', *World Politics*, 44/2 (Jan. 1992).

SIKKINK, K., 'Human Rights Issue-Networks in Latin America', *International Organization*, 47/3 (summer 1993).

SMITH, P. H., 'The Political Impact of Free Trade on Mexico', *Journal of Interamerican Studies and World Affairs*, 34/1 (spring 1992).

SMITH, T., 'In Defence of Intervention', *Foreign Affairs*, 73/6 (Nov.–Dec. 1994).

STARR, H., 'Democratic Dominoes: Diffusion Approaches to the Spread of

Democracy in the International System', *Journal of Conflict Resolution*, 35/2 (1991).

Tovias, A., 'The International Context of Democratic Transitions', *West European Politics*, 7 (Apr. 1984).

Tsakoloyannis, P., and Verney, S., 'Linkage Politics: The Role of the European Community in Greek Politics in 1973', *Byzantine and Modern Greek Studies*, 10 (1986).

Van Klaveren, A., 'El Apoyo a la Democracia en América Latina ¿Hacia un Nuevo Regimen Internacional?', *Sintesis*, 21 (Madrid, July–December 1993).

Zak, M. A., 'Assisting Elections in the Third World', *Washington Quarterly*, 10/4 (autumn 1987).

Index